57
Varieties

of

TALK
SOUP

By **BARRY CAIN**

Text © Barry Cain 2016
This first edition © Red Planet Books Ltd 2016

Publisher: Mark Neeter
Editors: Hazel Orme and Matt Milton

For photo credits see www.redplanetzone.com

Thanks to John Lydon for coming up with the title for this book

ISBN: 978 1 9059 5987 7

Printed in the UK by CPI

57
Varieties

of

TALK
SOUP

CONTENTS

Introduction   13

March 1978
Linda and Paul McCartney   17

1971–75
Court reporter and cider soul boy   25

1976–7
Eric Burdon, Marc Bolan, Robert Plant   30

Part 1: Record Mirror   35

January 1978
Blue Oyster Cult, Meat Loaf, Bethnal   35

February 1978
Sham 69, Earth Wind & Fire   43

March 1978
**John Miles, The Buzzcocks, Squeeze,
Linda McCartney**   51

Part 2: Pop Publicist   57

March–June 1978
**Modern Publicity, The Stranglers,
Tanz der Youth (Brian James)**   57

Part 3: Freelance Writer   65

June 1978
Skinheads, staff photos and Mink De Ville   66

July 1978
**Iggy Pop, Steve Jones & Paul Cook,
Joan Armatrading, restaurant reviews**   72

August 1978
**The Hollies, Dirty Berty, Thin Lizzy,
The Jam, Sham 69**   88

September 1978
**The Who, The Stranglers, X-Ray Spex, 10cc,
The Jam, Blondie, Boney M**   95

October 1978
Sylvester, Smokie, David Essex,
Kevin Keegan, Bill Shankly   114

November 1978
Hot Gossip, Public Image Ltd, Mike Oldfield,
Dan Hartman, Blondie, The Shangri-Las, Pere Ubu,
David Johansen, Bruce Springsteen   122

December 1978
Devo, Bryan Robertson, Rory Gallagher   151

Part 4: The Farringdon Agency   155

January 1979
The Village People, The Clash, Dr Feelgood,
Inner Circle, Bob Marley   155

February 1979
UFO   167

March 1979
The Stranglers, Motorhead, Steve Jones   175

April 1979
Squeeze, Frank Warren, Blondie   193

May 1979
Rush, The Tubes   203

June 1979
Ronnie Wood, Malcolm McLaren   210

July 1979
Wayne Fontana, Gerry Rafferty, Queen   225

August 1979
Whitesnake, Ian Dury   232

September 1979
Earth Wind & Fire, The Beach Boys, Sting   237

October 1979
The Jam, Andy Williams   248

November 1979
The Specials, The Selecter, Madness   253

December 1979
Alex Harvey, The Damned   255

January 1980
AC/DC, The Stranglers, The Clash   260

February 1980
The Stranglers 271

April 1980
Spandau Ballet 275

May 1980
Barry White, Devo, Mrs Constantia Cain 280

June 1980
Malcolm McLaren, Don McLean 288

July 1980
The Stranglers 292

August 1980
Bow Wow Wow 296

September 1980
Malcolm McLaren, Ozzy Osbourne 303

October 1980
Randy Crawford, Malcolm McLaren 305

November 1980
Adam Ant 306

Part 5: Magazine Publishing 309

1980–1981
Flexidiscs, pop mags, Sex Pistols 309

1982
The Jam, John Denver 320

1983
Last ever interview: Hall & Oates 330

1983–1988
Let's make lots of money 334

1988–91
**Link-Up, Pop Shop, Michael Hutchence,
Jason Donovan** 339

1991–1992
18 Rated, Zodiac Mindwarp, Elvis Aris 351

1992-1998
Property ads, Princess Di and the death of pop 360

Foreword

My life has been full of Megan moments.

Take the other night. I'm at a reception for a cruise company held in a sumptuous members-only club deep in the heart of Mayfair where toilet attendants are mandatory. I'm holding a glass of pink champagne, my third, and frequently swallowing exotic canapés distributed by red-jacketed waiters of various nationalities.

Around me, journalists, PRs and cruise executives hip-hop-hippity-hop. It's the same old song but it's comfortable and the faces are familiar. I'm there in my capacity as editor of *Cruise Trade News*, a glossy magazine for travel agents and the industry. I started the title fifteen years ago and although it never paid the rent, the perks – free cruises – are worth the odd minor sacrifice like no income.

So I'm chatting to a couple of girls, sharp and blonde and charming, when the presentation begins and I head for a tall side-table where I can put my drink down, stand and take notes. A voice ushers the room to silence and the MD begins his speech.

A few minutes in I accidentally knock my glass over, sending its entire contents flying across the table and over another journalist's notepad. The glass falls to the floor and explodes into a million pieces. The MD pauses while every face in the room turns and looks at me.

'Sorry,' I squirm and stare down at my notepad.

A waiter appears with a dustpan and brush and frantically sweeps up the hazardous shards as the MD resumes his speech. I move away from the table and position myself next to the closest wall where I watch the waiter clear up the mess.

A minute later my mobile phone starts to ring. I'd only just got it and was convinced I'd changed the phone profile to offline as I sat on the tube on the way down and messed around with it, like a first date, to see how far it would go.

It'll go far tonight. I'd accidentally switched the ringtone to a spoof airport public address system message:

'Attention! Could the man with the ten-inch penis please come to the phone? Could the man with the ten-inch penis please come to the phone immediately? Thank you.'

The message is loud and clear and keeps repeating itself because, in my panic, I can't find the phone – a super-small slimline special – and when I finally do, I don't know how to stop it. The MD breaks off, again. The journalist with the wet notepad grabs the phone, switches it off and hands it back to me. He's got the look of death in his eyes.

'Thanks. Sorry.' I stare down at my notepad, again. That's when you know everyone in the room thinks you're a wanker.

That's a Megan moment. Megan Davies, the singer from the Applejacks. A pop star whom I never met and who doesn't know me from Adam. But she unwittingly brought ridicule back to my place to watch the late, late show. I'll explain shortly....

This book is about hating the world for stripping me of self-belief, for not pulling me out of the quicksands of other people's dreams, for kicking me in the bollocks before they'd even dropped, for generally lying and cheating and hurting but for passing by far too quickly.

This book is also about taming that hatred through memory. 'Only by acceptance of the past can you alter it,' said TS Eliot, probably recalling the eight years he worked in obscurity for Lloyds Bank. Slipping into memory for me is like slipping out of Clark Kent's suit: by reliving the past I become immortal. 'The distinction between the past, present and future is only a stubbornly persistent illusion,' said Albert Einstein, while watching the 6.05 special heading down the track.

But this book is mainly about a shedload of pop stars. Pop stars I grew up with, from the Beatles to the Spice Girls. My generation invented pop music as we know it today and we alone have lived through all its guises.

It's dying. It has to. One generation's dreams are another generation's sorrows. Kids've got heads full of ringtones and *Grand Theft Auto* and music ain't enough anymore. That's why a tiny piece of equipment can store a million love songs and also double-up as a phone, digital recorder, games machine and camcorder.

In the Sixties we had radiograms as big as sideboards covered with family photos framed in silver plate, and vases overflowing with plastic tulips courtesy of Daz washing powder. They played big, bold records from big, bold packages.

And when I got my first record player for my first room, the evenings would melt away under the spell of the Beatles. It was mine. It was all I had. As I got older, the music machines got more elaborate, right up to a Toshiba music centre my mum bought in 1976 with built-in cassette player and radio.

The cassette was the first nail in the coffin of pop. Cheap, plastic and portable, you could even play your pet sounds in the car. But you can't listen to music when you drive; you can only *hear* it. It's a cheat. Music doesn't deserve that. If you can't play, there are only two things you can with music: listen to or dance. The rest is tomfoolery.

The musical gap between 1948 and 1978 is immense, but between '78 and now it's indiscernible. My parents grew up with songs populated by guys and gals falling head over heels in love under an eternally shining June blue moon floating in a heaven full of pennies. That all changed in the mid-Fifties and pop music continued to develop well into the Eighties. When it started to lose its way. Punk was the last great white music (indie is simply punk with melody). House, garage, drum & bass, hip-hop, R&B are all souped-up disco and Motown with bollocks. It's yesterday's news.

Live concerts are popular today with those who go to relive memories – acts and fans – when once they went in search of them. Pop music is now part of showbiz because my generation can't let go. We really are the oldest swingers in town: forty- and fifty-and sixty-year-olds buying albums made by twenty-somethings.

When I was sixteen, pop music was my domain. Middle-aged men would never have dreamed of walking into a record shop to buy *Beatles For Sale* or *Their Satanic Majesties Request* or *Paranoid*. It would've been just plain weird. It wasn't for them, it was for us. We'd succeeded in stripping the 'ular' from popular.

But now pop music belongs to everybody thanks to the cross-generational *X Factor* and Facebook and David Beckham and Prince Harry. It's been sucked into the showbiz swirl and now five hundred 'fuck's on a rap album mean fuck all. Pop, in whatever guise, has become the music of the people and got its 'ular' back. The young don't need it now like I needed it. Now you could get Cliff Richard and 50 Cent doing the 'Bachelor Boy' rap on the Royal Variety Show and nobody would bat an eyelid. Imagine Joe Strummer doing a duet with Des 'O Connor in '77 and you get the picture.

A recent study revealed that nearly half the fanbase of One Direction are old enough to be their mothers. The game is over; youth has lost its music and, as a result, its youth.

Music was my life for thirty-five years, but I checked out in 1998 when the Spice Girls sued me, and it's been painful watching it die. The weekly music press has long gone, apart from the death-defying *NME*, now just a commuter's freebie. *Smash Hits*, like the brilliant big girl's blouse it was, went on a crash diet and managed to slim down to 40,000 copies from a million, becoming the skinniest magazine in the skinny magazine graveyard. Before wasting away. The record companies dotted across London in funky offices have vanished like VHS, replaced by a few smirking conglomerates snorting up what they can before the Internet finishes dishing everything out for free. This book traces that demise.

Shit, this book is about a lot of things. Maybe it's time to tame some hatred. Time to get off this train and walk the rest of the way. Time to count moments, not months. Time to see what's been hurtling by all these years while my eyes were closed and my heart was stranded.

But it won't slow down as it heads, inexorably, to the last stop and if I jump, I'm toast. So I walk back to happiness through the empty carriages away from the engine in a desperate attempt to slow down time and commit myself unashamedly to memory, because it soaks up speed like a '77 nostril.

Whenever possible, I like to escape my now and head back to my then – when I was young and in love and only disillusioned with myself. I don't want to listen to the rhythm of this runaway train anymore, telling me what a fool I've been. The pouring rain does that already.

I do most of my time travelling in Colindale, home of the British Library, where dead words come to life in the kiss of an eye. Everything I ever wrote about music is enrobed in blue leather and stored lovingly in rooms where the smell of old paper is as intoxicating as Dune Spice.

It's my youth that smells so sweetly.

Where else will I again share a dressing room with the McCartneys, get pissed with Paul Weller, re-discover the boyhood secrets of Iggy Pop and fly Concorde to see Earth, Wind & Fire defy gravity like the funky box of tricks they were?

Where else will I relive the day I spent with Barry White at his place in the Hollywood Hills watching the rivers flow, or hear, once again, John Denver slag off his beloved Annie?

And, tell me, where else will I see the Stranglers play the pants off Japan (the country, not the band) or go on a guided tour of Bob Marley's Jamaican home with the be-dreaded man himself?

Fancy lunch with the Beach Boys on a Santa Monica beach? Your table's booked and may I suggest the Meat Loaf? Fancy a night of excess with Ronnie Wood and Keith Richard, in the Playboy Country Club, Milwaukee? Roll up that hundred dollar bill and inhale gently. The ol' heart may not take to heat, especially deep heat.

Fancy chewin' the fat with Bruce Springsteen in Maryland? C'mon, don't be chicken. Or howzabout sharing an afternoon with the sexiest woman in the history of pop? Share away.

Fancy a touch of Rotten, a Strummer bummer, a shock from Sting, a diamond ring? Snow in Texas and pain in Iceland? Fancy eavesdropping on the most embarrassing Megan moment of my life involving Blondie and Frank Warren? Or hearing Paul McCartney call me a bastard?

Fancy reliving some of the greatest concerts in pop history?

Fancy seeing a grown man's arse cry?

'Got live if you want it.'

Now don't get me wrong; my memory is a blur and I never kept any cuttings from the publications that employed my services. But at the British Library they're all dressed up with nowhere to go. I want to take them where the music's playing and dance all night long.

Paul Simon once said, 'Preserve your memories, they're all that's left you.' I wonder if he knew how right he was.

Six years later Marvin Gaye asked, 'Where did all the blue skies go?' It took me thirty years to figure out the answer.

Into the British Library, Marvin. Into the British Library.

Since writing '77 Sulphate Strip, I've been asked on more than one occasion (three actually) what Katy did next.

Well, for you three guys, I guess it went something like this...

INTRODUCTION

A medley of Megan moments

Between 1978 and 1980 I changed career five times.

OK, they all involved music, but they were all very different. With two of them I had to constantly sell myself and that particular skill wasn't in my repertoire. It was once. Up until the age of twelve I was awash with confidence, but it was the perishable confidence of an only child accustomed to being the centre of attention and eager to please.

I became a member of a local drama group and acted in productions at Finsbury Town Hall and wrote and starred in plays at my junior school. I was an oik from Oiksville but I knew how to turn a card.

So in my first year at Owen's, an all-boys' secondary school in Islington, I thought nothing of raiding my mum's wardrobe and dressing up as Megan Davies – the girl bassist in the Applejacks – and performing their song 'Tell Me When' in a miming competition (we were beaten by the Four Pennies with 'Juliet').

I was very competitive.

That was quickly followed by a magic show I presented in front of the whole school at that first Christmas concert. I even had the temerity to sing solo in the choir at the carol service the following day.

Grave mistakes, all.

I got away with it that year – eleven and twelve-year-olds back then were still standing in the shadows of tooth fairies – but after we were streamed I found myself in a form surrounded by some B-movie bastards. Life was no longer about classrooms lined with splodgy self-portraits, pine cones and home-grown plants all swaying gently to the sound of a hamster on a wheel. Now it was shit and piss and impromptu hard-ons and ignominy.

The Megan incident was recalled one dark day about four weeks into the new school year. And so began eight consecutive terms of warp-factor-six intimidation.

First they dubbed me Sheila after someone mistakenly thought that was the name of the Applejacks girl. That was replaced by 'Worms' because my hair was excessively straight and greasy. Kids would stick used pieces of chewing gum onto my scalp because they were 'Wrigleys' (quite witty actually – well, it was a grammar school). I could only get them out by slicing off chunks of hair with a penknife I carried purely for that purpose.

This was something I couldn't beat – there were just too many persecutors. It was my school nightmare and it didn't help that 90 per cent of them were more intelligent than me. Outside the classroom with the guys on my estate it was different. There, you knew where you were, you knew what you were. None of them had a glimpse of my nightmare – and they were my best friends.

At primary school nobody really got into major fights, apart from the odd bully boy, one of whom pulled a knife on me during morning break when I was six. I had a few street fights – it was unavoidable. As an eight year-old I once had to defend myself from serious injury with a dustbin lid when a mad Greek Cypriot kid, who later went on to gain notoriety as a mercenary in Angola (where he was executed) under the name of Colonel Callan, tried to stab me with a sharpened broom handle.

A year or so later three members of a rival gang – two heavies and one lunatic – dragged me into an alley and cut off the soles of my shoes with carving knives. Did ever you see such a thing in your life?

Those were the days.

But I'd never before experienced the violence I endured at grammar school because it wasn't physical. The thirteen and fourteen year-old boys who surrounded me in class tortured with their words. Forget that sticks-and-stones shit. Names hurled relentlessly for nearly three years hurt more.

I tried to compensate by acting a bit spivvy – bunking off, working on a pet stall in Chapel Market in the Angel, Islington, shouting, 'Two quid the dog, thirty bob the bitch,' as I walked up and down with a puppy under each arm. But it was all to no avail.

But, thanks to the Beatles, a trendy haircut and a handmade three-piece suit, this worm eventually turned.

Just before my thirteenth birthday we moved from a one-bedroom council flat in Kings Cross to a two-bedroom council flat in King's Cross, and the first thing I got for my bedroom was a record player. I bought it at Headquarters & General Supplies in Oxford Street and it cost a tenner. At the same time I bought my first single – 'Baby Let Me Take You Home' by the Animals, followed a week later by my first album – *A Hard Day's Night*.

It had to be the Beatles. They were like gods to me and I've never felt like that about anyone before or since. Each album was an introduction to another phase of my life and the deeper the albums became, the less they needed to release.

From '63 to the middle of '65, The Beatles brought out five albums full of six-month songs. During those years I was down at the end of lonely street with a barnet full of Wrigleys and I needed those quick fixes. Then they released the one-sided album *Help* and the fixes were cut with talc leaving me gasping for more. The lyrics were the problem. With a couple of exceptions, they were nothing more than flash Bobby Vee.

I started to panic. What if they were just another Gerry & the Pacemakers? What if their juice had coagulated in my veins and didn't flow anymore?

My soul was leaking. I needed a rubber one, quick.

They delivered, being the gods they were, with a bunch of songs that took the ribbon from my hair and helped me make it through the night. For the very first time, I could actually *identify* with the words. They made me feel more grown up, able to embrace the jibes and join the tribes.

Rubber Soul made things cool. It was December 1965. But there was still a long way to go for them, and for me. *Revolver*, released in the summer of '66, was the last of the 'six-monthers'. *Sgt Pepper* came out almost a year later and the extra wait coupled with the album's madcap songs kinda tripped me into adolescent maturity. To celebrate, I got a haircut to suit the times – smart skinhead. It freed the worms and freed my mind. People stopped taking the piss and even girls started to notice me. Well, the ones with glasses and a slight limp.

I was fifteen when my dad took me to Alfie Myer's tailoring shop in Old Street to be fitted with my first suit – dark blue three-ply mohair, single ten-inch vent, fifteen-inch bottoms with turn-ups, narrow lapels, waistcoat for those more ostentatious moments in life. Four fittings and one month later, I collected the thirty quid golden fleece and wore it for the first time at the Boathouse Club by Kew Bridge with the white button-down tapered Ben Sherman, college tie, white silk handkerchief peeking out the top pocket, fob watch gleaming from the waistcoat and shimmering classical black brogues. I danced to the Equals and Marvin Gaye and felt like a million dollars.

Incidentally, that night I was attacked by about ten mohair-suited skinheads, the worst kind, as I walked over the bridge to catch a bus. I escaped a beating – I had the gift of the gab back then – but the-ten-inch vent turned into an eighteen-inch vent during the initial chase when someone grabbed hold of my jacket.

I grew up overnight. It happens.

The limbs of my confidence had been blown off on a D-Day beach. But, thanks to the Beatles, Stanley Kaye's barbershop off Liverpool Road and Alfie Myers, I still had my knob. Just.

I don't remember meeting Stanley Kaye, or Alfie Myers. But I did meet Paul McCartney once, probably the most Megan-tragic meeting of my life...

I wrote it like this:

I've admired Paul McCartney since he stood awkwardly on a round pedestal during a 'Please Please Me' session on Brian Matthews's Thank Your Lucky Stars.

He had charisma. He had a flimsy leg style. He had a cosy puddin' face more appropriate in an Ovaltine ad than a pop show. More importantly, he had me.

But when I met him for the first time this week I would dearly have loved to shove the cherubic smile right down his throat and maybe follow that up with a swift right to his rubicund cheek.

There's a very good reason for this sudden urge to indulge in unmitigated violence as I will now endeavour to explain…

So began my epitaph, my final interview for *Record Mirror* (at least, that's what I thought at the time), which I'd joined at the tail end of 1976.

MARCH 1978

Linda and Paul McCartney

An interview with Linda McCartney, with the chance of a few words from Paul. It was the one I'd been waiting for. I always knew, deep down, the moment I heard 'Love Me Do', that I'd meet a Beatle. It was my destiny.

This was my chance to proclaim to the world my undying love for Paul McCartney and the purity of his voice, the bittersweet songs, the arrogance, the tenderness, the heart full of soul.

Nobody knew if Paul would show but my stomach still floated like a butterfly on the off-chance that he would as I sat on the train heading south to Twickenham, where Wings were filming a video for the song 'London Town'. I looked at the other passengers and secretly gloated: I might be meeting a Beatle in half an hour; what will you be doing?

I had been waiting weeks for this interview through endless postponements. OK, so it wasn't Paul I was meeting but Linda. Still, she was loved by a Beatle, and not just any old Beatle. It was the next best thing.

But I wasn't going to give her an easy ride. I'd loved Wings for as long as I could but I'd been hanging out in Cynic City for nearly two years. If it wasn't cool, slag it. Wings weren't cool. Me, Mr- long-hair-and-shaggy-beard-living-at-home-with-his-mum-and-dad-at-twenty-five Dude, what the hell did I know about cool?

Linda McCartney ruined Wings – that was the general feeling among those who considered Paul McCartney to belong exclusively to fools like me. There were a few highs – he was a Beatle after all – but, according to us, the minute she walked into his life he died.

I'd compiled an impressive list of questions. Did you stifle a dream? Do you consider yourself a professional musician? Have you ever felt you were a burden to Paul? Were you a groupie? Did past members of the band leave because of you? Are you a hippie? A mover? A shaker? A manipulator?

When I reached the huge studio in Twickenham I was greeted by Paul's PR, Tony Brainsby, one very smooth operator. He wore glasses, had shoulder-length, straggly red hair and when he spoke you could hear the laugh in his words. He was one of the most cynical men I'd ever met, with the confidence to be a complete bastard if the situation demanded. I once stood in his office waiting to interview Iron Maiden when he called his bank manager a 'total cunt' over the phone. Never mind the bollocks, here's Tony Brainsby.

'Paul's here,' said Tony, matter-of-factly. 'Would you like to meet him?'

Would I like to meet him? I didn't say – couldn't say – anything. I was about to shake hands with a living legend who had left his imprint on my soul.

Tony showed me to a table where two other journalists, veterans from *NME* and *Melody Maker*, sat drinking Coke. Denny Laine strolled in and we were introduced. 'You've always been in my ears and in my eyes,' I said to him in a lame attempt at a joke. I think he may have heard it before.

Tony handed me a Coke and I took a seat next to the vets who said they'd met Paul on numerous occasions. I already envied them.

'I'll go and find Paul,' said Tony and my heart skipped a beat.

I could think of nothing else during the idle, Coke-infused conversation that lasted for five minutes. Then...

'Paul, this is Barry.' He smiled. He raised his hand. I reached out to touch the fingers that had shaped my thoughts, that had lifted me higher and higher with their heavenly power. I reached out to hear that universal voice which, for the very first time, would say, 'Hello Barry.'

'Hello Paul.' I thrust out my hand and knocked an entire glass of Coke across the table, some of which ended up on his trousers.

'Oh, shit!' said Paul, and laughed.

'Oh shit!' I said, and didn't.

'Linda is ready to see you now,' said Tony who had realised I was in desperate need of rescuing. He gave me directions to her dressing room.

I left the bar as quickly as I could and turned right out of the door.

That was my first mistake.

It should've been left. Megan. Megan. Megan.

I got hopelessly, completely, depressingly lost. There wasn't a soul around to ask the way and I walked up and down a maze of sterile corridors feeling like Arthur Clennam trying to negotiate the Circumlocution Office in *Little Dorrit*. I should've reached Linda McCartney's dressing room in absolutely no more than two minutes. It took me twenty-five.

'Where the fuck have you been?' Tony stood outside Linda's dressing room. He wasn't a happy man.

'I got a bit lost.'

'A bit lost? We've been looking for you for ages. You do know you only had an hour with her? You're the last interview of the day, which means you've got precisely thirty-five minutes starting from now...'

He opened the door and pushed me inside.

'Here he is! The man got lost would you believe?'

'Lost?' I loved the way Linda said it, like she was really concerned.

'Lost? My God what happened?'

The first question was sublime. The second made me feel ashamed of myself.

'Are you all right?'

'I'm fine. I feel a bit stupid.' A bit stupid? I'd just knocked a glass of Coke over Paul McCartney and then get lost on my way to interview his wife. That gives stupid a bad name.

'Hey, Barry, don't worry about it. Sit down. Would you like a drink?'

'You probably think I've had too many already.'

She laughed. She looked nervous. She was lovely. She had to be. She was married to Paul McCartney. She wore multi-coloured socks, denim culottes, a waistcoat and a T-shirt, topped with a dollop of hair that looked like it had been squeezed out of a Mr Softee machine. I guess you couldn't really call her stunning. She was, well... nice. A nice person. A person you feel at home with, like a newsreader. Nice Linda.

'I'm really sorry about all this. It's not exactly been my day. Did you hear about the –'

'Yes.' She laughed again. 'I'm sorry but you do sound a little, uh, accident-prone.'

'I'm known as the Norman Wisdom of the music press.'

'Norman Wisdom?'

'Er, yeah. He was the poor man's Charlie Chaplin. Very English.'

'So was Charlie Chaplin, but I get your drift. Now what would you like?'

'A Coke will be fine.' I could have murdered a beer but it didn't seem prudent in the circumstances.

'Only if you promise not to spill it over me.'

She laughed as she got up to fix the drinks. This woman who had given birth to Paul McCartney's babies was fixing a drink for me.

No interview had affected me quite like this.

'I'll leave you two alone now,' said Tony. I'd forgotten he was there. 'I'm afraid you've only got about thirty minutes.'

Just then a nanny came in carrying Linda's six-month-old son, James. Linda took the baby and sat down, holding him like a bouquet of fresh roses. The nanny and Tony left together so now it was just her and me and sweet baby James in a dressing room with the name Sacha Distel smacked like a French kiss on the door. It's the good life.

Do you like being interviewed Linda?

'I guess I'm not a great person to interview. I'm really ordinary, y'know. Ordinary and relaxed. I didn't do very well at school ... I'm not a showbiz person at all. I find it difficult to write about myself so it must be nearly impossible for anyone else to do so.'

But if you were writing about yourself what would you say?

'Oh, that I'm very easy-going, nice...' See? Told ya, "...and like life.'

Did Paul groom you musically?

'Oh, no. More than anything he wanted a friend near him...'I do have an instinctive feel for music. I've always been a fan. I was a real New York Fifties gal. I'd go and see Alan Freed's rock'n'roll shows and listen to Buddy Holly. That's where I got my musical training. To me the Fifties was the best period ever for music.'

Linda refused to read the music press. 'So much of it is untrue. When they slag off Paul it makes me sick.'

Aren't you a little biased?

'Sure. But I'm biased for anyone I love. Paul is an artist, make no mistake.'

You once said, 'John was my Beatle hero. But when I met him the fascination faded fast and I found it was Paul I liked.'

She smiled. 'Well, John comes over on stage or record much heavier than he really is. He just isn't like what you think. In truth he's just a nice guy, not Mr Cool."

You've been married nine years. Don't seem a day too long?

'I feel newly married because it's all gone so quickly. There are some things I would've liked to change, like getting rid of all the pressures which drastically affect your home life. When you're famous, people need things from you. I've no regrets. I think in a marriage the essential thing is to be good friends – only then you can have a life. I take things less seriously now.'

It was like the perfect first date. My preconceptions were hideously wrong and when she said, 'Hey, Barry, I get the feeling you like me and I think this is gonna be a great interview,' the stars fell from the sky. But I needed to get to the nitty-gritty. We were fifteen minutes in already, which meant I only had another fifteen.

There was a loud knock on the door and Paul came in. 'Five minutes to curtain call.'

'Hey Paul, we're just having a really good chat,' said Linda.

'Right, but we've really got to go. Have you finished your interview?'

'Well, no,' I said, feeling short-changed. I'd been promised over thirty minutes, plus I'd been hanging around for weeks waiting to do this. Just because I got a bit lost didn't mean I should be penalised. This ain't on son, this ain't on at all.

'Could I ask just a couple more things?' I said gingerly. Shit, I was alone in a room with Paul and Linda McCartney and they were talking about me.

'OK, but if you could wrap it up as soon as you can,' said Paul.

Linda looked at me and smiled.

Right, er, if you weren't married now, what would...

'I'd be living out in Arizona just taking pictures.' Lovely Linda.

'Anyway,' said Paul, 'we are married and that's the way we intend to stay.'

The spell had been broken. Paul paced up and down and occasionally interrupted to hurry things along. I really wanted him to piss off. I'd just scratched the surface with Linda and this could have been the best ever.

Then Linda said something so magical it took my breath away.

'Maybe we could continue the interview back at the house.'

The house! Yes! The three of us would pile into his Mini, the one with the black windows, and drive over to St- John's Wood to the house I'd been reading about all my life. The one just around the corner from Abbey Road Studios, the one where he wrote 'Paperback Writer' and 'Yesterday' and 'Lady Madonna'. Where he slept with Jane Asher and entertained Mick Jagger.

Paul McCartney's house.

And Linda would maybe knock up a meal in the kitchen, something healthy like alfalfa beans, and we'd open a bottle of wine and talk late into the night and Paul would tell me his secrets and fears and dreams and finally explain to me the true meaning of life.

'No,' said Paul. 'That's out of the question.'

What are the worst words you've ever heard? 'I'm sorry but I don't love you anymore'? 'You've failed every exam'? 'The dog's dead'? 'Oh – have you come already?'

They aren't even close to what I felt when Paul said, 'No. That's out of the question.'

At that moment I'd have traded my mum's life for the opportunity of going to Paul McCartney's house. 'No. That's out of the question'.

Didn't he realise what he meant to me? What he did for me? How I could never thank him enough for simply existing?

I wish I could've said something glib – 'Don't beat about the bush Paul – do you want me to come or not?' But all I could muster was a feeble, 'OK, I think I'm just about finished. I'm sorry I was so late and I'm really sorry about the Coke.'

'Don't worry,' said Paul.

'No, it was my fault.'

As we walked down the stairs I was overcome by shyness. He said something to me but I didn't know what.

The three of us went out of the building together. I tried to talk to him, tried to penetrate that force-field I'd erected between us. I crazily expected Paul to know me like I knew him and the fact that he didn't was, I concluded, totally his fault.

A polite goodbye and I watched them climb into the Mini with the black windows. Linda waved.

I tried to imagine their conversation.

'Paul, how could you be such a bastard? That guy was about the best journalist I'd ever met and I sensed he was gonna write a great article about me. And you went and ruined it.'

'I'm sorry Linda, I didn't know. Shall we turn back?'

'Oh, it's too late now.'

But it was probably more along the lines of:

'He didn't seem like a bad guy. A bit stupid though. How could someone get lost like that?'

'Right. And fancy you asking him back. He'd have knocked over the Ming vase and then got lost on his way to the toilet.' And then they'd have laughed and driven back into dreamland.

I was angry because I felt cheated. Meeting Paul McCartney should've been deeply significant. But, like making love for the first time, it was a complete disaster. And, of course, in my eyes he alone was to blame.

My *Record Mirror* article ended:

'You've got enough, haven't you?' says Paul, obviously anxious to be rid of me once and for all.

'Yes,' I reply – meekly, I'm ashamed to say. And they left. The interview lasted twenty minutes.

I always liked John Lennon better anyway.

Wonder if Yoko fancies a chat?

Not surprisingly, Paul took exception to my piece and the following week, while doing an interview for *Melody Maker*, he apparently referred to me as a complete bastard and admitted he would've liked nothing more than to smack me in the face.

The *Record Mirror* article was written by someone I didn't know. Someone still clawing his way out of bombsite '77, covered with the dust of fallen stars. Someone who felt a little cheated because '78 was just another '76 without Barry Biggs. Someone who still sneered behind his beard at the ugly-bug ball. Someone jealous of an *NME* writer because they got all the glory. Someone jealous of Paul McCartney for being rich and talented. Someone with a grudge against everyone. Someone. But not me.

Of all the graffiti splashed on the whitewashed walls of my soul by vindictive ghosts, 'Barry Cain is a complete bastard, PM' hurts the most.

But it was the demon inside guv.

It wasn't cool to dig Wings and I went along with the cool cats. I couldn't be arsed to write nice when it was easier and more fun to write bad. I lied to myself by distorting my dreams.

I quit *Record Mirror* soon afterwards.

I never met Paul again and I shed a tear when Linda died. She was a sweetheart and would no doubt still have been married to Paul to this day.

The Beatles inspired me like nobody else before or since, but I lost them when they split. George was only good for one album, his debut triple-epic *All Things Must Pass*. John produced two classic albums – *John Lennon and the Plastic Ono Band* and *Imagine*. *Mind Games* was an intense disappointment and, apart from the *Rock'n'roll* album, he did nothing else of real note. The last, *Double Fantasy*, was drivel. Ringo?

Ringo joked about with photographs, sixteen-year-olds with lips like strawberry wine and sentimental journeys.

Paul released two truly great albums and three or four good ones. Maybe he still does. I stopped listening to his music twenty years ago. Mind you, I haven't listened to much else in twenty years so who am I to judge? I've taken an extended vacation from my house of music, returning, now and again, to collect the post and make sure the pipes haven't burst.

I always regarded Paul as the most beautiful Beatle, which was why I went for John with his hook nose and pounding hips. Paul sang the prettiest Beatles songs and yet 'I'm Down', 'She's A Woman' and 'Oh Darlin'' revealed an achey-breaky vocal that gave my heart a hard-on.

So, I take my hat off to you Sir Paul. You came in through the bathroom window and stole the show. I'd like to have written that back in March 1978.

Now back to the future – or, rather, forward to the past where the Intro still lurks....

1971–75

Court reporter and cider soul boy

I left school at eighteen with two E-grade A levels in English Lit and History and vague ideas of becoming a journalist. I wrote vague letters to my local papers like the *Islington Gazette* and the *St Pancras Chronicle* and I got vaguer replies declining the offer of my services.

Then I applied for a year-long pre-entry course at Harlow College run by the National Council for the Training of Journalists. After filling in a very long application form, I was invited, along with thirty other hopefuls, to attend one of the selection days that involved several written tests to determine the extent of my literacy and an interview with five solemn-looking tutors. The tests were pretty straightforward but I knew I'd blown the interview when one of the tutors asked me if I liked music.

'Yes. Modern music.' I meant pop. Never knew why I said 'modern'.

'Oh, early twentieth century music?' he enquired. He looked interested.

'Er, yes.' Never knew why I said that either. The next question was the killer.

'Who's your favourite composer?'

I had to think fast. I'd never heard the term 'modern music' in a classical context. Who did I know who might be an exponent of 'modern music'?

It came to me in a flash – of course, the composer featured at the start of the Blood Sweat & Tears album. French: wrote, what was it?, 'Trois Gymnopédies'! That's it! And the composer's name was, that's it! Erik, Erik…

'Erik Sartre,' I replied confidently.

'You mean Erik Satie,' he said.

'Yes. Satie. My favourite composer. Yes.' Not only ignorant, but a liar too.

Ten days later the rejection slip eased through my letterbox. Maybe journalism wasn't for me.

I then applied for a year-long creative-writing course at Watford College that was supposed to lead to a career as an advertising copywriter. They sent me a test paper, which involved questions like, 'Describe a colour to a person who has been blind since birth' and 'Write a short play about a cat and a dustbin.'

I had a go and sent it off. That Saturday I got a call at home from the principal of the college, who told me they loved the stuff I'd written and I'd better start thinking about arranging my student grant. I just had to attend the college for a quick interview that, judging by his attitude, was a formality.

Went down three days later, screwed up the interview by not being able to string two coherent sentences together and no doubt convinced them all (five again) that the paper they'd received from me was actually written by someone else who understood plain English.

Ten days later, the rejection slip eased through my letterbox. Maybe advertising wasn't for me.

So I blamed the Applejacks and signed on. Money wasn't really a worry. I lived at home with my mum and dad, who both worked. They liked having me around. It's easy to be a bum in the city when you've gotta mum, so I became one. Bum, not mum.

And then a woman who worked at the local labour exchange where I signed on, took a shine to me in a strictly motherly way. I told her casually one signing-on day that I'd once harboured dreams of becoming a journalist. She remembered, and when a job came in for a trainee court reporter she rang me.

'Are you interested? It's at Great Marlborough Street Magistrates' Court in Soho. Right next door to the London Palladium. Just pop down there tomorrow for an interview.'

Shit! What was the point? I'd only fail.

'I don't know if I can do tomorrow. Actually, I don't think it's for me. I'll leave it for now.'

'I thought you dreamed of becoming a journalist? Whatever it is you're doing tomorrow at 4.30pm, cancel it and head down there. A Mr Len Almond will be waiting to see you. He runs the Almond press agency and his office is in the courthouse. He sounds like a decent bloke. Go for it.'

She was my guardian angel.

I met Len in an empty Court Two. He was about sixty, glasses, double-breasted *Dad's Army* brown suit with a white pinstripe, impressive head of wavy dark grey hair. Five-foot-two, eyes of blue, He was all of Dickens' nice guys rolled into one.

We sat on the deserted solicitors' benches and after we'd chatted for five minutes, he offered me the job.

So, in the autumn of 1971, Len, four laddish reporters and I, now nineteen, covered Great Marlborough Street and Marylebone Magistrates' Courts in the West End. The heartbeat of the agency was the tiny 19th-century office that backed onto the gaoler's office in Marlborough Street courthouse. Its stained green walls housed three wooden desks and chairs, a similar number of typewriters from the Roaring Twenties, and a young shit-kickin' enthusiasm that wriggled through the cigarette smoke and plucked intros from thin air.

I sat on the press bench every day from ten am until four pm with a one-hour break for lunch that I spent writing up the notes I'd taken in the morning session. I covered every case so shorthand was essential and I studied it three nights a week at Pitman's Secretarial College in Russell Square. The reports were mailed to all the relevant local papers because the offenders' full addresses were read out in open court.

I sent shame through the post but Len, who completed *The Times* crossword every morning on the Bakerloo Line between Kilburn Park and Edgware Road, insisted it was a public duty.

If I thought the case had more than just local interest, I'd slip out of court, ring up the features' desks of every national paper and try to sell them the story. I then had to write it up in the style of the paper ordering it, phone it over to the copy desks, then go back to court to catch some more humiliation and degradation.

I went home on the tube every night with a headful of gypsies, tramps and thieves and the odd perverted accountant thrown in for good measure. One guy, who was in his early thirties and lived with his wife and two children in stockbroker Surrey, was caught jerking off while ogling the Carnaby Street boutique babes through shop windows in broad daylight. Now that's what I call a nineteenth nervous breakdown.

Another accountant got absolutely pissed in the West End one Friday night, met a woman in the street and was later spotted by an eagle-eyed copper shagging her under a bush near the bandstand in Hyde Park.

The next morning, when they stood together in the dock, the accountant, who was no more than twenty-four, turned and stared at the woman whose body he'd ravaged the previous night. I shall never forget to my dying day the look of horror on his face. She was a seventy-eight year-old in a filthy brown overcoat and bright green nylon socks that had more holes than Blackburn, Lancashire, revealing terminal varicose veins. Her thin, matted white hair fell across her grubby, wrinkled face and strands dangled on the dried snot that covered her top lip. She had barely a tooth in her head.

The night before he'd seen Julie Christie in a river of Red Barrel. I doubt he ever recovered.

I quit the job in the summer of '73. I was well and truly armed – 120wpm shorthand, a nose for a story, a master of the intro.

But I was also in love with Dina, a Greek goddess I met at shorthand classes. When she returned to Cyprus, I quit the job and went on a 2,000 mile trek in a beaten-up Ford Consul to that island paradise where, to this day, it's still easy to trace the tracks of my tears. But that's another story in another book. As you three guys know...

After that ill-fated trip – the first time I'd ever ventured abroad – life in '73 London at home with my mum and dad was just too mundane, too achingly trivial, too *Sing Something Simple*.

My tiger feet pounced out the door and into the gun-metal grey Hillman Imp I'd bought for thirty-eight quid at a car auction in dodgy South London. After my successful bid I went to check out the car and almost collapsed when, upon opening the bonnet, I discovered there was no engine. 'The engine's in the boot, mate,' said one of the dealers and laughed hysterically.

The engine in the boot took me to Gloucester where I started work as a trainee reporter on the *Citizen* evening newspaper around the time Fred and Ginger were dancing on the corpses of teenage girls down the Cromwell Road. I lived for a while in a converted barn on a farm in the heart of the Cotswolds, just around the corner from the Woolpack in Slad, the pub in Laurie Lee's *Cider with Rosie*.

I spent just over two years in Gloucester, two very happy years in which I acquired the art of interviewing, the knack of living alone, the desire to get to the front of a club queue and a lifelong addiction to freebies.

In '74 and '75, Tracy's and the much larger Mecca-owned Tiffany's, were the only guys standing in the shadows of the city's magnificent cathedral after eleven pm. Outside both venues on Friday and Saturday nights the West Country cider soulboys would gather, the velocity and spirit of Wigan Casino coursing through their pill-stained veins. Tracy's would occasionally feature a top-notch live act – we're talking Edwin Starr, KC and the Sunshine Band, and sad sweet dreamers Sweet Sensation – because the punters just loved to groove, their huge baggies billowing on the lager-sticky dance floor where their feet spun at the speed of light.

 1976-7

Eric Burdon, Marc Bolan, Robert Plant

I moved back to London at Christmas '75 in search of a 'glittering career' and blagged a job on the *South-East London Mercury* as entertainment editor.

Suddenly I was laughing and joking with sexy Sally James in a TV studio alongside the Bay City Rollers in the days when they frolicked in the autumn mist.

Suddenly I was sitting next to Eric Burdon on a coach from London to Cardiff where he was playing at Ninian Park stadium on a bill headlined by Bob Marley and the Wailers and featuring the Pretty Things and Country Joe and the Fish. I'm talking to the man who sang on the first record I ever bought. Shit.

'Do you know, there are a lot more fucking police sirens in London than when I was last here three years ago.'

It wasn't a question. Eric was that kinda guy. If it wasn't for the music – and, apparently, the acid – that accent and that face would have put the shits up anyone. It was like sitting next to a gangster from *Get Carter*.

'The city has gone up ten notches in violence. It's the overspill from the States. People are into violence these days. Many Americans I've spoken to would rather spend a thousand dollars on arms for the IRA than on a holiday. They got better guns than the British Army, man.

'It's like in the movies where there's too much violence and not enough sex. Sure you get the porn. But not the eroticism. The American sex object today is a gun.'

The rain continued to beat against the window. Fifty miles from Cardiff and Eric Burdon was talking to me and me alone.

'And do you know the biggest weapon the Vietcong used against the US Army was dope? There are more ex-soldiers walking about in the States with pin-pricks in their arms than gunshot wounds.

'The '67 generation tried to teach people the difference between good drugs and bad drugs. But we were put down. There was a successful movement on the streets of San Francisco in 1968 to get rid of LSD and turn kids on to speed and junk.

'Acid has almost disappeared.'

And maybe the music didn't turn him on either.

'I know rock'n'roll too well. For me there's no danger zone anymore, no sense of the unknown. I've never regarded myself as a singer.' (But your record cost me 6s 8p! I want my money back!)

'The movies always did it for me. I'm a celluloid junkie, man. I moved to LA to be close to the business. There are so many things I'd like to make movies about. My life on the road, the second invasion of Hamburg by the rockers in the early Sixties, the 'Day In A Life' concept that Lennon used on *Sgt Pepper*, my life in America in the late Sixties. That period was like an iron fist strangling me. I was manipulated in the rock'n'roll business. I was lived off because I never cared about money.'

One of his projects involved Jimi Hendrix.

'So much mysticism surrounds the man. Most of his concerts were diabolical. Maybe one in ten he really played. He was such a brilliant artist. He told me he was going to kill himself four years before he died. He tried to at Woodstock, and re-arranged the billing to carry it out.

'How many great Americans have died in foreign lands rejected by their own people? From Hemingway to Hendrix, from Bessie Smith to Billie Holiday.'

What of the Animals?

'We recorded an album together and that will come out after a few legal hassles have been sorted out. I see a lot of Chas Chandler and Hilton Valentine.

'But nobody sees Alan Price. I don't even think he does.'

Suddenly, a few hours after chewing the fat with my new mate Eric, I was interviewing Marc Bolan in the Cardiff City players' changing rooms at Ninian Park. Torrential rain had turned the day-long festival into a washout. At the time, 'I Love To Boogie' was a huge hit. It was also his swansong. 'The song's suited to the present climate,' he said, while reclining on the player's' massage couch, like Elizabeth Taylor on the *Cleopatra* poster. 'It's part of the cosmos. And anyway, my stars are with me this year.'

He wore a white suit and red silk shirt and was at least four stone overweight. The cute Bolan locks were gone, replaced by a short forties-style haircut. His face was beginning to show what living in the pop world was all about, if you were Marc Bolan.

So what had happened to the skinny idol who broke a million teenybop hearts?

'I just got bored with playing music seven days a week and appearing on television every night.' His voice was glitzy and giggly and so, so sweet. 'It was time to re-evaluate. I found myself putting out virtually the same record every three months and watching it zoom to the top of the charts. I was being likened to Richard Cassidy and Donny Osmond – and that just ain't me.

'So I took a gamble. I packed my bags and went to live in New York City. I'm twenty-eight years old. I'm a musician. I'm a raver. New York was the place to be.'

Marc had written a film script with David Bowie and they were also recording an album together. 'I went to Stockholm with him and we were just hanging about. I had my hair cut there. The front of it was green and the back orange.'

He was proud of his career.

'I played to the public. We were the purveyors of public rock. 'Ride A White Swan' took off in 1970 after T. Rex were four years of being an album band. 'Hot Love' was number one for nine weeks. We sold millions. But I could see the end of glam rock and I was into longevity, man.

'Look at the bands around today. Slik died after a week, the Bay City Rollers are finished. Even Donny is giving up the classics. And guess what? I'm gonna get married.'

The lady in question, Gloria Jones, had been his constant companion for a few years. She was appearing at the festival backed by Gonzalez.

'I went along to Rod Stewart's party which was lovely until someone got smacked in the mouth, then people started having fights every two minutes. I met David Essex there. He's had his haircut too and looks a completely different person.'

I figured that back in the glam days he wouldn't have name-dropped like that. Marc was the only being in his universe when he was getting it on.

We left the dressing room together and went to the bar where his old friend, Robert Plant, was drinking a beer and wearing an 'I Love To Boogie' badge.

'I haven't heard Marc's new song yet,' Robert told me, 'but it's bound to be good.' He looked to have completely recovered from the horrific car smash he was involved in the previous year. They both agreed to a quick exclusive pic for the *Mercury* with Robert's finger planted firmly up his nose.

Marc Bolan and Robert Plant in one hit. Jesus.

Suddenly I was swamped with review albums and concert tickets and offers of interviews and backstage passes to amazing concerts, like the Who's greatest moment at The Valley, Charlton Athletic's home ground, on 31 May 1976 – officially the loudest rock show in history and as wet as Woodstock.

The concert was part of a short UK *Who Put The Boot In* stadium tour that also featured Little Feat, the Sensational Alex Harvey Band and the Outlaws.

I sat in the covered VIP section immediately behind the band and it pissed down. I watched sixty-thousand people dance between raindrops as laser beams bounced off mirrors high up on the floodlights and punched holes in the moon.

It was some night.

The last and only other time I'd seen the Who was at the Isle of Wight Festival in 1970 when they performed the whole of *Tommy* at midnight and were preceded by the Doors, Emerson Lake & Palmer's debut gig and my festival faves Ten Years After. I fingered a cute hippy under a sleeping bag during 'Pinball Wizard' and it was the best version I'd ever heard.

At the Valley they disembowelled the saturated night. I managed to keep dry while the crowd shook off the torrential rain like dancing dogs. On their way to the stars, the lasers (the first time I'd ever seen them) cut through the damp steam that curled and twisted from sixty thousand rapturous souls. It was a concert I'd like to take with me six feet under.

At the end of 1976 I landed a job at *Record Mirror* and my first year on the paper was recalled in my book *'77 Sulphate Strip*.

Fast forward to '78. And the five careers...

PART 1

Record Mirror

When I return from the Deep South in January 1978 after the Sex Pistols' disastrous, but ultimately wonderful, US tour, the world has changed.

Sweet soul '77 has died and taken a piece of me with it. Nothing again in pop will prove to be as pretty and witty and wise as those tatty '77 showmen, from the Clash to the Damned, who could've danced all night (excuse the mixed musicals). Punk was the sunshine that gave pop an incurable melanoma.

Now everywhere you look there are passionless, prosaic, quasidodo bands, indiscreet and out of time. I'm a '77 boy looking for adventure. There's some serious money to be made in music for shrewd brains sharpened by '77 steel and I want to have me some.

But, first, I have a piece of winter '78.

JANUARY 1978

Blue Oyster Cult, Meat Loaf, Bethnal

I duck out of the Pistols US tour in Memphis. This is a rare one – my entire trip is financed by *Record Mirror* because the band's record company, Virgin, shrewdly didn't offer any press trips, confident in the knowledge that every Fleet Street paper would send their boys over the top at their own expense to get all the hot Stateside Pistols poop.

The money is running out so I jump a plane to New York where CBS kindly agree to set me up for a week in a fine Manhattan hotel overlooking Central Park in return for a few features in *Record Mirror*.

Record labels foot all your bills, including room service and the mini-bar, and then arrange a couple of interviews with some of their newer, juicier acts. They often fly you to another city in the US and pay for everything there as well. Coverage in the UK weekly music press is the holy grail because of the vast readerships involved. They carry a lot of clout and the staff writers are in the front line, hoovering up ligs and freebies and 24-carat trips. I'm anybody's after a slap-up meal, a river of vintage red and a few lines of Charlie. Throw in a hotel suite in a big foreign city and you can tie me to the radiator for a gangbang. Yep, you could say the music business has given me some tainted love.

So, first up, Blue Oyster Cult. Step inside, loves.

A car picks me up at the hotel for the ninety-mile drive to Poughkeepsie where the Cult are performing at the Mid Hudson Civic Center.

I don't know much about them, but I do know they ain't your average US hard rock band. There's a certain whimsicality in their make-up, coupled with a peek-a-boo intelligence. Their biggest hit, 'Don't Fear The Reaper', was a pussycat of a record when compared with the clenched-fist mojo marathons of so many of their airhead contemporaries.

I'm intrigued, but not enough to look forward to the show. Punk has petrified my ears. Three minutes is enough for any pop song and punk is the real deal of the late Seventies. The pedestrian pomposity of rock bands in leotards is obscene by comparison. I've learned to love my music in single shots; a rapid brainbust bursting with chaotic guitar and violent drums is infinitely more exciting than the contorted skulduggery of windswept rock played by a penis in blue jeans.

But tonight, the Cult napalm the place, then douse it with hosepipes, then napalm it again. But they do it all with a smile. A Blue Oyster Cult smile. A sly grin behind the amp, a snigger in the solo.

OK, they're loud. But it's a smoochy, candlelit-dinner of a blast. Wild, woolly and wonderful.

And then there's the lasers.

Razor sharp green beams carving elaborate patterns on walls, colliding with rotating crystal balls strategically suspended from the ceiling and cascading into the hypnotised audience like electric rain.

Lasers shooting out of the accusing finger of sinister Eric Bloom like the Green Lantern. Lasers like barbed wire, where the shreds of a Donald Roeser guitar solo hang like ripped clothes. This is close-encounter ray-gun rock.

A Blue Oyster Cult concert cuts you open and bandages you up at the same time.

And then it happens.

The band blow a fuse, literally, and all the lights and all the heat and all the can-openers go bang in Poughkeepsie, New York State, on Wednesday, 11 January 1978.

A smoke bomb had dissolved and the Cult had just begun to disseminate 'Born To Be Wild' when it happened. A fitting finale 'cos they'd pumped enough volts into that Civic Center on that icy cold night to blow the minds of an army of Frankensteins encased in ice.

'In unenlightened days, a VD victim had to be bombarded with what was then referred to as "Heavy Metal" drugs. Unfortunately they were so heavy that they turned the poor bastard's gums blue. Then penicillin and all types of cunning-device drugs came along and your gums didn't turn blue anymore.'

The Cult are the blue behind the squeaky clean red. Your girlfriend will never know. How's your gums?

Blue Oyster Cult drummer Albert Bouchard tells the blue story as he inhales the mindsteam, breathes out oh-so-slowly, and talks about his wife, life and the blues.

I like these guys although that could be something to do with the wonderful smoke I have in the back of a limo with BOC founder member Albert, en route to Manhattan after the gig. We talk for ninety miles and I can feel the smooth engine and soft leather. I'm twenty-four and life can't possibly get any better than this. Can it?

I bid Albert and the chauffeur goodnight and watch the Cadillac head off towards Central Park. The street is sticky with hard snow and my smoke-addled feet make heavy weather of it. But when the doorman smiles I feel fine and the walk to the elevator isn't nearly so desperate. The minute I open the door to my suite – yep, suite – I switch on the TV and fall into bed. Not only am I getting paid for doing this, I also get expenses.

I pick up the phone, dial long distance – Islington – and amaze my mum with the six-hour time difference, the proliferation of TV channels, the size of my room, the snow, the food and the whores on 42nd Street. Then the old man gets on and I repeat it all to him. The bill will be astronomical. But, shit, it isn't public money and CBS would have to pay a lot more for a double-page ad. Because that's the space they were getting from me in a paper that sells 160,000 copies a week.

So, naturally, after I hang up on London I dial for a little TLC from my room-service man – steak sandwich, salad, fries and a bottle of red. I have a half-pack of Marlboro, twenty-five channels on the TV, snowflakes on my windowpane and a couple of joints. Who needs women at a time like this?

The next day in Room 5C on the thirteenth floor of the immense Black Rock CBS centre in a snow-covered New York City, Cult keyboardist Allen Lanier sugar-sweet waits for me with a couple of glasses of red wine and an interesting selection of words.

'People are always ready to come up to your expectations when they're dazzled,' he says intellectually. 'There's this great cathartic experience at rock shows – a very necessary explosion of inner sensibility and feeling. A chance for the inherent anarchic senses to be released.

'There's got to be some phenomenon that gets a big crowd together and then sends the whole lot of 'em raving. The kids smoke, drink, get wiped out and explode the pressures. Religion has its escapes too – like revisionist meetings.'

Lanier actually looks intelligent, which is sometimes difficult when you've got long hair these days.

The BOC have just completed their most successful ever tour and are hitting Europe next month. Interest has been rejuvenated, thanks to their first hit single in six years, '(Don't Fear) The Reaper'.

Allen Lanier is a highly articulate man who likes to get drunk now and again. His lady also happens to be Patti Smith – but we can't all be perfect. Just kiddin', Allen.

'The Sex Pistols won't make it here,' he says. 'For starters, no radio – they won't get the airplays. Second, no hardships to play on. America is doing quite well thank you. We had the Vietnam war, we killed all the Indians. Hiroshima is our Dachau. We've had all that.

'Rock'n'roll was all about a frustrated generation of kids hating their mothers and fathers and getting wrecked. But those revolutions have been won and it now reflects in the music – soft and radio playable.

'The greatest rock'n'roll records I remember being raised on were flamboyant, youthful, energetic, yet with the expertise of old musicians. One of the weaknesses of punk rock is the fact that they don't have a Charlie Watts.

'You don't understand the temptations you face in this business. You can have a lot of ideals – but they can vanish in a champagne and caviar onslaught. I ain't a real extravagant guy – except in the sense that I spend all my money.'

Blue Oyster Cult play cruiserweight metal – it's flightier than its heavier counterpart but still packs a seismic punch.

Another night in New York, another new fango dango. And all I have to do is interview some band called Meat Loaf the next day. Apparently no other UK journalist has met them. In fact, nobody knows much about Meat Loaf in January 1978.

The album, *Bat Out Of Hell*, has been knocking around for a few months but isn't setting the world alight, and there are rumours that people at the record company – Epic, part of the CBS empire – actually hate it.

An interview with Meat Loaf and Jim Steinman, the real Batman, is arranged in a Manhattan apartment and I take along my blankety blank notebook and pen for company.

Meat Loaf and Steinman may sound like a firm of quirky lawyers but in reality they are the Laurel and Hardy of soda-pop soliloquy.

Bat Out Of Hell is an hour-long adolescent insurrection. Its Bazooka Joe passion comes, quickly, over motorbikes and breasts, Coupe de Ville's and football games, lubricated love and fat wet dreams.

The hero, wearing faded Levis that can apparently burst apart at will, feels 'the fever grow' and Meat Loaf's fat, wet voice grows along with it, splish-splashing through the Spector-sized production, courtesy of Todd Rundgren.

Jim Steinman has written all the songs on *Bat Out Of Hell*: songs concerned with the amplification of reality, his words told to yours truly as Meat, Jim and I sip brandy from crystal glasses.

Meat Loaf, a.k.a. Marvin Lee Aday, is as big as the biggest night club bouncer you've ever laid eyes on. But it's a syncopated bigness – sometimes, when the moon's in the right place, he looks half the size.

'I left Dallas when I graduated,' he recalls. 'I was always drunk, playing basketball and running.'

Running? You did say 'running'?

'Yeah, I ran five miles every day for eleven years.'

I wonder what would he have looked like if he'd only walked?

Jim, with his long hair and cute eyes, is a front man waiting to happen. 'We started work on these songs in '76 after some exploratory sessions the year before.'

'We would have completed it earlier,' Meat interjects, 'only we're both perfectionists.'

I mention that the album has been compared, in feel, ambition and technique, to Springsteen at his finest

'Yeah, but when I hear Springsteen I think of the Who,' says Jim dismissing the comparison. 'It's the resonances, the reverberations, the echoes. It's simply 1966 rock'n'roll.

'Our songs are a series of heroics. An amplification of reality, a glorification of fantasy. There hasn't been a lot of that in the last few years. Fleetwood Mac are a glorification of what's already real. Everything musical at the moment seems so homogenised. The Seventies has been a decade of languidness. The Sixties was a decade of rock'n'roll.

'But everyone got older and left rock behind them. They've dispensed with the heroics and are now dealing with interior forces. We all live too comfortably. That's why we like FM radio. Universal fantasies are projects in a changing environment. Impulses and sexual desires haunt rock'n'roll songs. A Stevie Wonder arrangement can be just as fanatical as an Elvis Costello arrangement.

'The songs on the album are a combination of all my dreams, all my obsessions. But it's essentially sarcastic. A lot of the most dramatic moments on 'Bat' are sarcastic. That doesn't mean to say I find "teenage" a disparaging term. Rock'n'roll is teenage. It's narcissistic. Teenage is one of the most pure American terms I've ever heard.'

Jim has managed to vinylise his dreams. And vinylised dreams last longer. The last thing you see is your heart.

After initial doubts on the part of their record company, the meaty, beaty, big and bouncy Bat Out Of Hell went on to worldwide sales of over 50 million. The record is more famous than Jesus, or something. Meat Loaf has appeared in a shitload of movies including Fight Club, Wayne's World and with Tenacious D in The Pick of Destiny. He has continued to release albums – most notably Bat Out Of Hell II in 1993 and Bat Out Of Hell – The Monster Is Loose in 2006. He lives in California and is a supporter of Hartlepool FC. It takes all sorts…

Before I go home, CBS insist on flying me to Fort Worth to catch an Earth Wind & Fire concert and I duly oblige. Texas is covered with thick snow, the first they've seen in these here parts in years. As I walk along the city's supersonic streets, I know this is the shape of things to come and it gives me a warm glow inside. And the women are dynamite, as the bell hop informs me, 'If you're interested.'

Why must I be a teenager in love (give or take a few years)?

Earth Wind & Fire are magnificent. I loved the *That's The Way Of The World* album back in the early Seventies and these guys are now really well hung, like a good salami. I'm in Texas; I'm in love; I'm in phone booth, it's the one across the hall. My positive review in *Record Mirror* puts me one step closer to the trip of a lifetime.

Then I return to London. It's back in the old routine. A great routine, sure, but it'll never make me rich.

Funny, I'd never thought about money until I proposed to Dina. Greek Cypriots are, in the main, devoutly avaricious and it does rub off after a while. I start to look at pop stars and music moguls, who laugh and dance and sing till dawn, in a different way and I realise I'm merely a guest with blisters on my fingers and bells on my toes. I'm renting but they own the freehold. Dina makes me want to own the freehold.

For the first time in my life, I feel the itch of ambition in my boxers.

The *Record Mirror* Readers' Annual Poll Awards make for grim reading. T. Rex win best group and best album with the awful *Dandy In The Underworld* while the male singer award goes to Marc Bolan, who's been dead for months. The sympathy vote prevents Queen winning everything, though they do get best single with 'We Are The Champions,' narrowly beating 'God Save The Queen'.

Gloria Jones, Marc's lover and the original Northern Queen of Soul who was also injured in the fatal crash, even wins best female singer, and all she'd done last year was work with Gonzalez, who had a solitary hit with 'I Haven't Stopped Dancing Yet' (which she also wrote). Gloria was the first person to record 'Tainted Love' in 1965.

The best new band category is won by the Boomtown Rats followed by the Tom Robinson Band and the Stranglers.

Record Mirror readers are weird.

My first back-in-town feature of the year is getting down and dirty with cosmopolitan London combo Bethnal, made up of two Greek

Cypriots, a Jamaican and a white man in Hammersmith Palais. They're talented musicians who play souped-up hard rock dressed as punk, and their USP is the strong-arm violin of George Csapo.

The hard part is the PR.

Hence the idea to hold the interview at lunchtime in hand-job's fair city where the girls are so pretty. A Soho strip club in 1978 is *Midnight Cowboy* meets *Eraserhead*, dark and deceitful, a Fanny by Gaslight flashing parlour for the deeply disturbed. I love it, but that's probably down to the line of speed that has just stormed up my nose. How's *your* day at work?

It turns out the main stripper has been chatted up by one of the guys in the band in the pub over the road an hour earlier. He's blissfully unaware of her occupation and is made up when he manages to get her telephone number. Now, as she sits on a swing with her legs apart, wearing nothing but a bonnet and a smile, the look on her face when she spots Michael is priceless. The look on his is pricier and he takes some monstrous piss-taking, but I'm kinda envious. A date with a stripper sounds pretty cool, especially if she brings her own swing. And bonnet.

FEBRUARY 1978

Sham 69, Earth Wind & Fire, Concorde

I find myself in times of trouble in Glasgow with Mother Pursey and his band and some of the worst fighting I've ever seen. We're sitting in a cafe in the city centre. Sham 69 eat muck and chips. It's that post-soundcheck wait-till-the-midnight-hour limbo feel.

Jimmy makes enquiries. 'Ere sweet 'eart – where's the Goebals? Or is it Gerbals? Or fuckin' Gorbals?'

'Och, quite a way.' Elderly Scottish waitress, bewitched, bothered and definitely bewildered.

'Tell me, luv, is it really 'eavy there?'

'Sorry?'

''Eavy. Y'know, 'ard.' Jimmy raises his fists like a boxer.

'Och no. Things like that don't usually happen in Glasgow.' She wanders away, stops and turns around. 'Mind you, last week a mob of sixteen-year-olds did go on the rampage there, mugging everyone in their path. But things like that don't usually happen in Glasgow.

'Oh, yes, and someone was murdered in a club the other night – but things like that don't usually happen in Glasgow.'

Jimmy is trying hard to smother his laughter when the waitress returns with the teas. 'Och and last week a man was shot outside a pub but...'

The band in unison, 'Fings like that don't usually 'appen in Glasgow!'

Punk gigs are banned in the city. Oh, sure, you could play the Apollo but you might get belted by a security man if you put one foot in the aisle. So Sham are playing the university tonight. But only students in the know are allowed to attend and the entertainment committee on the door – all suits and ties and windscreen wipers on their horn-rimmed glasses – are there to ensure the unemployed mind haemorrhage kids with the diesel fuel fists don't make their mark.

Fat chance, I think, as a kid covered with blood tumbles down the stairs in the entrance before the show has even started.

It's hard to make out support band Backstabbers because about fifty people are on the stage ripping the shit out of each other.

Jimmy wades in. 'Ere!' he shouts.

The fighting ceases immediately and the Jocks cheer. Jimmy pulls the guy from the stairs onto the stage, his head now swathed in blood-soaked bandages. 'We don't want fings like this to 'appen, do we?'

I say to myself instinctively, 'Cos they don't usually...'

'NO!'

'We wanna 'ave a good time, don't we?'

'YEAH!'

'They fink we're gonna riot. Let's show 'em we can 'ave a fuckin' good time wivout fings like this.' Pointing to the bandaged pawn.

'YEAH!'

OK, so the gig doesn't pass without further incident, but Jimmy has taken the sting out of the tail. He appeals to your sense of inferiority. The squashed kid's champion always accusing a nebulous, nefarious 'they' of being responsible for all of their woes and frustrations.

Jimmy's a big brother warning you of Big Brother. He's effective because Jimmy loves the limelight, the smell of the greasepaint, the roar of the crowd. Like Bette Midler (with a bit of Henry Cooper), he's a performer.

He sings like he talks. He's having an intimate chat across a table in the corner of a restaurant, totally focused on you. Swap a serenading violin for tower-block guitars and a DM-in-the-bollocks drum and that's a Sham 69 concert.

Crash, bang, wallop, what a picture. Wherever the band go, the reaction's the same. The stage becomes the crowd. The kids glorify in Pursey freedom. Close your eyes and you're transported back a year to 1977 BC – Before Clash. Before excitement became subjugated to stance, style and indoctrination.

It's a memorable show for all the wrong reasons, which eventually become all the right reasons.

Back in my hotel room I'm a little disappointed that Jimmy left with a bonnie lassie straight after the show. I've known him for a year and I'm one of the first people to write about the band after he bombards me with phone calls at *Record Mirror* telling me how good he is. And when I finally see the band at the Roxy I know he'll be a star.

So I think he might at least have said goodnight. I mean, who wants to come to Glasgow on a cold, wet Thursday night to watch the William Wallaces get it on?

It's two am when I get into bed – seven am call. There's a bang on the door.

'Open up – police!' I recognise the voice. Jimmy strolls in with a bottle of Scotch under his arm. 'Well I couldn't let a bird come before my pal Barry, if you excuse my French.'

Jimmy Pursey can talk. A lot. He can talk corks out of bottles, forks out of mouths, porks out of pigs, hawks out of hunger. He's the geezer in the boozer who corners you and never lets you go; the spiv in the market effortlessly selling cheap crockery with immaculate spiel; the Deep South preacher breaking the backs of the gullible and weak.

Hallelujah!

He talks himself into trouble: he talks himself out of trouble. Talking Head '78. He'll tell you about his life, his strife, his knife, his aspirations: 'I've done everyfing I wanted in music so far, 'ad a free single and a live side on me first album.' His fears: 'I 'ope to God I ain't never gonna change.' His past: 'They stuck a broken bottle in me mate's neck and then stuck 'is 'ead down the toilet while they broke both 'is legs wiv an iron bar. And a few weeks later they beat me up, only worse.' His fans: 'All I want them to understand is they should be able to stand up and say anyfing they want to. Don't let other people tell you what to do.' And his soul: 'I used to wear Dr Martens too.'

We polish off the bottle in an hour and the world seems a nicer place. It's about to get nicer. Much nicer.

Sham 69 broke up in 1980. They reformed in 1987 and knocked around for the next ten years during which 'If The Kids Are United' was used in a McDonalds' ad and by the Labour Party. A new version of 'Hurry Up Harry' was released for the 2006 World Cup and made the top ten. Jimmy left the band in 2007 and formed Day 21. After a brief reunion tour in 2012, Jimmy parted company from them again. But you can't keep a good man down, and he's now back with the band once more.

Writing for *Record Mirror* in 1978 can make your dreams come true, probably far too early. My aim isn't so true anymore, doesn't have to be, because shit just happens. Like being around when a bunch of newly released albums land in the office one morning. I'm immediately attracted to the foxy fantasy cover of Earth Wind &

Fire's fancy pants album, *All 'n' All*, and, my recent trip to Fort Worth fresh in my mind, I take it away to review. Whoosh, it's a belter. Erudite dance music you can listen to – the ultimate accolade.

So I write a 150-word review praising its dynamism and desire to inject some off-the-shoulder soul into a late-Seventies disco scene sadly lacking any fever of the Saturday-night variety. In other words, this is hot stuff.

Someone somewhere high up likes my review.

A week after it appears, my office phone rings.

'Barry, Ellie here.' Ellie Smith is the PR for CBS in Soho Square. New Yorker, sharp, sassy and great company. 'We liked your review and were wondering if you'd care to see the band play live again.'

'Are they coming over to promote the album?'

'Yes, they're planning a European tour for the late summer.'

'Stick me down. I'd love to see them.'

'Well, the idea would be for you to preview the show – as you know, it's pretty spectacular – before it actually comes over. The band are currently on a US tour and the show we're looking at is in Atlanta. Next week.'

At the end of 1977 I'd never been to Atlanta in my life. It was as far off the radar as Borneo or Billericay. Within barely the first four weeks of '78, I'd have been there twice, first with the Sex Pistols and now with EW&F. So no difference there, then.

'Sounds great. Thanks very much.'

'Wonderful. Now, let me tell you the itinerary.'

She sounds a little excited.

'You fly out in the afternoon, first class from Heathrow to Paris.'

'First class?' That's never happened before. And why Paris if we're flying to the States?

'You then stay overnight at the George Cinq where you'll dine with some other European journalists who are also going to the gig.'

See what I mean? Dreams.

'How many?'

'I think it's about thirty.'

I can't believe CBS would fly all those journos over – it's unprecedented.

'Any other British writers on the trip?'

'Yes, Richard Williams for *The Times* and Pauline McLeod for *The Mirror*.'

A touch of class.

'The next day you go to Charles de Gaulle airport where you catch a flight to New York on Air France Concorde. There you change planes and fly down to Atlanta on a private jet, stay for five days in a five-star hotel, see the show, do an interview and take in the sights. Then you get the private jet back to New York where you check in at the Plaza, have dinner and spend a night on the town. Next day, Concorde to Paris, Paris to London...'

'First class?'

'First class.'

Amen.

'Gee,' she said, 'I hope I get to go too.'

This is like an incredibly upmarket *Price Is Right* where I almost expect to be asked how much it will all amount to. Come on down!

'Take a ride in the sky on our ship fantasy / All your dreams will come true miles away...'

We break through the sound barrier off the coast of France, the George Cinq a distant memory. As the head chef from Maxims prepares dinner in the galley, I toast Concorde with a glass of vintage champagne and a medallion of fresh foie gras followed by fillet of turbot in lobster sauce and a slab of chateaubriand with green pepper sauce. It's the least I can do. This is Heaven in a tube for 128 passengers. The seats are tight but the speed is cool.

And the silver-plated futuristic cutlery is even cooler. I slip what I can into my inside jacket pocket and then feel terribly guilty for the rest of the journey. When we land in JFK, a passenger drops her handbag as she gets out of her seat. Its contents spill into the aisle and include several place settings' worth of Concorde cutlery. She looks embarrassed as a smiling stewardess picks them all up from the cabin floor and puts them back into the handbag.

I don't feel so guilty any more. Neither does virtually every other passenger. They must go through a shitload of Concorde cutlery.

I get to know Richard Williams a little that week. He's an influential figure in music and the first presenter of *The Old Grey Whistle Test*. But I don't take advantage of the opportunity.

Pauline McLeod is attractive and laughs a lot, which makes her even more attractive. She's a top Fleet Street music writer. But do I ever call her? Mind you, does she ever call me? Does Richard? And there you see my problem: my inability to cultivate in order to progress. I suffer from don't-ring-us-we'll-ring-you syndrome – I'm constantly auditioning and never getting a call back. Sad bastard, really. My face still doesn't fit.

Earth, Wind & Fire are the most successful black group in America, elevating the slick choreography and jump-suit harmonies of elementary soft-soul outfits to a Cecil B. DeMille extravaganza.

They're a Mafia funeral, Tubes with a straight face, a drug-free, festival-free, booze-free Sly and the Family Stone for the late Seventies. I love everyday people – but Earth Wind & Fire?

Well, is their music lipstick on your collar or on your knob? Judging by their show at the Omni Coliseum in downtown Atlanta, there she blows...

An essential ingredient for an EW&F show is a vast sports arena that seats fifteen thousand people. And what people. Smoking dudes in whippersnapper suits and Bogart Panamas, smoochy Astaire spats with gold laces and matching shades, emerald teeth, silk shirts, silk walk, silk talk. And their hoochie-coochie wet-dream girls just one step away from obscenity, daubed in soft-porn *Vogue*, all legs and smiles and joy. Money to burn.

In the US, EW&F had reached the apex of a career spanning

eight years, seven gold albums and a Papa's brand new bag full of accolades. Bassist Verdine White, brother of Maurice, tosses an elegant glance across the room. To say he's smart, intellectually and sartorially, is an understatement. Pride in appearance is an important part of Verdine's life. 'You gotta look good,' he says. 'Brush your clothes every day. Comb your hair right.'

He sits a little stiffly on a stiff chair in his hotel suite sipping orange juice. 'I used to drink but then the process of trying to get high just seemed to become more and more unnecessary, plus I broke up with two ladies because of it. None of the group drink or take drugs.

'A lot of people figure that if you're clean you're square. People admire crazy people. Lennon was more liked than McCartney because everyone thought he had guts, y'know, the experimenter. But I preferred McCartney because he was more sophisticated.'

Verdine was once quoted as saying that if EW&F weren't black they'd have been bigger than the Beatles. So?

'We've had to cross a racial barrier in music. We're black and it's much harder to get in on any success trip when you are. For starters you don't have many people buying your records and, second, black managers are notoriously inept. There's also less channels for black music to pass through.

'It's taken us a long time to become acceptable. We could never be like the Beatles, but now we've opened the door for future black bands, one of them will be.

'EW&F have helped to change a lot of black lives. Kids today are too wild. They get away with murder. Everyone needs direction and guidance. See, blacks take success differently from whites. A lot of black guys ask me what the white guy knew that he didn't. Success is a mystery to them whereas to whites it's a way of life because he's been taught in the ways of dynasty.

'Young black people in England are different. They're more Rastified. We just don't look like them. They'll check us out, though, simply because they want to convince themselves we're a hype. But we don't get upset.'

Their current album, *All 'N' All*, is their most successful to date and has attracted a whole new white audience. Though it's teetering on the edge of an MOR abyss, it's nevertheless impossible not to be impressed by the music – a black Chicago fused with the incestuous naiveté of mid-Seventies disco.

'I guess we'll have to change things, tone it down, when we get to Europe.'

So, Verdine, are you looking forward to the European tour this summer? A natural enough question, in the circumstances.

'Oh, I do believe that was cancelled yesterday. We're going early next year now.'

I think about that last line a few nights later in New York as I yank another Jack Daniels' miniature from the mini bar in my huge suite at the Plaza and settle down to watch a little TV before going into the restaurant for dinner with the other twenty-nine.

And another trip on Concorde in the morning.

The music business is like that in 1978.

Money to burn.

MARCH 1978

John Miles, The Buzzcocks, Squeeze, Linda McCartney

I'm beginning to lose touch with reality. Planes, hotels, lavish meals, deafening concerts, lines of fascinating powders, bathfuls of booze, world-famous rock stars. I'm living the life of a wealthy man on thirty quid a week. It's time to start living the life of a wealthy man as a wealthy man.

I've got enough contacts. I really feel I should be taking advantage of the music. I've loved it for a long time and I want to marry it. It's only natural.

It's time to hang up my dancing shoes and get serious. I've proposed to Dina. I'm going to get married, have kids, live in Cyprus, float in the pool at my villa on the coast and watch the waves break on white sand, laugh and joke with the locals in impeccable Greek and die in the sunshine. I need money. The job is great but the pay is lousy. Anyway, punk is dead.

I finally decide to quit after being invited to run Albion Records with leading pop publicist Alan Edwards. Albion is the name of the management company behind the Stranglers and they decide to launch a record division. Alan and I are to have complete control – signing bands, dealing with promotion, the works. It's too good an offer to turn down. Fat Lou Grade cigars beckon.

But first I've got four more interviews to do – John Miles, Pete Shelley, Squeeze and Linda McCartney.

John Miles is the first person to tell me that Rock Hudson is gay. 'Allegedly he lives with Rod McKuen and they're known as Mr and Mrs America.'

We're having breakfast in the dining room of a Glasgow hotel and I nearly choke on my tattie scone.

John Miles is – uh – blond. Cutie-pie blond, Clearasil blond, cabin-boy blond and, now, permed blond. It's also not unknown for him to be regarded by some as a dumb blond. Each to his own. Me? I simply find him blond. Natural blond. In fact, he's probably the most natural blond I've ever met. (Actually, I used to think a certain Californian lady was until I got to know her better.) The only thing a natural can stick to is what he's good at. John Miles happens to play the guitar like a god. So he sticks to that. He realised long ago that he was faceless. He tells me as much over a cascade of burgundy, a pool of port, and a fountain of brandy – all in the back of a Granada en route to Scotland on a promo tour. John likes a drink. It makes him feisty.

Over burgundy: 'Maybe not having an image is detrimental to my career, but there's not much I can do about it. Sometimes I try and think

of something out of the ordinary to be, but I just don't know what.'
 Over port: Do you often get lost for words, John? ... John?

   'Er, yes, I guess I do. If your face doesn't fit, some people just say
fuck the music, and my face definitely doesn't fit.'

   Over brandy: 'I may be old-fashioned but I still think people buy
records because of the music.

   'I saw Frampton play in the States. He was the American dream.
The face and not a lot more. Same with David Essex. Sure he was
OK on ditties like "Hold Me Close" but then he started to get over-
ambitious and it just didn't work out.

   'Maybe people don't know too much about music. It gets so
frustrating when you look at so-called artists making a living out of
image while professing to be musicians. It eventually destroys your
fucking faith in human nature.'

   Brandy can affect you like that.

*After he'd knocked out a few more albums, John's solo career waned.
He never quite recovered from the 'Highfly' image but, as our chat in
the back of the Granada revealed, the suit of pop stardom was a little
too tight under the arms and around the crotch. John eventually became
Tina Turner's musical director.*

   The day after I return from Glasgow, I head back north to seek out
the band of the moment, the Buzzcocks, Manchester's answer to
punk-pop artistry, with a leader who can spot a Tretchikov quicker
than you can say, well, Tretchikov (more later).

   They're the new darlings of the broadsheet music paper brigade after
the release of their debut album, *Another Music in a Different Kitchen*.

   And so, to a terraced quarter where headscarf houses wink in the
rain and Pete Shelley lives in comfortable squalor. He sleeps on the
floor in a two-up two-down squat – at least, I think it is. You don't
like to ask, really.

   'I'm thinking of buying a carpet,' says the wistful northern punk, looking at the bare boards. There's no furniture to speak off in any of the rooms, the roof leaks and the windows haven't been cleaned in twenty years.

'It's better than living in a bedsit on your own. I enjoy living with friends. It beats living at home.' Pete sounds like he does a lot of living.

We're sitting in his bedroom, I think. Pete, Steve Diggle, John Maher and Steve Garvey. In a time of punk recession, the Buzzcocks have emerged as a powerful but insular force. They've been around just as long as the Clash and the Jam with nowhere near the same degree of success. But that's because they adopted an intransigent policy of concentrating all their efforts in Manchester and deliberately avoiding the London blitz.

'We have as much fun as any band based in London,' says Pete, with a Woody Allen intensity. 'What's the point of going to London looking for ephemeral success? The only really good thing about success is it enables you to obtain the resources to do more things.'

That's when he starts talking politics, with a *p* and a *P*.

'The lowercase *p* denotes every day, personal politics. The way people react to each other. Politics with a small *p* is people. But when it's spelled with a capital *P* it means creating a new order to change people.

'That's why politics with a *P* is shit. People, not an order, should change people. Capital *P* politics doesn't concern itself with the individual who is simply not part of the equation. But that, unfortunately, is the political system we have.

'I want people to have healthy attitudes. When I write lyrics I try and get across as many different sides to an argument as possible. I deliberately insert ideas I firmly believe in, others I'm opposed to and others which are totally unproductive.

'That way I can create moods, ploys. The songs that sound the happiest are the most anger-ridden. The dirge-like tunes contain the happier lyrics. That's when you get the guy singing the nice tune in the bath when suddenly he notices the words and it jolts him.'

Pete was jolted while watching *Crossroads* the other day. He recognised a painting on one of the motel walls.

'It was by Vladimir Tretchikov. He's a Russian-born South African artist.'
He suddenly sounded like Pete to my Dud.

Following the release of the Product box-set in 1989, Shelley, Diggle, Garvey and Maher re-formed the band for a reunion tour. They went on to support Nirvana and have continued to record.

The penultimate interview is with a little-known band called Squeeze, whose debut single, the semi-novelty 'Take Me I'm Yours', has sneaked into the charts. I've seen them play live and they're shit hot.

The band come up to the *Record Mirror* offices in Covent Garden, above the underground station, and I take them round the corner to our local, the White Lion in James Street. They're a hoot.

Chris Difford smiles a hairspray-ad smile as he gently pulls petals off a pink rose.

Chris: He does, he doesn't, he does, he doesn't, he does. He does! I knew it. Our drummer Gilson Lavis does like girls who have strange sexual fantasies.

Glenn Tilbrook looks shocked.

Chris: You mean you never knew? Did Gilson never tell you?

Glenn: No.

Chris: Well, when he was seventeen he played with a dance band in Glasgow...

Glenn: I- I never knew he was...

Chris: Drums.

Glenn: Oh.

Chris: Anyway, one night after the show he went to a party. He's never really drank that much before and well, it went to his head. The party got out of hand and turned into one of those orgy things. Next thing he knew it was morning, he was naked and lying beside a girl in a similar condition. Well, the next thing that happened...

Jools: Did I hear someone mention girls?

At this juncture, Jools Holland joins us. He's a torrid little fellow who plays piano like a dream and dances like a Cotton Club dandy. He's forever chewing a cheap cigar which makes him look like an emaciated Edward G. Robinson.

Chris and Glenn in unison: Yes, Jools, you did.

Jools: Good, because I like girls in Nazi uniforms. I've also got a very large collection of Dinky cars, including a rare Chrysler Airflow. But I like bigger ones too. Cars, that is. I've got a 1959 Dodge.

Chris: Really? I don't wear undies 'cos it's a nuisance to clean them.

Glenn: I like to wear women's undies, preferably belonging to someone with whom I've had sexual relations.

Chris: I like plain girls who go horse-riding and have three A- levels. That way I know I'm goosing an intelligent girl. My favourite films are *The Night Porter* and Piesporter. I also like yachting.

Glenn: I know what you mean, that men against the sea feeling.

Chris: I think I like yachting because I'm convinced I'm a reincarnation of Christopher Columbus.

Squeeze's 'Take Me I'm Yours' is spitefully hypnotic, consistently clever. And the lyricist – that's Chris – has been known to stutter. Live, they're togetherness personified, Siamese quins even. On record they're meticulous, possessing a soap-clean mean sound.

Glenn: If I can make just one person happy in this world by what I've done then my life will have been worthwhile. That's really all I can say. Apart from hello Lawrence Impeney and all residents of Bournemouth.

Jools: And I'd like to say hello to my mum and dad and brothers.

For my final interview, I check into the Linda McCartney Home for the Criminally Insane. (You've read that part already, back in the Intro.) I'd love to turn, you, on...

A week before I'm due to leave *Record Mirror* and those spacious Long Acre offices, Alan rings to say Albion are pulling out of the deal.

'That's all right, though' he says. 'You wanted to leave the paper anyway, so why not come and work here with me, at Modern Publicity?'

Yeah, a publicist. I can do that...

Pop Publicist

Alan operates Modern Publicity from the third floor of a squat in Covent Garden, just around the corner from *Record Mirror*. He has two rooms, both used as offices, and he and I share the larger one at the back. The smaller office is sometimes occupied by a part-time secretary. Upstairs, several rooms are taken by impresario Andy Czezowski, the brains behind punk wonderland the Roxy.

Our desks face each other about ten feet apart. Alan sits with the only window behind him, and when the sun is in the right position once a day, he disappears into a black shell, gradually emerging a minute later, when the rays slide off the window and onto the crumbling brick wall outside, bit by bit. I look forward to that minute every day. It keeps things in perspective.

MARCH-JUNE 1978

Modern Publicity, The Stranglers, Tanz der Youth (Brian James)

Every time Alan picks up the phone he sparks up a Marlboro Red. Smoke drifts seamlessly all day long because when Alan isn't smoking Marlboro Red, I am. It's a stressful job. The artists can be a pain in the arse, the managers can be a pain in the arse and the journalists, especially, can be a pain in the arse. And these are the only people I deal with. My arse aches like fuck on the tube home every night. I think I preferred the gypsies, tramps and thieves.

The bands we represent include the Stranglers, Blondie, the Buzzcocks, Generation X and 999. They each pay up to fifty or sixty quid a week for Modern Publicity's services, which means getting as much press coverage as possible. I've entered the business end of music and this is where it gets serious. Music had always been a dream but now it wears curlers and no make-up. I'm a fantasy man and I think I want to be a music writer again.

It's far more difficult to become a successful PR than a successful journalist – look how few of them there are – and that's why the financial rewards for that success are often, deservedly, much fatter.

Music PRs sell people, not brands. They earn more respect than money. They're the good guys. When I was a journalist they plied me with alcohol and gourmet food and bought me a ticket to the world. I've never met a PR I didn't like and I've met a ton of them. It's an art that I, sadly, soon realise I don't possess. Sure, I can chat the chat but it churns me up inside. I have to simultaneously impress, coax and charm, and as the weeks at Modern unfold, I start to feel like a juggler on the high wire with no net. Journalists hide their self-doubt behind questions. Successful PRs have no self-doubt.

I miss seeing my words in print. I miss the fascination of interviews. I miss the wooing and the cooing and the feel of a typewriter key at three am on deadline morning. I miss the lunches and the hunches and the expense-form lies. Most of all I miss the freedom. Becoming a journalist set me free, allowed me to roam and write and discover.

During my time with Alan I write new-wave press releases for new-wave bands, canoodle with faces because big clients make big PRs, capture a couple of accounts – including George Thorogood and the Destroyers no less – and help to organise an epic press trip to Iceland to watch the Stranglers in concert promoting their new album *Black and White*.

Oh, what a night? Reykjavik, Iceland, 2–4 May 1978: it's my first, and last, large organised press event – but what a way to enter and exit. The Stranglers have released their third album in a year – 'Black and White' – and Modern Publicity is charged with the task of promoting it through the nationals and the weekly music press. The record company decide to fly the band to Reykjavik for the opening night of the *Black and White* tour along with around fifteen journos, management and record-company people, Alan and yours truly, for some serious nights in white satin. It's the leave-the-light-off season, daylight 22/7.

I arrange for the invitations to be delivered by hand in empty *Black and White* Scotch bottles, collected direct from the distillery in London. Inside each empty bottle is a piece of rag with a handwritten message (scrawled meticulously by my dad no less, each and every one):

Reykjavik, Iceland.

HELP!

Anarchic Arctic alcoholics slashing their wrists and 20-hour days. Blood streams in the white. Ice 'n' sleazy in Reykjavik. No night, no black, just a northern light frostbitten whiteness. Follow the instructions in the bottle and all this (and more, much more) can be yours. And you can even get to bring home a dead husky, if you play your cards right.

Not seeing darkness for seventy-two hours does something to a man. This is my first trip abroad as a PR and it strings me out. I crave the night life like a vampire, or Alicia Bridges. These few endless days are full of thrills and spills and danger that all belong big time to the night time and make everything disarmingly surreal. Great if you're a journalist but not so hot for PRs who have to *organise* while they're day-trippin'.

And Iceland isn't the best place to trip in. Outside the city the landscape is comic-book Martian – the sky is flecked with red, and never-ending streams of volcanic hot water pour out of tortuous rocks onto little green men. Inside the city there's a thousand things I wanna say to you.

Stand-out white-light, white-heat moments:

Black attack! Being mistaken for Jet Black as I walk through the airport lounge on arrival.

Shark attack! At a special Icelandic buffet put on by our hotel, the manager urges me to try 'Iceland's most expensive delicacy' and hands me a plate containing a slice of what appears to be a small white saturated flannel. I place it gingerly into my mouth and I can honestly say, hand on heart, it's the worst thing I've ever tasted. And believe you me, I've tasted some pretty horrible things. My immediate reaction is to spit it out but the manager is awaiting my praise.

'What is it?' I ask, after forcing this fiendish thing down my throat and draining a glass of red wine to kill the taste.

'Well, it's raw shark marinated in cow's urine and buried underground for three months. Very nice. Have some more.'

'Er, no, thank you.'

Of course! That's the taste – old fish soaked in cow's piss. Shit, you wouldn't want to pick a fight with an Icelander.

Cock attack! Standing in the middle of a hotel room with a naked Hugh Cornwell painting half of his body black and the other half white for a *Record Mirror* cover shoot. Painting his knob is a fairly sobering experience but I'd do anything for love and seven column inches. Or eight.

Chair attack! The journalist from the *New Musical Express* looks a little apprehensive. I've arranged for him to interview the band in one of the hotel rooms and we're waiting for the elevator. The Stranglers are universally feared by journalists, and with good reason. Reports of kidnappings and violence against writers reverberate around the industry. It's all really heavy duty, so the *NME* guy's obvious agitation is only to be expected as the elevator arrives.

I become a proper PR in that eight-floor ride.

'I've never seen them so laid back,' I say convincingly, as we get into the lift.

'Really?'

'Yeah, Jean has assured me' (and he really had) 'that they've stopped all their antics. This album means a lot to them and they really want people to appreciate it.'

'Great.' He looks relieved. 'I really like the album.'

We hit floor eight.

'You'll have a great interview. I know it. Like I said, I've never seem them so laid back.'

Jean-Jacques opens the door. 'Hi.' He smiles warmly. 'Come in.'

I do the introductions, but as the journo goes to sit down, Jean pulls the chair from under him and he falls flat on his arse in the most ignominious fashion. I quickly help him to his feet and kinda remonstrate with the band, who apologise profusely. But the damage has been done and I don't know whether to laugh or cry. So I leave and laugh. Out loud.

Massive attack! And the Icelandic young blades, deprived of beer (you can't buy it anywhere) but awash with whisky, smash the shit out of each other in Reykjavik Exhibition Hall on the night the band play. The blood gets on your shoes as broken bottles hit vacant faces and life suddenly seems cheap. I'd seen London dancehalls erupt but not like this, not with such hatred. This is drunkenness blinded by the light; all reason extinguished by a 50 per cent proof flood and some hard-assed Stranglers sounds.

It must be the raw shark.

Applejack attack! On the final morning – or was it night? – of our stay, a pony trek has been arranged for the whole party. A small band of pissheads and I opt for some extra hours in our luxury hotel rooms followed by a long, slow comfortable, swim up against the pool. Besides, horse-riding seems far too hazardous a pursuit after a night – or was it day? – of skuldruggery.

However, I badly sprain my ankle after treading awkwardly on one of the stairs leading down to the hotel pool. At least, that's what the doctor tells me three hours later after checking my X-rays in Reykjavik General.

What a klutz. I'm supposed to be looking after everyone, getting them on the coach to the airport, checking them in, attempting to prevent them getting too pissed in the airport bar. And now, here I am, a cripple who can't walk without assistance. They even radio Heathrow on the flight back to ensure there's a wheelchair waiting for me.

It's a glorious Megan moment.

Jean pushes me in the wheelchair when we get to Heathrow. I'm surprised and a little flattered, but also have a vague fear that he'll whip it away as I try to sit down. That would've been stretching the boundaries of taste way too far.

But I'd have laughed. Out loud.

Heart Attack! – One of the reporters – pissed morning, noon and night – is the inadvertent clown of the party because he's a bit of a toff who works on a national gossip column, carries a silver-topped cane and is too drunk to care. On the plane journey home, JJ bets that nobody can drink the full bottle of whisky he has in his bag in half an hour and the toff volunteers, pouring the lot down his throat in fifteen minutes, with a little help from his friends. He also needs a wheelchair at the other end. The perfect end to the perfect day – or was it night?

Independent PR is hard work with no expenses. The hours are anywhere towards the latter end of ten a.m.– six am because you have to be *about*, to be part of the scene. You also have to constantly convince people to have confidence in you. Tricky when you've got no confidence in yourself.

As a music journalist I only had to do that once, maybe twice, a week in a one-to-one interview. But an independent music publicist has to deal with a lot of shit from a lot of people and deal with it swiftly and competently. That's hard. You have to be made of the right stuff and, frankly, I'm not.

When I join Modern, Alan has just started to manage 'psychedelic punk' band Tanz Der Youth, led by ex-Damned mainman, Brian James. It takes up a lot of his time, yet he still manages to stick in a full day of PR work every day. Alas, the band never really get going – usual story, too many cooks – but it's fascinating watching the whole thing unravel slowly before my eyes in that smoky Covent

Garden squat. Alan learns a lot from the experience. And I doubt he ever really considered management again. Until he bumped into the Spice Girls one night twenty years later.

After three months I decide I've had enough.

It's Alan's business, not mine. His dreams are big but his expectations are bigger, sleeker, fuel injected and heading down the highway. My expectations are more handlebars and high street and were achieved the moment I wrote the first word in a notebook on the press bench at Marlborough Street Magistrates' Court.

I want to be a journalist again.

Each morning I wake up from a dreamless sleep in a dreamless world stripped of all desire. This is no way to live. So I resign.

I'm twenty-five and fucked when I step into the fruity Friday sunshine of a 1978 Covent Garden evening, Alan's firm good-luck handshake still warm on my palm. I suspect he's a little disappointed in me and I don't blame him. I'm a little disappointed in me.

I'm an out-of-work music writer and failed PR. The bells aren't ringing for me and my gal.

Within a few days I get offered the job as head of PR at United Artists but I decide it would be disrespectful to Alan to accept. Besides, I want to write. That's all I've ever really wanted to do. Delusion is tragic. It makes the train go so much faster...

It'd been nearly a year since I proposed to Dina but, just like the Phoney War of 1939, nothing has happened. No plans are made. I mean, it's still plain to see she is my destiny but I guess I'm too young to die.

The subject never comes up so I guess she feels the same. It's awkward. She hasn't told her family in Nicosia about me and they certainly wouldn't have approved of an Englishman with long hair and a beard, especially an unemployed Englishman with long hair and a beard. So we dance in limbo and it's delicious. Screw marriage. Screw work. There's always Mum and Dad. I'll sign on. There's plenty of time...

I'm just starting to warm to the idea of turning misspent youth into misspent manhood when *Record Mirror* editor Alf Martin and assistant editor Roz Russell become Guardian Angels: The New Batch, and introduce me to Career Three...

PART 3

Freelance Writer

Another dreamless night. Another new fandango. Another farce in the crowd. The phone rings and I'm trying to focus on the sound, y'know, scheme it's a dream. But it's for real. The clock says 11:10 and it's light outside so I figure it must be a.m., unless I'm still in Iceland.

I'm home alone, both the parents are at work, so I get out of bed and limp to the phone in the hallway. My ankle still aches.

'Hello Barry, it's Alf. Fancy doing some stuff for *Record Mirror*?'

'Absolutely,' I say the next morning in his office, face-to-face. He offers me a fifty quid a week retainer.

Yeah, I can be a freelance writer. I can do that.

Next day. 'Barry, Roz here.' It's three p.m. Civilised. A nice time to ring.

'The *Daily Record* in Glasgow is looking for a pop writer and I've recommended you to the features editor, John Burroughs. They want a piece on Bob Dylan. And include something on his love life.'

I didn't know he had one.

'Dylan's doing a UK tour shortly so I suggest you write something and get it over to the *Daily Mirror* pretty damn quick.' The *Mirror* is the *Daily Record*'s sister paper and drop-off point for London-based hard copy and photos heading north.

I know absolutely nothing about Bob's bedroom antics but I cobble together a few old press cuttings and pump up the volume a little. My very first piece of tabloid freelance journalism and amazingly I get the gig. Freelance. The *Daily Record* is the second biggest selling paper in Britain after the Mirror, and here I am with my own twice-weekly column. Pop is hot stuff and getting hotter. In a perverse way, punk has made the music scene more glamorous, more exciting and, shit, am I excited! I get another hundred quid a week for keeping it that way.

'Is that Barry?'

'Yes.'

I don't recognise the voice. A soft-lights, sweet-music voice. Relaxing. One p.m. That's fine.

'Hi, it's John Blake here, from AdLib on the *London Evening News*. I wondered if you wanted to fill in for someone next week.' AdLib is a nightly entertainment/gossip column heavily slanted towards music. David Hancock, who works alongside John and is an ex-*Record Mirror* staffer, has mentioned me to him.

'Absolutely,' I say, the next morning in his office, face-to-face, in Fleet Street. A hundred quid for a week's work plus expenses – and, boy, what expenses. That'll do nicely.

JUNE 1978

Skinheads, staff photos and Mink De Ville

John invites me back to write gossip on a regular basis: no by-line but the drinks are free. Every Saturday there are AdLib specials across the centrespread and I tentatively mention an idea for a feature – the re-emergence of the skinhead.

Two days later I'm in a pub in Canning Town, interviewing ten-year-down-the-line skinheads braced and booted and hot to talk.

Light and bitter was the drink, the complexion and the attitude of that unique Sixties animal – the skinhead. He appeared quite suddenly on the street – a mod derivative but more violent and classier than the marauding Margate model. The hobnail hobo was the personification of working-class youth with time on its hands. A youth that could no more identify with flower power than the House of Lords.

The bootloose and fancy-free summer of '68 was the skinhead sartorial peak. Daylight hours required spotless Ben Shermans (tapered naturally), clip-on braces, Levi's or Sta-Prest that wavered nervously a clear two inches above the demon black Dr Martens, which seemed to pulsate with a life of their own.

The night demanded an infinitely more elegant approach. The Mecca machos pulled during dream-time wearing two-tone mohair suits (all made to measure – off-the-peg whistles had the perpetual piss taken out of them), scrupulously polished brogues, college ties and the customary Sherman.

I, for my sins, was one – or more accurately, an unsuccessful one. I never possessed as much bottle as my mates, my braces used to fly up my back every five minutes, which was distinctly uncool, and I couldn't afford Dr Martens because I was the only skin on the block who still went to school after sixteen.

But that whole era was doomed. Sheepskins and Crombies shot up in price. Flared bottom strides became fashionable because music dictated it and somehow they just didn't go with boots. 'Django's Theme' and Desmond Dekker didn't seem to matter much anymore.

Fashion goes in cycles and now the Rabelaisian rabble-rousers are pedalling back.

But this time the circumstances are a little different. Most of the skinheads you see today are ex-punks disenchanted with the middle-class infiltration of that particular cult.

The spokesmen are Gary Dickie, a twenty-year-old labourer who became a skinhead to avoid authority, and his mate Vince Riordan, a nineteen year-old roadie for a rock band (and later bassist with Cockney Rejects), who wanted to identify with something.

Both are dressed like their ghostly Sixties ancestors – with the addition of two-tone Slazenger jackets which weren't around then.

'We get most of our clothes from Oxfam shops and stalls down Brick Lane market,' says Vince. 'I bought a pair of loafers the other day for three quid. I reckon you can look like a skin for twenty-five'.

The compulsory crop is now 70p. 'It's merely a question of telling the barber whether you want a number one, two, three or four cut. Number one is the shortest – the Kojak cut,' says Vince. Gary maintains the new breed of skinhead is not as violent as his Sixties predecessor.

'We're just working-class geezers looking for a good time. But I guess we've got something to prove – we're not scum. People think 'cos you come from the East End you're a gangster. Birds won't let you take them home from a dance when you tell them where you live, so that limits your choice 'cos there ain't many skinhead birds around and the soulies just don't wanna know.'

Skin girls are recognisable by their gypsy-cut hairstyles and monkey boots or astronauts.

Vince says his parents prefer him being a skinhead to a punk. 'They even give me money to buy clothes now 'cos they realise it's a lot smarter.'

'People think we're either National Front or Marxists,' says Gary, 'and that's shit. I'm fed up with being asked if I was involved in that racist riot down Brick Lane the other day. I just don't want to know about any of that crap. I don't get taxed any lower for being a skinhead, do I?'

Jimmy Pursey, darling of the skin world, has been accused of spearheading the crop-top revival and of being responsible for perpetuating rock-gig violence.

'Sham 69 were the first band to really appeal to the skins,' says Vince. 'I suppose it's the equivalent of going to a football match when you see them play. As for the violence, you can get that anywhere. Like we said before, we go for a good time and nothing more.'

Pursey himself seems to be feeling the strain. 'The reason I welcome all the skinheads to our gigs is because I preach peace not violence. If they didn't have me telling them how stupid it is to be violent then, well... But I'm alone and it's about time somebody gave me some help.

'They're a nice bunch of geezers though. Most of them had never been to a rock gig in their life until Sham came along. But I want to make it absolutely clear – Sham 69 is a punk band, not a skinhead one.'

Vince and Gary have both been in trouble with the police, mainly after football-terrace rucks. 'At one time the police picked on you for being a punk – now it's for being a skinhead,' says Vince, who once had five jobs in five months. 'I just couldn't take authority on any level – I still can't. I don't ever want to work for anyone. I guess that's why I became a skinhead. The future looks pretty bleak. I can see us all ending up as suedeheads wearing suits and going to discos. Not much to look forward to when you're 25 is it?'

The following Saturday I pick up the *Evening News* in my local newsagent and open it in the shop. There, under the headline 'Skinheads Rule OK', is my name, which I quickly point out to Steve, the owner's son. He's a printer at night and a black-cab driver by day and earns a fortune. He also doesn't sleep much.

'Great,' he says, wide-eyed and couldn't-care-leg-less.

So, later that week I'm sitting at my Fleet Street desk when suddenly a photographer pops up, takes my picture and *voila*! it appears beside my name in the following Saturday's column.

I buy the paper in the same shop and open it up like a woman's legs.

'Great,' says Steve, bleary-eyed and couldn't give a toss.

I'm in seventh heaven. I look mean, moody, magnificent ... and bearded. Well, you can't have everything.

Dina is terrified at the prospect of me returning to the lonesome road. She wants a man with a stable career and I don't know where the fuck I'm going but I know I wanna go there. I explain to her that I'm back doing what I really want and appeal to her Greek nature by boasting that I'm getting paid five times more. That seems to appease her, for now.

The fact is, music writers are like footballers – we've only got short careers. None of us knows where we'll be ten years from now and none of us really cares. Life's just too good.

I'm easing back into the flow and slide on down into Mink DeVille territory where all the Pachookas are chewing bazookas in the shadows tonight...

Wily Willy's with them, his skyscraper quiff bending in the breeze, his willowy frame winding down the alleyways, like a cartoon cat on a Spanish stroll.

Hey Willy, Willy DeVille.

'Yeah, what is it, man?'

What's a Pachooka?

'Hell, man, you don't know what a Pachooka is? Wow. A Pachooka is a guy who only cares about looking sharp, real sharp, on the streets. It's a style, man. A real style.'

He falls back into the black-leather sofa at his London record company clutching the remnants of a badly rolled joint.

And is he stoned, man. I mean, really stoned. Eight hours of solid interviews, eight hours of tinny lager, eight hours of pushing broom. Yeah, Willy DeVille's back after nine months of anonymity, holed up in a New York recording studio and hanging out with those Pachookas.

In this state he's no fun guy. He's bored with the questioning, bored with honeydew hacks shipping the same expression, bored with the whole record company rumba. What he wants is sleep, man. What he wants is food, man. What he wants is for me to get the fuck out that little room in his Soho-based record company where the smoke hangs like portraits. Man.

But I ain't going. I'm a freelance now. I get paid by the word and I'm hungry for them.

OK, Willy, let's talk about clothes. Now, you're a real tasty dude, huh?

'Y'know,' he says, pausing to pour a drink, get rid of the joint, ruffle his barnet and light a cigarette, 'most people when they walk on stage dress up like hippies. They don't look cool and one thing you gotta be up there is cool. I mean *real* cool.

'Y'know sumthin? I like to look cool on stage. I like to look like I'm going to a dance and at that dance I'm gonna jive with my chick. You don't ever want to look like a hippie at a dance. There ain't no way I'm gonna look uncool in front of 6000 people man. No way.'

He looks down, almost dejectedly, at his feet. 'So, anyway I can,

I've got to look cool. Really cool. Real cool.'

Now, I don't know about you, but I get the distinct impression that Willy likes to look cool.

'I've got some hot shantung suits, y'know Chinese silk, in black, canary yellow and peacock green. Real classy. They cost around five hundred dollars each.'

He takes a long hard look at me.

'I like to get jazzed when I sing. I'm escaping from everyday life and I ain't afraid to say it. I take all those people sitting out there. I take them all.

'Hey man – I *heal* them!'

Ever been to a rock concert, Willy?

'I swear on my mother's grave, I've never been to one in my life. They're for hippies and I don't hang around with hippies. I don't want people saying, "Hey, look, there's Willy DeVille hanging out with hippies." Hippies are lambs man. Lambs.'

'Listen, man, I left school when I was fourteen. I had no education but I know I've got the power to do what I want. See, some people are leaders and some people are followers – lambs. Whatever you believe is real – so what you have to say to yourself is, 'I wish I wish I *wish* so *bad*,' and if you wish hard enough you'll get it.'

So you wished, Willy?

'Yeah, but I wished for the wrong shit. I'm telling you, man, if I'd have been smart and made the right decisions I could have gotten out of this whole thing and got into something much bigger.

'So I'm left with the lambs – and I love 'em cos they're so easily misdirected. But I'd do it differently if I could go through it all again.'

How differently?

'I'd be governor of Louisiana.'

A photographer laughs somewhere in the smoke.

Willy continued to release albums – the last, in 2008, was Pistola. He also wrote for movies and in 1987 he got an Oscar nomination for his song 'Storybook Love', the theme to the film The Princess Bride, which he performed at the ceremony that year – not, however, while wearing a shantung suit. He died of cancer in 2009 aged just 58.

JULY 1978

Iggy Pop, Steve Jones & Paul Cook, Joan Armatrading, restaurant reviews

The *Evening News* asks me to do restaurant reviews. Unbelievable. And what a scam.

I dine out with a mate or Dina and after I pay the bill I ask to see the manager and explain that I'm reviewing the restaurant and how I really enjoyed the food – which I invariably do. Who wouldn't? Then I claim the whole bill on expenses.

A week or two after a glowing review appears in the paper, I wander on back to the restaurant, with a guest, where a beaming manager greets me and says the review has done wonders for his business and insists my money is no good. I eat out two, three nights a week for absolutely nothing.

Plus, since grabbing the gigs on *Record Mirror*, the *Record* and the *News*, I get taken out to lunch twice a week by sexy record company PRs, hungry for column inches, who seduce me with wine and crème brulée.

And then one of them asks if I want to interview Iggy Pop.

I take the tube down to RCA's luxury West End offices but claim for a cab. It's hard to be a saint in the city. I'm a little nervous. I'd heard some very heavy things about Iggy Pop and his hatred of journalists.

He turns out to be a pussycat.

My last glimpse of him was brief. Shelter out of the midnight rain in the Music Machine. Iggy on stage beating his hairless chest with chimp hands. He was wearing a leotard and fishnet stockings, like the ones kept in the back of a housewife's wardrobe and brought out on special occasions, in the dark.

Pop of the Iggy kind turns you on like that, in the fishnet-stockings dark.

He vanished after the Music Machine show. 'I'd just had enough. After every gig I need to get away – it's a psychological trick. I use the simplicity of distance, in miles, to enable me to gain a perspective of where I've just been. Then I can sit back and evaluate in a totally clinical way.'

Iggy the ego hero is sitting opposite me. It's just the two of us. I've got an hour. He's limiting himself to just two interviews. After that he loses patience.

He looks as healthy as a visiting tennis player, but his virginal white is marred by the odd pubic black poking through the racket. His hair is Sassoon-slick, his dress despicably tasteful.

So where's the demon?

Defunct.

And where's the diesel-powered snake body?

Decelerated.

Or so it seems. He's just so friendly. The drug-ravaged piss-artist that I'd been told so much about turns out to be little more than a lovable rogue with a neat line in vilification and Detroit demagoguery

'This is a real dirty business – a filthy business. I hate it. It's a big industry built on precarious foundations. So I try and keep myself apart from it as much as I can. I give everything I've got on stage and steer clear of the industry after that.

'I'm afraid I'm a member of that terribly unfashionable school which adheres to the rule of giving people entertainment. My life revolves around my work. I'm not a very interesting international playboy.'

He's got a perpetual grin that erupts into a full scale smile every so often. For a moment, a very strange moment, I think I'm talking to a member of Blue Oyster Cult or maybe even an Eagle. So I pull myself together by asking about his relationship with Laughing-boy Bowie.

'Things I read about him and me bear so little resemblance to what actually goes on. It's so predictable. I value everything we've done together. And there are things between us that will come to light in time. Projects we're working on now are years ahead of this era.

'I seem to have found myself in a position to always be ahead of the next man. Everything I do is interpreted later. That why there's so much press about me. People are unable to understand what I'm at so all they become interested in are my attendant features – like vomiting a lot.'

Pretty understandable, if you ask me.

'I'm often regarded as a boil, y'know, a big boil that has to be lanced.'

But doesn't he like to be thought of in that way? Don't you capitalise on it. Huh?

'Sure I capitalise on it. Instead of ignoring it I embrace it, accept it, and it brings me more fame and fortune. And the more fame and fortune I get the more it enables me to play my music.'

Simple. But what about that music, the sonic that freezes your brain? Know what I mean?

'My music is like a high-pitched dog whistle. You either hear it or not. To me it's soothing. I need volume to drown out the rest of existence. It has this soporific effect, weakening almost, on me. But at the same time its sheer buoyancy keeps me afloat.'

Would you like to die on stage? Y'know – Iggy goes Pop in public?

'I get very scared about death – but I guess I wouldn't mind dying that way. It's bound to happen anyway. There are a lot of guys out there that hate me. One of them is gonna get up one night and – BANG! – shoot the fuck outta me."

That put the wind up him. How do you live up to the undoubted richness of your character?

'Oh, I occasionally go into bars and jerk off over women's legs.'

That put the wind up me.

You really done that?

'Yeah, really.'

Nah – really, Iggy's a mummy's boy at heart. 'My parents are pretty important to me. They have a great deal to do with whatever position I've attained now. They're the best.

'A lot of guys in rock don't talk much about their folks. That's 'cos they're now fighting the battles they should have fought when they were seven. Y'know, they say now, "Hey Mum. I don't wanna eat my eggyweggy," when they should have said it years ago. Me, I always told my mum if I didn't want my eggyweggy. Sure my parents are shocked by some of my actions. They always wanted me to be reasonably in one piece. Still, better shocked by me than strangers, eh?'

Hands up all those who knew there was an Iggy Junior. Eric's his name. Eric Pop, born out of wedlock eight or nine years ago, Iggy's not absolutely sure about the time.

'He's in California at the moment riding horses all day. I don't see much of him. I provide for him but that's all. I guess looking after him financially is my way of doing something worthwhile.'

What about Eric's mother?

'I don't see much of her either. That's the way I like it. I move around a lot. Don't like the same surroundings.'

Say, didn't you once describe yourself as the King of Failures?

'That's apropos. I'd just been reading Cocteau when I said that.'

Of course.

'See, all the successes I know are really boring little cheeses. Once those guys are exposed to that dirty thing called the public they become ignorant and inhuman.'

And what was that stockings and leotard get up for the Music Machine show all about?

'I don't like to disappoint my fans. Besides, I looked really beautiful in that outfit. I mean that. I'm their superman and before I walked out on stage that night, I looked at myself in the mirror and thought, Wow, Iggy, you're pretty good looking. You know something? I think I'm the greatest.'

I think I'm the greatest when, after the interview, the PR invites me into the label's record library. 'Help yourself. I've got to dash. 'Bye.'

Help yourself? Well, sugar pie honey bunch, I can't help myself. I take as many albums as I can possibly carry, including the entire Bowie back catalogue, three Kinks, a couple of Jefferson Airplane, an Elvis greatest hits, a brace of Don McLean, several Nilssons, a ZZ Top and a Fats Waller. There must be forty albums in my arms as I struggle through the reception, smile and push open the door to the street with my foot.

Needless to say, I get a cab back to the office.

In 2009 Iggy was the face of a £25 million TV ad campaign for Swiftcover insurance. The same year, original Stooges guitarist and one of Iggy's closest friend's Ron Asheton died aged sixty. Iggy's solo album, Préliminaires, was released in June 2009. In 2010 Iggy and the Stooges were inducted into the Rock and Roll Hall of Fame

As part of a *Record Mirror* disco special, Tim Lott, who works at the paper, and I are to go to the Hammersmith Palais on a Friday night, try and pull two girls, take them to a flash members-only club in the West End and record their reaction.

It's quite an evening.

We're standing at the bar down the Palais admiring each other's creases, when I see her.

You know that feeling you get when you see someone in a dancehall? Someone who stands out from the rest of the girls as they twirl in the gloom. Like it's Christmas, y'know, and you're about to unwrap the flashiest package.

I say to Tim, who's looking pretty sharp in his off-white linen suit, 'Ere, Tim, what d'you reckon of her, then?'

I point. He looks. He sips his lager. I wait. 'She's ...' he sips his drink again, '... not bad.' Tim's seal of approval is all I need.

'Fancy her mate?'

'Her mate?' He sips. 'Yeah, all right.'

Now, walking up to a girl to ask for a dance is one of the most frightening things known to man. But somehow with this one I think my chances are good. And I suppose I've always had that extra spark of originality in chatting up technique. My opening line was guaranteed to destroy.

'Heaven must be missing an angel.'

She glances around, looks me up and down and turns back to face her friend. 'Push off,' she says through the back of her head.

'Do you wanna dance?"

'No.'

'Look, stop beating about the bush. Can I dance with you?'

'No.'

'Please? I ain't too proud to beg.' I touch her hand.

'Don't manhandle me. Stay there and we'll dance.'

It was 'Boogie Oogie Oogie'. My favourite. I danced.

'What's your name?'

'Mary.'

'Where do you live, Mary?'

'Northolt.'

'How long have you been coming down here?"

'What is this? The Spanish Inquisition?'

I discovered a long time ago that people like nothing more than to be asked about their lives and there is no better chat-up technique.

'I'm interested. Is that so bad?'

'About five years.'

'Why?'

'It's just what you make of it. People take you for what you are down here. You don't have to try and be anyone else in a place like the Palais. It's simply up to you whether or not you want to enjoy yourself.'

She's blonde, blue-eyed, beautiful. Her smile is Colgate fresh and full of promise.

'If you saw a bloke you fancied, Mary, would you ask him to dance?'

'I've never asked a guy to dance and I don't intend doing so. It's a man's duty to ask for a dance.'

I ask her if she wants to come with me up west to the Embassy Club – home of stars and stargazers and members only. I tell her it's for a feature in *Record Mirror* but she doesn't believe a word.

'No, thanks. I'm very happy here, thank you. I know that if I went to a place like that I might enjoy it and get a taste for the high life.'

'But, Mary, it's really difficult to get in for the likes of...'

That stops her in her tracks.

'What do you mean by that?' she snaps. 'I'm not good enough for it, eh? Well, I wouldn't go with you if you were the last man here. Go away and find somebody else.'

Her friend, Sue, clocks what's happening and leaves Tim midway through a particularly tricky oogie.

Tim and I walk dejectedly back to the bar. On my third pint I look around at the other girls but none of them holds a candle to Mary. I think it's when the band start playing, 'If I Can't Have You I don't want Nobody Baby' that I decide to act. It's now or never.

She's sitting alone at one of those intimate circular chatting-up tables, handbag at her side like an obedient dog.

'Look, Mary, I'm sorry about earlier. Why don't you come down the Embassy and we can compare it to the Palais? Just for a laugh. Drinks are on me.'

I kneel by the chair. She flashes one of her smiles and something breaks. It's the comb in my back pocket.

'I wouldn't expect anything else. Oh, all right.' So Tim and I leave with the girls and head for town.

The cavernous dancehall with its big-band sound, rococo interior, dicky-bow bouncers and two-tone-six-pint-too-pissed-to-care customers is a dodo waiting to expire. It belongs to a bygone age of air-raids, seamed stockings, American GIs and Joe Loss. The only reason they continue is because the alternative – the disco – is too pricey and too fast for the dancehall diehards of 1978, older but none the wiser.

You can pull with relative ease in the vastness of a dancehall without fear of recrimination if you fail. Discos are still too tight to mention for many, predominantly working-class, punters, but as music gets sleeker and more sensual it will demand a more appropriate environment and the Palais, the Locarno and the Lyceum will crash and burn.

The Embassy is too pricey and too fast and too full of sleek, sensual people. It's not open to the public and a fairly hefty membership fee combined with a long waiting list makes it Fort Knox cool. The drinks are nearly four times the Palais price and there's not a pint in sight. The canned music is loud, incessant and accompanied by a Charlie Atlas go-go dancer. There's a light show, including lasers, flash enough to make any rock band cry into their coke (and consequently ruin it) and the barmen walk around in football shorts and nothing else.

'Well, Mary, what do you think?

'I don't like it. The people are too old."

'But there's a lot who are younger than us.'

'I mean old in mentality.'

We get some drinks and sit down. Mary looks a little overawed by the whole thing. Clearly she's not enjoying herself.

'I can't relax because I get the impression the people here demand that you be like them. It all seems so false. People down the Palais are just being themselves but these people come across like they're trying hard to be somebody else.

'I don't think it's a matter of money. Maybe everyone here is just chasing a rich reputation. I mean, there's no way I would've got in on my own tonight and I don't think that's fair.'

She sips her scotch on the rocks like it's cat's piss.

'But I do like…'

To be beside the seaside?

'…the style of some of the people. The guys are really nice-looking but a lot are very effeminate. Going with someone like that would turn me off men for life.'

Inferiority complex?

'It's *not*! People have told me that before and it's definitely not true. There's not a straight person here except me and my friend, Sue. The rest look like a bunch of dropouts to me.'

She takes another sip. The conversation turns to music. She says she doesn't listen to any and would never dream of buying a music paper. The only time she hears new songs is when she goes to the Palais.

But she can't forget my earlier remark.

'Look, the people here have their own little world, I have mine. I think they try a bit harder than me to be something but that's up to them. It doesn't worry me. I'd never come here again. It's just not my scene.'

At that moment Pistols Steve Jones and Paul Cook come and sit with us. Mary and Sue jump up when a photographer flashes.

'If you dare print any pictures of us with those animals I'll sue,' shrieks Mary.

'You fuckin' ol' cow,' says Steve. 'Who the fuck do you think you are – Elizabeth Taylor or sumfin'? You fuckin' tarts make me sick, you're so fuckin' snobby.'

Mary is shocked. 'I don't expect men to swear in my company. It's not right.'

'Why don't you go and fuck yourself, then?' replies Steve, master of the witty retort.

'I want to go,' says Mary. I'd promised her a lift, and fortunately a record-company PR girl has agreed to drive her home.

Steve follows us outside and the two continue to argue.

Mary and Sue sit in the back of the car with Steve, who decides to tag along.

'What do you do?' Steve asks Mary.

'I'm about to start work in an airport.'

'That's right, a fuckin' air hostess – every little working-class girl's dream, to be a fuckin' air hostess.'

'I'm going to be a secretary.'

'Fuckin' secretaries are just as fuckin' bad.'

It continues like that for the entire journey but by the time we arrive in Northolt, Mary has started to find the curly-haired ex-Pistol rather cute.

'Goodnight, Steve,' she says, as she gets out of the car.

'Fuck off,' says Steve.

And with that my little Mary walks off into the Northolt night.

On the ride back to town Steve agrees to an interview and invites me round to his flat in Marylebone a few days later. He's wearing nothing more than a skimpy towel and a few soapsuds when he opens the door.

'All right Baz. Just 'avin' a baff. I'm going out later so to save time I fort we'd do the interview while I'm 'avin me baff. Don't worry,' he laughs, 'the baff's full of fuckin' bubbles and I don't mean Greeks. You can't see nuffink.'

No one is innocent – not even plebian *pistolero* Steve 'Calorie Counter' Jones.

It appears this gay young blade, often spotted arm in arm with Paul Cook doing the Continental at London's fashionable tête-à-tête nite spots, has rather a dark past.

In fact, Steve has had no less than thirteen brushes with the Old Bill for burglary, shop breaking and... peeping tomfoolery!

He admits his criminal adolescence while soaking away the day's cares and night's traumas in a bubble bath at his rock-star pad in the Waste End.

'I was eighteen when I got done for being a peeping Tom. I wouldn't mind but I was only trying to break into this house without realising there was some bird changing next door.

'She thought I was looking at her tits and rang the police. I was nicked and got fined fifty quid.'

Steve was a member of that exclusive members-only club when he first joined the Pistols – the Order of Probationees. No subscription required, merely an unfortunate tendency to get caught a lot and an uncontrollable urge to drive around in stolen Rolls-Royces.

'I was in Northolt one night – not that night – when I downed a couple of mandies and nicked a Rolls,' recalls Steve, while gazing lovingly at the rubber duck floating merrily on his bubbly tum.

'I was skidding all over the place – but I pulled a darlin' bird.'

But, Steve, I mean, didn't you have any, well, qualms about stealing other people's property?

'Nah. Anyway, I never used to break into council houses – just places where it was obvious the owners had plenty of dough. I did a year in approved school once for taking and driving away.'

Why did you do all this?

'Boredom, I guess, I dunno. I never knew me ol' man. He was a boxer who ran off before I was born. Then this geezer moved in with me mum. He never liked me so he refused to let me have a key for the front door. He used to lock me out of the house when I came home late from the boozer. He made life a misery for me. One night it all came to a head.

'I came home late as usual and he just wouldn't let me in. I began to bang on the door and swear and he finally came out. Before I could say anything he went for me. We started fighting and Mum came rushing out, screaming and crying.

'I left home that night and never returned.'

Steve didn't see his mum again for years.

'She was working in a hairdresser's and I happened to be passing. 'Doing all right for yourself then son?' she asked. But I don't think she cares much either way. Maybe she feels a bit proud of me now – but she should have felt like that ages ago.'

He's covered from head to toe in soap – not a commodity you would usually associate with those grubby, gruesome Sex Pistols. But then Steve ain't a Pistol any more, and neither is his flat mate Paul Cook, the blonde rapscallion skinsmaaan who has just joined us in the mirrored bathroom.

These two guys, the quiet ones in the Rotten camp, have undergone a unique change over recent months. The chintzy ragamuffin chicanery – it was considered both unethical and unprofessional for either of them to be seen out at one point – has vanished, making way for a softer, boy-next-door image.

They got fun, they got videos, they got sixty pounds a week, they got their own hit records. And they got each other. You mean they're… no. Strictly hetero. Metro heteros enjoying their reputations.

'When we're seen in nightclubs,' says Paul, 'everyone immediately says, "Oh, yeah, street credibility slashed." But we ain't got no money. Sure, we've got a video, a hi-fi and a flat, but no hard cash. We ain't even got bank accounts. We're just two healthy young fellers trying to enjoy ourselves. What's wrong with that?'

'Right,' splashes Steve. 'Why should I sit at home every night crying my heart out? I wanna enjoy meself.'

Unfortunately, ahem, Steve does tend to overdo it a bit. 'I seem to get VD every week. But it ain't nothing to be embarrassed about. I can't help it if I like screwing. I've never been in love. Hold it. If being in love means you want to keep seeing the same bird all the time then, yeah, I think I might be at the moment. But generally women are all right when you're pissed.

'Don't get me wrong, I like women's company, but I'd rather be with blokes. They've got a better sense of humour. You can't have much of a laugh with birds – and you couldn't nick cars with them around!'

I guess you couldn't describe him as a Casanova – more a legova. But he's happy. And he's more than happy that the Pistol pressures on him and Paul have vanished.

'I just woke up one morning and felt so free after I finally realised that the Sex Pistols were no more.'

'But,' interrupts a slightly melancholic Paul, 'it's sad when you look back on the whole thing. The scene seems to have gone back to where it used to be. There's nothing, nothing. People won't let us die. Why can't they realise that the Pistols simply don't exist anymore.'

'There will always be a Sex Pistols,' says Steve, defiantly. 'I don't want it to die because the kids don't want it to die. We started so much.'

'I'll never regret anything,' says Paul. 'There was no other way things could have gone. Everything just happened so quickly. The whole episode has made me more wary of people. I'll never trust a soul again as long as I live. I may have been naïve once – not any more.'

Do they still see Rotten? 'We've seen him once since we came back from the States,' says Steve. 'I ain't got any grudges against him. I hope his new band works out – but he's gonna face a lot of problems. Still, our record company seem to think a lot more of him than us.'

So let's just leave Jones & Cook Ltd. with the shaky finances and the flaky scruples in that soapy bathroom in that smart flat in that grubby block in that side street they call home. No one could argue that they've earned the right to indulge themselves.

The Sex Pistols may be the ex-Pistols but the malady lingers on.

Dina is visiting Cyprus. The switchboard girl at *Record Mirror* is an incurable romantic and when Dina rings from a phone box near her mum's house – her family still don't know about me – she takes the number, rings it back, puts me through and we talk for half an hour. Wonder if anyone ever checks the phone bills? There aren't many Cypriot bands in the UK charts – i.e. none – so a phone interview a day to an unspecified Cyprus number should probably ring a few bells.

Dina's away for three months. It's the first time she's returned since becoming a refugee after Turkish troops rampaged through her village in 1974. Why do I keep getting the feeling she's not coming back?

As I'm living at home, I'm sticking away over a hundred quid a week. The only bills I get have pictures of the Queen on them, exchanged for travellers' cheques at Heathrow while I'm waiting for flights to New York and any place else where a big band could get it on in front of twenty thousand hot dogs with mustard on the side.

I'm a PR's dream. Get me an interview and I'll hit you with my rhythm stick – the triumvirate of *Record Mirror*, *Daily Record* and *Evening News*, plus the odd *My Guy*, *Smash Hits*, *Revue* (the new *Reveille*) and another monthly retainer from *Jam*, a Japanese version of *Rolling Stone*, in return for being their UK correspondent. I'm a one-hit wonder, spreading my interviews like NSU. The days of writing in different styles at Marlborough Street are finally paying off.

After the wine and the crème brûlée come offers of flights to five-star hotels in far-flung cities to see rock legends play and talk to them about life, the universe and everything for an hour or so in a room with a view.

It's the stuff of dreams and I'm turning Japanese.

I really think so ...

But now I've got to check my heart for a little love and affection because Joan Armatrading ain't exactly my idea of a carnival ride with a mouth full of candyfloss.

She's never really appealed to me. Adored 'Love And Affection' but not much else. Maybe only women bleed...

So the prospect of an interview is kinda intriguing. I'm not in love, but maybe open to persuasion. You don't get to interview many women in my line of business. And the ones you do get to meet are pretty special. They have to be.

Lester Bangs got it right – 'The only hope for rock'n'roll, aside from everybody playing nothing but shrieking atonal noise through arbiter distorters, is women. Balls are what ruined both rock and politics in the first place, and I demand the world be turned over to the female sex immediately.'

During the interview I suss out a few things about Joan. She talks intimately only to close friends. She could be the little girl who never grew up – she taps her knees together throughout the interview and fiddles incessantly with her cap. She answers each question immediately and there's not of hint of the 'er's that rampage through the words of a considerable number of pop stars. This is one erudite lady.

She adores flat caps. Well, she never told me that exactly but she wore one throughout the interview and didn't even bother to doff it in a gentleman's presence. What is this ultra-feminine make-up bag of a world coming to?

What of the current race problems manifesting themselves in the Bengali twilight zones of the East End? Not the coolest opener.

'Journalists are always trying to make out I have a problem because I'm black,' she says. 'Let me tell you something ... I don't. Journalists are always trying to make me say I grew up in a deprived Birmingham ghetto. Let me tell you something ... I didn't. Sure, it happens in some cities, and don't think I had it easy.

'I was one of six kids and we were very poor. We just didn't happen to live in a ghetto. I never had to fight for anything on that score. So don't ask me about contemporary race problems. I refuse to voice an opinion publicly. I may talk about it to friends but I don't want to see what I think, politically, in writing. Besides, people in my position who do talk openly on political matters have the unfortunate tendency to influence the thoughts of their fans and I don't think that's quite ethical.'

She doesn't like journalists much. 'I just get disappointed when I read my interviews.'

So do I, Joan. So do I.

Time for an up question – the Blackbushe festival.

'Bob Dylan contacted my agent and asked him if I would play at the festival. I've been told he really enjoys my work. I must admit, the first Dylan album I bought was *Blood on the Tracks* so I guess I'm not an ecstatic fan. But I do like some of his stuff.'

That's one of the most refreshingly disarming answers I've ever heard. Joan is as straight as they come and you can't help admiring her honesty in the face of such an accolade from a rock god. Ordinary women are more fascinating than extraordinary men. Special women are goddesses.

Don't forget, I am only twenty-five.

'The last time I played an open-air festival was Reading – and I spent my entire set untangling the chains around my neck, which I fiddled nervously with beforehand.'

Shy, huh?

'I was very shy. When I was younger I had to spend a lot of time with my brothers. But they didn't really want anything to do with me so I found myself alone most days. They were too busy having boy fun, so more and more I had to rely on myself for company. I just reached the point where I couldn't relax with people.

'Suddenly it was a case of having to. I had to teach myself to be natural around people and I had to tell myself that it was pointless making a hard job of it. Eventually I got the message and from then on I started enjoying myself. But I won't relax completely until I do everything I want – like playing more gigs and making more records and having more people like me.

'That's not to say I'm a different Joan Armatrading from the one that first started out in this game. I once wrote, "No, you haven't changed – I've just got to know you better." You don't really get to know someone for three years.'

What type of person do you take the trouble to get to know?

'Unselfish, considerate people. People who think of others – though not necessarily putting others first. How can you help others if you can't help yourself?

'I guess I've only got one really good friend. She would do anything for me and I would do anything for her. She was very good to me when I first started out and let me stay with her until I found my feet. My income then was six pounds a week and my rent was five pounds – but I didn't want for anything. That's how good she was.

'I'm not really very close to my family. I occasionally see two brothers and a sister but not my parents. They still live in Birmingham and it's just a question of time.'

One of those memory bubbles seems to burst.

'My dad kicked me out when I was fifteen. I'll never forget, he was fixing the television, which had gone wrong for the umpteenth time, and I made a silly remark and he just blew his top. It was the damnedest thing. I ran into my room and packed my school satchel with some books, a toothbrush, limericks I'd written over the years and a camera. Know something? To this day I've never been able to understand why I took a camera. No food, no clothes, no money – but a camera.

'I went and stayed with my brother's girlfriend for a while – until my parents begged me to return home. But when I walked back through the front door I finally realised I could never stay. I'd looked after my brothers and sisters for most of my childhood. I knew that was no way to carry on and I couldn't spend the rest of my life doing that. So the row I had with my dad just brought everything to a head. I left home as soon as I could.'

Sometimes, just sometimes, this non-smoking, non-drinking introvert, does give a little bit more than she realises. And it's hunky-dory.

Joan's album Into the Blues debuted at number one on the US Billboard Blues Chart in 2007, the first by a British female artist to do so. The album was nominated for a Grammy Award. Her follow up album, This Charming Life, reached number 4 in the US Billboard Folk Albums chart. She was awarded an MBE in 2001 and a Lifetime Achievement Award in 2012.

AUGUST 1978

The Hollies, Dirty Berty, Thin Lizzy, The Jam, Sham 69

Life is pretty sweet, but my smile's only trying to fool the public because I ache for Dina. It's the longest we've been apart in two years and pretty sweet soon turns to shit without a focus. Maybe I should've married her before she went back to Cyprus.

Meanwhile, I'm mastering the art of mainstream journalism, skimming across the ocean like a stone and ending up on the doorstep of a Holly...

After fifteen years in the pulverising world of pop, Keith Richard doesn't look too well, Bob Dylan is positively ancient and John Lennon looks just plain weird. But Tony Hicks of the Hollies looks, well, like he did fifteen years ago. He confounds the axioms of the live-now-pay-later brigade with his pristine features and boundless enthusiasm. Those big, doleful eyes have surveyed the erratic eccentricities of rock'n'roll – Merseybeat, psychedelia, glitter, punk and power pop – but the guitarist has steered round them all, preferring to chart his own course to stardom.

Result? At thirty-two, Tony has escaped unscathed. His rewards? A pretty wife, a four-year-old son, a beautiful home in South Kensington, a pair of Stan Bowles football boots and an album standing at number two in the charts.

The band's *20 Golden Greats* record has caused something of a nostalgia wave. Every song showcased is a pop classic. Every song bears testimony to the fact that the Hollies are Britain's oldest surviving pop band.

'I've looked after myself over the years,' says Tony, sipping vintage red wine in the pinewood splendour of his spacious lounge. 'Sure, I've raved it up in the past – but I've never gone over the top. I've merely kept myself on a separate level to the music business. I feel sorry for the new bands around today. They're virtually forced into "enjoying" themselves, with all the consequences that entails.'

Tony is laconic – the sign of a contented man. And who wouldn't be with his bank balance?

'I guess I've always had enough to buy what I wanted for most of my life. But money does slow you down. If I didn't have the music anymore and was just left with the bank account, I'd go out of my mind with boredom.'

The Hollies were the epitome of the pop boom – John-Collier-dummy lookalikes who pierced the Sixties with gems like 'Stay', 'Just One Look' and 'I Can't Let Go'.

'I suppose it'll be hard to shake off that old image. And you know how it came about? Our first manager was a tailor who insisted on pushing his latest lines – with us! But it didn't prevent the band going through changes. First there were the Hollymania days of screaming girls and seven-week tours with the Stones. Graham Nash was with us then, before leaving to form Crosby, Stills & Nash. Then when all that eventually died away, we were confronted by a very boring period of ultra-smart suits and violins. But now, who knows ? Look at the Bee Gees. Five years ago you couldn't give them away.'

And it was five years ago that the father of an attractive blonde called Jane gave his daughter away to Tony. That's not very long, considering the time he's been in the business.

'I don't believe in early marriages,' he says. 'I figure a man shouldn't even consider marrying until he's at least thirty.' He keeps his wife and son Paul hidden from the music glare. 'Family and music just don't mix. I'll never take them on the road with me. But I decided a long time ago that I should live well while I'm on the road for my health's sake. I've spent a lot of money getting around in comfort.'

He doesn't smoke and plays squash. 'I've got into sport a lot recently – especially football. I have a pair of Stan Bowles' boots which he wore at Wembley when he played for England.'

His main ambition is to see his son become a Wimbledon champion and then throw a celebration party at the wine château he dreams of owning one day.

The Hollies may be an institution, but the Holly-days can't last for ever. Or can they?

Tony rings me after the article appears in the *London Evening News* to say it was the best interview he'd ever read about him and the band. 'If there's anything I can ever do for you, please don't hesitate to call me.' The sweetheart even gives me his number.

I was always a big fan of the Hollies, especially the Graham Nash days of 'I'm Alive' and 'I Can't Let Go'. They poured honey on my lemons as I tried to break free and they looked cool on stage. Never, in my wildest dreams, would I have imagined that baby-faced guitarist on *Ready, Steady, Go* would one day compliment me. I feel like I've been touched by King Midas.

Tony still tours with the Hollies, accompanied by original drummer Bobby Elliot. When lead singer Allan Clarke retired in 1999, he was replaced by ex-Move man Carl Wayne, who died in 2004. Peter Howarth took over vocals and they released the album Then, Now, Always in spring 2009. In 2010, the band was inducted into the Rock & Roll Hall of Fame.

I'm liking this freelance malarkey. The more interviews I do, the more money I make; the more people I meet, the more money I make. But late nights partying and writing will take their toll.

I'm lost in a forest of snappy intros and staccato paragraphs. The tabloid effect haunts everything I write, so I leap at the chance to replace *Record Mirror*'s resident gossip columnist, Juicy Luicy (who shall remain nameless) while she's on holiday. I adopt the alter ego of Dirty Berty, Luicy's public-school nephew who doesn't give a toss.

The first column goes well, and contains some juicy items, including the fan who breaks into Wilko Johnson's dressing room after a gig at the Marquee, covers the ex-Dr Feelgood man in kisses before dropping his trousers to reveal a multitude of running sores. A member of Wilko's band, Solid Senders, is about to throw a bottle of disinfectant over him when the fan grabs the bottle and proceeds to drink it before running off into the night. 'Police are looking for a man with very clean insides but very dirty outsides.'

I also mention that Sid Vicious is playing a one-off gig at the Electric Ballroom, fronting a band comprising Rich Kids' Glen Matlock, Steve New plus Rat Scabies. They're calling themselves Vicious White Kids. Every paragraph is an intro and I'm hooked. I'm living the part: I *am* Dirty Berty, the tabloid hack with the adolescent brain. A lethal concoction.

But the second column almost ruins my career.

I run a piece about Phil Lynott and his relationship with the now-pregnant model Caroline Crowther and hint the father might be thin and answer to the name of Lizzy. But naturally, as a naughty-boy gossip writer, I embellish it. Anyway, somebody up there doesn't like it and the day after the paper hits the streets, everyone of note at *Record Mirror*'s publisher, Spotlight, is hit with a heavy-duty libel writ accusing Dirty Berty of all sorts including allegations of homosexuality and bestiality!

I find one on my desk addressed to Dirty Berty. My sulphate-soaked blood collapses and I can feel it gushing through my body and cascading over my trainers.

Thank God they don't know my identity.

Alf Martin is on holiday when publishing director Mike Sharman, calls me into his office.

'I take it you've seen this?' He waves the writ in the air.

'Yes.' I'm suddenly back at school and Megan is calling.

'It's pretty damned serious. What have you got to say for yourself?'

'Er, it was just a bit of gossip. It's not that heavy.'

'Well, these writs suggest otherwise. I can tell you now, you'll never write another word for *Record Mirror*.'

I'm speechless, but manage to stand up and go to the door.

'Oh, and Barry...'

'Yes?' Maybe he's changed his mind. Maybe they'll laugh the whole thing off. Maybe, just maybe, the world is full of goodness after all.

'I suggest you get yourself a very good lawyer.'

I nearly shit myself on the spot.

After collecting my stuff, I say my goodbyes. Someone mentions a strike, but someone else points out that I'm only a freelancer and, besides, she couldn't afford it. I guess I'd have said the same. You could replace the entire editorial staff overnight with the freelancers who've contributed to the mag over the last year. Plus, regional newspaper journalists across the land would jump at the chance to work in Covent Garden, writing about pop stars and flying around the world. A strike is definitely a no-no.

The next few days are a nightmare. I'm not worried about being sued – they can't get blood out of a stone. I live at home with my mum and dad in an Islington council flat and have about five hundred quid in the bank, for Chrissake. Thin Lizzy won't get fat on that. My fear is of not being able to write about music again. God in his infinite wisdom decided not to give me the fingers of a musician so writing about music was the ultimate consolation. To deprive me of that while my heart is flapping around like a dying fish on a Cypriot beach would be a blow from which I might never recover.

Pass me that axe, Eugene.

Maybe it's destined to end like this. Maybe 1977 is as good as it gets. Maybe this is my 10th Avenue freeze-out. Maybe it's nature's way of saying pop music is dead, that I'd only be shagging a corpse if I carried on. While I'm busy patting myself on the back for not being a necrophiliac, Alf Martin returns from holiday. When he finds out I've been tossed aside like a snapped plectrum, he does his nut.

'If he goes, I go,' he tells the suits and, within a day, I'm reinstated. The following week a big retraction appears at the bottom of Juicy's column and, as far as I know, that's the end of it. I meant no harm. It wasn't me. It was someone else. I swear I'll never write another gossip column as long as I live. On my first day back in the office the switchboard girl puts Dina through.

Bearded *Record Mirror* writer Robin Smith lives up the road from the Reading Festival site with his mum and dad. I think we're the only two guys working for *Record Mirror* who still live at home. Must be something to do with the beards.

Robin's covering the event and I tag along. I've never been before but the Friday night line-up looks a bit tasty – the Jam, Sham 69, Ultravox, Penetration, the Pirates, Radio Stars – so if I'm going to lose my Reading cherry, tonight's the night.

I drive down in the afternoon, park in the VIP area backstage and meet up with Robin, a teetotaller inhabiting a drug-free zone. He's without doubt the straightest man in music journalism, possibly the entire music business. But he's open and honest, and his self-deprecation is unashamedly charming.

I, on the other hand, could murder a beer and, as the day progresses, turn into a serial killer of the bottled lager that abounds in the caravan dressing rooms dotted around the backstage area. My two favourite caravans of love belong to the Jam and Sham 69. One of the roadies backstage shares a few lines of sparkling crystal speed.

Both bands are riding high again after a '78 hiatus and they're eager to please. Predictably, Sham 69's performance is interrupted by skinheads in the crowd beating the fuck out of each other.

While Ultravox are playing, I sit in the backstage bar with Paul Weller and Jimmy Pursey, drinking lager, smoking endlessly and bemoaning the state of the industry. We talk for ages and I can't believe they want to spend so long in my company. Good job I'm pissed and speeding, good job they're pissed, but not speeding – they're not those kinda guys. Jimmy may be the chalk to Paul's cheese, but when it comes to illegal drugs they're both no shows. But they can drink for England and most of northern Europe and smoke fags for Scotland and southern Europe.

Jimmy, at twenty-three, is assertive and loud and determined to get his point across. Paul, just twenty, is more uncertain, his timidity revealing ever-changing moods and a nascent passion. His opinions are still taking shape while Jimmy's are set in stone.

At twenty-six (barely), I'm just happy to listen. I don't have any opinions on any subject whatsoever because I'm pissed and speeding. I just want to smoke and drink some more and hope the night never ends. And the Jam show is some kinda wonderful.

Robin has arranged for me to stay over at his house. The car cannot remain where it is, so I decide to drive, much to Robin's horror. By the time we arrive at his house I'm feeling really ill. I drive onto the front lawn, jump out and spew, almightily, over the grass.

I recover sufficiently to make it through the front door but that spinning sickness sloshing the booze around like a washing machine hits the back of my throat like a train and transports six packed carriages across the kitchen floor, hurling splashes of sick onto most of the pinewood cabinets. It's a Megan moment, all right.

I'm incapable of cleaning up the mess and collapse on the settee.

Waking up at six am – I always do in strange houses no matter how fucked – I stumble out the door, reverse the car back over the lawn and speed off. On the way home I have to stop nine times to vomit, four of those on the M1.

Two days later I contract pneumonia. I blame the sparkling crystal speed and the fact that my life is empty without Dina. But mainly I blame the sparkling crystal speed.

SEPTEMBER 1978

The Who, The Stranglers, X-Ray Spex, 10cc, The Jam, Blondie, Boney M

When my temperature creeps up to 107, the GP decides to call the hospital. It's the least he can do. But by the time the ambulance arrives, I'm dead. Or is that Keith Moon? Who gives a shit? They're coming to take me away hohoheeheehaha. The funny farm burns down and my temperature drops and the ambulance guys decide I'm over the worst of it, so I stay in my steaming bed and vow never to touch drink and drugs again.

That's something Keith Moon vows when he downs 32 Heminevrin pills – one for every year of his life – to combat the withdrawal symptoms of chronic alcoholism before dying in his sleep at Harry Nilsson's Mayfair apartment.

Mandy Bruce from the AdLib team at the News rings me at home, enquires after my health and asks me what I know about Keith and the Who in general. I tell her – which isn't much – and crawl back to my bed.

My own favourite Who tale was related by John Entwistle when I once went to interview him at his West London home. He didn't come across as a particularly generous bloke – I remember we sat in a room with an enormous bar that stocked every drink imaginable and he never offered me one the whole time I was there. OK, so it was eleven in the morning but, shit, I was a guest. Still, he did tell me the best LSD story I ever heard.

'I was never tempted to drop acid,' he said. 'The idea of losing complete touch with reality was just too terrifying for words. One night in 1969 at a party, someone gave me some punch and after a while I started to feel strange. Then it clicked: the punch was spiked with acid.

'I panicked. I tried to reason my way out of it but the strangeness was getting stranger. Then I knew what I had to do. I grabbed a bottle of Jack Daniel's from the bar and ran upstairs to a small bathroom. I locked the door behind me and my intention was to drink the lot, pass out and hopefully sleep off the whole trip. But I was suddenly overcome by a fear that I'd inhale my own vomit like Hendrix because not only would I be out of my mind, I'd be drunk and out of my mind.

'Then I saw it – a small window above the bath. I figured I'd drink the entire bottle very quickly, open the window and poke my head and shoulders through until I got wedged in. Then, even if I wanted to inhale my own vomit when I passed out, I couldn't.

'So I drank the bottle in ten minutes – I was that scared – and then squeezed the top half of my body through the window. I woke up ten hours later staring down at a garden patio, still jammed in the window and suffering the worst hangover I'd ever experienced. And every part of my protruding body was covered in pigeon shit. At that moment, I wish I'd fucking inhaled my own vomit.'

I can't afford to stay ill and within a few days I'm up and at 'em. I've added a few more publications to my portfolio and the cheques are making dents on the welcome mat. My mum, who's left work through ill-health, spends her day answering the phone and taking messages for me. It's all getting too hot to handle.

Enter Tim Lott. Tim is still on staff at *Record Mirror*. He's a marvellous writer with ambition and is currently doing a few stints at Capital Radio. One afternoon, about a week back into the swing of things, I'm sitting with him in the Nags Head in Covent Garden. We've always liked each other's company and got pissed together on several occasions. I'm telling him how much work I've got on and how sometimes it gets a little too much, and he suggests we team up.

By the time we leave the pub, we've already decided to set up a press agency supplying local newspapers across the land with weekly pop columns, including interviews, reviews, the works. In return they would each pay us just twenty quid. We'd mail every paper with a freebie taster to get the ball rolling. If only ten took it up that'd be two hundred quid a week, Imagine if we had fifty, or a hundred.

Great idea. On top of that there's all my stuff that Tim can start helping out with, plus his Capital Radio spots.

We start to look for a suitable office.

Saturday, 16 September: the Stranglers are playing in Battersea Park. What fun. I interviewed bassist Jean-Jacques three days ago and it appears in today's *Evening News* so I thought I'd toddle off to see the boys in blue watching the boys in black, while holding my feature, tightly…

You could be forgiven for assuming The Stranglers are essentially nocturnal creatures. That their eyes squint in strong daylight, that they go about their work under cover of darkness, that they pursue their prey along the corridors of the night. Such is their expertise.

Their music instils in the mind twisted visions of decay and depravity, all acted out in a scenario of everlasting night. Edgar Alien Poe reads like Enid Blyton by comparison.

All the more surprising then that they should decide to play at Battersea Park this afternoon, home of stray dogs, defunct funfairs and a Pink Floyd album-cover power plant. To top it all, they're making a grand entrance on a tank – apparently they intended to fly in by way of rocket-packs strapped to their backs, only to discover at the last minute that such a stunt required a two-year training course. They maintain the GLC (Greater London Council) has made life difficult for them and prevented the band from playing more suitable venues.

'They hate our guts,' says bassist Jean, 25.

'This is simply a PR exercise on their part. They never exactly ban you, just quietly nobble you.'

Maybe the council is simply bored with washing down paint-splattered walls all over London that boldly proclaim, 'The Stranglers Must Play', or sick of being inundated with petitions from irate fans.

For the Stranglers can rightly claim to be the first dinosaurs of punk. They are the only band to have emerged from the grand old days of new wave with a cast-iron reputation of almost Zeppelinesque proportions. Three gold albums, a succession of memorable hits and bang! Superstar status. They're assured of a tax-haven future. But all is not well. Indeed, the band is in danger of forgoing the lot for a little bit of peace and quiet.

'There are many people out to destroy us and it's getting us down,' says Jean. 'Sure, it's nothing new, we've always been the band everyone loves to hate because our clothes aren't cool and we're all over twenty. But it's getting out of hand. What with bans – though none of them will admit it – by the BBC, radio stations, journalists, it's all beginning to look a little hopeless.

'Even America is turning its back on us. I've received three death threats this week from the States over comments the band made about the smallness of American brains compared to English.'

Quelle surprise!

So Jean has decided to lie low after today's show... in Japan. 'I'm going to live there for three months to continue my karate studies. I'm already a brown belt, but I want to attain black-belt status and return to teach the art. Karate has taught me self-control. I guess I was a little headstrong as a kid, maybe because I was French and living in London. I had to fight a great deal to prove myself.'

His battleground has now switched from the street to the concert hall. At a recent gig, he jumped off stage into the audience and got into a fight.

'This guy kept spitting in my face. It's no fun trying to play with spittle dripping down over your guitar. The rest of the band came to my assistance.'

Was he hurt?

'We never get hurt. The Stranglers always win their battles.'

Such flagrant displays of nihilism have earned the band a dubious reputation and a money-spinning fascination.

'We seem to attract intellectual psychopaths at our gigs. Sentient beings who like to exercise a little muscle. We don't encourage them. It's not such a good idea to have a uniformed group in attendance at concerts.'

But they do have the Finchley Boys, a gang of fanatical fans with good intentions. 'We've learned a lot from them, and they from us. See, we're one of the most intelligent bands around. That, and a determination not to take anything from anybody, is the real reason for our longevity. There's a biochemist, an economist/historian, an international gourmet and a cosmic cowboy in this band – a winning combination if ever there was one.'

Jean, the economist/historian, has achieved a certain individual notoriety. Although reports are often grossly exaggerated, he *did* punch a journalist who vilified one of their albums, he *was* once a Hells Angel and he *does* have love affairs with motorbikes and an endless stream of women.

'I hit the writer because he attacked me personally and that is totally uncalled for. But, contrary to opinion, I'm not a stud. I just have a habit of sending myself up occasionally. The only guy I would honestly call a stud was George Simenon, the creator of Maigret. He's supposed to have slept with around fifteen thousand women in his life – give or take a thousand. In comparison, I'm just a good, clean, wholesome chap.'

Although Jean has made a great deal of money, he still hasn't found a regular place to stay. 'The last time I lived in a flat permanently I kept getting raided by thieves who would smash everything up. That's how I came to write "Five Minutes". What do you do with money? Lose it, I guess. Some of it appears to be vanishing mysteriously recently.'

Few can deny that the quality of Stranglers' music is extremely high. But many question the ideals they reflect in their lyrics – in particular, a so-called preoccupation with misogyny.

'It's amazing how many people believe what they read in the papers,' says Jean. 'Some women are actually afraid of seeing us play in case we beat them up. Even representatives from our record company refuse to come along and see us. It's just an excuse. We're back to the same old problem – people hate us and that's that. But I must admit, recently the band is getting pretty depressed about the whole situation.'

Jean, what do you think you would've been if you hadn't joined a band?
'A yob.'

The show? It's nice. And sleazy.

On the opposite page there's my interview with Poly Styrene. That means I have the whole centre spread of the *Evening News*. And a photo by-line thrown in for good measure. Who's the man, the man bringing punk music to Fleet Street instead of punk mayhem?

And it turns out Poly isn't as cool as we all think, cos when the lights went out in her Day-Glo world, the princess of punk found herself flat on her back in a psychiatric ward. Doctors pumped her full of drugs, and when she emerged from a chemical coma two weeks later, that famous bracing smile wasn't quite so wide.

'The band had just come back from the States and we went straight into another tour,' says the twenty-year-old lead singer of X-Ray Spex. 'We kept playing gig after gig and I started to feel exhausted. I couldn't sleep. I lay awake every night, fighting to close my eyes, desperately trying to rest. Everything seemed to be closing in on me. It was all so claustrophobic. Finally I collapsed, and the next thing I knew I was waking up in a hospital bed.'

Poly says the main reason for the breakdown was exhaustion. 'But there were other reasons. Things like kids pretending they knew me and trying to find out where I lived really got me down. And I used to hang out a lot after gigs. I chain-smoked – but that was all I did to calm my nerves.'

Now Poly has made a complete recovery. 'But it's taken a long time,' she says. 'I haven't played in front of an audience for ages. My body was really wrecked and I still have to take things pretty easy. In the future I'm determined to be more selective with gigs. I'm not going to play sweaty little clubs any more. I want to stick to bigger venues.'

She's sitting in the garden of her manager's Fulham home, sipping coffee in the rain. Those recent traumas are swept aside in one glistening, metallic smile revealing a mouthful of braces. 'I use them like jewellery, complementing my ear-rings and bracelets. I still have to wear them for a while yet.'

Poly is an anti-glam heroine, singing anti-melody songs for an antiseptic world. She writes of rayon trees and synthetic fibres and germ-free adolescence.

'We all seem to be preoccupied with cleanliness – but the type pushed in adverts. A clean, tooth-pasty love is used to sell anything from washing powders to floor polishers. Sex and romance help to sell food – what on earth is romantic about that? Especially today's junk food. I get this recurring dream. What happens when we die after years of eating all this chemical muck and are buried? Can you imagine all the plant life that will grow up around our chemical-ridden rotting bodies? It'll be like another planet.'

Strange thoughts from a half-Somali girl raised in Brixton, who left school at fifteen to pursue a fashion-buying career. Predictably, the job only lasted a few months. Poly, restless by nature, wanted to see what life was like outside the confines of the city. She travelled all over the country, sleeping rough when she had to, and taking a succession of jobs – including a short spell as a mushroom-picker.

She finally settled in Somerset and remained there for eighteen months before returning to London to form X-Ray Spex.

'I guess I love doing different things. I like changes. I like creating images around me. But I don't think I would embark on such a journey now. When you get older, you become aware of the dangers of hitchhiking and sleeping on beaches and meeting different people. I was young and naïve, ignorant of the fact that the world is full of odd people, cranks. Sure I met them, but I didn't realise they meant me any harm. Simply by thinking along those lines, nothing happened to me. Lucky, I guess.'

It was a logical progression for Poly to venture into rock. She had nurtured an interest in fringe theatre for some years and regarded music as an artistic pursuit on a similar level. Attired in obligatory plastic bin-liner and sporting a decadent pose, she acquired both notoriety and a fan club. Many thought her appearance a cheap trick to gain fame – she was spending hours in front of the mirror trying to look ugly.

Not so, says Poly. 'I'm not women's lib, I'm myself. People have said I try so hard to be ugly that I become beautiful. I'm myself. For some people it's a struggle to be themselves. Sometimes I'm shy, sometimes I'm not the person you see, sometimes I may be myself, but I'm also schizophrenic – an entirely different person on and off stage. I used to fantasise at school, and the songs I write now are merely extensions of those fantasies.

'I used to hang out, posing, going to endless parties. But that's all over now. Whenever possible, I flee to the country and lead a separate life.

'I also ride around London on my bicycle, looking at museums and buying clothes from street markets. Cheap clothes, preferably. Clothes I can wear just as easily off stage as on. I go for those styles you see in old English films of the thirties and forties.'

One more brace-ridden smile. One more sip of coffee. No more Poly. Poly-gone.

Poly, real name Marian Said, went on to join the Hare Krishna movement. She released a solo album, New Age Flower Aeroplane, in 2004. In 2008 she fronted the re-formed X-Ray Spex for a live show at the Roundhouse. She moved to St Leonards, near Hastings where she lived alone. Funny how so many punks turned into hippies, the original objects of their venom. She sadly died of cancer in 2011 aged just 53

10cc are shrewd hippies who used to be a good band, verging on greatness. Loved 'The Dean and I', and, of course, 'I'm Not In Love', but when Kevin Godley and Lol Creme split to pursue the bizarre and make ingenious pop videos, the writing seemed to be on the wall for 10cc.

Eric Stewart and Graham Gouldman continued the good name but their first few releases – 'The Things We Do For Love' and 'Good Morning Judge' – were running alive with mediocrity, even though both were hits. And now they've hit the big time again with 'Dreadlock Holiday' for cricket lovers everywhere – and it's number one with a rubber bullet.

I'm in Bristol with the band, near the end of their mammoth UK tour. The show is slick and safe and the dreamers in the audience light-up the twisty lanes of 'I'm Not In Love' with flaming lighters held aloft in the darkness. After, we head off to a night club where we drink champagne like cherry cola.

'We've found that certain chords can make you laugh while others make you cry,' says sleepy-eyed Eric Stewart. 'In one tune we can make you feel down, then up, then back down again just by altering the structure very slightly.'

No wonder they've been dubbed the Professors of Rock.

That don't worry Eric none. 'That nickname is meant to be derogatory – but I consider it a great compliment. We do analyse, we do create in a very technical way. Our aim is to achieve perfection,'

Some may argue they've already attained such dizzy heights with the classic 'I'm Not In Love' – recently voted the best song ever written.

'It's a total love song. Look, you can only say the words, "I love you", once in your whole life and really mean them. If you happen to say them again it's nothing more than an aside. Wives are continually asking, "Do you love me?" They shouldn't have to be told over and over again. I've only said those words once and I don't intend repeating them. That is what the song is all about. When I first heard the completed version, I broke down and cried. It meant so much.'

Yet it wasn't so very long ago when 10cc looked like a washed-up 5cc. When Lol Creme and Kevin Godley quit the band everyone assumed that was the end.

'When they went, there were many hoped Graham and I would decide to scrap the whole thing, go home and bloody die,' says Eric.

'We were criticised for perpetuating the name,' adds Graham, who has just torn himself away from an army of autograph hunters in the club. 'But what people tend to forget is that Eric and I were responsible for 80 per cent of the singles hits the band had. We parted with them on very friendly terms and they were only too pleased that we carried on with the name.'

'Right from the start, we knew we could survive without them,' says Eric.

Eric and Graham are the antithesis of your average rock stars. For starters, both are happily married.

'Neither of us has ever gone out with Britt Ekland,' laughs Eric. 'And we always telephone in advance when we're planning to wreck a hotel room.'

Eric lives in Dorking in a house he designed himself. Graham has decided to stay in his native Rochdale. 'I'd hate to live down south. Up there, I can be anonymous. I can relax with my family away from all this. See, if you're truly dedicated you'll find yourself married to your band and your wife but the two just don't go together.'

'Working ridiculous hours has kept my marriage strong,' says Eric, as he opens another bottle of champagne.

'If I did a nine-to-five job, I reckon I would've only been married for two years. I'd have gone stark raving mad. I need to work all the time. It keeps me alive.'

10cc celebrated their 40th Anniversary on May 10, 2012 with a concert at the Royal Albert Hall. Kevin Godley performed several songs with the band

Y'know what keeps me alive? Seeing the Jam live from time to time. Listening to Paul Weller whistle while he works.

Paul thinks there's one in every classroom – he's teacher's pet, team captain, top scholar and goes out with all the best-looking girls. 'David Watts' is his name, the title of the Jam's new single.

'I had a kid like that in my class,' recalls Paul, twenty with a bullet. 'He really used to fucking infuriate me, y'know. While I was smoking in the toilets, playing truant and generally being one of the lads, he swept the boards both academically and on the sports field. The last I heard he was a copper.'

The single, written back in the Sixties by the Kinks, is the Jam's first big hit for almost a year. 'Everyone was saying we were all washed up. But it doesn't worry me if I never have a number one single. But a number one album ... that's a different story.'

We're sitting backstage at *Top of the Pops*. Neat. I've never been here before. The dressing room ain't up to much but, shit, I'm on *TOTP*. And it's just as you imagine it would be – kids, clumsiness and catchy chaos.

The boys are casually slipping into suits sharper than samurai swords. It's just another day.

'I was really depressed earlier this year,' says Paul. 'Nothing seemed to be going right. I kept looking at myself and thinking I'd sold out. I always thought it'd be great to get everyone together, audiences and bands. Just one united force with a common dream. I now realise that was idealistic dream shit. OK, I miss coming off the stage after a gig and walking straight to the bar for a drink and a laugh. But you've got to progress. To keep the same lifestyle is ridiculous and it's only human nature to try and better yourself.'

Meanwhile, Rick Buckler is trying to butter (sic) himself. He's left home. 'I got sick and tired of my mum giving me brown bread. I fucking hate the stuff,' the twenty-one-year-old blue-eyed blond – though his hair is dyed jet black at the moment – told me as he slipped into his strides. 'I only ever eat white bread yet, for some reason, when I came back home after a tour, my mum insisted on serving up brown. She even started toasting and frying it to disguise the colour – but she couldn't fool me.'

So Rick cleared off and now shares a flat in Croydon with a friend. He says that living on the breadline was only half the problem. 'When you play in a band you tend to keep strange hours and it begins to affect the lives of everyone where you live, in my case my parents and twin brother Pete, especially when they have to work regular hours themselves. After setting up home on my own, I've never looked back.'

But Bruce Foxton is a happy home boy. He's flicking his neat barnet and nervously clapping his hands. 'I prefer it. The only time I've ever had any hassles was when I brought a bird back once. My mum and dad weren't too keen on that. But that's the only grouch. Why should I move out when all my friends still live in the area? Besides, I'm away half the year touring so it doesn't matter much anyway.'

I get to Heathrow an hour early only to find Dina's flight is delayed by two hours. I haven't seen her in three months – what's three hours? The time now is two fifteen p.m. She's due in at five twenty-five pm.

So I have a coffee and read the paper.

Shit! Two thirty pm.

I take a walk. I've never been so full of longing and desire and friendship. It's too hot a potato for my patience to handle and I'm on fire, a chunk of burning love, a many-splendoured thing. I sit down and read the paper and have a coffee.

Shit! Two fifty-three pm.

I honestly never believed Dina would come back. Everything she ever wanted in life was in Cyprus – sunshine, laughter, the comfort of family and friends with a clear blue sea and pine-clad mountains never too far away. And here there's me, full stop. OK, I know she enjoyed the freedom that London offered, freedom from the shackles of a traditional Seventies Cypriot mother – but I ask you, sunshine, laughter, the comfort of family and friends with a clear blue sea and pine-clad mountains never too far away, or me?

Well, she chose me. Maybe she knew she'd never find another

living soul who loved her as much I did. Maybe it's women's intuition. If it is, then it's not as sharp as women make out because if you ask the 2015 Dina she'd stab me a million times to get through to the sunshine, laughter, the comfort of family and friends with a clear blue sea and pine-clad mountains never too far away. I thought you gals had something going for you, but it turns out you're just as dumbarse as men are.

Shit! Three twenty.

I get up and wander around the shops. WHSmith is full of Stephen King, Robert Ludlum and John Le Carré – ghouls, guns and gumption. I read the first pages of half a dozen novels, glance through the *NME*, scratch my arse, check out the latest Louise Brown story in the *Guardian*, scratch my arse again, have a coffee and read the paper.

Shit! Three fifty.

I've booked a hotel in Windsor for the night – sex, dinner, sex, dance floor smooching, sex, breakfast, sex.

Shit! Three fifty-one.

Will this plane never come?

Shit! Five ten.

I've written to Dina while she was away and spoken to her, courtesy of the Cupid on the switchboard at *Record Mirror*. Her face was beginning to fade, with the trace of a smile the last to go like a Cypriot Cheshire cat. Suddenly I can see her again. She hasn't passed through the gate but I see her perfectly, see her loveliness. She's close by and my memory can sniff her out. She's still at the baggage carousel but she's all I can see, all I can hear, all I can *feel*.

And there's my dream, come true.

My first meeting with Debbie Harry starts a chain of events that alters the course of my entire life. It's a funny old game. Picture this if you will: Debbie Harry in black, in transit, incognito, in shades in London.

Incandescent coffee-cup laughter in the hotel garden. Cheesecake smile, creamy frown, peachy patter. The Fifties starlet without a Tab

Hunter shoulder to cry on. Forget the odd bark line of maturity – it's just another dream gone wrong.

She's younger-looking than I expected. The Bitch Brothers had instilled in my innocent mind visions of a hoary, gum slithering club hostess with honeycomb features. Instead, I encountered a face of eyes; two Roaring Twenties crystal balls reflecting the miasma below.

Yes, below. For Debbie more than any other female singer of the Seventies has been elevated to those untouchable heights reserved for movie stars. Y'know, every guy's gossamer sexual fantasy – blissfully unattainable combined with a masturbatory elegance. Visions of her swathed in and out of a focus wonderland on *Top Of The Pops* wearing silk shorts – looking for all the world like a blonde Ava Gardner pickled for thirty years to preserve that pristine promiscuous look – only serve to perpetuate the myth.

If ever there was a Venus in blue jeans it's Debbie Harry.

But moments before she was in schoolgirl regalia for a national-newspaper photo shoot. All black stockings and suspenders peeping out from beneath a short pleated skirt like war wounds.

'I don't mind posing for photographs. It's part of my art form.' A disposable voice. It's there, you listen, it disappears, you forget. 'Being a photograph, being an actress, being a sculpture. It's all creating image simultaneously.

'OK, so maybe that whole image thing can backfire. Now people review Blondie less in terms of music and more in terms of how I look. All I know is, I've always tried to stimulate interest in this group through whatever channel's possible. Sure I have some regrets about that, but I've learned to accept them. I used whatever advantages I might have to sell records.'

Hence the wet-lipped Marilyn Monroe come-on.

'I used that kind of image a lot in the early days because it was convenient and made for easy reference. But I'm not at all like Monroe. She got sort of lost inside. I have more creative outlets.

'She was a legend, but not in a Da Vinci way. All she really did was turn people on and that's not what I want. Anyway, I don't cultivate that image any more. I'm more sure of myself now ... and the music. I don't ever want to end up a legend.'

But she's already halfway there with a history that reads like a B movie. Left her comfortable home, where her mother ran a candy store, for the bright lights of New York. Predictably the bulbs went out, leaving a twilight zone of Times Square druggies and groupies. Debbie became an addict with a pillowcase view of the rock world.

'I finally decided it was about time women took the initiative in rock and roll, so I formed a band, the Stilettos with Chris Stein, and kicked my habit. I have no regrets about those days. I had to get away from home. I had to experience life to the full. I had to.

'I suppose I was lucky to come through unscathed. I've been left with an inner feeling of contentment. I made up my mind to do those things and it's all turned out worthwhile. Surely that's better than sitting in front of the TV all your life wishing you had done the things you're watching other people doing.'

That indeed may be so – but the corpulent bozos among us would rather watch in their claustrophobic cells of splendid voyeurism than venture one step beyond.

Stardom appears to have landed her with one hell of an age hang-up. When asked that delicate question she pauses, lowers her shades and replies, 'My published age is thirty-two. I think most people lie about their age when they pass twenty-five. And being in this business only makes things worse because the accent is on youth, so I guess it's crucial that I should be marketed in the right way.

'What these marketing men tend to forget is that rock'n'roll is a part of everyone's life now, no matter how you react to it and what your age might be.'

She is wary, forever on guard against giving any kind of reply that could be misinterpreted, thanks to previous interviewers, she says, who managed to carve her up nicely. Sometimes she looks older than those thirty-odd years, sometimes younger – it depends where the sun happens to be in the sky.

So, what of persistent marriage rumours with guitarist Chris Stein?

'Totally unfounded. Sure, Chris has proposed, but I'm just nowhere near ready. We have a great relationship and I'm sure marriage would ruin all that, leaving at least one of us unhappy. I sort of feel sorry for the man in a married situation. For a woman it's a business proposition and since I already have a career I don't need it.

'A wife has to help her husband's career, which limits her chances of doing something stimulating with her life. If I had a kid I'd like to make it legal to give the child some kind of identity. But I think Chris would rather I gave birth to a guitar anyway.'

She says it's only the true love she's found with him that has helped her overcome her fears of sexual come-ons.

'I don't worry about them any more, thanks to Chris. Now I can even let girls approach me after a show and I think it's flattering. It's the drunks in bars who spit in your face while they try to chat you up that I can't stand.'

And it's not only the drunks. The era of the Blondie slag-off is upon us. It was just a matter of time. You're heralded as the next big thing and before you know it you're given away free in a packet of cornflakes. Blondie's sex-on-the-beach sound has, according to some sources, lost its Alka-Seltzer.

'On the new album *Parallel Lines* we've tried to make as many singles as possible. The songs are better than ever simply because we're now a fully fledged band. The image and the music are working together for the first time. We're touring again in the States, which is a great challenge and gives our music a bigger bite. And the lyrics, which were always third-person transsexual anyway, are improving all the time. I was always a Walter Mitty character and that whole romantic detachment is beginning to show in the songs.'

Walter Mitty, huh? There surely can't be much left she can imagine.

So that's it. A quick chat with a production-line dream. Oh, and there was something she asked me as I motioned to leave. 'Listen, er, do you think you could mention the rest of the band? See, er, everyone seems to just talk about me and it makes me feel kinda guilty, y'know.'

Blondie are: Chris Stein guitar, Clement Burke drums, James Destri keyboards, Nigel Harrison guitar, Frank Infante bass and Debbie Harry vocals.

A few days after the interview appears in *Record Mirror*, I receive a phone call from a guy called David who says he wants to reproduce it in a magazine he's publishing about Blondie.

I enquire what sort of magazine and he tells me it's an unofficial poster mag.

'What's a poster mag?'

'An A4 magazine that opens up into an A1 poster.'

'In that case I don't think it's appropriate ...'

'I'll pay you two hundred and fifty pounds in cash.'

'Er, yeah. OK. Go ahead and use it.'

The next day, in a pub around the corner from my house, he plants the cash onto my palm and I feel like I've just participated in a smack deal. David is of indeterminate age – anything between twenty-five and thirty-five. He wears a cream suit with a couple of stains, teeth likewise, and appears to be a slightly eccentric chancer. He intrigues me. A few days later he gives me another £250 for my Boney M interview.

Speaking of Boney M, I have just uncovered an innovative marketing ploy that takes advantage of the faceless mass of people otherwise known as record buyers. (And it has nothing to do with unofficial poster mags.) The ploy, which should catch on like a forest fire, is based on the assumption that they never play the B-sides of the singles they eagerly dash out to purchase on pay day. Now, bearing that in mind, if a B-side happens to be catchy but has been overshadowed by the immense popularity of the A-side, what are you going to do with it? Wait for an incompetent radio DJ to play it by mistake? Enclose a leaflet with each single begging them to flip it over occasionally?

Or do what Boney M's record company, WEA, have just done and re-release the single but swap sides? Sounds inconceivable? Well, why don't you just wander over to your record collection, pick up your copy of 'Brown Girl In The Ring' and take a peep at what's on the other side. Surprise, surprise 'Rivers Of Babylon'. And while you're about it, have a quick butcher's at your copy of 'Rivers Of Babylon'. See what's on the back? Need I say more?

'Brown Girl' has been selling so well – around thirty thousand a day – that there are those of you out there who must've bought the same record twice. Mugs.

'Isn't it incredible?' beams Marcia Barrett. She's wrapped in a towel on the edge of her bed. Nope, I'm not there. We're speaking over the phone.

'People were showing interest in "Brown Girl", which is a West Indian school song, so the record company decided to put it out. I guess people aren't playing their B-sides.'

You guessed right, Marcia. So how come you're all dripping and dreamy and drowsy at this unearthly hour – nine am – with the sun caressing your towel like a Lifebuoy soap ad? Huh?

'Well, I'm just off to Jamaica for a month-long holiday.'

And where's the rest of that deliciously textured European disco warrior wagon – Boney M? (Wonder what the M stands for? Mouth, Mind, Meringue, Missile, Morony, Moko-Moko – that's a New Zealand bell bird by the way – or maybe just plain Mammoth?)

'Well, Maisie's in Italy, Liz is in Paris and Bobby's still back in Germany.'

And who are you going to Jamaica with?

'My mum, who now lives in Croydon, and Wayne.'

Who's Wayne?

'My son. I'm not married, never have been. I had Wayne when I was sixteen and very naïve. It was a strange pregnancy. I was still at school and I had him in the Easter holidays.' Quite some egg.

'I went back to school when the headmistress told my sister I should. But it was difficult. I had to get up in the morning, bath and dress him and take him to nursery before going to school. I lived with my mum and sister then. My father was in Jamaica and that made things even harder. I went to night school during the holidays and got various jobs to help my mum make ends meet.

'Before I had Wayne I was scared of life. But those experiences helped me grow up quicker than I could ever have expected. Wayne has always understood the situation and has had a better life than many kids with two parents. At least he hasn't had to listen to parents arguing in the middle of some cold night.'

So what have you gained from all that?

'To be careful with money and men. I used to dream a lot before I had Wayne, but not any more. I just take life as it comes. I never saw Wayne's father again and I thank God I never married him.

'I went out with a German guy for ten years. He's still around but there's no way I'll marry him. Sure, I'd like to get married one day – wouldn't every woman? – but a girl in my position has to watch herself. There are a lot of guys around unscrupulous enough to marry for a fast buck.'

Will you marry me, Marcia?

'Listen, life is so short that you must have fun, you must enjoy yourself. That's all I ask.'

Nicely dodged.

'Rivers Of Babylon' was a revelation, the tail-end of a chain of massive but disposable hits and the one record that has given them a broader acceptance and got lascivious bodies dripping in diamonds to boogie the night away in indulgent risotto-resort discos oblivious to the morality of it all.

'Sometimes I'm not too crazy about our music. Y'know, when you're on a long tour and you keep singing those same old songs I get to thinking I wish I was singing something else. Something that I can get off on. And as for the critics, let them think what they like. I'm not bothered. We sell, don't we?'

You sure do, Marcia. You sure do.

Boney M split up in 1990. During the Nineties, Marcia contracted cancer and overcame it. She continues to perform and record. In 2007 she played before the president of Georgia. The following year she gave a concert in the palace grounds in Bangalore, India, in front of an audience of thirty thousand. Bobby Farrell died of a heart attack in December 2010 aged 61.

OCTOBER 1978

Sylvester, Smokie, David Essex, Kevin Keegan, Bill Shankly

Sylvester. Now that's a real wild one. '*I tought I taw a puddycat a cweepin' up on me / I did! I taw a puddytat as plain as he can be.*' I hum that immortal tune as I dial his number in San Francisco. At last, my long-time ambition is about to be realised: an interview with Sylvester. How many times have I gasped at his heroic adventures? How many times have I admired his spurious groans, his devious plots, his surreptitious methods to exterminate that infuriating little shit Tweety Pie?

I wept, I can tell you, when his efforts were thwarted at every turn. Oh, how I wished I could be at his side, vanquishing that disgusting yellow squirt with the squawk impediment. But, alas, the little bastard always ended up swinging, defiantly, on his perch in that Fort Knox of a cage. That butter-wouldn't-melt-in-his-mouth expression has haunted my craziest nightmares.

Now's my chance to ask him about his frustrations, his suffering, his interminable battles personifying the struggle between big and small that the latter always seems to win.

My heart races as the ringing tone burps out of the receiver.

'Hello.'

Now, that's strange. The voice is free of a soaking-wet lisp. Hello ... Sylvester?

'Yes.'

Er ... *the* Sylvester?

'I guess.'

How's Tweety Pie? The question doesn't appear to go down too well. It feels like Sylvester is a Buckaroo ready to explode when asked one question too many. Either this cat has taken night school lessons in cool, or this cat ain't a cat at all.

Why, it's none other than Sylvester James, the cutesie-pie, slick, soft soprano singer who jettisoned his surname and whose delicious 'You Make Me Feel (Mighty Real)' has just twinkle-toed into the hot twenty and got the boutique bootie boys jiving all night.

This guy ain't gonna know much about cartoon canary carnage. But he will know about style. I seem to remember him to be veritable *Vogue* when it comes to dress sense. What you wearing, Sylv?

'Well, I got khaki trousers, an Indian cotton shirt with a white silk shirt over that and a pair of plastic oggs [fisherman's sandals].'

Tolja.

'I'm standing in the hall. The sun's out.'

His answers are pert but laced with a note of boredom. Like he doesn't really want to talk but has been told to and is reacting with schoolboy sulkiness.

So let's wander through Mr Sylvester's multi-mirrored life. But beware. Sometimes it's rather like walking on a bed of flowers.

He was born into a wealthy LA family. 'My dad was a cameraman, my mother did absolutely nothing.' He became a coy gospel singer touring the South at the age of eight. Young Sylvester started noticing he was a little – uh – different from the other boys. In fact, it was his granny who set him 'straight'.

'She was a great blues singer in the thirties and met a lot of gay people,' he recalled. 'She knew the signs. Knew what to look for, you might say. But by then I'd already made myself aware of who I was, so she used to tell me things about it.'

At this point Sylvester stopped singing. Was it because his new-found awareness scared him?

'No. Look, nobody can make you gay and that certainly wasn't the reason I gave up singing. I just wanted to do other things. Sexuality doesn't enter into it. When you grow up you have to leave home and do the things you have to, so I read books, I moved, I went shopping – everything everyone else does.'

Ahem, everyone doesn't live as a woman for a couple of years on Sunset Strip.

'I don't want to talk about that. Listen, honey, I don't think about my sexuality. It's no big deal in my life. I very rarely write love songs. There are enough love songs in the world, like there are enough children – we don't need any more. OK, so I'm in love right now, but that's between me and him and I ain't gonna tell the whole world about it in a song. As long as he loves me and I love him, that's all that matters.'

Sylvester lives with John, a male model, and five Borzoi Wolfhounds.

After the mysterious period on the Strip, Sylvester lived in San Francisco, where he found freedom and acceptance. In 1970 he joined The Cockettes, an outrageous musical revue, and quickly became the star.

At this time he was a fragile character, unable to surmount the problems that sprang up like weeds in his flowerbed. He supported David Bowie in San Francisco but was dropped after two shows. 'Because my act was better than his – that's what people told me anyway.

'I started to freak out. I wasn't prepared to be that kind of singer. I couldn't handle money, managers, record companies. I didn't like what I was doing. I had to escape. I always escape when I'm unhappy. I hate things that bother me.'

He found solace in London and did … nothing. He's proud of doing nothing. In fact he'd rather do nothing than anything else in the world.

'I remained in London for several months until the money ran out. I got myself together and by the time I returned home I was prepared for anything. I got a job singing and then became attracted to the disco scene because disco makes money and I wanna make enough money to retire at an early age.'

How early?

'Thirty-five.'

How old are you now?

'Never mind, dear.'

You hate singing that much?

'No. I enjoy it immensely. I have a great time – but I don't want to do it all my life. Why should I work till I'm old? Who ordained that I should? I just want to get enough money together to live comfortably and do whatever I want. In five years' time I want to be able to stop everything, dear.' Giveaway. That makes him around thirty.

'I don't want much – just a fabulous time. Not that I don't have that already. I have quite normal feelings but I like to take on a little bit more excitement than most. I am what I am, I do what I do, I know what I am, and I live for what I feel.

'If I died tonight I'd say I've had a great life.' Difficult if you're dead. 'I'm easy to get along with. I'm a happy person. Happy with just living.'

He's being very sincere but I like him when he's angry. What do you think of Tom Robinson singing about being gay?

'I don't particularly care what the subject matter of other people's songs is. Look, dear, being gay means absolutely nothing except to straight people. They, and that means you too, honey, want to find out what it's like. Why can't we just be left alone? I don't ask straight people, "Hey, what's it like being straight?" Maybe you ought to have a homosexual experience yourself, dear, and then you won't have to ask me what it's like. You would never understand if I told you. Go out, find yourself a gay guy and fuck him. Then you'll know.'

Now here's one calculated to make his curly, cascading locks stand to attention. Are you a drag queen, Sylv?

'NEVER! I live my parts on stage. I leave them on stage.'

That sounds a bit painful. But his stage act sounds little short of sensational. Along with his band he has a couple of girl singers lovingly called Two Tons of Fun.

'Izora weighs three hundred pounds and Martha two hundred and sixty. I just adore big lady singers.'

He's also just made a film, *The Rose*, with the other darling of the gay circuit, Bette Midler. 'Bette plays a Janis Joplin-type figure and I'm a Diana Ross impersonator at a nightclub that Bette visits. We sing a duet.'

But, really, all Sylvester wants to do is hang around at home with John collecting art-deco clocks. He doesn't have much time for anything else. Geddit?

'Hey, if I'd have been interviewing you I wouldn't have asked all this gay crap. I would want to know what was important to you as a person.'

What's important to you as a person, Sylv?

'Nuthin'.'

Thufferin' thukertash!

Ten years after that interview Sylvester succumbed to AIDS at the young age of forty-one. Two Tons of Fun went on to become the Weather Girls.

In this job you get to meet all sorts. When I worked exclusively for *Record Mirror*, I usually cherry-picked the interviews I wanted to do. The Pistols, Clash, Stranglers, Damned, Heartbreakers and Jam were my stomping grounds, with the occasional foray into Demis Roussos territory to keep the girlfriend happy. But being a freelance means that beggars can't be choosers, so I fly to Hamburg – a city on the Brits' radar because that's where Kevin Keegan plays his football – to meet and greet Smokie, who've been living next door to Alice for quite some time.

Their singles are trite, monosyllabic gestures calculated to appeal to that susceptible region of the brain prone to costume-jewellery tears. Smokie are the undisputed masters of mellifluence.

They succeed because the ugly, out-of-tune public craves pretty, in-tune opiates. A ditty a day helps you work, rest and play. Their insidious sophistry is difficult for critics to swallow but, in reality, Smokie are more than capable of producing worthwhile music without resorting to such artifice. But it sure pays the rent.

'It's true, our singles do tend to resemble each other – but the problem lies with my voice,' says singer Chris Norman, as we drink a couple of beers in a Hamburg hotel bar. The band are due on stage in a few hours. 'The Beatles had the same "trouble" on their earlier songs. They all sound the same to me now. The fact is, we played music on our own terms for eight years and it got us absolutely nowhere. For the last three years we've had all these hits. Now we've got another three years to attempt something different.'

As we climb onto the band's coach to head off to the gig, Kevin Keegan is waiting to greet us. Turns out Kevin is a huge Smokie fan and Chris and Pete are writing a song for him called, 'Head Over Heels In Love'. The perm is a doosie.

A few weeks later I attend a reception to launch Kevin's single and end up talking to Bill Shankly for most of the night. When he tells me, 'Football isn't a matter of life and death – it's more than that,' I thought I got the football quote of a lifetime till I found out the next day he'd said it to all the boys.

Chris Norman and Pete Spencer quit the band in the mid-Eighties and Norman was replaced by Black Lace's Alan Barton. They had a hit with Roy 'Chubby' Brown in 1995 – 'Alice? Who The Fuck Is Alice?' – and are the only band to have a top ten hit with a song featuring the word 'fuck'. Who would've thought it? Barton died shortly after the song hit the charts, when the band's tour bus crashed in Germany.

I make a point of hearing everything. I know every song in the Top 50, I see a live band at least five nights a week; I can have any record I want whenever I want. Song lyrics pepper my conversation and even my mates in the flats call me the music man. But much of it is unqualified shit and when you hang around shit long enough you become immune to the smell. Music – my blood, my soul, my heart, my sweet, sweet love – is slowly turning into Muzak in my ears.

I need to listen again, not hear. I need the fix of insane harmony. Letting punk in was like smoking three packs a day while hanging around Bikini Atoll in the late forties. I have an insidious tumour in my hearing and it grows fat and pink and bold. And one day I will never hear music again. There is no cure.

In the meantime, there's always David Essex…

God knows why, but I've always had a soft spot for David. I thought 'Rock On' was cool and 'Lamplight' interesting. He was impressive in *That'll Be The Day*' and consistent in *Stardust*. Even 'Hold Me Close' held me close and you can't say more than that.

But he's getting older and those glorious looks are no longer the stuff of dreams. Where does a teen idol go when he ends up with an adoration overdraft? When the portable fourteen-inch monochrome kids on the block switch to colour and a flashier model? When the feline fans never close their eyes anymore when he kisses their lips?

So, does he borrow a revolver, venture into some sun-kissed field and shoot himself, because this world was never meant for one as beautiful as him?

Or does he star in a hit show, release a song from that show – 'Oh What A Circus' – and sneak back into charts and hearts.

Of course, David is no newcomer to the stage. He cornered the market in cool Christs in *Godspell*. Then 'Rock On' came knocking and he swapped his loincloth for a trendy demob suit and neckerchief and become the cheeky parvenu with the face of a god.

But when it became clear he wasn't comfortable in the teen zone, that he wanted to actually be regarded as a thinking artist, he was rejected. Oh sure, there were still a few loyalists who continued to haul his singles into lowly chart positions – but as a big-draw-peek-a-boo star, Essex was *finito*.

And then the Girl from Argentina – tall and tan and young and lovely – glided past and he went, Aaaah! David Essex playing Che Guevara does seem an odd choice on the surface – but it works and *Evita* is more popular than Big Ben.

I follow the aroma of hamburger down a labyrinth of grey corridors backstage at the Cambridge Theatre until I reach David's dressing room. He's wearing the jungle-fighter khaki outfit in preparation for the matinée and stuffing a Big Mac and fries.

His dressing room is spacious with a colour TV in one corner and a fridge full of vintage white wine in another. An adjoining room has nothing except a bed. He eats as we talk. His voice has that attractive quasi-Cockney intonation – cheeky chic. Although he enjoys playing Guevara, David has no intention of growing old gracefully in the role. In fact, he's leaving the show in a few weeks' time.

'I'm getting into a routine now and it's becoming too much like a real job. But I'm rejoining the cast when the show goes to Broadway next year. Having this hit is like a whole new beginning for me. Oh, don't get me wrong, I never resented being a teen idol. I had a long life in that capacity. It was a wonderful experience. To get that reaction when you play a concert is unforgettable and unique.

'I feel a lot easier now. Like a heavy weight has been lifted from my shoulders (George Foreman?). There's a lot more space around me, personally, these days. Being a teen hero is only a point of fashion anyway and consequently very short-lived. You can't rely on your looks for ever.'

Personally, I always thought you were a bit of an ugly bastard, David. 'No, you're getting confused with you looking in the mirror.' He smiles. He can take a joke. Thank god for that.

Success has given him the freedom to explore his creative abilities. But it's arguable that it also led to commercial suicide.

'I just wanted to be able to write and record my own songs. What's so terrible about that? I never became a musician for the money. I believe I've always done things for the right reasons. I can honestly I say I've never been complacent at any point in my career. Look, I'm not a male model, I'm not one-dimensional. I'm an artist. If I wasn't then I'd have become a promotions man for a record company after the teen thing collapsed.'

At thirty-one, David appears to have transcended the showbiz image he seemed to be cultivating a few years ago. 'I don't think there's another person like me in the world.'

He seems to have enjoyed my company. How can I tell? After the interview I shake his hand and turn to leave.

'Hey, Barry! Fancy seeing the show?'

Tickets are like gold dust. I immediately think how much I could make on them. I really hate, 'Oh What A Circus'.

'Should help with the article, don't you reckon?'

Absolutely, David.

'Good. I'll arrange for a pair to be sent to your home.'

I think I should go and, in the absence of Dina, I take Versa, a Greek PR girl, who reciprocates by treating me to dinner at the restaurant of my choice after the show. I decide on Langan's in Mayfair. Cheers, Dave.

David was awarded an OBE in 1999. He continues to record on his own Lamplight record label and tours regularly. He has appeared in the shows Boogie Nights 2, Footloose and Andrew Lloyd Webber's musical Aspects of Love. In 2009 he toured the UK with a musical play, All the Fun of the Fair. He lives in the US, continuing to sing and act.

NOVEMBER 1978

Hot Gossip, Public Image Ltd, Mike Oldfield, Dan Hartman, Blondie, The Shangri-Las, Pere Ubu, David Johansen, Bruce Springsteen

It's funny going round to Dina's after spending a few hours on a date with Sarah Brightman, the girl from Kenny Everett's Hot Gossip that Mary Whitehouse couldn't shut down.

And now they have a top-ten single, 'I Lost My Heart To A Starship Trooper', which proves they have voices to match their shapes. 'We never deliberately set out to be sexy,' says sexy eighteen-year-old Sarah. 'It's simply our style of dancing. We were very surprised when we heard Mrs Whitehouse had complained.'

We sit in a coffee bar just around the corner from where Hot Gossip have been rehearsing. I feel like I'm on a date with Salome – being castigated by Mary Whitehouse really gives a gal an edge. Sarah has big, bouncy black hair and lips like Kate Bush. Lots of girls have lips like Kate Bush these days.

'I want to make as much money and be as successful as I can before I get too old for this business,' she reveals, and tentatively sips a black coffee. 'But it's really hard work. I get up at five-thirty most mornings and don't get back home until midnight. My time teems with constant rehearsals, filming and strenuous exercise.'

Sarah danced with Pan's People when she was sixteen. 'I decided after eighteen months with them that it was time to give another girl a chance, so I joined Hot Gossip. I much prefer working with this group. Their dancing comes more from the heart. The funny thing is, we only wear those flimsy costumes because it's much easier to move around.'

Oh, I see.

'We try to be different. The public had ten years of Pan's People and Legs and Co., but now they want something more exciting. We've all had classical training and we put a great deal of thought into our sets.' One routine involved a French chambermaid in suspenders and sexy schoolgirls. Her boyfriend Andrew, a twenty-seven-year-old rock-group manager, is very understanding.

'Most men like to watch pretty girls bopping around wearing next to nothing.'

Not me.

'But they hate it if one of those dancers happens to be their girlfriend.'
I wouldn't mind.

'But Andrew knows the work we put into our act so he doesn't mind.'

Right on, Andrew. Hold on. Shit, she's got a boyfriend. Well, I ain't buying her another coffee.

'Somebody once said this is the century of the dance. And suddenly in the Seventies everybody wants to do it like Hot Gossip.'

Of course they do, Sarah, of course they do.

Sarah married a different Andrew – Lloyd Webber – in 1984, and the couple divorced six years later. She has received 160 gold and platinum awards in thirty-four countries, and is the only artist to hold the top spots on the Billboard classical and dance charts simultaneously. She's been ranked by the Recording Industry Association of America as the best-selling female classical artist of the twenty-first century, and has a Guinness World Record for the success of 'Time to Say Goodbye', the most successful single in German recording history. She has sold at least 26 million albums and more than two million DVDs and is rumoured to be worth £30 million. My, oh, my.

It's time to enter the Twilight Zone again.

Time to renew my acquaintance with public enemy number one, Spanky and his gang. Time to nip round to his place in Gunther Grove and meet the directors of his company.

And it's not a bad gaff. Wallful of posters, floorful of pretty good carpet, teleful of interference, speakerful of Public Image, fridgeful of lager. Rottenful of bitter (draught). Wobbleful of quips. Sidfool in NYC.

John Rotten looks like he's ready to take over from David Essex in *Evita*. Khaki jungle-fighter outfit and black barnet. Clambering around Epping Forest gunning down picnickers and courting couples.

Whatever happened to the incandescent revolution? Maybe Malcolm McLaren sold it at a profit. Maybe straight bottoms held the shit in too long. Maybe, just maybe, it's in a kind of splendid hibernation, ready to stretch and pounce on some future crazy kid.

So what remains?

Public Image Limited for one thing.

'Oh, you're talking about the Sex Pissups...' John, lost in his huge sofa, spits out the words. 'There weren't many songs that band wanted to do. They were such a bunch of arseholes.'

'They wanted to chug, chug, chug, chugchugchug,' adds Jah Wobble, grinning.

'Yeah,' continues John, 'they're only really happy doing "Johnny B. Goode" and cover versions of Everly Brothers' songs. If I'd have asked them to listen to this,' indicating the PiL sound on the speakers, 'they would have gone, "Oooh, that's a bit heavy, ain't it, John?" Anyone who expects us to come out with "Cosh The Driver" ditties is in for a big surprise.'

Like the Teddy Boys' Picnic?

'We've written 469 songs already,' says Jah. They also found dog shit on the moon.

'That's exactly the way we want to hear music,' says John. 'Danceable but good. High, high treble.' They play me the album and it's a million miles from the Pistols. It's a million miles from anything.

He's just read a newspaper report that detailed his life as a drug addict. The actual article confusingly said he took 'smack (cocaine)' and also mentioned how punk stars fell into a life of drug-taking, 'smoke, cocaine, sulphate and speed'. Damned well-informed lot these journalists.

'The article was merely an excuse to get me on the subject of Sid,' says John. 'Contrary to popular opinion, I've never taken heroin. Oh, sure, they used to say it was in my eyes and all that shit, but taking that stuff is totally against everything I stand for. I'll sue.'

So, uh, while we're on the subject what about...

'Sid, eh? Nope. I'm not giving out any sensationalist copy. There's nothing to say anyway. See, the geezer has always been a failure. He couldn't play bass and he couldn't even cope with his image. And as for him being violent ... He met Nancy when she followed

Heartbreakers' drummer Jerry Nolan over here from New York. He just picked her up and that's when he started on heroin. Right away she tried to interfere with the Pistols. Y'know...' He and Jah begin to mimic a ramshackle, nail-across-the-blackboard, feline East Coast voice: '"Oooooh, Sid, you're really good. You'd be *soooo* much better off without those other guys."'

'She was a starfucker,' says John. 'I spent a year trying to get Sid off his habit. A year. And every time I turned my back he'd start shooting up again, thanks to Nancy. And when he did eventually try and kick it he got hooked on the cure – methadone.'

Would he like to help Sid out of his predicament?

'If I could help him personally I would. But he'd have to get rid of McLaren for a start and then stop trying to kill himself. I know a few people think I got jealous of Sid grabbing some of the limelight in the States. That's absolute crap. Steve and Paul never wanted him in the band at all. It was me who got him in. Me. And when we were in America it was Sid and me who decided we didn't want to get involved with a failed bank robber. McLaren was infuriated and he never even bothered to book hotel rooms for us over there.

'There was no reason for the Pistols to bust up. No reason at all ... except for McLaren. Sid agreed with me. Steve and Paul were over-concerned at finding themselves on their own. They were scared of that 'cos they need someone else to do everything for them. They like people telling them what to do. It was all just a nine-to-five job with them – and that's a contradiction of what the band was all about.

'Consequently, whatever Malcolm said, they would do. I spent a lot of time writing lyrics I felt were important and valid. But when I confronted the others with them they'd say, "I don't think Malc's gonna like these words, John." How can you run a band like that? As a group we had regular talks about his role. It used to get me down, but at the same time I kept thinking at least the songs were getting out. Getting across to people.

'And all the time Steve was happy with his Chuck Berry impressions and Paul with his never-sounding-different drumming. It was me who had to bear the brunt of the studio work. They would fuck off leaving me and producer Chris Thomas to listen to the final mixes. Chris trying to make us sound like Roxy Music and me trying to fight it. We were just too limited.'

And there's me thinking they were a great band. It's easy to slag off in retrospect but what Rotten feels is unrefined hatred. Are we to assume, then, that he never liked anything the band achieved? 'I like the good things. I like "Problems". I like "God Save The Queen". I like "Anarchy". Not much else.

'But what I loathe most of all is being set up, taken for a mug. And that's exactly what happened. Malcolm would tell me we were banned from playing everywhere and I believed him. It took six months to discover he was lying. At the beginning he was great. It was all so perfect for us to dominate the world. And then he changed. We never saw him from one month to the next. And when we did try to ring him a strange voice at the other end of the phone would say he was in LA or Paris or anywhere."

John demanded and received £12,000. He bought the flat with the money. And that, according to him, was all he ever made.

Still, no more bad times, eh, John? No more stitch-ups. No more misanthropy. No more midnight beatings. No more torrid TV.

'At last I'm not limited to the old ways of doing things,' he says. 'At last I find myself in a situation that far surpasses my wildest dreams – I feel totally proud of being in the same band as this bunch of cunts. Christ, it took me so long to realise that these people have always known what I was about. They're old friends. Friends I've known so much longer than the Pistols. Public Image Limited is a collection of friends.'

Ten minutes later we've adjourned to the boozer around the corner from John's place. The girl who wrote the article that John hated walks in, and when she tries to explain how the sub messed around with her original piece, John's reaction is a peach.

'Piss off, shitbag.'

Over a pint he gets real. 'I never realised the consequences of being a member of the Pistols and talking the way I did. The press had never seen anyone like me before. Never anyone so sensational, so personal, so hateful. Normal situations suddenly became extreme situations.

'But, fuck, as much as people try to put me down at least I've done something. Something they'll never do. People who have attacked me are so, so silly. Now I've managed to get myself into the best possible set-up. Now I'm more involved with the way things should be rather than the way things are.

'This is not Johnny Rotten's band. If anything, I'm probably the weak link.'

We follow Johnny back to the flat. He's sprawls out in front of the TV watching *The Hustler*. Jah and I decide it's time to split.

A toddle with a Wobble on Chelsea cobbles is an altogether illuminating affair.

His jacket collar upturned, his head submerged, the headless phantom of the King's Road avoids the pavement cracks and basks in the shadows between the lamplights.

'Let's go in here,' says Wobble, indicating a flash Frenchie establishment custom made for garrulous, three-piece-suit execs with Chicago tapes in their TR7s.

John met Wobble at Kingsway College of Further Education when both enrolled for their O levels. The two remained firm friends.

'Do you really wanna know something?' he asks, over avocado and prawns. 'This whole thing, Public Image and all, means absolutely nothing to me. Nothing. They put me away, y'know. Put me in a psychiatric ward for cutting up a copper. Said I went a bit mad, they did. Truth is, they're waiting. Always waiting. Waiting for months, years. Ready to pounce when you crack. Then they're on you like vultures. Then you're in the hospital.

'And that's only like being on the outside, but more acute. Then they "calm" you down. That means they stick electrodes in your brain and drugs in your arms. I shit myself. I really shit myself. I quietened down. I conformed. You always lose. Nobody ... nobody's gonna stick up for you. So I said I was sorry, "sir". If I hadn't they would have certified me and I'd have been in there for the rest of my life. I stuck my neck out, I lost.'

Wobble is a twenty-year-old Whitechapel waif into reggae and prawns. He acts as unofficial minder of Public Image.

'Put this down.' He picks up my pen, which I'd placed on the table so I could eat my veal, and pushes it into my hand. 'All these people in the restaurant . . .' he frantically rubs the top of his head and looks around with psycho-killer eyes '. . . are never gonna stick their necks out. They're all following their little set patterns. Look at them, look at their stupid fucking grins.

'They've watched me bang my head against the wall. All through school – I hope some of those ex-pupils are reading this – all my life. I feel impotent. My spirit is gone. Please, please, never let them kill your spirit. Keep stoking the fire of your hatred. That's all you've got left. Let me make myself a martyr. Let me try to break down their huge, indescribable rubber wall. The one that everyone bounces off.

'See, the rest of the band think they're going to break it. I know they won't. They'll try, try, try. But they'll fail because the wall is 360 degrees.'

I pay the bill and we leave. There's no way he's a new Sid in town.

It's all becoming a game. Public Image will obviously succeed but just exactly how long they will last is entirely up to them. The public don't really matter much anymore. Like Wobble says, 'You can sell people bags of shit and they'll be happy.'

Public Image Limited ain't crap, as their tapes confirm. It's just that it doesn't really matter anymore. Wobble's paranoia doesn't really matter. It's up to him whether he enjoys himself or not. Eighteen months ago it was a different world.

Now we're back to the same old shit. And it really doesn't matter.

Jah Wobble left PiL in 1980. He now runs his own label, 30 Hertz Records, and tours regularly throughout England and Europe with his current band, Jah Wobble & the English Roots Band. He also writes book reviews for the Independent, and his autobiography, Memoirs of a Geezer: Music, Life, Mayhem, was published in 2009. John Lyden fronted the Sex Pistols for varous reunion gigs and tours; he continues to front PiL and has appeared in butter ads on the telly. PiL played a few concerts in 2011 and the following year released their first studio album – This Is PiL – in twenty years.

From the ridiculous to the sublime ...

Virgin have arranged a phone interview with Mike Oldfield, who's currently promoting his fourth album, *Incantations*. I'm at home in the King's Cross council flat with my notebook and pen, and Mum's in the kitchen preparing dinner. It's a familiar scenario.

The interview is set for four thirty. At four twenty-five the doorbell rings and my mum answers it.

'There's a man outside says you know him,' she tells me. 'Strange-looking bloke.'

Shit, who's that? The phone's gonna ring any second.

I open the door.

'Mr Cain? Hello, I'm Mike Oldfield. Look, I've got my chauffeur waiting in the Rolls downstairs, but if it's all the same with you I'd like to have a chat here. I'm sick to death of sitting in the back of that car. Put the kettle on.'

'I'll tell me mum,' is about all I can say, as he walks past me and wanders into the living room.

I know Mike Oldfield is supposed to have changed his hermit-like image, but this is ridiculous.

I'm flabbergasted, in a Frankie Howerd way, but that's nothing compared with my mum who, wearing her cotton housecoat, hides in the kitchen making endless cups of tea for the thirsty superstar.

In between the Typhoo, Mike tells me how he clawed his way out of a 'living hell'.

It turns out the twenty-five-year-old millionaire composer of

Tubular Bells has been trapped in his own bleak house in the wilds of Gloucestershire for the past five years, shunning the outside world.

'I was hanging on the edge of a cliff, terrified of falling into the unknown,' he reveals. 'I began to lose my mind and had two nervous breakdowns, each lasting for three months. The idea of killing myself even entered my head. I started to really hit the bottle. I was petrified at the thought of meeting people or leaving my home. The only way I could face those doing those things was to get drunk.'

So why did Oldfield – hailed as rock music's greatest composer – become a hermit?

'I was determined to prove to myself that I could have a bad time. I always believed my parents didn't like me. My mother was one of those really neurotic housewives – but she took it one step further. She became addicted to tranquillisers and alcohol after giving birth to a Down's syndrome child. She spent many years in and out of mental hospitals. My father is a doctor and he treated her like a sick wife. She finally died four years ago – a wreck.

'Right from the first I realised what was happening to her and decided that if this was how people lived, forget it. So I retreated into myself, striving to find my own world in music. I've tried to make some sense out of the whole thing ever since. I've tried living with lots of women, but I couldn't have a proper relationship with them because I had to make them hate me.'

Tell it like it is, Mike. Maybe I should be charging him for this. By the hour.

He married a mystery girl – whom he refers to simply as Diana – this summer. But it wasn't exactly George Burns and Gracie Allen. Within two weeks they'd split up and are now in the process of getting a divorce.

But now Mike has had enough of the past and wants to 'play at being a superstar'.

'I always wanted to be one, but I felt too guilty. I'm just waking up to the fact I can enjoy life if I want to. I can have loads of money and loads of girls. It's so easy to change.'

Mike has shaved off his beard, cropped his hippie hair and now looks like a Vegas playboy.

'I've even started going to discos and dancing the night away. It's great.'

Oldfield currently lives in the Bahamas and has seven children from three marriages – there's a man chasing rainbows. His autobiography, Changeling, was published in 2007. A year later he released his first classical album, Music of the Spheres, which topped the UK classical chart and reached number nine on the main UK album chart. Man On The Rocks, his 25th studio album, was released in 2014.

And then it's New York again. Instant replay. This is getting seriously close to commuting. Every time I set foot on a plane I think I'm going to die, but after a line, a large brandy and Coke and a cigarette, the cabin looks a rosier place. I'm here for Blondie sans Debbie and Chris. But I also check out the intriguing Dan Hartman, whose hot 'Instant Replay' is up there in my chart of fave 45s in '78 style.

This trip to New York is all part of the conspiracy to change my life forever. Remember what I said about the Debbie Harry interview – that it started a chain of events that would alter the course of my entire life? First, David the itinerant publisher tentatively stepped in, but his real influence would come later.

Debbie's final words as I got up to leave gave me an idea for a feature: 'Listen, er, do you think you could mention the rest of the band. See, er, everyone seems to just talk about me and it makes me feel kinda guilty, y'know.'

I sell the idea of a non-Debbie-and-Chris-Stein Blondie interview to *Record Mirror*. Next stop, Manhattan.

I mean, did you know there were four other people in Blondie apart from the sugar-candy kisser of Debbie Harry and Chris Stein, the man who bought his eyebrows from Axminster?

Yeah, it's true; I've seen 'em with my own eyes. Seen 'em on their home ground too – in ol' numbland New York, that necropolis with neon tombstones where... Oh, so you think it isn't dead, huh? Listen, any city that shows *The Partridge Family* twice every morning on TV, split only by *I Love Lucy* and *Brady Bunch* re-runs, just has to be dead, or severely wounded.

Like a Victorian explorer venturing into fleshy foliage in search of an obscure tribe, I take a cab to a nocturnal recording studio in one of the more uncivilised districts where the natives eat strange exotic food they call 'Burrgakeeng', which they claim possesses health-giving properties, and drink copious amounts of the 'Pepsee'. The taxi winds its tortuous way through narrow streets infested by an unfriendly creature known locally as 'deemugger'.

Alighting from the cab, I ask a statuesque black guy where I might find the Unknown Blondie. His eyes freeze and he utters a primal scream before fleeing into the night.

My God, what have I let myself in for? Just then, a wizened old man taps me on the shoulder, like they always do at such moments, and rasps, 'The Unknown Blondie is a taboo tribe in these parts. 'Tis a curse of a thousand McDonalds to merely mention the name.' 'But you mentioned it!'

'Yes – and I'm only nineteen!' he wheezes, and points to a dilapidated building. 'There. But beware...' A tangled web of close-circuit TVs guards the door. I beat my way through, slide into a waiting elevator and press the button for star-filled limbo. The doors open onto a recording studio that shows no sign of life. I hear a rustle and a figure dashes from behind one speaker to disappear beneath a control desk. Nervy. Not used to strangers. There's some indecipherable chatter. I reach for my Pistols album...

'You're a journalist?' It's the voice of Clem Burke. He touches me in what appears to be an Unknown Blondie ritual. But I soon realise he's just making sure I'm real. 'Hey, you guys, it's a journalist.'

From the vinyl gloom emerges Jimmy Destri, Frank Infante, Nigel

Harrison and several Elvis Costello lookalikes.

'Wow.' It takes some time to convince them that it's them I intend to write about. Not Debbie or Chris, the Sonny and Cher of the lacquered New Wave. 'Wow.' It transpires that Clem is involved in producing former Unknown Blondie bass player Gary Valentine and the tribe has gathered to listen and rave. 'This guy is sure talented,' says Clem, in cute, cumbersome, cocktail tones. They decide to show me their native ways. 'Hey, let's take a drive to McSorley's,' says Nigel, an English muffin with fluffy curls.

On our way we pass a giant plastic lizard recently erected on top of a bank. 'Could cause a lot of trouble – sure scared the shit outta me,' says Frank, who looks like he could make it as a movieland method myth – y'know, all corrugated cheeks and Mogadon eyes.

McSorley's Old Ale House (established 1854) is a soiled, silent-movie straitjacket of a bar in Greenwich Village (where the nuts come from). Fatty Arbuckle could have been filmed here, looking clown-sad and lovable but all the while immersed in crazed sexual fantasies. When it was built, women weren't allowed into bars so there's no ladies' john. Local libbers have complained but McSorley's virginity remains intact.

An Irish waiter asks if we want dark or light beer, both brewed on the premises. The party go for light.

'No, I'm not at all jealous of Debbie getting all the attention,' says Jimmy, teen-dream face. 'See, I think she sees it from our level too. I'm very happy having a face like that selling my music. I wouldn't be in the position of selling records for Chrysalis if it wasn't for her. She sells my music. I know that if I was in a record company and was responsible for marketing Blondie, I would market Debbie Harry as a viable commercial product simply because she is the obvious thing.'

The table is now overflowing with glasses. A dollar for less than half a pint. 'In time,' Jimmy continues, oblivious to the stains and the ascending banter on other tables beneath timber walls covered with badges and original photographs of cloth-cap five-o'clock-shadow debauched ghosts, 'people will begin to realise that Blondie is a conglomerate of ideas. All of us can do other things. We're good musicians. It's really cool being in this position because I have the opportunity to do other things. See, I get the respect that being a part of Blondie brings – and so you get asked to do things.

'OK, I admit being in the shadows was frustrating at the beginning, but now it's just perfect for me. I don't want to be a star. I'm happy everyone's looking at Debbie on stage and not me. I'm content playing keyboards, writing and producing. Besides, it ain't all that much fun being in a band. Richie Blackmore's mother . . .' What the hell has she got to do with this conversation? But Nigel is insistent. 'Richie Blackmore's mother once said to him, "Why don't you get yourself a decent job, son?"'

'So?'

'Well, I love being in a band. It's been my ambition since I was sixteen,' says Jimmy. In case you're wondering, Clem and Frank are embroiled in deep conversation. 'I was anxious to get somewhere. I came from a bad neighbourhood in Brooklyn, which ain't that different from poor parts of London except for the accent and colour of the police cars.

'I worked fourteen hours a day to get through college. When I was twenty-one my father gave me fifteen bucks and I felt like a king. Fifteen bucks!'

'I lived in Hollywood for a while,' says Nigel, 'and many kids I bumped into who were in the music business were so rich. And you know why? Their parents organised trust funds for them from an early age. Y'know, twenty bucks a week for years. So these kids live a real maniacal life. It's easy when you know you've got twenty grand coming to you in a year or so.'

The waiter brings another round of beers. Jimmy starts getting angry. 'Yeah, some people are born lucky. I worked in a hospital emergency room strapping up junkies. I saw people who had no determination or energy try and get on simply because they've always had it easy.

'That's why when a dude becomes a pimp or pusher and starts making money, he becomes very ostentatious and buys every flashy thing he can lay his hands on. He ain't ever seen 'em before.'

Jimmy then relates the tale of the frozen stiff.

'One day Chris and Clem were walking in the Bowery and found a wino who was frozen solid dead. And they call this a rich country. You're kept on a certain level and if you can't transcend that you rot.'

Or freeze. The bar starts to empty like the glasses. The band decide to move on to CBGB's in search of the Demon White Powder – an act causing a big stir in New York. In the contrived decadence of the club, about as meretricious as the iceberg wino, the four guys disperse, checking out the depravities and emaciated faces. Someone hands me a bag of coke, which I take with me to the toilet.

'Hey, I'd like to introduce you to a coupla friends of mine,' says Clem, when I emerge from the cubicle. He ushers me to the bar and interrupts a conversation between two typical electrical-appliance American housewives.

'This is Mary.' She wears golden glasses to match her long, straight hair. Her eyebrows are the same shape as her top lip, which gives her face a strange symmetry. 'Hi.'

'And this is Marge.' She's heavily tanned and her skin has suffered. Her smiles are tired. 'Hi.'

'They're the Shangri-Las!' I have visions of waking up in a hospital bed with a nurse above me full of reassurance and comforting words: 'You're OK now. You've just been in a state of shock for awhile. Take it easy . . .'

When I was twelve, the Shangri-Las had epitomised everything that was dirty and sexy. Libidinous teenage punkettes inhabiting a voodoo vestibule where jailbait languished on stained plastic sofas. I remember seriously starting to think about thighs when I saw them singing 'Remember (Walking In The Sand)' on *Top Of The Pops* one Fireworks Night. I'd never heard a song quite like it before.

Time kills. To be confronted by these thirty-year-old women makes me suddenly very depressed.

And, believe it or not, they're making a comeback. Well, just these two, Mary Weiss, the blonde in the brunette pack, and Margie Ganser.

Maybe Mary's singing voice still overflows with that rub-sucking venom. 'We broke up originally,' says Mary – straight voice, like the steam from the spout of a kettle – 'because we were young and there were too many people out there trying to squeeze every last drop of money they could get their hands on out of us. That left a really bad taste in our mouths.

'For a long while we've been running away. But now it's time to face the music. Besides, the business was much more dangerous in those days. There's a child in my soul and I don't want it to die. I can't let it perish. When that goes you're dead.

'I really got screwed up when the band split. I was nineteen. I'd never been out with anyone while I was on the road. Christ, I'd been a rock'n'roll star at fifteen and I was only just getting over my first period.'

Margie tried to talk over the band on stage (it was audition night and they were playing 'God Save The Queen' like they were a Woolworths cover job or a too-dark Xerox). 'We never knew what was going on. How could we at that age? We got to do things 15-year-olds never dream of. It started off with high-school dances – we were younger than the punters – and just escalated. We played parties where the kids used to make their own wine because we were all under age.' Mary's looking a little spaced out. She offers to drive me back to my hotel.

In the car she says they met with little success at New York record companies. 'They expect us to be completely punk. Y'know, they say things like "How does it feel to be the Queen of Punk?" And one guy wanted us to be the female equivalent of the Ramones. I'm twenty-nine years old. I'm serious about my music. I don't care for punk that much.'

I say I'll call her for some more gen. She says OK. I say goodnight. She says seeya.

'Hey, what happened to you last night?' says Clem, straightening his collar in the dressing room at My Father's Place. 'We had a real great time. After we left CBGB's we all went on to Max's Kansas City and met up with Elvis Costello and Nick Lowe. Real nice guys.'

My Father's Place is a club on Long Island about forty minutes' drive from Manhattan, and Blondie are playing two shows tonight. It's a converted bowling alley and the long tables where the punters sit are the original lanes. Pin-table pyrotechnics with free pizza thrown in.

Backstage the Greenwich weirdos are out in force. It's all prurience and strawberry-blancmange brasses eager to lavish praise on what looks like becoming New York's creamiest cult band.

Debbie doo-doos past in white culottes, takes a seat opposite a reporter from the strike-ridden *New York Times* and churns out the same old spiel while doting dykes strain their ears.

A guy comes to the door and asks a sound man for Debbie's autograph. As he says the words 'Debbie Harry' his hand automatically reaches down to his crotch and he mimes a jerk-off, smiles and leaves.

Blondie are as big in the States as they were in the UK a year ago – in other words, they ain't very big. My Father's Place seats about five hundred, all diehard fans who gasp the moment Debbie appears looking like Sandra Dee on sulphate. Blondie's three-minute bam-bam is the ultimate in pop perfection. Sanguine satisfaction in every rooty-toot-toot nuance, in every aphrodisiac phrase.

The set is predictable. Highlights from the first two albums, a substantial segment of *Parallel Lines* and the obligatory 'Get It On' encore. The only real difference is the slight corpulence around Chris Stein's stomach and jowls. The second set is the same, except for Debbie's loose-fitting orange dress. But the audience is cut by half, and most of them are the first-set patriots.

Still, *The World About Us* was never like this. And they've already found their Shangri-La in the verdant pastures of the English charts.

But will they ever make the 'Leader of the Pack'?

I have a drink with Debbie at the bar after the gig and she tells me she loved my interview and thought the Venus in blue jeans line was neat. I think I'm in love. Again…

Clem and Jimmy are still in Blondie, along with Debbie and Chris. The band has sold over 40 million albums. They toured the UK in 2016.

Within a week of returning to London, I head off to Toronto with Alan Edwards and photographer Chris Gabrin in search of a nice Pere. Pere Ubu cling to Cleveland, the spot that spawned them, nurtured them and will probably kill them. David Thomas, singer and co-composer, is a walking Billy Smart's with eyes that curl away from you like a Victorian fire-eater's moustache. The rest of the band look like they missed the 5.45 special out of Woodstock and have been waiting for the next bus ever since.

They're gathered in the Horseshoe Tavern, Toronto. I still can't figure out on which side of the city the bar is situated because one part of Toronto looks very much the same as another – shops, offices, homes, roads with cars, people (but not at night). It's undistinguished, achromatic, and the nearest major town to Niagara Falls.

The Tavern reflects its mother.

Thomas and company amble on stage. The Big Top looks uncomfortable in an ill-fitting suit that covers his six-foot-two-inch 20-stone frame – it's a pair of silk pyjamas on a rhino. His brow is perpetually creased, but it's a feigned seriousness, as is the passion of his pleas to the audience.

Thomas is a unique performer. He looks terribly uncomfortable on stage, like he knows every movement, every word, is a hideous *faux pas*. Yet you know it's an act. The guy's been doing it too long for it not to be.

It appears the audience are diehard Ubu fans and they actually call out requests. 'Hey David, what about some "Chinese Radiation"?' 'We want "Drinking Wine Spodyody!"' '"Blow Daddy-O"!' And when it's all over, Toronto dies again.

There's no doubting Pere Ubu possess a morbid sensibility – each track on their album is like the dismembered victim of a sex murderer. A leg in the long grass, a head in the hedge, an arm near an arch. All mean nothing until gradually pieced together on the bloodstained pathologist's slab. It takes time, but the cadaver begins to resemble somebody, somebody you've known in the past, somebody who might have meant something. Long ago.

Backstage, Thomas sucks grass fumes from underneath a glass, up, up into the wide blue yonder. Almost immediately he has a coughing fit that renders him incapable of speaking. His face puffs up, turns crimson. His eyes bulge. You can just see the whites, which ain't as white as maybe they should be. He finds a chair and flops, still wheezing. We all take no notice and form an orderly queue behind the grey fume-filled glassful of grass.

The dressing room is tiny and, with Thomas the tank engine in it, positively claustrophobic. He's wearing a cheap blue mac that's as ill-fitting as the suit underneath. He looks like a character in a Samuel Beckett play.

'I was a high-school drop-out," he says and, right away, the eyes begin their darting movements – movements that persist throughout our little tryst. 'It didn't seem to make much sense staying on. Everyone appeared to be pretty uninteresting. I was going to be a teacher like my father, but that lasted six months. Then I started writing for a music paper. I wrote under the name of Crocus Behemoth. But I got tired of writing about music. I wanted to go out and do it.'

The room is getting smokier, the Mac is getting bluer, the body bigger, the ceiling lower. I feel like Alice after drinking the shrinking potion.

'We're described as an industrial band but that's wrong. I can understand when some people say our music has nightmare qualities but we're really a folk band. We approach the whole thing like one. The Velvets used to be described as a folk band.

'I can't imagine ever being popular. It would be fun if it happened – I've nothing against making it. But I still can't really see it happening.'

'Industrial rock is nothing more than a hook. In the early days we used to talk about it and its relevance to Cleveland. But it's just not important. What is important is getting away from Joe Public expecting something from a show just because he bought a ticket. That's old thinking. He's as much part of the show as the artist, of equal importance in fact. I have a job to do, the audience has a job to do.

'I've never gone to a show and expected something. Whether I'm listening to a record in my room, or having some friends round, or watching a Western, I never expect to have a good time. That causes too much trouble because then it starts getting into "Am I having a good time or not?" and that's a waste of time.

'The only thing I ever expected was to get accepted in Cleveland. I just hoped that at some point, some day, Cleveland would come around. I was wrong.'

Pere Ubu – named after the protagonist of Ubu Roi, a play by French writer Alfred Jarry – have disbanded and re-formed on several occasions, and David Thomas remains the one constant. In 2013 they released the album The Lady From Shanghai.

We stay at a five-star Toronto hotel for three nights, during which I get three calls from a local escort service Alan keeps contacting in my name, as a joke, requesting a girl. On the third night the very sexy-sounding voice warns me, after I deny yet again booking a girl, to 'stop pestering us or we'll have you thrown out of the hotel'.

Alan denies making the call but his hysterical laughter is a total giveaway.

The three of us then head down to New York for interviews, photos and fun.

In a bar on 42nd Street I bump into ex-New York Doll David Johansen and assure him I don't want to talk about the New York Dolls because, let's face it, the New York Dolls are dead. Kaput. And what's the use of reminiscing? What's the point of checking out that whole sordid, Biba-stained past?

I mean, who wants to remember all that?

I'm sure the geezer serving cold beers in this bar the size of a high-street barber's couldn't give a toss. In fact, I'm sure he couldn't give a toss about anything, the way he bangs the bottles on the counter.

I'm sure David Johansen doesn't care that much either. Just because he happened to front the band don't mean to say his needle nose is stuck in some gluey groove revolving on a time warp turntable. He's got a band of his own now anyway. This lonely-planet boy is back to the front.

David has a squashed face but it's a subtle kind of squashiness, like blancmange. This naturally makes him all the more interesting because every time he opens his mouth you expect his cheeks to wobble. They don't, of course. Not even a raspberry ripple. Funny how some people make you think of food. I see Johnny Rotten and pilchards spring to mind. Bob Geldof brings visions of meat pies, Kate Bush gherkins, Freddie Mercury walnuts, Elvis Costello peas.

With David Johansen it's definitely blancmange. I guess that's what makes him attractive to sweet-toothed women.

He's often likened to Jagger, but in fact he's better-looking. Jagger is like a half-eaten jaded jelly. Johansen is pristine blancmange.

'I'm an unassuming, rambling kind of guy.' He smiles. 'I went to high school in Staten Island.'

Seeing how this guy never says 'er' or 'y'know' or 'yeah' but proceeds with a perfect line in spiel, I'm going to take a short break while he, with the aid of untipped cigarettes and an endless stream of Carlsberg, tells a bewitching tale.

See you in a wee while ...

'We lived in a residential area, rather like a part of London, on the Island. There were six of us. My father used to sing Gilbert and Sullivan stuff when he was young before joining the air corps and going off to war. We lived in a real working-class neighbourhood. I remember eating tuna fish a lot, sleeping in a warm place and selling Kool-Aid on the street when I was about six. In those places the most you can hope for is a nice jacket, two or three pairs of pants, a pair of shoes and a job in a grocery store earning fifty bucks a week. There's a good community spirit.

'All the guys used to hang out in gangs. My gang consisted of the nuttiest guys around and all the other gangs used to like us because we were so crazy. I never used to fight much; it wasn't my scene. But I did hang out with one bunch whose warlord used to beat up three guys at a time in a rumble and throw them over his head.

'I used to listen to Bob Dylan and when I was fourteen I joined a band playing school dates. Sometimes, just for a laugh, we'd throw a musician in because we were pretty bad. I also had this mad girlfriend and we used to write poems to each other.

'School dragged on. I still get this recurring dream. I'm sitting, breathless, in my old classroom. That's all it is but it's a fucking nightmare. See, I used to set the alarm every morning for eight thirty, get up, take a shower at eight thirty-two, dress, shake my hair, dash out, catch the bus, travel the two miles to school and arrive at eight forty-four. 1 got everything down to a fine art so I could sleep till the last minute.

'But as I got older I just couldn't get up and my mother would come home around eleven thirty am and I'd still be in bed. I'd just wander round Greenwich Village. School didn't seem important.

'Around this time me and another guy used to play acoustics and harmonicas for the Madras crowd. Those guys had check shirts and desert boots and used to hang out at ice-cream parlours. My pals used to find out where we were playing and come around to beat up the Madras mob 'cos they were pretty namby-pamby. They also used to beat up the New Jersey guys who trespassed on Staten Island territory, drinking pints of Tango and pop wines.

'I was working at a supermarket as a cashier making fifty bucks a week, which was cool. I gave my mother twenty and spent the rest on clothes – T-shirts, black leather jackets and roamers, which were boots that came up to the ankle and made to last for no more than two months. All the girls used to dye their hair black too.

'Then I moved to the city and joined Fast Eddie and the Electric Japs. We won a battle-of-the-bands contest cos we had a Puerto Rican drummer and a black bassist. The night we won I knew I wanted to be a star. I walked on stage and started singing. Then I closed my eyes 'cos I thought they were going to kill us. But they cheered .

'People said we were the best band around –but that's 'cos we were the worst. We were entertaining. Bands, that time, made everything look so boring, taking everything so seriously. We stood out because of our conspicuous consumption. Then the New York Dolls. Right?'

Whoops. I'm back.

'Our lifestyles in the Dolls didn't radically alter – we always used to stay up all night before we were in the band. I think one of the main things we achieved was to get a lot of record companies interested in bands they would never even have considered before.'

After the band disintegrated – an appropriate word – David was not interested in making any records. 'I just wanted to sit around and dig myself for awhile.'

It was while he was digging himself he met drummer Frankie LaRocka on the Staten Island ferry and the David Johansen band was born.

He smiles incessantly, like the Joker. He's a professional raconteur gently unfolding stories that tell you more about the city than the man.

'This is my life – it doesn't really change. I'm happy with this band and confident about the future.'

But will it ever attract mass interest?

'Who knows? But I know one thing – I'd rather be popular in New York, the Shanghai of the States, than anywhere else in this country. This place has more of a creative spirit, streets ahead of any other town.

'These days, if you're the hottest band around you have to be homogenised 'cos you've got to be hip with the people that eat white-bread sandwiches. Yeah, it's true. There are actually people in certain States that grill two slices of white bread and then slap another piece of white bread covered in margarine in between and eat it as a sandwich. Who in their right mind wants to be popular with them?'

David has since appeared in several movies, most notably as a taxi-driving ghost in Scrooged and alongside Mick Jagger in Freejack. He has toured with a re-formed version of the New York Dolls and has contributed songs for movies, including The Aviator.

Photographer Chris Gabrin and I are invited to the CBS offices in Manhattan by executive Perri Chasin to watch a video of Bruce Springsteen in concert, singing 'Rosalita'. I've loved him with a passion since first hearing the *Born To Run* album. This guy was serious shit.

'Would you like to see him play?' asks Perri.

Would I like to live forever?

'We're flying you and Chris down to Washington tonight to catch the show in Maryland,' says Perri, 'and we're trying to arrange an interview, but it's proving to be a little difficult. See what you guys can do when you get there.'

We can do a lot as it turns out.

Christ it's hot in here.

The guy behind me is pawing my neck with his heavy on the onions hot dog breath. The fulsome closed-circuit system above my head revels in zoom-a-loom close-ups.

You can almost see the microbes getting it on in each sweat droplet racing down Bruce's face.

It's a 15,000-humanwatt heat, fulminating on stage, unleashing microwaves that permeate the cavernous Capitol Center in Largo, leaving the snow covered outside untouched but burning the shit outta them pumping organs grinding away inside.

A smile has been superglued on each and every face. No matter how hard you try it won't peel off. You're stuck with it for three hours. Then you realise there's something wrong with your legs. You know you should sit down because the stewards keep telling you, but they won't respond. It's a three-hour clockwork wind up and if you force them they'll snap.

Your eyes refuse to leave his face. The lids won't close because you'll miss something if they do. You're waiting, just waiting to respond. The song climbs to its climax. You're straining to shout. Not yet. Not yet...

"I am a prisoner of rock 'n' roll," he screams.

"BROOOCE, BROOOCE, BROOOCE!"

A Springsteen show is a joyous celebration of rock'n'roll the way it should always be played, with huge dollops of elation and passion. Its extravagant length is the fulcrum, its black-magic secret the E Street Band, especially saxophonist Clem Clemons, a veritable Empire State of a man dressed in one those fer-lashie white pimp-pusher suits found in *Dirty Harry* movies. But when he pumps up that sultry sax swing, it's like you've caught a glimpse of heaven.

The songs mean so much more when you see them performed live. Like you've spent all your life with only one eye and they've just given you another for Christmas wrapped up in starry paper. If they told me I was dying, I'd spend the rest of my life watching Bruce Springsteen.

Thirty minutes after the fourth and obviously final encore hardly anyone has left. That Pythonesque sheep-shearing Christian-name chant continues long after the show has finished, 'Broooce Broooce, Broooce,' and even an announcement over the tannoy that there will be no further encores fails to quieten them.

I'm hanging out with the 'Broooce' brigade on the off-chance of grabbing an interview, though it looks a pretty remote possibility.

I'd be surprised if the man is still standing, such was the intensity of his performance.

Fourteen-year-old girls queue up at the backstage door armed with photos of their idol and handkerchiefs soaked with tears.

It seems strange that a twenty-nine-year-old New Jersey urban cowboy who talks of love and death and streets of fire should attract the hordes who've been playing Andy Gibb records at home before the show.

But it's the kids who Bruce sings about. It's their town that rips the bones from their backs, their town that's a death trap. When he pleads, 'Get out while you're young,' you know he really means it.

Suddenly Chris grabs my arm. 'I think we're in.'

I follow him to a backstage door, which a mean-looking dude lets us pass through. Chris is one helluva blagger. Three floors up we're led into a room. We sit down and I frantically write down some questions as we wait for the man to appear... ...

Bruce Springsteen walks into the room with a towel draped over his shoulders, like a boxer who's just gone the full nine yards. He looks different. His hair has been slicked back and it makes him seem leaner but not meaner.

This feels like a great honour.

He's extremely polite and has an almost childlike demeanour. He's genuinely surprised that he's popular in Britain.

'I try to do as much as possible,' he says, of the gruelling nationwide marathon tour. 'The kids want to hear 'Born To Run' so I sing it. I've got some new numbers so I sing them.

'We originally started off with a two-hour set. But when the tour got under way, we found it impossible to restrict it to that. It's hard for me to leave anything out. So now I play as long it feels right. Some nights it's too long and others it ain't long enough. Tonight was one night they were about ready for a double dose!

'I guess most of the songs are pretty durable – at least, from the reaction they still get, they seem to be.'

Darkness on the Edge of Town is a lot bleaker musically and the trademark cinematic lyrics make way for blue-collar blues.

'It's been a real progression,' he says in mellifluous five-o'clock-shadow New Jersey tones. 'The characters on *Born To Run* and *Darkness* could be the same people in the same town only years down the line. You can see the difference. It's, like, older. Some people have called it a depressing album. That's untrue. It's just that when you have one successful album people tend to expect the same format for the next one.'

Ah, now seems like the appropriate time to probe. I wonder if his work is autobiographical.

'No.'

Oh.

'Oh, sure, some of the characters on a track like "Rosalita" are people I've come across in my life. But my songs are fantasies. Should a song reflect imagery or the performer? You can't get away from the fact that you're making the statements – but then again, is it the song that does that? There comes a point where the song becomes more and more like a movie. And when that happens you cease to become its creator and assume the role of director. You have to be so many different characters and it's better to let them have lives of their own. My songs have a kinda drive-in quality about them. They may be about factories, they may be about something else. I'm just there, quietly directing.'

So all those songs about crazy gangs in city heats and fights and drinking – you never lived any of that?

'Not really. I was always pretty much on my own. I didn't hang out with a crowd or anything. See, ever since I was fourteen I was playing. Clubs, YMCAs, high-school dances, you name it. As a result I felt OK playing to people but not actually being with them.

'And I'm still like that. I am by myself. If there's one other person around, well, that's OK. You tend to find that attitude in most rock'n'roll musicians.'

Never in a gang. Wow, and I'd always thought this was one hell of a heavy dude. Er, how about the drinking, then, Bruce?

'I haven't taken a drink in around two years.'

Gulp!

'I guess I don't really have the time. I never did drink much. Oh, there was one time. For a while I used to hang out with this really big guy – I mean really big, y'know. And together we'd head out to the bars. I was underage but nobody guessed or cared. We'd really shake those bars down. I had a great time with this big guy. But then I never saw him again.

'I had time on my hands. Now, I suppose if I wanted to get drunk I'd go to a bar on my own. But I wouldn't want anybody else to see.'

And what about those early sexual – uh – travels?

'I was fourteen when I first made love. And when I'd done it I didn't know if I'd done it or not!' He starts to laugh, all shy and secretive. Well, at least he's done something he can sing about.

Funny how preconceived notions get their noses rubbed in the dirt. No matter. This guy could never be a letdown. For starters he's too sincere and, besides, somebody with a show like he's got could give an interview with a mouth full of marbles and still gain my respect.

The Asbury Park apparition found himself alone in the rundown seaside resort when his parents upped and headed west to California.

'I was around eighteen at the time and still at high school. I decided I didn't want to go with them. I had a local reputation as a musician and I didn't intend losing that. I tried to live there for a very short time but I soon found out the place held nothing for me. Musically I preferred what was going down in New Jersey. I didn't need a job to get by 'cos I could make enough money playing in the clubs.'

Jon Landau wanders in. He looks a little perplexed. The wrinkles in his brow suggest it's time for us to head back to the hotel.

The moment Bruce emerges into the chilly night hundreds of kids who've been waiting patiently for a glimpse go berserk. 'Give me a kiss, baby – sign this, pleasepleaseplease?'

'I'll always love you, Bruce. Ain't he just so damned cute?"

He signs everything flashed in front of him. And that smile's not false. He loves it.

We climb on the luxury tour bus that boasts a colour TV, sofas, beds and built-in stereo and head for the hotel. 'Hey, ain't it just amazing?' he says. 'I came out on this tour 'cos I wanted to enjoy myself again. I never dreamed it would turn out like this. I've done eighty-eight shows, we've got thirty-three more to do, and everywhere the reaction is the same. You get the young kids from the suburbs and they're such a great audience. It's funny ... At the start the girls would jump on stage, then, after realising what they'd done, just stand there and freeze. But now they're getting used to it – and so are their tongues!

'I like running among the audience while I'm playing, and the other night I thought I'd take a little trip up into the balcony. But as I got in the foyer about ten fifteen-year-old girls hit me. They just grabbed me and wouldn't let me go. I guess they're more demonstrative at that age. They even come around to my house and wait for hours outside. I got a kid sister back in San Francisco and when she tells her friends who her brother is they go wild. Ain't it just amazing?'

Bruce still lives in Asbury Park. 'It's still the same as it always was. If you got enough gas in your car you carry on to Atlantic City. If not, then Asbury will just have to do. But it'll always be my home. I like Arizona and Holland. London's pretty cool too. My first show at Hammersmith three years ago was tough but the second one was great. I guess I'll never leave Asbury, though.'

During the long encores at every show, Bruce asks for the houselights to be turned on, and they stay on till the end while he goes through his usual rock'n'roll medley fare. 'When you see all the people, everybody, right up to the back, it's such a great feeling.

'It's their night. You may get sore, you may get hoarse, but when you see all those kids out there it's like the first show all over again. They may not have seen you before and they may not see you again, so you've always got to make it something real special. If you think like that every time you walk on stage you've got it made.'

And, boy, has this guy got it made.

Jon tells everybody to look out of the windows.

'Willya take a look at that?' shouts Bruce. The coach is being escorted back to the hotel by a convoy of cars stretching as far as the eye can see. And each car is stuffed full of screaming kids screeching horns, singing Springsteen songs and, of course, chanting, 'Broooce, Broooce, Broooce.'

'Wow, that's never happened before,' says Bruce.

But it's gonna happen again. And again. And leave us running burned and blind chasing something in the night.

I start chasing something in the night when I return to London. Tim and I check out an office in Mount Pleasant. We're weeks away from unveiling the Farringdon Agency.

Bruce is still The Boss. His album Wrecking Ball was named the number one album of 2012 by Rolling Stone magazine

DECEMBER 1978

Devo, Bryan Robertson, Rory Gallagher

It's cold. It's Liverpool. It's Devo. I'm talking to the guys in the Holiday Inn lounge.

Devo have just played the local Empire where the five Akron portables pumped it up precisely and with intent. Their indefatigable cohesion galvanised the Pudlians and there was scousely room to breathe at the front. The crowd more than simply enjoy the static, they worship these bespectacled college kids.

Behind those glasses (which most of them wear off-stage too) you get the feeling there's a world of victims, staring and expecting you to punch them on the nose and kick them in the bollocks.

Their show is Tubes without the Quaaludes, Clash without the accent, Vince Hill without the nose, Meat Loaf without the inches,

Blue Oyster Cult without the lasers. Yes, Devo are without.

But within, they're fine upstanding young spectacles with inveterate principles. They wake up in the middle of the night and cry out, 'Why are we here? What are we doing? Where are we going? Where's the toilet? Can I have a glass of water, Mummy?'

The boys have escaped the frenzied mob and are seated around a table reading reports about themselves in assorted music papers. They don't appear to drink much, smoke much or munch much. They sip tea sedately, and nibble biscuits conservatively. Gerry Casale does most of the talking.

Three fans stroll into the lounge with posters which they ask the boys to sign. They talk of the heavy stewarding at the gig.

'There's two thousand of you and only twenty of them,' screams Gerry. 'If you all worked together you could trample over them. But none of you would do that, would you?"

The fans shrug and walk away. Gerry turns to me. 'Those bouncers really want to hurt the kids. It's a totally Fascist attitude and overtly sexual. They hate the kids because they have the ability to get off on something. The kids represent a kind of healthy sexuality. The bouncers feel threatened by this because they see life as a situation that has to be controlled. People like that find jobs where they can give vent to their repression in a socially acceptable way – like being a bouncer. In future we'll have a say in the security before we set one foot in this country to tour."

After initial raves, Devo have come in for piss-take upon piss-take in the music press.

'It was a real Devo situation,' explains Gerry. 'We read all the laudatory British press and then came over. We did all these interviews and gave truthful answers to every question. We told them about Akron, we told them about us, about why we wrote our songs, everything. And they really laid into us.'

'What they resented was the fact we didn't tell them we liked to wank and pull chicks and eat hamburgers and watch TV. We simply told them what motivated us to create.'

Now that's asking for trouble. Gerry smacks his teacup on the table.

'Yet they can tell kids to go along to a Clash show and lose their front teeth or an eye and then go back to the factory. See, when they realised we were in no way similar, they got offensive. They found Devo a threat and that's typically human.'

'But the press really believe they're deities – "The Lord giveth and the Lord taketh away."'

I feel distinctly uncomfortable at this juncture. I adopt the false-laugh method of interrogation. Ha, well, haha, boys, hahaha, your album wasn't too, hahahaha, hot.

'It was a three-and-a-half-week Devo classic,' says Gerry.

'Today's noise is tomorrow's music.'

Hahahahaha, today's music is also, hahahahahaha, tomorrow's noise. I sit tight waiting for their reaction.

They laugh.

'We are sensitive to change and use it. We won't repeat our music,' says Gerry. 'Change is what keeps a band going. What you start out to do is ultimately changed from what you intended. Of course, you could end up like Jefferson Starship, a band who know exactly what's going to happen to their music at any given time. When you stop moving you become a statue and then you fulfil middle-class expectations.'

And he goes on into the wild blue yonder . . .

I decide to leave as Gerry admits he finds it difficult to accept the fact that Siouxsie and the Banshees are praised by the rock press and Devo just get systematically slagged.

Don't know what they're worried about. Once you start getting ripped to shreds by the press you're on your way to a fortune.

Bryan Robertson's mesmerising guitar solo on 'Still In Love With You' from Thin Lizzy's Live & Dangerous album is just about the finest guitar solo I've ever heard and I get the opportunity to tell him just that down at the Speakeasy one night.

I swear to God, he starts to weep, gently. OK, he's probably pissed and I'm probably standing on his foot, but I've never managed to make a rock star cry before – in a nice way – at something I've said, and it's one of the more poignant moments of my life.

Just before Christmas I have a quick chat over the phone with another guitar god, Rory Gallagher, currently on a massive tour. 'I do enjoy the way I live,' he says. 'I wouldn't change it for the world. Touring is the lifeblood of rock'n'roll. All those endless hours of finding places to eat and not sleeping, it's all part of it. If I took all those things seriously I'd lose my bite. I'm into brass-knuckles music. I want to woo the public.'

The next day I interview the Barron Knights, not really renowned for brass-knuckles music... But, hey, it's Christmas. And, hey, it's that time again...

PART 4

The Farringdon Agency

Tim and I face each other across two large desks in a small office in Mount Pleasant, both of us still slightly stunned by the fact that we've actually started the Farringdon Agency and are renting an office and getting phones installed and buying furniture and filing cabinets and stationery and having letterheads and a partnership bank account.

We've upped the ante with all the publications and the money is enough to cover everything with a nifty few bob on top. Plus Tim has a regular Capital Radio spot that doesn't pay much but helps our Farringdon cause look more kosher.

I get about a bit – trips, receptions, fine white lines on the freeway. I am that hitcher...

JANUARY 1979

The Village People, The Clash, Dr Feelgood, Inner Circle, Bob Marley

There's a sudden deluge of tabloid tumbling, of dots and dashes and punchy intros and jaunty exclamation-mark-ridden prose. How about this brazen bunch...

It's the most bizarre combination to ever hit the charts!

A cowboy, an Indian, a cop, a GI, a construction worker and a leather-clad motorbike stud all extolling the virtues of the YMCA!

That's the wild and wonderful Village People who sell as many records in the States as John Travolta.

They call their act a celebration of the all-American male and their biggest fans can be found in Gay Lib.

'We go for a Mae Westian approach,' says David Hodo, the construction worker. 'When we started, we aimed for a gay audience simply because we're a disco band, and most of the people that went to discos in the States originally were gay.'

The Village People are the brainchild of French producer Jacques Morali. He visited a bar in New York's Greenwich Village, and saw a group of male go-go dancers, including Felipe Rose dressed as a Red Indian chief, performing on top of the bar. 'I decided it was time to have a group specifically for such people,' he recalls.

So he got the other guys together, dressed them in American stereotype male outfits and took them into the studio. 'I never thought it would catch on with straight audiences – but they loved it right away,' says Morali.

The band's first single, the aptly titled 'Macho Man', went platinum. Their stage act is sensational, and the audiences they attract are zanier than the band themselves!

Says Hodo, 'A lot of people overlook the humour of our act. It's incredible. We're not a Gay Lib band, we're a People Lib band!'

At a recent gig they attracted a record audience of 110,000. When they appeared on one US TV show it got the highest ratings in its history.

The cop – Victor Willis, a high-school football star – maintains he has no connection with gay people. So isn't it all a bit awkward?

'Sometimes it gets a bit uncomfortable because I won't let that sort of image be connected with me. I'm just dealing in disco. Songs like "YMCA", "My Roommate" and "Ups And Downs" can be interpreted either way. It's entirely up to the listener.'

'There's a mystique about us,' adds Hodo. 'And women love it because there are six real manly looking guys onstage.'

Village People sold over 85 million records and were awarded a star on the Hollywood Walk of Fame in 2008. Morali died from AIDS-related illness in 1991 and Glenn Hughes, the Leatherman, died of lung cancer in 2001. Mark Mussler, the construction worker, died of AIDS in 1987

Even the Clash can't escape my exclamation-mark clutches! The leader of Britain's most exciting band lives in a squat!

Joe Strummer of the Clash, whose new album *Give 'Em Enough Rope* has shot to number two in the charts, can't afford a place of his own.

'People think because you've had a few hits you're rich,' says Strummer, twenty-four. 'Bands like the Who and the Stones never got any money until years after they started making hits. I hope it's gonna be the same with us. But if you think I'm hard-up, you should see our drummer Nicky Headon – he sleeps rough!'

The Clash have come in for some heavy criticism recently from those who reckon they've sold out.

'We haven't changed,' says Joe. 'We've still kept our integrity and we still know what our duty is – to make a stand. Times have changed, standards are all different. But the music business doesn't know that. There's a whole new world of kids out there – but those mugs in the industry close their eyes to it. Instead, they continue to go out at lunch times and get drunk on other people's money.'

Joe went through a nightmarish time earlier this year when he was frightened of going out alone.

'It was all getting too much for me. I kept thinking I would be attacked because of what we've always stood for.

'But I soon got over it. You have to or you're dead!'

Rat-a-tat-tat! Check out Mr Brilleaux.

Doctor Feelgood have found the perfect cure for the winter blues.

While we've all been dreaming of castles in Spain they've bought one ... complete with hundreds of squealing pigs!

And the band are hoping to bring home the bacon when they visit their newly acquired pig farm next month.

Lee Brilleaux, the Cockney hell-raiser with the hung-over eyes and the hangdog voice, explains that the Feelgoods had money in Spain which they couldn't collect.

'We've played shows there, but the money we get is subject to high taxation if it goes out of the country. We heard about this farm-owner who had got into heavy debt, so we used our money to bail him out – and we bought the property. We've kept him on as manager but it's ours – all four acres of it. So now we're going down in a few weeks to rehearse in the barn where the pigs sleep. Besides, it might be a profitable sideline. You can't get good bacon in Spain 'cos the pigs are too scrawny. In fact, everything in Spain is skinny – except for the birds! And I like a nice bit of crackling now and again!'

Lee, twenty-seven, is delighted about the success of their new single, 'Milk and Alcohol'.

'It looks like being our first Top Twenty record! It's great because the lyrics are all about how drink gets you into trouble – and everyone thinks I'm a hard drinker. I like a pint as much as the next man, but once reporters see you with one in your hand they think you're an alcoholic. I go down to the pub most nights because I hate the rubbish they put on the telly.'

Lee, a bachelor, has never moved away from Canvey Island where he was born. 'Why should I? I spend most of my time on the road anyway, so home doesn't have to be somewhere glamorous, just where you can hang your hat. Nobody bothers you when you nip out to the boozer for a drink. Only problem is, the pubs close too early!'

'Milk and Alcohol' was the Feelgoods' only top-ten hit. Brilleaux continued to front the band, through various line-up changes, until his death from lymphoma in 1994. The Lee Brilleaux Birthday Memorial concert is held every year on Canvey Island.

They don't close too early in Jamaica, where the cocks never crow before ten am. The blistering sun devours haste and time is a thing of the past.

To the musicians who congregate outside Randy's record shop in the heart of Kingston, the hour is of little consequence. It's all just a matter of hanging out – until the heat on the street becomes unbearable. Then they split for a spliff in the shadows and play a little reggae, Jamaica's sweet soul music.

And I'm watching all this courtesy of Island Records, thanks to some well-placed punctuation and even better-placed publications. Maybe the Farringdon Agency is finally paying off. They want me to interview Inner Circle and I know fuck all about 'proper' reggae. Doesn't mean to say I can't write about it. Right?

Over the last ten years, reggae in its many guises – like ska and bluebeat – has become big business. The classier exponents have earned fortunes and Bob Marley, the richest of them all, has brought his island's joy and tears to the masses. In the last year reggae has burned through the rainclouds to tan a whole new market in America and Europe.

'I've been very disappointed at the indifferent reaction the music has had up until now, although it's always been a major industry in Jamaica,' says Chris Blackwell, who, as head of Island Records, is the man responsible for breaking Marley. 'But this year I'm confident all that will change mainly because reggae is beginning to assimilate other kinds of music and consequently growing stronger.'

There are two radio stations on the island, more than a hundred record-shops and around twenty recording studios. There is precious little live music. If an artist wants to play, he gives an impromptu show almost anywhere and passes the word round his friends beforehand. The locals tend to rely on the numerous mobile deejays to catch up on the latest sounds. The deejays' influence on the music scene is considerable – especially at a 'rockers' dance, although dance is altogether an inappropriate word since the thousand or so people who usually attend the functions are predominantly male and spend most of their time getting stoned.

Yeah! Tell it like it is. Reggae, reggae, reggae, here comes Johnny Reggae, lay it on me...

OK, I admit I've always found roots reggae totally inaccessible.

For me, it's a mystifying mixture of incomprehension and repetition enjoyed only by guys far across the sea or in Shepherds Bush basements, and vaguely condescending middle class honkies who like to "identify" with the black man's plight and can't dance a step.

Now Desmond Dekker, I could get off on. Never had the faintest idea what he was rabbiting on about, but I felt flash swaying to it down the local Birds' Nest.

And then I get offered this trip to Jamaica by Island Records to interview Inner Circle. At first it seems both exciting and alarming. I'd read about the poverty-stricken ghettos and drug-driven violence in Kingston, the murder capital of the world. But an island capable of producing sweet airs that have danced across oceans and grooved nations can't be so bad. And there's always a chance of drifting on a Jamaican breeze. Come on, man. It's roots, and the Maytals.

So I go, and prepare to be shocked. And I am, but it's not the shock I was expecting as I find myself being chauffeured up to a mansion in Beverly Hills. Can you get that? Lavish houses peppered over verdant hills on the outskirts of Kingston and home to Inner Circle.

Their mainman, Jacob Miller, who, someone whispers in my ear, is 'legendary', is holed up in New York. Apparently there's some friction between him and the police regarding gorgeous ganja and he's decided to prolong his stay. So we're left with the mighty Lewis brothers – Roger and Ian.

I tell ya, if these two ever decide to visit Venice, all those charities to keep it above water might as well jack it in. The city would sink without trace. Roger weighs in at twenty-three stone and Ian ain't far behind. By comparison, Meat Loaf looks like Twiggy after a six-month bout of anorexia. Oh, yeah, and Toto the keyboardist is hanging around in this year's fashionable Jamaican outfit – a football kit.

They give me a glass of iced coconut milk, an inch away from nectar, and we start talking. You never know what you're gonna get when you sit down and interview someone you don't know from Adam. So you indulge in chit-chat to suss them out and weigh up whether to use a lot of foreplay and beat about the bush or just go straight in because they're moist and eager to please.

Now, as it turns out, the guys are friendly, happy to communicate their thoughts and downright hospitable. There's only one snag – I can't understand a fucking word. It's a real heavy accent, almost indecipherable. Ian does all the talking initially, and it's like trying to hold a conversation with a geezer operating a road drill. But the more he talks, the more I hear.

They've just released 'Everything Is Great' as a 12" – and if you're gonna try and kid me that's roots you may as well add that the Queen's a smackhead.

Maybe I'm not comprehending the subtleties, but I can't find a trace of reggae on this Earth, Wind & Fire visitation. It's disco with guts and it's as hot as Colman's.

'We want everyone to understand our music,' Ian tells me, in a grim voice, as we step out onto the patio where a hummingbird hovers like a gargantuan bee. 'It's energy. It makes people really start rocking. A lot of people from outside Jamaica think that all people like here is reggae. But Jamaicans love all music, from Billy Joel to soul, from the Eagles to disco.'

The band have been together for five years and before that they were all part of the Third World set-up. They've been making and producing records for most of that time (which explains the affluence) but it was only at last year's Kingston Peace Festival, attended by the world's press, that they really came to the attention of the uninitiated.

'We were really good that day," recalls Ian as he scratches his beard for the umpteenth time.' Mick Jagger approached us afterwards and has since become great friends. The vibes were right and–a–everything.'

But what you play ain't exactly reggae, is it?

'It's reggae all right. We'll never forget our roots. We're always reggae. It's just that we add a few things, like a synthesiser. They've never been used correctly in that context but we know how to make it sound right for reggae. Jacob Miller is roots. He'll always be roots.'

Ian becomes more adamant. 'Reggae can't be left out. It's always got to be there. You have that first and everything else is secondary.

But you've got to do it the right way. We ain't afraid to experiment. We're more theatrical than most bands. As long as you know where you're coming from, it's OK to use backdrops or even lasers. It's not a deviation, it's a transition.

'Everything is great. It's a laugh. Simply a matter of seeing things in a revised form. You just gotta make the people feel happy, that's all.'

I can tell Ian is running out of things to say 'cos he stops scratching his beard and peers longingly back into the comforting solitude of the lounge. Happily, Roger is now cultivating a communicative mood and wanders onto the patio like an articulated meat lorry.

I ask him what he feels about the writers who are more patronising than pure when it comes to black music – and I don't mean Boney M.

'I don't feel they check their facts. They write all this stuff about lifestyles related to music and what's roots and what ain't and if you ain't you're not worth listening to. Why should I play music to please them when they don't know what they're talking about anyway? Either they've never seen Jamaica or they come over here with preconceived notions which they refuse to change even though what they see contradicts those notions.'

His voice wavers. His lips tremble. He shuffles backwards and forwards on the patio cutting a strange, wild figure in this pacific, wealthy garden of joy.

'It makes me feel bad. Don't write about my lifestyle. Don't write about my personal existence as a human being. Don't say, "Roger Lewis is not crying from the streets of Trenchtown." If you criticise me then you must criticise Bob Marley for living in a hundred-thousand-dollar house or Joe Gibbs or any one of a number of reggae singers.

'I was brought up in the ghetto. So what? All I'm doing is trying to bring reggae to the marketplace of Britain, Europe and America. You either like the music or you don't. It's not a question of culture. We all got different ones anyway. We play reggae music because we come from Jamaica. But that doesn't prevent us getting into other areas of music One of the biggest disco records of all time was "Kung Fu

Fighting" and that was sung by a Jamaican – Carl Douglas.

'And look at Boney M.'

A year after the interview, Jacob Miller was killed in a car crash. Inner Circle's biggest UK hit came in 1992 with 'Sweat (A La La La La Long)', which was new roots and panties. The band now run Circle House, a famous Miami recording studio.

'Hello, Bob.'

'Hi, Baree. Welcome to my 'ome.'

Bob Marley leads the way into the heart of 56 Hope Road, Kingston, and my heart skips a beat, strolls, and skips another beat. Back in the UK we call that atrial fibrillation – here they call it reggae. I watch his dreadlocks wriggle like a nest of funky snakes as he bounces along the corridors beneath the minatory ceiling fans that spin the heavy air into gold through seven rooms of gloom. He points out a few interesting objects of memorabilia before taking us – that's Alan Edwards, who's organised the whole trip and spends much of his time on the phone to the UK running Modern Publicity, *Sounds* journo Hugh Fielder and the *NME*'s Chris Salewicz – into the Tuff Gong studios, which he founded in 1970.

He plays back something he's just recorded and I know this is a moment I'll carry to the crematorium.

'Fancee a kick around in da yard?'

And that's how I get to play football with Bob Marley. Honest. You ask Joyce and Vicky. He's a blinding passer of the ball but his dreadlocks smack you in the face when you try to tackle him, which I think is a little unfair so I give him a sly dig in the ribs next time I try to get the ball off him. He gives me a friendly kick as he leaves me standing, minus the ball, in a cloud of dust. Fucker, in a nice way.

As a parting shot he gives us all a chunk of Lamb's Bread, the island's most potent ganja and his personal favourite. Mr Marley is a true gentleman and a musician touched by God.

The next day the four of us are driven to Chris Blackwell's house for tea. Chris isn't around but we're given a guided tour of his beautiful colonial property, high on a hill, before lighting up the Lamb's Bread. I've never smoked such dope – three puffs and I'm paralysed. I can't get out of this unfathomably deep armchair and when I eventually do, I struggle outside to look at the sunset. Shit, I'm smoking a joint given to me by Bob Marley while standing outside Chris Blackwell's home watching the sun go down on Jamaica. What have I done to deserve this? Maybe I did my time during those three nightmare school years. Maybe in return I get a sweet life. Maybe, just maybe, this is payback time.

We leave the house and while on our way to a Rasta party in downtown Kingston, we crash the car. But we still make it to the party where the smoke is thick as smog, pierced only, like luminous moths, by the flash of a green, gold and red Rasta tam worn by a Tribesman with a point to prove and a joint to roll.

After a couple of days' lounging round the hotel pool, Island tell Alan to fly us all to New York to interview Jacob Miller, stay a few days, then return home to London. But it's snowing in New York with temperatures below freezing. Why do I want to go there? Besides, the average *Record Mirror* reader won't have a clue who Jacob Miller is anyway. So I decline and spend the next two days in Kingston before agreeing to meet up with the others at Kennedy Airport en route to Heathrow.

I persuade my unofficial guide, Maurice, to accompany me on a cab ride around Trenchtown, although he assures me we won't find a taxi driver willing to take us to a place where white light spells danger. Sure enough, the first six we hail refuse. Lucky seven, who obviously needs the money more than the other guys, agrees but insists he won't be held responsible if anything happens.

Maurice is not happy. He's only eighteen and drowning in roots. 'You sure you wanna do this?' he asks, as we climb into the back of the cab. Why not? I walked home through Brixton on a few Saturday nights and nothing ever happened. I've been to Harlem in diamonds and pearls and nothing ever happened. I've searched for a cab in The Bowery at four am and nothing ever happened. I've tried to shit after four lines of speed and nothing ever happened. Trenchtown? Bring it on.

'Why not?'

The hype had hoisted images of zinc huts and chicken wire into my willing brain. Instead there's a proliferation of redevelopment. I expect murderous stares and get curious side glances.

'So, what do you think of Trenchtown?' asks the driver.

'Yeah, it's . . .'

'Wind your window up quick and lock the doors.'

Four guys are standing in the road forcing the cab to stop. One of them comes over and stares straight at me and, yes, it's a murderous one.

'Hey, man, you wanna fight me?' he screams. 'Come on and fight me, man. Come on and fight me now.'

I start to wind the window down with a milky, shaking hand.

'I wouldn't do that, man,' warns Maurice.

Shit – I'm getting called 'man' a lot. I undo the window just enough to make my terror audible 'Er, no thanks.'

He smiles and, without looking away, says, 'Hey, guys, he don't wanna fight. Maybe he'll buy some ganja. You wanna buy some ganja, man?'

'I'd buy the ganja if I were you, man,' prompts Maurice.

'Yeah, man.' My words are stumbling out. 'I'll buy some ganja, man. How much, man?'

'Easy, man. Easy.' He produces the dope wrapped in a tissue. 'Give me ten US dollars.'

I hand over the money, the four guys walk away laughing and the cab proceeds.

'You're a very lucky man, man,' says the driver.

'Yeah, man, yeah,' concludes Maurice.

Oh, man!

The cab goes to Tuff Gong studios. Bob's away but there's six or seven guys kicking a ball around the yard. Maurice recounts the tale of Trenchtown and I produce the ten-dollar deal. One guy takes the dope and starts filleting it.

'Too many seeds. See? Not good qualatee.'

He rolls a few joints and hands me back the remainder of the deal. For the next few minutes the group puffs in silence. Not good quality? A raging storm of paranoia buffets my brain and I convince myself that everyone around me is talking in code because I can't understand a word. I feel terribly isolated. I'm a long way from home and everybody has got it in for me. Infamy, infamy, they've all got it in for me. A toga-clad Kenneth Williams flits across the yard kicking a ball. Shit, I'm fucked.

I decide to leave before they kill me and spend the next hour trying to lose them because I know they're following me, swords drawn in a bloodlust frenzy. I finally make it to the hotel in one piece and collapse on the bed. An hour later I wake up feeling good and craving food so I order a steak sandwich, fries and a beer from room service. I also feel mightily embarrassed. Shit, what must those guys back at the yard think of me, leaving like that? This Jamaican weed makes the dodgy London black smoke like weak piss.

Thirty minutes later a knock on the door wakes me up again.

'It's room service with your order, Mr Cain.' The guy looks about sixty. 'Where shall I put it?'

'The table will be fine.'

When I glance at the table to indicate, there's my deal, spread out on the tissue for the whole world to see.

'What have we here?' he asks.

I start to wonder what Jamaican jails will be like.

'Got any skins?' he asks. 'It's quiet tonight.'

'Er, no.'

'No problem.' He looks around the room and espies a brown paper bag containing an ornament I'd bought for my mum. 'Can I use that?'

'What – the ornament?'

'No, the bag.'

'Er, sure.'

He then proceeds to perform the best room service I've ever had. Like an origami master he transforms the bag into a perfect – very large – joint, which he hands to me and which we polish off in no time.

Fifteen minutes later he's dancing on my bed.

'If you want I can get you a lot of this and you can take it back to London, no problem,' he says, as we sit out on the balcony. It wasn't that long ago I saw *Midnight Express* and a dancing bell hop who can roll joints like a magician could easily be a passport to violent beatings and rape behind Kingston bars of sodomy. So I graciously decline his very generous offer and fly home the next day, zonked but ganja-free and a little more appreciative of roots reggae.

FEBRUARY 1979

UFO

As Billy Idol splits from Karen O'Connor, Des's daughter – 'I knew when it was Des on the phone 'cos he kept singing "1-2-3 O'Leary"' – I spend a couple of nights on the road with heavy-metal gorillas UFO where I get to wonder, 'how over-the-top is over-the-top?'

A question that has vexed many a lonely soul.

Oh, sure, several people have sussed out the answer – Gandhi and Sid Vicious, for example. One doused himself with petrol and asked a passer-by for a light, the other pumped himself full of five-star smack when he only had a two-star engine and met his maker in a two-bit Greenwich Village laundro-flat.

It transpires that UFO have often pondered the very same question, searching for an answer as some men hunt for El Dorado. Then, out of the blue, they found it . . .

One night during a show, lead singer Phil Mogg was accidentally hit in the face by Pete Way's bass. The gash required ten stitches and left an ugly scab. A week later Phil turned to Pete in the dressing room after a particularly forgettable gig and asked yet again . . .

'How over-the-top is over-the-top?'

Pete didn't bother to reply. He grabbed Phil's head and ripped the stitches and scab off with his teeth, chewed them up and swallowed the lot.

'That's when I realised how over-the-top is over-the-top,' recalls Phil, as he drops his trousers backstage at Lancaster University in preparation for the gig.

UFO are the real deal.

Like some hideous hibernating creature, your average heavy-metal merchant comes to life only when he's touring and spends the rest of the year snoozing in a flash LA Brillo pad. UFO are no exception. Their tours are fantasies, peopled by soporific groupies with twin-carb tits, sneaky dealers, indifferent writers, emaciated, hysterical fans in trench coats and flares, demons, gods, sleazebags, all caught in the split-second blindness of a flash gun.

They go to bed when it's light and get up when it's dark. They get drunk, stoned, exhausted, all in the name of a glorious guitar solo and wailing vocal.

'There's only one thing that comes first in this band,' Phil tells me in his hotel room. 'Either you enjoy it or you don't. If you don't, don't do it. Whatever comes after that is secondary.'

I first met Mr Mogg in his manager's office just off Baker Street. I knew next to nothing about the band and only agreed to do the interview because *Record Mirror* commissioned it. He reminded me of a young Frank Marker in *Public Eye*, the suburban Phillip Marlowe with the hangdog look and the beat-up mac.

It's when he said, 'Bob Geldof is the modern day Eamonn Andrews,' that I decided I liked him and that his band would be worth checking out. I wasn't disappointed.

Theirs is a perceptive blend of pretentiousness and night-on-the-

Pre-concert with the Stranglers in Castel St Angelo, Rome, July 2, 1980. Later that night I interviewed each member in hot hotel rooms under starry skies. I travelled the world with this band and it was a mighty fine ride

Above My wedding reception above a mate's pub in New North Road, Islington, a couple of weeks after Dina and I were married – it took that long for the immigration authorities to accept it wasn't an arranged marriage and let her remain in the UK. That's me and the missus with Bruce Foxton and his wife, the sadly missed Pat Stead, who I knew from the very start. The late George Bodnar took the photo
Below Mr McLaren during his 'Duck Rock' Days, in a shoot for *Flexipop! Pic: Neil Matthews*

The photo from *Flexipop!* in 1983 that I thought had upset Paul Weller so much that he refused to talk to me for over thirty years. Turned out that wasn't the reason at all. But he did mention in a text that the last time he saw me was back in the Eighties, when I apparently blanked him in a restaurant. There's proof that drugs don't work – I actually blanked Paul Weller in a restaurant and I don't remember it. *Pic: Neil Matthews*

FREE A.N.L.
METEORS & DEFECTS
Punky Party Flexi E.P.

No. 26 65
USA $3·00

FLEXIPOP!

ON THE FIDDLE
MALCOLM McLAREN
up to his old trick

BLANCMANGE
Get Set

SPECIAL WALTER & DENNIS ISSUE

Plus: Southern Death Cult,
Blue Zoo, John Peel, Haney Bane,
Brilliant, Flock of Seagulls,
Flexipop Records Of The Year,
Blitz, Shalamar.

Above Issue 26 of *Flexipop!*, December 1982, with exclusive Malcolm McLaren interview
Opposite Annabella Lwin, on stage in Southampton with Bow Wow Wow, 20 August, 1982.
Annabella was the last person I interviewed for *Record Mirror*. Pic: Neil Matthews

Jools Holland at the office of
Faulty Products, March 11, 1980.
Pic: Neil Matthews

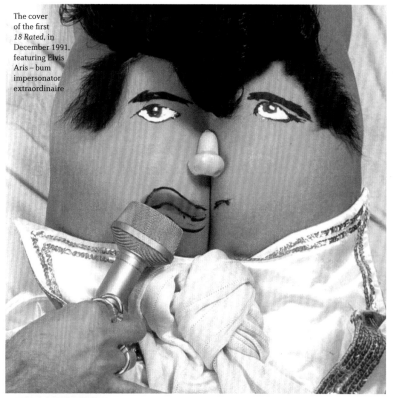

The cover of the first *18 Rated*, in December 1991, featuring Elvis Aris – bum impersonator extraordinaire

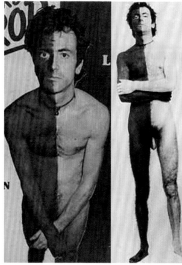

Left Hugh Cornwell insisted we paint every bit of him, including his genitals, in black and white during the infamous trip to Iceland in 1978. It was an idea I cooked up that, brush in hand with a naked Cornwell, I suddenly regretted

Above Roger Taylor taking time out during the shooting of the 'It's A Kind Of Magic' video in 1986. I got lost in his house once. *Pic: Neil Matthews*

THE WORLD'S FIRST SINGING MAGAZINE

FLEXIPOP

FREE
SELECTER
RECORD

No.1 60p

SPECIALS

JAM

BOW
WOW
WOW!

U.F.O.

BAD
MANNERS

WENDY
WU

Above The first issue of *Flexipop!*, November 1980, a weird and wonderful time
Opposite (above) Captain Sensible was John Travolta in a *Flexipop!* photo story, shot in the Music Machine in June 1982. *Pic Neil Matthews*

Opposite (below) Cherished memories of bygone days in Reykjavik, Tokyo, Poughkeepsie and Farringdon. Mind you, I'd swap them all for an ounce of that Lambs Bread Bob Marley once slid into my grubby paws…

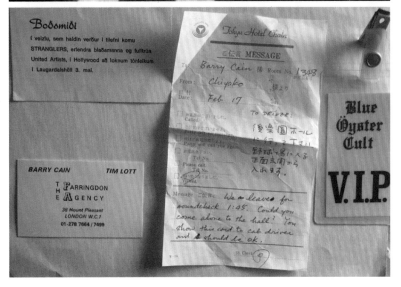

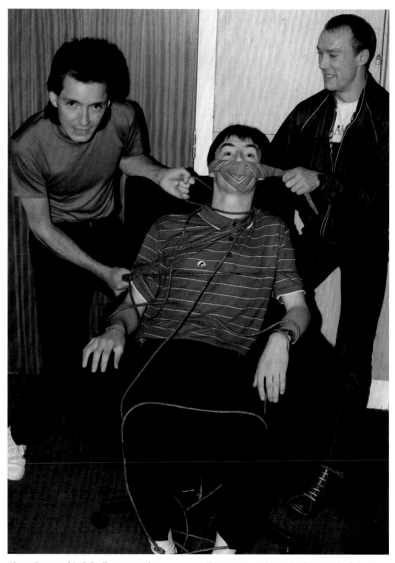

Above Bruce and Rick finally get a word in. *Flexipop!* certainly injected a bit of fun into a fairly maudlin world, *Pic: Neil Matthews*

Opposite: Top left The relaunch issue of *PopShop* that was unwisely advertised during the break on *Coronation Street*. I guess I was one of the few people that made money out of Robert Maxwell. Rumours he was clutching a copy of *PopShop* when his body washed up on shore are unfounded

Top right Is that a gun in your pocket…? Gary Kemp in 1980 at Manor Studios in Oxford, during the recording of Spandau Ballet's first album *Journeys To Glory. Pic: Neil Matthews*

Bottom right The cover of our last issue in July 1983, starring Aleister Crowley and numbered 666. Reasons to be cheerful

Bottom left Nice New Years' Eve 1978 statement from the *Daily Record*, with an even nicer cheque. I got paid more for the Clash piece than anyone else, including Barbara Streisand and Mike Oldfield

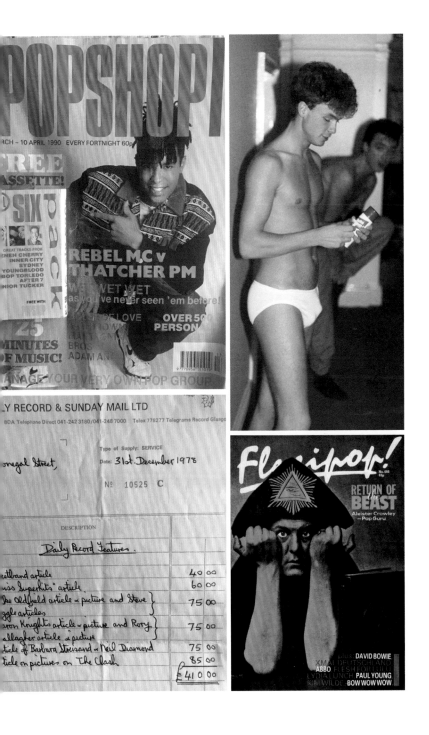

1. THE BAND STOP PLAYIN
WAIT FOR SECURITY G
TO GO AWAY AND STO
BEATING UP THE FAN
(BRUSSELS JULY 1980

3. HORACE COMES
OF THE CLOSET

2. RODDY WITH COMPANY
SECRETARY SARAH AND
ROAD CREW.

5. LYNVAL ASLEEP
ON THE JOB.

4 JERRY IN BELGIUM.

In the first issue of *Flexipop!*, the Specials gave us this bunch of personal pics
taken on the road during their 1980 tour. Lovely chaps

6. PROFESSOR HALL INSTRUCTS THE JAPANESE RUDE GIRLS & CONCERT SECURITY GAURDS IN THE THOUGHTS OF CHAIRMAN JERRY.

DAMMERS— MUSIC CAN'T CHANGE ANYTHING. IT'S ALL CAPITALISM!

7. TERRY ATTEMPTS TO PLAY THE GUITAR.

8. BRAD.

9. NEVILLE RELAXES AFTER A STRENUOUS PERFORMANCE.

One of the greatest shows I've ever seen – Bruce Springsteen at the Capital Center in Largo, Maryland, November 2, 1978. I even got to interview him backstage after the gig. *Pic: Chris Gabrin*

In December 1980 the second issue of *Flexipop!* – featuring two exclusive tracks by the Jam – really put the mag on the map and we sold nearly 70,000 copies. Not bad for a flash fanzine

town fun. They scream songs of teenage dementia and the beer-and-bum-fluff audience lap it up. Mogg, the Tottenham toreador, looks suitably all-powerful, cultivating the character of tight-arse demagogue as he whips through the songs like a whirlpool, making me spin.

Meanwhile, Pete Way runs around the stage like he's dying for a piss. Pete Pete Pete . . .

By contrast, lead guitarist Paul Chapman, who's recently replaced misfit German Michael Schenker, is immobile. 'It's natural that a lot of people are going to compare me with Schenker,' Chapman tells me, after the show. 'But I find it difficult to accept writers accusing me of dressing funny and not blending in with the rest of the band on stage. Before you can think about image you've got to think about more important things –like music.'

Chapman was a former member of UFO anyway. 'The first time I was with them I wanted to go back to Wales and play with my friends.' He formed a band called Lone Star and when they folded Chapman rejoined UFO on a Stateside tour after Schenker mysteriously vanished. 'Three days after I got married I went on that tour. And I took my wife with me. Can you believe that? Taking your wife on the road with UFO for nearly three months!'

He wants the band to be associated with 'strong songs'.

'I tend to see music in songs rather than guitar solos. But it's down to me to prove to people that there will be no difference in the style of UFO because I've joined.'

'I've told him he's got to wear a Nazi uniform and sing "Deutschland über Alles" between songs,' jokes Mogg.

All five members sit on Phil's bed in his Preston hotel room two hours after the encore. UFO, unlike most of their contemporaries, like to hang around in their dressing room and meet the fans.

Paul Raymond – nope, not the stripper-dipper king – takes a back seat tonight and drummer Andy Parker looks tired. So it's down to the Mogg/Way team of incessant lunacy to provide the action.

'I used to be in the Enfield Harriers,' says Pete, 'and I was the third fastest athlete over my distance in the country.'

'He keeps telling me that,' says Phil, 'yet when I challenged him to a race around a hotel in Cleveland I slaughtered him.'

'Oh, yeah?' says Pete.

'Yeah.'

'Yeah?'

'Yeah. And I'll prove it. Race you along the corridor.'

'Nah, don't be stupid,' shrugs Pete, as he lights another fag.

'C'mon. Or are you too chicken?'

'No, I'm NOT!' says Pete, looking and sounding like a little-boy-lost Terry Scott. He puts out his fag while Phil limbers up. The others watch incredulously as they stroll out of the door like pathetic gunfighters and mosey on down the hall.

It's three am.

'On your marks, get set – 'ere, tell 'im to stop movin'. Cheat,' says Pete.

'No, I ain't.'

'You are too. A fuckin' cheat. Go!'

They tear down the corridor, crashing into each other as they burst through the doors that lead to the staircase. Phil wins.

'You fucking cheat. You bastard,' yells Pete, tears in his eyes.

'No, I ain't.'

'Let's do it again, then.' The two wander back to their starting blocks. Go! Pete wins this time. Both are far too breathless to argue but Phil demands a recount. Pete collapses on the bed.

'I used to box, bantamweight,' says Phil, still trying to regain his breath. 'I was doing quite well too, until I met our local milkman Reg Hicks in the ring. With one punch he gave me a nose from eye to eye.'

Phil, ebullient, buoyant, Sterodent, is 26 and married with two kids. He seems to have a morbid fear of being left alone and begs for me to stay up talking long after the others have gone to bed. His words are as multifarious as the snowflakes strangling Preston tonight as he conjures up visions of insidious UFO exploits during their ten years together.

He loves spontaneity on stage. 'It's easy to become just another Vegas act acting out well rehearsed, clinical shows night after night.

"Know something, I used to love B.B. King until I heard he did the same rap every night. That's a big difference between English and American bands. The former ride with the moment, the latter have it all written out."

He smiles his words, embellishing them with a pair of impish eyes. He tells me UFO have broken on 46 radio station in America, that he doesn't particularly love the place but that living there means they can at least begin to understand it.

Last time I saw Phil Mogg he was singing in a hotel corridor in Preston at five in the morning, looking for company. I reckon Phil's a boy who's afraid of the dark. He also happens to be great fun, a natural showman, athlete and the leader of one terrific band.

Lights out . . .

UFO released their twenty-second studio album, A Conspiracy of Stars, in 2015 to universal acclaim. Shit, over forty years of playing heavy metal. Wonder if Phil and Pete are still racing down hotel corridors?

During the late-night interview I discover I saw a friend of Phil's being murdered in Manor House when I was fifteen ...

My own personal song of death and kisses is 'Try A Little Tenderness' by Otis. It's the one I remember most from that hot summer Saturday night in 1968 when I was fifteen and women were goddesses.

There was a schizophrenic club above the Manor House pub at the junction of Green Lanes and Seven Sisters Road. On Friday it was called the Bluesville and showcased some of the hottest blues-rock bands in town, like John Mayall, Chicken Shack, Fleetwood Mac and, best of all, Ten Years After. The punters were hippies and local dudes like me, who loved a fast guitar and a puckered lip. I always wore jeans and a T-shirt and succumbed to the slick chords and heavy-duty four-play.

On Saturday nights the Bluesville slapped on a suit and tie and became the Downbeat, a juicy soul-searcher packed out with skins in mohair and girls you could occasionally dance with when you got a little pissed and Brenton Wood was waiting for the sign. There were also a lot of black guys who occasionally hit the Royal dancehall in Tottenham on a Thursday like drugstore truck driving men and sometimes met the wound-up, woolly-bully white boys head on. Black guys never got drunk. They didn't need booze to fuel their domain. They took the women and song away from the wine – it was their secret. Oh, and the fact that most of them could dance the hind legs off Nureyev.

The Downbeat was a place for a fifteen-year-old boy to grow up, and that night I shot up like fucking Godzilla.

There were three of us. Terry was a sixteen-year-old print apprentice. Being a printer – especially on Fleet Street – in 1968 was a licence to print money and some of them even found time to do the knowledge and become black-cab drivers. Ray was twenty, the son of the caretaker on our estate. He worked for Robert Dyas and was handy for getting the drinks in.

These were the light-and-bitter days at two bob a throw. I had an after-school job cleaning a nearby office block every night. I was flush. My semi-hippie Friday clobber was replaced by the blue mohair three-piece my Dad had bought me. Terry wore a pale green mohair suit and Ray, not a fashion god by any stretch of the imagination, had the suit he wore to work.

After several pints we headed out on the highway to the dance-floor. It was the third time I'd been to the Downbeat on a Saturday night and I'd never danced with anyone. None of us had. We'd stand on the edge of the floor and look at the girls and dream.

But tonight I was determined to walk out of my dreams and into a heart and as 'Hold On I'm Coming' segued gently into Otis Redding's

'Try A Little Tenderness' I took my chance. I entered the void...

Oh, she may be weary...

Would you like to dance?

'OK.'

Them young girls do get wearied . . .

What's your name?

'Mary.'

Wearing the same shabby dress . . .

I've got an aunt called Mary.

'What's your name?'

Barry.

And when she gets wearied . . .

'I've got a boyfriend called Barry.'

Oh.

'Only joking. How old are you?'

Eighteen.

All you've got to do is try a little tenderness . . .

We suddenly kissed. It was my very first and when her tongue searched for mine I nearly fainted. That was the moment I realised I was tongue-tied: the membrane that attached my tongue to my mouth was at the front instead of the back and although I could welcome visitors I couldn't make any house calls. I kept falling at the first, my bottom teeth.

I know she's waiting, just anticipating ...

In the end she gave up.

The thing that you'll never, never, possess, no, no, no . . . Three months later I had the unwanted flesh snipped during a five-day stay at the Royal Free Hospital. I assumed Mary was the only girl to have a slut tongue and I adored her for it. I thought of marriage and kids and a little house on the prairie before realising I was fifteen and in blue. I never saw her again.

As Terry, Ray and I walked out at closing time, down the long, wide flight of stairs that led from the club onto the Seven Sisters Road, I noticed that on either side of each step was a line of white dudes in suits – members of a notorious local mob – each one brandishing a cutthroat razor, each one checking the punters, each one desirous of seeing twisted flesh and internal organs made external on these stairs with stares. I was shitting myself. When I reached the bottom with my bollocks still intact, I asked a guy what was going on. He said it involved strangers and women. Don't they all? Someone asked a girl he shouldn't have to dance. When she refused he got stroppy. It was time to die.

'Who is the guy?' I asked.

'No fucking idea.' He shrugged. 'He's with a couple of mates. I wouldn't want to be in their shoes for all the money in the world.'

I looked back up the stairs at the gamut of flashing blades and I knew what he meant. Suddenly, a guy came hurtling down the stairs and ran out of the door pursued by an army of razors. He managed to jump on the luckiest bus in the world as it sped past down the Seven Sisters Road into infinity. The number 38 saved his life that night.

The boys from the black stuff returned, disconsolately, to the club and waited like clay pigeon shooters for the next target. Sure enough, another guy – the one Phil Mogg knew – came bounding down the stairs. Alas, there was no bus, just a warm breeze and a heartful of soul.

He turned right. Wrong move. He turned right again into a quiet residential street. Really wrong move. About twenty or thirty guys were on his tail. Terry, Ray and I stayed outside the club. I was curious – it was the latent journo in me.

A few minutes later most of the guys strolled back to the club. They looked elated. Their work here was done.

The three of us decided to go and see what had happened. The guy was lying face-up in the gutter. A small crowd began to form and an ambulance pulled up. We stood just a few feet away and he didn't look too bad. I said to Ray he'd had a result as two ambulance men lifted the guy onto a stretcher. Splashes from the impact of his brains spilling out of the back of his head and plopping onto the pavement danced on my blue mohair turn-ups, and Terry fainted. I'd never seen someone so dead.

From that moment on, I knew it was unwise to argue with strange guys in sharp suits with lipstick on their collars, especially on a Saturday night. A few years later Diana Dors took over the club but I never went again.

Couldn't get the splashes out.

 MARCH 1979

The Stranglers, Motorhead, Steve Jones

So the self-styled Queen of Pop, Nina Myskow, and I board a plane for Japan. She's in first, I'm in economy. She works for the *Sun*, I work for myself. She wears red, I wear black. She's a sweetheart, so am I.

The same can't be said of the Stranglers ...

And I tell you what – it's definitely not true what they say about Japanese girls. So tell me more ...

They wait, these Nipponese nymphs, on stations, in airports, in hotel lounges, in the shadows of afternoon corridors, in vain, in rain, armed with heart-shaped chocolates, flowers, love letters, sugar-sweet smiles, bird-wing eyes, all things feminine, for ... the Stranglers.

It could've been any other band, any other full-cream hard-ons in Brylcreemed trousers, any other bunch of matinée idols with false bollocks and painted smiles.

But the Stranglers?

As the band alight from the bullet train onto the platform at Osaka station, they're immediately surrounded by a mob of girls, all manicured giggles and stiletto-heeled admiration, looking as incongruous as dogs on hot tin roofs. Some even wear surgical masks because they have colds and don't want to infect the air around them.

'They don't think of us as idols,' says Jean in the cab on the way to the hotel where another gang of honeydew peaches is waiting to pounce. 'They're really into what the band says. They understand.'

To back up his statement he flashes some letters written in over-formal, shaky English. They'd been thrust into his hands at various points of his journey across Japan by girls anxious to identify with his admiration of the writer Yukio Mishima and to provide a few enlightening anecdotes on the subject of his decapitation after committing suicide, or *seppuku* (sounds like a word game).

Not exactly love letters in the sand.

Osaka is around two hundred miles from Tokyo. It's like a brass rubbing of Birmingham but more curvaceous and sparkly.

It's the second concert into the Stranglers' Japanese tour. The previous night in Fukuoka – many Japanese words sound vaguely obscene – they apparently went down so well they were banned from ever playing there again due to audience overreaction.

Tonight, the barriers in front of the stage again don't prevent the fans rushing down to the front to get close-up and personal with sour-faced Jet, doe-eyed Dave, lustful Hugh and jumping Jacques flash.

After years of heavy metal conditioning by clapped-out, podgy, monolithic dross kings from far across the seas, it's not surprising they find the Stranglers something to write home about. These normally placid people from the valley of the dolls are even starting to spit! What other race would go berserk for an hour, kick stewards in the bollocks, mob the band and then politely bow to each other afterwards as they file out of the hall?

I expected order. I expected rules. I expected the Stranglers to be regarded as a novelty act whose only redeeming factor was Jean's romantic attachment to their country and his cutie-pie smile. But with a kind of indomitable elegance, the fans accept the moribund meat the band relish chewing before their very eyes.

They understand, without understanding a word.

Back in the Osaka hotel basement bar, Jean intimates, in no uncertain terms but with a snappy smile, that he wants a fight. And he wants a fight with Judas Priest, who'd just played a concert of their own and who sit like Madame Tussaud's rejects with their entourage in a corner being ogled by a dozen leopard-skinned groupies.

Jean scrawls, 'Judas Priest R Fucking Women' on the back of a menu and places it on a silver platter held by an unsuspecting waiter who proceeds to deliver the message to the Birmingham metalheads.

No takers.

Jean snaps another smile and leaves. Judas Priest may not have even heard of the Stranglers. The evening culminates in manager Ian Grant insulting a concrete-arsed groupie, tour manager Tom playing tunes loudly on a silver tray and Ian banging nails into the ceiling. None of the band participate in such on-the-road antics. They're parsimonious with their off-stage energy. Apart from Jean's occasional muscle flexing (he does tend to tread on your toes a great deal: I put that down to him being French an' all), they're more inclined to exercise the larynx than the inebriated soul.

I guess that's part of their attraction.

The following day we coach it to Kyoto, the ancient capital awash with Buddhist temples all made entirely of wood and without the merest hint of a nail. Despite the overbearing symbolism that pervades the ornamental parks in which these edifices are set, it's difficult not to snigger when confronted by 'Get your souvenir of Buddha here' signs.

The band pose for the *Sun*'s Queen of Pop outside one temple. Nina's probably still feeling a little freaked out after seeing Jean's balls swinging like church bells in the dressing room the night before when he emerged naked from the shower. Still, he didn't seem to mind.

The venue tonight is Kyoto University. There are holes in the ceiling, holes in the walls, holes in the floors, holes in the hearts, holes in the holes. This black hole of Kyoto is tailor made for the band. No police are allowed on the campus. No chairs are allowed in the main hall. No holes (sic) barred.

But without the barriers and red-jacketed stewards, the element of anarchy is dispelled and it becomes just another gig.

'No, I don't mind Jean getting all the attention at the moment. After all, he makes a prettier cover than me.' Hugh, wearing the tongue-in-cheek sincere look he cultivates so well, pours another beer in his hotel room at the Nagoya Miyako Grand the next day. Initially, he was the Strangler who grabbed the attention but in recent months he's taken a back seat.

'Last year I got pissed off with being pushed into situations. We've had a very depressing time on the business side but things are looking up. Now we are a very successful band and there are a lot of things we have to do. Now I feel I have the time to know what I want to do and what I want to see the Stranglers doing. I haven't got time for the pain.'

There's a knock on the door and the tour manager wanders in with a leather-jacketed boy who looks around eighteen and a slightly older girl. 'You said you wanted to talk to some fans. Here's two.' Hugh leaves.

Aya is a student and has saved up for months just to accompany the band on every gig and he's taken a week off work to do this. Why?

'Because the Stranglers are unique,' he says. 'They sing about our lives and I understand and identify with what they think. Other rock bands sing about love between men and women, they sing about the government. People are afraid to sing about the government, but they're not.'

Ayako Shimizo is twenty-three, works for a bank and lives in the dormitory her company provides for its employees. She has a record player in her room, a boyfriend in LA and a thing about Jean. Or she did have.

'He was my favourite. I liked his playing. I liked his philosophy. I think he is very strong and very manly. More manly than Japanese men. But I was disappointed when I met him because a friend told me he had gone to bed with a Japanese girl while here. I was surprised. I didn't think he would be just another rock star.'

She leaves. Hugh returns and I mention the conversation.

'She's just like anybody else,' he says 'She can't cope with reality. She hasn't sussed out yet that there are no more heroes. You'd have thought the Zen way would have taught them to think otherwise.'

Nagoya lies sixty-seven miles outside Kyoto and is the fourth most populous city in the country.

Before going to the soundcheck, I corner Jean and tell him what Ayako said. He's clearly upset. 'What her friend told her just isn't true. No. We don't behave like rock bands with their idiotic on-the-road antics. I don't want this band to be like any other. The Stranglers are all I've got. No. Shit, man, that's a drag. I didn't expect to hear something like that, something so palpably untrue.'

I mention my chat with Hugh, as Jean slips into his Dr Martens.

'At the beginning I felt Hugh had a lot more going for him than me. He's got a regular place to live. He can concentrate on higher things. I've never had security, just the Stranglers.'

The show that night is a triumph. The stewards are really coming on strong and at one point the band stop playing and direct an accusing finger at a particularly venomous one who's hounded out of the hall.

The crowd's excitement is infectious and turns this into one of the great Stranglers' shows.

Backstage I meet up with Marl Takahashi, a bespectacled twenty-year-old, and the president of the Japanese Stranglers' Information Service. She, too, has been travelling with the band for the duration of the tour.

'At the moment there are seventy members,' she says, 'but I expect that to really increase after all this. The average age is eighteen but we have a few thirty-two-year-old members. We also have a fanzine.

'For me the Stranglers are so different from other bands. They have opinions and they point out all the wrong things in England. Other bands just sing and wear pretty clothes and I'm tired of all that. I know the band look so wild, but after meeting them I know they are gentle. But all the girls that come to the hotel don't understand them. They just want to go to bed with them. I don't. I just want to be their friend. If I went to bed with Jean I wouldn't be his friend any more.'

And you thought the Stranglers were a boys' band.

Despite the obvious temptations, I never fool around at home or away. I sussed out a while back that sex without love was intensely unsatisfactory and not worth the hassle. Hey, but if you're a rock star it's part of the nine-to-five.

Besides, I want to get married one day. I've been going out with Dina pretty solidly for nearly two and a half years. I love her madly but I know she's unsure about me, about the kind of job I do, about the way I live my life. She could hardly be described as a rock chick. She hates receptions, doesn't matter how glitzy, she doesn't bother with most of the music, no matter how good, and she definitely won't dish the dirt with the rest of the girls. It's part of the attraction.

So what am I doing walking down this endless corridor to my room at the Nagoya Miyako Grand holding the hand of a girl called Haroko with oriental sex on my mind?

The foyer had been full of girls when I returned to the hotel with some of the band and their entourage after touring the city's hot spots straight after the gig and meeting some real, live Yakuza in a club full of semi-naked women and malt whisky.

Many of the fans are actually staying at the hotel after booking double rooms months in advance and sneaking in some of their friends to keep costs down without the management's knowledge.

We went to the bar where the girls giggled at tables in corners. At around three am we decided to call it a night and strolled to the elevator followed by a bunch of around eight girls, and we all squeezed in together.

I'd been drinking solidly since 6pm and I was pissed. Really pissed.

And that's why, as the elevator stopped at my floor, I shouted, for a laugh and for the first time in my life, 'Right, who's coming back to my room, then?'

'Yes, please.' Softness is a thing called comfort. Her voice sounded miles away. And then, there she was, suddenly, magically, standing next to me in the corridor as the elevator door closed to the sound of applause from the roadies.

'Hi.'

'Hi.'

'What's your name?'

'Haroko.'

She wore shiny red boots with heels, a shiny red mac over a shiny red mini skirt. Her shiny black Stranglers T-shirt was as shiny as her shiny black lipstick.

Her eyes stretched into infinity and beyond, I was pissed. When she smiled my heart skipped a beat, I was pissed. She was gorgeous, I was pissed.

And now here I am, outside my door, fumbling for the key. I may be pissed but I'm as nervous as hell. What if she thinks I'm Jet Black? After all, we are the only two people with beards in this travelling show, maybe in this entire country. Do I play along?

When we get inside I don't quite know what to do. Does she expect sex or is she just being polite?

Then she starts to cough.

Shit, it's a nasty one. And it's persistent. And it's a bit wet. Knowing my luck, the only time this happens to me I get someone with some weird oriental flu for which there's no known cure for westerners. Why isn't she wearing a surgical mask like everyone else?

I convince myself she's OK. The gallon of sake has distorted my judgement.

'Bad cough,' I say, pointing to my throat, like a fucking jerk.

'Sorry. Very sorry.'

'That's OK.' I tell her I'm feeling tired and indicate by closing my eyes and resting the side of my face on my clasped hands, like a fucking jerk. I point to the bed and start to undress. Like a fucking jerk.

'Would you like to sleep here?' I ask. Like a fucking jerk.

'Yes, please.' She starts to undress and we both get into bed, my pants still firmly intact. We kiss. She coughs. We kiss again. She coughs again. I feel like Benny Hill.

'Sorry. Very sorry.'

'That's OK.' I tentatively touch one of her breasts and immediately feel a lump. She coughs. No! Japanese flu and cancer? Maybe you get the cancer as a result of contracting the flu. Oh my God! Infectious cancer!!! You've got to be fucking kidding me.

Then she starts to cough again. I convince myself she's at death's door and whatever she's got, I've probably got now. I've just signed my own death warrant, and all I did was kiss a Japanese girl in the dark.

I have to get her out of here.

'Are you staying in the hotel?'

'Yes, with some friends.'

'Look, let me take you back to your room. You'll feel more comfortable.'

'Yes, please.'

We both dress and before we leave the room I give her a signed copy of the band's X-Cert live album. She starts to cry. 'Thank you so much. Sorry. Very sorry.'

My heart breaks.

Her friends welcome her, and me, with open arms, and Haroko sniffs, and coughs, as she proudly flashes the signed album and they all go, 'Oooh!'

None of them has a cough.

I'll never ask anyone back to my room again, and even think twice about asking myself.

'It's amazing,'' says the normally diffident Jet Black the following day on the bullet train to Tokyo 'The girls are everywhere. We get off the train and they're there. We go to the hotel and they're there. We go to our rooms and they're waiting outside. Sure, that happens in England – but there it's not girls, it's the fucking police!'

I know what he means, not the police, the girls. It's like being an eighteenth century European sailor in the South Seas greeted by a bevy of lei-bearing beauties with Bali Hai's to die for.

Jet admits he'd rather think than talk. 'I leave all that to Jean and Hugh. If I wasn't an introvert we'd probably be fighting all the time. I'm in the classic drummer mould. When bands try putting the drummer up as a front man they fail.'

Dave Clark Five, Genesis?

'The only thing that gets me annoyed is incompetence when we tour. I've come across people who can't organise a bunk-up in a brothel.'

About the disparity. 'We have all the ingredients for failure. But the pressures, all that we've gone through, have given us a mutual respect for each other. We're all very strong individuals. That's why we've got so much more to offer than anyone else.

'We've been managing ourselves for the last six months, although things on that front are improving. I tell you something – show me a good manager and I'll show you a Martian.'

It's raining in Tokyo. The coruscating skyscrapers are wet yet still they gleam, still the cars are polished, still there are no stains on the pavements, still the women out walking their dogs bend down to sweep the steaming damp turds into polythene bags to deposit in nearby litter bins, still the victims of flu wander around in surgical masks to prevent spreading their kamikaze germs.

Tokyo is straight out of *The Shape of Things to Come*. It's more advanced and consequently more civilised than London or New York or any other major city on earth. Wells envisaged the vertical aspects perfectly. He just didn't latch onto the horizontal aspects of the inhabitants.

The magnificent metropolis of the east is dripping and glistening in the glare of a billion neon lights while the Stranglers prepare for the show. . They're pretty pissed when they find out it's an all-seater tonight at the Korakuen Hall.

'You two keep playing,' Jean says to Jet and Dave in the dressing room, like someone planning to break out of Colditz, 'while Hugh and I jump into the audience and start wrenching up the chairs. If that doesn't get them going, nothing will.'

They did. And they did. Result – the most immaculate Stranglers' show this side of the Nashville.

When you see them perform it live you realise just how underrated *Black and White* is. 'No More Heroes' was merely a stepping-stone, a transition between the singalongastranglers of *Rattus* and the psychopathic delusions that course through the veins of *Black And W*.hite There's death and night and blood in Toytown tonight. And the Woodentops are loving it.

In the band's dressing room I start talking to the very glamorous Kato, who insists she's not a groupie. She's bright and sassy and twenty-one with a bullet and no bra. She taught me *oppai* (tits), *shakuhachi* (blow-job), *senzuri* (wank), *omeko* ('girl's one'), *ochinko* ('boy's one') and *omekoshiyo* (fuck). That's all you really need to know to get by in any language.

'Before they came, Japanese girls thought The Stranglers would rape them,' she tells me. 'See, English bands often make fun of Japanese girls, but this band seem more friendly than most.

'Also, in general, English men have bigger *ochinko*s than Japanese men. It frightens the girls, y'know. They had to make a slightly smaller condom especially for the Japanese market.

'There's no doubt we are hampered by our lack of English. Usually the only thing a Japanese girl can say to a guy in a band is, "Can I come to your room?" That doesn't give you much of a start! And the girls then get very sad because they know the guy will leave shortly.'

When you get right down to it, rock stars are just singing sailors. It's all in the game and many a tear has to fall.

Oh, Kato? I love hearing her pronounce my name – not only is it sexier than a French accent, it also makes me feel kinda important. Kinda big and crisp and tall.

'Yes?'

I just wondered, do Japanese girls wear stockings and suspenders?

'No. They're too uncomfortable.'

I find Haroko sitting outside my hotel-room door when I get back from the gig. She's followed me to Tokyo. I can't believe it.

Then I start to worry that she's some kind of mad stalker. That she'll stab me repeatedly, mercilessly and tomorrow in the Tokyo Daily under the headline 'Coughing Killer Strikes Again', they'll report that Jet Black was found stabbed to death in his hotel room

Fate has decreed that Dina is my last, my everything.

So I tell Haroko she can keep a-knockin, but she can't come in.

Tim and I decide we should use the Stranglers in Japan story as the main feature of our first syndicated column along with record and concert reviews. We do a mass mail-out to every local paper in the country with a covering letter saying they have permission to use this free of charge, then pay twenty-five pounds for each subsequent weekly column.

Lots of papers use the column, but only two agree to pay for a regular supply. Tight bastards. The road to riches is closed for extensive works and won't be opened again for a year. It's back to the bread-and-butter stuff of phoners and phonies.

It's a never-ending story of love, hate and redemption. An orgy of celebrity that demands cynicism. The boy can't help it and it leaks out during a speed-fuelled meeting with Motorhead in their manager's London office ...

Well, first of all there's Lemmy. A couple of protuberances on his face (de rigueur for a heavy metal beast) – or is that a face on a couple of protuberances?. Quo coiffeur (that's long, no-nonsense greasy). Hirsute top lip (curling Zapata moustache currently fashionable among London taxi drivers). Mean look (very effective behind a mike). Hairy chest with medallion (the Greek pose) and leather jacket. Bassist.

Then there's Phil 'Philthy Animal' Taylor – thin eyebrows (sign of a psychopath), narrow, piercing eyes (sign of a psychopath), Sid Vicious barnet (sign of a psychopath), two days' facial growth (sign of lazy psychopath), not so tall as other members of the band (sign of a short psychopath) and leather jacket. Drummer.

And, of course, there's Eddie Clarke – er, no painfully obvious physical characteristics (is this man really a member of Motorhead?) and leather jacket. Guitarist.

These men actually appeared on *Top of the Pops*.

And they are probably the most slagged band of our time. Just a few years ago they were voted the Best Worst Band. They've been ridiculed, accused of having no musical talent and even disliked a bit too. And because of that they now have a single and an album in the charts. Nobody could accuse them of being insidious.

'We're resigned to the fact that we'll never be accepted on a musical level by the critics,' says Lemmy, lounging on the lino of his manager's office in West London. 'All they ever review is our stance. OK, at the beginning it's a laugh, but after a while it becomes both boring and annoying.'

That attitude has recently escalated with the release of their aptly titled second album *Overkill*. *Record Mirror*'s lithe, libidinous Chris Westwood has just been awarded the coveted Motorhead Intellectual Nerd of the Year Trophy. His album review really got to their dandruff.

'He said I should grow up,' Lemmy complains. 'Christ, if I grew any bigger I'd be out of reach! He wasn't constructive at all. It was just one big bitch. Fancy some speed?'

I acquiesce. Hot stuff. In fact, I'm sitting here eating my heart out, baby…

'Yet when we met him he was really nice – drinking our drinks, smoking our fags. Maybe we didn't give him enough.'

'People like that are really beginning to get to me. I seriously think they regard us as three geezers wandering around in leather jackets and gun belts causing mayhem. Well, I regard them as pseudo-intellectuals who lock the world out when they sit behind their little typewriters. I've got a really good wall for them to bang their heads against.'

So we're confronted by two opposing Motorhead schools: (1) the pupils who think the traumatic trio are just another bunch of metal gurus; (2) the pupils who like Motorhead quite a lot.

'Rock'n'roll refused to die and now heavy metal is refusing to die,' says Lemmy, white speck in a nostril hair, white heat in a brain cell.

'I hate that term "heavy metal",' interrupts Phil. 'It immediately conjures up visions of heeled boots, Spandex trousers and demented fools.'

'Right,' says Lemmy. 'I think we're more a molten-metal band.'

A molten-metal band that was just a solid mass four years ago when Lemmy first formed it after leaving Hawkwind. You remember them – unidentified flying objects in Lurex strides. Motorhead number one recorded an album that was never released. Lemmy drafted in two new musicians – Taylor and Clarke – and they've never looked back.

Mind you, they've never looked forward either.

Their first album sold around 50,000 and a single, 'Louie Louie', actually showed in the charts. Grown men were seen to break down and cry when they saw the record at number sixty. And now the new success, which has jettisoned Motorhead into the £45-a-week bracket – each!

But things weren't always rosy. 'We looked like splitting at one point,' says Phil. 'One night, just before a gig, I punched our tour manager on the head and broke my hand. It was over a chick ...'

Lemmy's eyes light up. Not sure if it's a chemical or spiritual reaction. 'Never take chicks with you on the road – they're bad news. Hawkwind were destroyed by chicks.'

'Now we've got a good manager and a great lawyer,' says Lemmy. 'With a combination like that we're impregnable.

'That's the thing about punk. They were all such a bunch of kids. If you don't get yourself organised in this business, people will walk all over you. People had been walking all over us for a long time. What do you do when people hate you? You just keep going. You fight back. You survive. That's why punk was destroyed – it never fought back. Mind you, heroin also helped it along the path to destruction.'

Lemmy and Eddie continue to slag off the use of heroin.

Lemmy: 'Smack has killed three musical movements – first acid rock, then pub rock and now punk. OK, I admit I'm a bit of a speed freak – and I'm afraid I'm influencing the rest of this band – but I'd never touch smack. People who like smack also like Lou Reed and that can't be anything in its favour.'

Eddie: 'I knew a guy who was into needles so much he once stuck an eye dropper into the veins of his wrist and bled to death in a public toilet.'

Lemmy is thirty-three, nurtured on Johnny Kidd and the Pirates, Gene Vincent and those other two tasty trios, Cream and the Jimi Hendrix Experience. He once worked as a roadie for Hendrix. He's a man who lives very much in that Middle Earth world of Trafalgar Square hippies and kimonos. 'I play the kind of music that I'd like to go and watch. There ain't a band in the world that enjoys doing what they do more than us. We're so happy doing what we're being.'

The indomitable Lemmy ensured that Motorhead – minus Taylor and Clarke – continued to record and perform for decades, becoming an institution and even picking up a Grammy in 2005 for Best Metal Performance. He died in December 2015.

Apparently, Lemmy, wasn't terribly enamoured with the intro to the article (unsurprisingly) and tells a colleague that he'll beat the shit out of me if ever our paths cross. I thought he'd laugh at what I considered to be an obvious joke but, in the cold light of print, it may not have come across that way. So it's official – I've turned into a cunt.

But not where Steve Jones is concerned. He's always good for a laugh. Hampstead in the rain smells like the countryside, but there's not much green down Jones Street.

'Yeah, come round to me gaff for a chat. I've moved up to posh ol'

Hampstead now.'

His phone words, still ringing in my ears during the solemn umbrella trudge from the tube station at midday, provide little solace since they have to compete with an insidious shoe squelch due to one tiny sole slit.

His newly acquired flat is on the second floor of a large house. I ring the bell for ten minutes on the main front door. No reply. I ring other bells, hoping someone might deign to answer and let me in out of this interminable wet.

Eventually, a little old woman opens the door. 'You're looking for Mr Jones? To tell you the truth, I don't think he's in, but you can try.' She leads me along a passage and up the kind of staircase you usually find in thirties musicals, full of lipsticky smiles and top hats. 'That's his door.' I knock. No reply. 'Yes, he's definitely out. This happened the other day when a young girl came to see him. And in this weather too.'

I try the flat next door. Another elderly woman answers. 'Mr Jones? No, I didn't hear him leave. I've been asleep all morning. Besides, he's such a nice quiet boy I wouldn't hear him if I was awake.'

'Yes, our Mr Jones is a quiet chap,' says the other. 'I live underneath him and the only sound you can sometimes hear is when he plays his records.'

I leave this distinctly unPistol-like situation cursing the Milky Bar kid but not before bringing in two pints of milk for the first woman. 'If I see him I'll tell him you came. But he's so quiet you don't hear him come in.'

Can I believe my ears?

When I get back to the office I ring him.

'Sorry 'bout that. I had to rush out and there was no way of contacting you. Come round again. I'll definitely be in.'

Take the motor this time. The hole in my shoe just got bigger.

Inside his flat, I take a close look at him. Steve Jones is beginning to look more and more like one of those photographs in the window of a flash barber shop. His hair is remarkably immaculate and enough to make Tom Jones reach for the curling tongs. Two-tone too. His face is chiselled like Burt Lancaster's and beneath the T-shirt he appears to have a Charles-Atlas-was-here physique.

All this, coupled with an indifferent attitude of almost swashbuckling proportions, and you have the Adonis-flavoured chewy pop star. He's as straight as a Yorkie, as interesting as a Topic and as durable as a Kit Kat.

His flat is epic. The lounge is predominantly black with no furniture except a few large cushions and a portable colour TV in one corner. There's even a stage, which maybe fulfils a certain need in those long gaps between his public appearances (although it was installed by the previous owner).

'The flat cost me fourteen grand,' says Steve, as he shows me the rest of the property, which includes a bedroom done out entirely in wickerwork that the handyman did himself. 'And then it cost me another six grand to decorate. It's all I've got in the world now. I ain't got a penny in the bank. Whenever I need any money I just have to go and sell a guitar or something.'

The word 'unfair' immediately springs to mind. The Pistols sell as many records now as when Rotten and Vicious called the tune and teased the media. There seems little doubt that, had they survived intact, the band would have transcended reputation and gone on to become the biggest selling ever, in this country anyway.

The success of 'Something Else' and 'Silly Thing' (best routine Legs and Co. have done in years) reinforces the fact that there are still plenty of people around who refuse to forget.

Unless, of course, you don't remember in the first place.

'It's really strange,' ponders Steve, strumming a guitar he hasn't sold yet. 'There's all these thirteen-year-old punk rockers wandering about who don't even recognise me. They don't know how it all started or why.

'Everything's really changed now. There's no fun any more. People are too straight. All these punk bands are writing songs that mean nothing. The reason rock'n'roll lasted so long was because the songs were great. But what's going down now is rubbish, so the bands don't last five minutes. Some journalist asked me the other day if the Pistols would ever get back together again and I told him I'd never team up with those sods – for a laugh, y'know. He printed it, and I tell you something, that was the only true punk thing I'd read in a paper for a long, long time.'

Fun is a key word in both Steve's vocabulary and lifestyle. It's fun to be a rock star. It's fun to be dubbed a charismatic cockney Casanova. It's fun to be young and curly and popular and twenty-three and to frequent bareback skaters' haunts full of creamy women and write hit songs and appear in movies and... in movies?

'S right. Steve plays a diligent dick in *The Great Rock 'n' Roll Swindle*. You've heard the soundtrack, now wait for the movie when you can: GASP as Sid jumps out of bed in his underpants; SCREAM as he rides a motorbike down the high street ('It was a three-wheeler 'cos Sid couldn't ride a bike'); MOAN as Steve hops into bed with sex queen Mary Millington; LAUGH as Steve is then pursued by Mary's screen husband, piano man Russ Conway; THRILL to Steve as a detective on the trail of Malcolm McLaren; CRY as they all die.

'It's gonna be really funny, although I think Malc is trying to make it all too political. He's rapidly getting away from the point of what he originally set out to do – have a bit of fun and make a few bob.

'Rotten's in a few scenes, like the early days of our gigs, but he didn't want to know about anything else. Irene Handl is also in the film and so's that Shaft-like DJ who does that ad for K-Tel records on the telly. I hear the distributors are queuing up for it. I only hope none of this legal wrangling will prevent the film from being released.'

Steve is convinced that people want to know what it was really like in the good old days of the Pistols. 'They just want to have a laugh, that's all.'

The movie should also reflect that Steve was, and still is, the original punk beast.

'It was me who used to get up to all the bother most of the time. Rotten was always pretty quiet. Funny, I knew he'd slag me off when the band split. Same with Matlock. If he got chucked out, everyone was to blame.'

I've no doubt that Steve could, if guided in that particular direction, hurl abuse at Rotten all day quite happily. But Pistols' in-fighting has become rather monotonous, vapid and documented to tedious length in other publications. Let's just say that Steve preferred Sid.

'He was better than Rotten. I really liked ol' Sid. Naturally I felt sad when he topped himself. It's not every day one of your mates dies. At least he was one rock star who lived up to the "hope I die before I get old" thing. Paul and me were gonna go over and do an album with him after he got nicked to raise some money for lawyers' fees. But the day before we were due to fly out we got the news that he was dead. I was looking forward to working with him again.

'I always knew he wouldn't last. He couldn't help but be in bother all the time. Always up to stupid things like fights and getting cut up when he started getting too flash. And what with the drugs … You could never imagine Sid at forty.'

Can you imagine Steve Jones at forty?

'I suppose I'll live to be a hundred. I look after myself,' he says, while chewing into a chocolate bar taken from a bowl of sweets he keeps in the lounge. 'I don't go around beating people up. I don't take any lethal drugs.'

It's true, he does look the picture of health. He's lost weight over the last months, leaving a pound or two of sunburned fat on Californian beaches.

'I had a great time over there. One night I went to a big party where the Runaways were playing and ended up mingling with loads of film stars like Gregory Peck and Zsa Zsa Gabor.'

Didn't I read that he pulled Miss Gabor? 'Nah – she's too old. I'd like to live in America for a while. They treat rock'n'roll totally different over there. It's much more of a big deal, while here nobody gives a toss. When you play at gigs everything runs so smoothly. Here you always get problems. Like when you travel up north you're never seen again. All that crap you hear about "friendly" northerners. They hate Londoners. Northerners are so thick . . .'

When he's not slagging off northerners, Steve is producing records for ex-Runaway Joan Jett.

'I've just done her new single, "You Don't Own Me", and there's a chance I might go to the States and do an album with her. It would be great to get away. I hate it here. It's all so depressing at times.'

Maybe a spot of, er, permanent female company might help.

'I don't want to live with a bird yet. I enjoy myself too much.'

Fitting enough finale, I s'pose. I think if I'd ever been a rock star, I'd be a bit like Steve Jones.

And old ladies would love me for my silence.

Steve went on to perform with such luminaries as Bob Dylan, Megadeth, Iggy Pop and Adam Ant. He lives in LA – as does John Lydon – where he was a radio DJ for a while, and has played at all the Pistols' comeback shows.

APRIL 1979

Squeeze, Frank Warren, Blondie

In a packed Greenwich pub, I share a few pints with Chris Difford. I always seem to talk to members of Squeeze in packed pubs. And you know something? Neatneatneat. Dat's Squeeze. Sweetsweetsweet. Dat's Squeeze too.

They're the doyens of cartoon-strip situation rock. Each song a two-inch-square excursion into the crazy caper world of big noses, dangling fags, words frozen in blurb balloons and painful domesticity.

Yet at the same time they're as slick as a Sassoon quiff, as succinct as a silicon chip. Squeeze are artifice with substance. Their dexterity is sometimes quite devastating, sometimes only partially successful due to an occasional lapse into Fantasy Land (a trap they have avoided on the new album *Cool For Cats*). But, then, a perfect Squeeze would be intolerable. Imperfection is half the fun.

A year ago the Deptford dickie-bow merchants clocked in with the a hit single, 'Take Me I'm Yours' and clocked out with nothing more than a five o'clock shadow and a few strangled dreams.

A series of indifferent reviews followed, interspersed with downright venomous assaults on the band's capabilities, too easily dismissed as lightweight and shallow. Then there was an album that made about as much impression as a hooker in an old people's home.

'You learn by your mistakes.' Chris Difford, lyricist, singer and guitarist, grips his pint like Steve Austin and raises it above the sticky beer mat. 'After the hit we decided, erroneously in retrospect, to try and break America.'

When Squeeze returned from their Stateside sojourn they found themselves back at cartoon strip square one. 'The press seemed to resent the fact that we'd stayed in America for so long. But I guess the press have never really been on our side. They don't regard us as being hip enough, a Human League or Gang of Four. That's fine by me because we see ourselves in the same bracket as the Faces or the Stones. Just good time rock'n'roll. When we played Hammersmith with the Feelgoods we got an encore. That meant more to me than anything we've done so far. It was more important than a hundred rave reviews in the papers. Christ, we're doing seven nights at Hammersmith with the Tubes. If we get an encore every night I think I'll retire.'

And so to the 'cheeky, schoolboy humour' (an Anne Nightingale *Old Grey Whistle Test* special) of 'Cool For Cats', which, by the way, was doctored by *Top of the Pops*.

'A few minutes before we were due to appear they told us to substitute "blinkin'" for "bleedin'." I was absolutely petrified because

I really didn't want to do it. But really the joke's on them 'cos they haven't sussed yet there are far worse lines in the song – like "Give the dog a bone", for example.'

Chris reckons he got the inspiration for the song while in a boozer, surprise, surprise. 'In the course of an hour if you're on your own having a drink your mind will wander over at least five or six different subjects. That's all "Cats" is, five unrelated images linked by the same phrase.

'We just get fed up with the acceptable structures for songs. Squeeze are influenced to some extent by Kraftwerk and there is a happy medium between the average rock sound and "Showroom Dummies".'

It's arguable that they occasionally went overboard with the dummies on the first album, but *Cool For Cats* is more yer strictly roots beer foam Bensons 33.

'It's a London album. The next one will be European. After all, life is just a railway track – once you've been to Scotland you've got to come back.'

He never said a truer word, although I'd have gone for Newcastle.

Chris's songs are littered with earthy references. 'Round here, women are sometimes called trouts. My songs are simply observations and you find men often refer to women in such terms.'

One thing young Chris thinks about is his ever-increasing folio of songs – around two thousand at the last count. 'I've sent some to Ian Dury because I think he's the best social writer around. I'd love to team up with him because I'm sure we could become the Gilbert and Sullivan of rock and write a new *Threepenny Opera*.'

Squeeze have got a new drive, a new bassist, a new series of cartoons, a new confidence. They've also got a first-class return ticket to Scotland.What more can you ask?

Difford and Tilbrook kept the Squeeze box going until 1999 when they both started to pursue solo careers. In 2007 the pair re-formed Squeeze

– minus Jools Holland and Gilson Lavis – and toured the US. In 2015,
Chris and Glenn released the album Cradle To The Grave.

The *Daily Record* version of that meeting leaves the Squeeze
PR Versa Manos livid. 'Chris is furious because his words were
misconstrued and it shouldn't have appeared like that.' I do appear
to be rubbing interviewees up the wrong way these days. One in
particular hits very hard, causing a landslide that blocks the way to
the biggest money-spinning opportunity of my life. And all thanks to
that Debbie Harry interview nine months ago…

My first, vivid, memory of Frank Warren – or Frankie, as he was
known back in the day – was getting a right-hander from him outside
my flat when we were both five years old. It was my first fight.

It felt more comfortable getting punched close to my front door:
I figured if the fight was going against me, my dad would come out
and break it up and, if not, he'd let it roll for a while before stepping
in. He came out double quick that day. I'd bloodied Frank's nose but
he kicked the shit out of me. My mum gave him a banana and we
shook hands, but from then on we were always on opposite sides.
He ran with the enemy.

I lived on the ground floor of Bevin Court near King's Cross and he
lived up in the sky on the seventh. He had a lovely mum but he was
always such a little bastard – forgive me, Frank. He'd throw other
kids' toys down the chute, tip up games of Monopoly, which we
often played in the stairwells, and generally cause havoc. He always
seemed to be itching for a fight.

He was of very slight build, a little below average in those below-
average days, but he could punch well above his weight. He was
kinda dangerous and I kinda liked that. I had one more fight with
Frank. It was in the street that led down to the flats. I guess we were
about nine. He had hardly grown out of his five-year-old shell but I
was rapidly turning into a tall, tubby kid. I towered over him and it

was a complete mismatch. I knew it but Frank didn't, and he steamed in like a raging bull and really hurt me. After a fierce struggle, my blubber managed to pin him to the ground and I placed both my knees on his outstretched arms.

We stayed like that for seconds, minutes, hours, who knows? My locker no longer contains such secrets. The older boys who had instigated the fight got bored and started wandering off. It must've been hurting Frank because it was really hurting my knees. I think we both wanted to cry but our hearts wouldn't let us. It was the way we were. And then I started to feel deeply ashamed. I didn't want to hurt this person, I grew up with him for fucksake. What was the point of this?

'Whack! 'You bully. Get off him.'

An old woman hit me with her umbrella and pushed me over. 'You're twice as big as him, you bully,' and she whacked me again. I got up quick and ran as fast as my tubby body would let me. I knew what Frank was capable of; I knew what all of us on that estate were capable of and, sure enough, a brick came heading my way. Luckily, his arms must've still been numb because I wasn't caught by the shrapnel as it landed, and for a big, fat kid that was a result.

'You bully.' I've been called a lot of things in my life but those words will always hurt the most. 'You bully.' Me?

That was the last 'straightener' I ever had. I didn't like the look of someone's face contorted with a pain that I was inflicting, someone that I actually, perversely, liked. I also hated getting hurt. But I hated the most being goaded by older boys who wanted to see a fight. We were a pair of prize suckers. Neither of us fell for that again. We were all beasts in baseball boots, but some of us were cleverer than others.

Frank passed his eleven-plus – hardly anyone from our area did that – much to the surprise of one particular parent who actually stopped me in the street and said, 'Can you believe it?'

I could.

By then Frank's family had moved to a nearby estate, Priory Green, but he was still a frequent visitor to our shores, organising football matches between neighbouring estates on concrete playgrounds with walls for goals. He didn't play, he organised. He made it happen. When you can do that at ten, the eleven-plus is a stroll in the park.

It was patently clear that the guy had brains. He shed the 'ie' from the end of his name, ducked and dived like we all did and became very wise very quickly, like some of us did. I'd see Frank around and we'd chat and it was easy, comfortable. He was flash, but in a good, unintentional way. Natural flash. Organic flash. And every time I bumped into him he'd grown appreciably taller, nicer, genuinely interested in what I was doing. As his reputation grew, I felt a sense of pride that a bloke from my flats could achieve worldwide fame doing something that really did come naturally.

Our paths cross on several occasions in 1979, one of which involves probably the most embarrassing Megan moment of my life ...

Frank is starting to make a name for himself as an unlicensed boxing promoter of mainly overweight fighters who beat the shit out of each other at the Rainbow in Finsbury Park. It's great entertainment and the media love it.

I bump into him in Chapel Market and he hands me a pair of tickets for one of the shows. I take Tim and I think he's surprised at the sheer number of spivs in suits that pack out the venue. The fights are more like boxing matches than I'd thought they'd be. Gloves, a ring, rounds, referee, shit, it's boxing. There's a few decent contests but no one suffers any really bad injuries.

When I meet Frank after the show, he's backstage sitting at a desk behind a mountain of cash because it's tickets in advance or at the door and loads of people leave it until the last minute to go. It's all legit and includes the fighters' purses, security payments and other staff and receipts are issued. He's now way out of my league. He's about to embark on his first trip to the States and I try to impress him with a few feeble stories about my travels.

'Do you know Blondie?' he suddenly asks.

I'm delighted. Why, only a few weeks ago I'd spent the night on the town in Manhattan with Blondie, snorting and smoking and scheming. 'Yeah, sure,' I reply, and proceed to relate my chemical soirée – naturally leaving out the bit about the chemicals. I figure Frank wouldn't appreciate that, him being a teetotaller and all.

'Look, I'll be honest,' he says after listening attentively. 'I've got first refusal on Stamford Bridge for a one-day rock concert this summer and I fancy Blondie to headline. Do you reckon you could set up a meet?'

Blondie are the biggest band in town. Their single 'Heart of Glass', released in January, has sold more than they could ever imagine. The band's PR is none other than Alan Edwards.

'No sweat, Frankie.' I instantly regret the 'ie' but he doesn't seem to mind. I tell him I used to be their PR and that they know me really well.

'Well, if this comes off you'll do very well. By the way, do you know the Stranglers too?'

Do I know the Stranglers?

'Well,' Frank continues, 'that Jean-Jacques Burnel would be a fantastic attraction if he stepped into the ring against, say, Lennie McLean. He's got a bit of a reputation of being shit hot at karate, hasn't he? It would be perfect.'

It's true. Jean must have had nearly every Dan in the book, including Desperate. He was as hard as nails yet supremely intelligent – a beguiling combination.

A few weeks later I'm sitting having lunch in a burger bar in Hoxton with Frank, ex-middleweight champion of the world Vic Andretti and, yes, Jean-Jacques Burnel. I originally introduced Frank to Jean at a gig to promote Jean's debut solo album *Euroman Cometh* and I'd driven JJ to the Ringside bar in Hoxton, which is owned by Vic. The unlicensed boxing shows at the Rainbow were making Frank rich and famous. He was becoming a celebrity and I loved it. Of course, JJ going one on one with Lennie McClean was never going to happen, but it's good to talk and the idea did receive some media interest.

Besides, there are bigger fish to fry ...

As I walk home from the Rainbow that night it suddenly dawns on me that this could be my biggest break – switching from observer to controller. A pop promoter with the biggest band in the world. Power, dosh, fame. Everything I'd always wanted, well, since meeting Dina. This was my destiny and I was going to share it with someone who beat the shit out of me when I was five.

I ring Alan the next morning to try to arrange the meeting. Debbie Harry and Chris Stein would be arriving in London in a few weeks. He'd see what he could do. He sounds sceptical but eventually manages to set up a meeting at their hotel, the Montcalm in the West End. Alan always comes through: it's the secret of his success.

It's an unusually warm Sunday morning. The meeting is arranged for noon and Frank picks me up in a smart S-reg something.

This definitely feels right. I lean back in the leather seat and decide I've finally arrived.

Frank and I breeze into the foyer and glide up to the reception desk.

'Room 221,' I say, in a voice brimming with such confidence it surprises me.

The clerk dials the room. 'They'll ring back in a few minutes,' she says, as she replaces the receiver.

We turn to find a seat and bump into Frank Infante from the band.

'Hi, Frank,' I say, like he's my long-lost brother.

He hesitates. 'Oh, yeah, hi.' I'm used to the pretty vacant look from new wave bands. A flicker of recognition crosses his eyes. 'Right, yeah. The other guys are in there having breakfast,' he says, indicating the dining room.

'Great, I'll catch you after I've seen Debbie and Chris,' I say, still confident, still surprised.

'OK.' He shuffles off.

The phone on the desk rings. 'You can go up now,' says the clerk.

Frank is wearing a beige suit and brown tie. He looks the part. I'm in a jacket and jeans. I think we make a cool pair, like Sinatra and

Martin or Starsky and Hutch.

Chris Stein opens the door. He looks like he's been up all night.

'Come through. Debbie will be right in.'

He leads us into an impressive living room and Frank and I sit down on the couch. Debbie walks in. She's wearing a plain white bathrobe and no makeup. She's the biggest pop star in Britain and walks in loveliness like the night across pubescent souls starved of glamour in the aftermath of punk.

But at noon on that particular Sunday, she looks like death warmed-up.

'So what's this all about?' Chris asks.

Frank hits the gas. 'I want Blondie to top the bill at a massive one-day pop extravaganza I'm promoting at Stamford Bridge, the home of Chelsea Football Club. 'Here's the deal. We'll fly the band over on Concorde . . .' I suddenly feel very cool when he says, 'We'll'. Chris and Debbie seem to like the supersonic words he's speaking. They start to listen more intently. This is going well.

'Then we'll---'

The phone rings.

'Excuse me just a moment,' says Chris.

Frank starts to make small-talk with Debbie as Chris picks up the phone.

'He's the guy who did what?' We all turn and look at Chris. He stares at me wide-eyed. After a few moments without saying another word he hangs up.

'That was Clem.' He's talking only to me. 'He says you're the guy who interviewed them in New York a few months back. They didn't like what you wrote about them, man. I haven't read it but I know they were pretty pissed. They're sending a couple of guys up to throw you out.'

He turns to Debbie. 'Shit, I don't know how these guys were allowed up here in the first place. Who arranged this?'

This Montcalm Megan moment is a doozie. Why me?

'Er, I'm sorry about this, Frank,' I say, still in a state of apoplexy and frantically trying to remember what I'd actually written that had caused such consternation.

'Don't worry.' He was taking it nobly.

There's a loud knock at the door.

I fear the worst. Frank and I had fought each other as kids – now we're united against a common foe: Blondie bouncers.

Chris opens the door. There's an exchange of words in the hallway.

He comes back into the room and says the guys outside want a word with me.

I go out. Frank, gratifyingly, watches my back.

A big guy in a black jacket, with the word `Security' emblazoned across the back in large letters the colour of blood, is waiting. His colleague, similarly attired, stands a few feet away.

'Is that guy you're with Frank Warren?' asks the first guy like it was Mick Jagger or Dustin Hoffman. Shit, Frank from my flats is a media celebrity. The boxing shows at the Rainbow are proving to be his stepping stones to fame. He really has caught the public's imagination.

I try to say, 'Yes,' like Al Pacino, but it comes out sounding more like John Inman.

'I thought so,' says the guy. 'Look, we've just been asked by the band to throw you out but I don't want any trouble with you or Mr Warren. I've seen you around at concerts and I know you're kosher. I don't know what it was you wrote about those guys but they're pretty fucked-off. I'll leave it up to you but I think, honestly, it would be better if you left.'

He's a straight-up guy and he's marking my card. And then the two of them turn around and walk away, though I think they were tempted to ask for Frank's autograph.

At that moment I realise I'd never be able to pin Frank's arms to the ground ever again. He's a well-respected man with more influence than I could ever have imagined. I, on the other hand, am a schmuck who still doesn't know what I'd written that had got them all so pissed.

'When we sort this shit out I'll get in touch,' says Chris. Frank and I both know we'd never set eyes on him again. Or each other come to that.

'What the hell did you write?' Frank asks, as we walk through the foyer and out into the April sunshine. We both laugh about it on the way home but we know we are never going make it as Barnum and Bailey. This was my last tango in Paris. From now on I have to set my sights lower.

Much lower.

What the hell I wrote can be found a few pages back. I actually did meet up with Frank over twenty years later. I heard that his mother had passed away. She was an absolute gem, always a smile on her face, always a kind word on her lips. I felt I had to write a letter of condolence to Frank and he replied with a wonderful handwritten letter awash with memories.

We met for lunch, two Finsbury boys with a boxful of chat, and he invited my sons, who were 16 at the time, and I to see Herbie Hide at the London Arena. He was fighting some unknown called Vitali Klitschko. My sons were well impressed when we were ushered into ringside seats and even more impressed by the Goliath proportions of the Ukrainian, up front and personal. The guy was a mountain and Herbie went down in the second round. It was a wonder he lasted that long. After the show, I introduced the boys to Frank who chatted to them for awhile.

'I tell you something,' he said to them as a parting shot, 'Your dad and I had better fights than that one tonight when we were kids.'

MAY 1979

Rush, The Tubes

I arrive at the Newcastle hotel where Rush are hanging out before their second-night concert at the City Hall.

Outside there are a dozen fans jumping in front of anything on wheels to catch a glimpse of the Canadian capers. They've been on ice all day – school's out and this is dole-queue rock, sonny. This is the punter's paradise. This is what mitigates their unconditional surrender to the inevitable grey. This is the early pay cheque, the visit to the movies, the undignified grope in the back row.

Rush and their ilk tamper with their dreams. Epic allusions, day excursions to Parnassus (where the nuts come from), huge diaphanous characters battling for Good in a galaxy far, far away.

Rush's music is an extravagant, electronic enema, complex and facile, gross but with the occasional delectable nuance.

One critic recently condemned the whole operation (and it is nothing less) as fascist. But there's no attempt to indoctrinate. Rush are simply true purveyors of pomp-and-circumstance heavy metal. Three-piece suites are their forte: some may be a little chewy and difficult to digest, but their music is a glorious overkill. In fact, it's a two-hour maim.

Alex Lifeson ('Hey, isn't that Schencker?' asks the air steward, peering over my shoulder as I read a Rush review on the flight from Heathrow to Newcastle) with the glittering Gibson solos, Geddy Lee of the stoned-choirboy voice and multifarious moogs, and drummer Neil Peart.

Neil has just ordered a steak, with sherry trifle to follow, in the hotel restaurant a few hours before the concert. 'It's really difficult to get trifles on the other side of the Atlantic.'

He's Rush's lyricist and was instrumental in changing the band's direction from a bottom-of-the-heap HM a-go-go band to top-flight spectacle when he joined four years ago. Neil, with the Edwardian moustache and Georgian barnet, came to London from Canada in the early Seventies to seek fame and fortune as a musician. After bumming around with a few bands he eventually ended up selling souvenirs in Carnaby Street.

His rock-star ambitions thwarted, Neil returned to Canada and started work with his father, a farm-equipment dealer. He was promoted to parts manager, selling the odd tractor track or combine cog and looked assured of a fairly affluent life in the agricultural world. It was around this time he was approached by Alex and Geddy who were on the lookout for a drummer after the departure of original percussionist John Rutsey.

There then followed a series of albums that showcased Peart's predilection for the myth, the fantasy, the sci-fi scenario, the magic.

They toured Britain early last year to a tumultuous reception. Their last two albums – *A Farewell To Kings* and *Hemispheres* have now gone silver over here and the current tour sold out weeks in advance. Yet their songs have been dismissed as immature and pretentious.

'That's ridiculous,' says Neil. 'I've matured a great deal during my association with Rush and managed to maintain my integrity. I've come to understand a whole new aspect of life which I've never been able to articulate before.'

Hence the 'message' accusations.

'OK, maybe there are messages in the songs. I just write about anything that seems important to me. If I have a "pure" idea to express I'll put it over in grand style to blend in with the structure of the whole thing and to illustrate my point. The songs are specifically aimed at people my own age, twenty-six, and younger.'

Another accusation leveled at Rush is that their songs praise capitalism.

'To make it clear once and for all, I believe totally in personal freedom. As long as I have the choice I don't care. I went through the stage when I was interested in politics but now I'm interested in other, more spiritual, things. Our integrity is not for sale, our art is. It costs us a lot – both financially and personally – to produce our music and we deserve a just reward. We are, first and foremost, a hard-rock band – and the cornerstone of all hard-rock is excitement.'

Neil in a nutshell: he'd like to write a novel if he ever gets the time. He reads voraciously, anything from Agatha Christie to Plato. The

Who were the first band he ever really got into. He has a sweetheart and a child back home and he visits them every fourth week during the tour. He never drinks before a gig and smiles when he talks about anything he considers important.

Then I get this headache.

It thumps through the journey to the Newcastle City Hall of the crimson kings, does a Chinese burn on my brain during the support, devours rational thought during Rush's two-hour set, and totally blinds me in the *après*-gig Rush dressing room. As I crunch a clutch of Anadin, I try to convince Geddy Lee that it wasn't their music that caused it.

Rush leave early and decide to drive through the night to the next concert in Glasgow.

I stagger back to the hotel. No dreams for me that night. No Apollo. No Dionysus. No Xanadu. No mighty oaks or shimmering palaces. Just a world of pain.

Rush went from strength to strength in the Eighties and Nineties. In 1997, Neil's daughter Selena was killed in a car accident and his wife Jacqueline died of cancer ten months later. Neil took off on a motorbike, rode across America and clocked up 55,000 miles. He remarried in 2000 and the band released a new album, Vapor Trails, in 2002. In 2016, Alex Lifeson said the band's 2015 R40 tour was to be their last on such a big scale, after Neil announced he was retiring from touring. To date, Rush have sold more than 40 million records.

Back in New York and I find myself asking the age-old question: what do you want from life? To watch a meretricious show pumped full of more costume changes than Liberace had in his entire career? To enjoy a showroom spectacle as transient as it's torrid? To whistle one song on the way home and wake up the next morning totally devoid of musical memory, just the routines, and the high heels, and the big tits, and the chainsaw, and the bondage?

Or... do ya wanna see some kick-ass rock'n'roll with the occasional embellishment to accentuate rather than drown? Me, I'd rather suck my choc ice while watching the TV Tubes!

Yes, by special request, brought to you at great expense (but not nearly so much as last time – or the time before that), we have the meticulous, the desultory, the alarming Tubes.

The San Franciscan sluggers with the neat line in swashbuckle have now become neophytes in the land of three-minute rock. The Tubes ain't so gross any more. Sure, it was fun while it lasted but they eventually discovered there are more important things to attend to – like making music without the blinding flash of techno-theatre, like making money. So they've stripped the Rococo trimmings from their show.

Now, how do I know this? After all, they don't play their first show of a sell-out British tour until this Friday. Come with me now to the backstage area of the Palladium in New York City where Fee Waybill pulls me to one side. 'Hey, do you know a reporter called Tim Lott?'

'Not personally,' I lie. 'Why?'

'Well,' he says, pounding his right fist onto his left palm, 'if I ever meet him again I won't be responsible for my actions.'

'Why?' Fee's a big guy. He looks a little menacing.

'Because when he did a review of one of our concerts he kept talking about the size of my nose. That's fucking wrong, man. It's not fucking relevant. So, you don't know him?'

'No.' *My* nose nearly grows a foot. Shit, I hope he doesn't find out in the next two days. Could be a little awkward. Gee, these guys are touchy.

Fee is brimful of nervous energy while watching Squeeze win over yet another bunch of fastidious Yanks. 'Great band, huh? I love 'em.' The feeling, I later discover, is mutual. 'Hope you like our show,' he says, continuing to boogie to 'Take Me I'm Yours'.

In the Tubes' dressing room the rest of the band limber up. Drummer Prairie Prince does a tricky little two-step twinkle around the floor, which percussionist Mingo Lewis paces conservatively. Tension around the huge plastic bins packed full of ice and cans of beer.

Out front, that unmistakable US rock-show smell pervades the air – grass. As pungent as fish and chips, as thick as cold porridge. The audience is curious. They've obviously heard of the Tubes' metamorphosis. Would they still cut it in that old cynical, spectacular style? Or would they now simply be another bunch of rock'n'roll rookies looking for somewhere to hang their burnt-out blues?

'Would you please welcome from San Francisco ... THE TOOBS!'

The show spells the end of Fee's alter-ego, Quay Lude, who is finally banished to that great exposed clit in the sky. Oh, it's still over the top, but the big bucks are missing. The technoflash may have gone, but the rock has really set in complete with a Who encore – 'Baba O'Reilly' and 'The Kids Are Alright'.

The show's an unqualified, unequivocal, underarm success.

Cecil B. DeMille has been replaced by John Cassavetes, but it's a change that had to happen.

And that's the point Fee makes in the Tubes' tour bus the next day on the road to Providence, Rhode Island, the submarine capital of the world. 'When we started this US tour we were really apprehensive of blowing it in front of the fans who only came to see the Tubes for their theatre as opposed to their music,' he says – he always looks so innocent with those big eyes and curly hair. 'Granted, we amassed an impressive following because of that – but that wasn't necessarily a following of record-buying fans. Christ, they'd see our show, then go home and build up their movie systems, not buy our albums.

'We'd been doing the show for four years and we were flat broke. Oh, sure, we'd make thousands of dollars on the road – but that was all spent on the show and providing for thirty people in hotels every fucking night. I got fed up with going home after a tour and having to borrow money from friends. I was killing myself. It was time to change. We had to become the new Tubes. We'd created a monster that just kept getting fatter. We had to kill it.

'But it's a lot more than just economics. We're trying to make a career out of this business. Listen, five years down the line I don't want to end up playing in a Bonzo Dog Band. They went on for years – lots of people know their routines, but how many remember their songs?'

Not the Urban Spaceman, baby, that's for sure.

'We decided we had to make people listen to the music, not just get off on the million dancing girls, the elaborate sets and the costumes. We wanted to become a kick-ass rock'n'roll band. The music had been suffering. Weak songs were being reinforced with extreme visuals. It got to be such a headache, thinking of different scenes to match the songs. I was spending more time on changing my costumes than actually singing.'

The initial dates on the tour were, as Fee put it, 'murder'.

'I was dressed in little kid's clothes, which was supposed to signify how I was brought up on TV and never left the set. But unfortunately nobody understood it. So there we were, changing the format of the show after two concerts.'

That night in Providence, the Tubes play an ice-hockey stadium this time without the Who encore because the Rhode Island dossheads thought 'White Punks' was the final song and left.

Silly puckers.

Fee left the Tubes in 1985 but rejoined eight years later to tour Europe and release a few, largely unsuccessful, albums. Vince Welnick committed suicide in 2006 and the following year the remaining members of the Tubes reunited in Phoenix for their induction into the Arizona Music and Entertainment Hall of Fame.

Within five minutes of my getting back home to London the phone rings. It's Tim. 'Can you do a phoner for me? I'm double-booked with Iggy Pop.'

Who is it?

'Your favourite, Billie Jo Spears.'

Throw that blanket on the ground, I think I'm gonna be sick …

By the way, Fee Waybill sends his love. Click.

JUNE 1979

Ronnie Wood, Malcolm McLaren

In Chicago 14,000 Stones fans gather outside the International Amphitheatre, which resembles an obese Roundhouse. Perusing the horde from the back of a cab, I conclude that spotting a Stones fan is a cinch. They always look younger than they really are and they're more fashion-conscious – not a flare in the world – than the average Who/Zep/Deep Purple partisan. They also can't tell the bottom from the top.

Yet there's a subliminal Sixties approach to their fanaticism, their rational exuberance, their walk. If they'd been born twenty years earlier, Liberace would've been the diamond-studded object of their indestructible affection.

But it's not the Stones that these predominantly hirsute resurrectionists have come to see. Well, not all of them. No, it's none other than Ronnie Wood, that desultory epitome of the hackneyed phrase 'good-time rock' who's about to brighten this domed Chicago night with a song in his heart.

Oh, and there's Keith Richards. A mite less lugubrious than Mr Wood but that's just his way. And, of course, there are a few other good-time Charlies in the shape of ex-Small Faces Ian McLagan and Kenney Jones, Weather Report's Stanley Clarke, saxophonist Bobby Keys and Meters drummer Ziggy Modeliste.

This disparate combo answer to the name of the New Barbarians, a title apparently suggested to Ronnie by Neil Young when it looked likely that the man with the bollock-squeezing vocals might join the band as well.

They were hastily assembled to promote a solo Wood album, *Gimme Some Neck*, on a hastily-put-together US tour neatly slotting into a Stones time warp of sunbathing, divorce suits and writing.

The crowd is plagued with 'Willy' rumours: 'Will Jagger play?'; 'Will Stewart show?'; 'Willy?'.

'Who needs guests?' yells Ronnie, at the outset of the show, to dispel all the rumours.

Woody nips around in blue jeans and musketeer shirt like a sub who's just been asked to warm up for an FA Cup Final appearance. He sings, predictably, the whole of *Gimme Some Neck*: the morbid infections of 'Buried Alive', 'FUG Her', 'Lost And Lonely'; the unadulterated optimism of 'Worry No More'; and 'Don't Worry', a suitable inscription for Woody's gravestone. Big cheers.

More cheers for Keith Richards's two contributions – 'Apartment Number Nine' and 'Let's Go Steady'. Biggest cheers for 'Honky Tonk Women' and 'Jumpin' Jack Flash'. Chicago becomes their kind of town. I even see a guy dancing with his wife.

A few hours later I follow the mesmerising scent of music and marijuana through a Milwaukee wood in the dark to a large timber building set in the grounds of the Playboy Country Club. The music, folded into the immobile shadows on the window, is vaguely familiar. I wander up and peer through the glass. The New Barbarians are huddled around an elaborate hi-fi, listening to a tape of their Chicago show like gaunt-faced pathologists slicing up a fresh cadaver.

The post-mortem is complete. All's well in Wood's wood.

'The deciding factor to actually make the album came during the *Some Girls* sessions with the Stones in Paris,' says Ronnie.

He sits cross-legged on a huge red leather sofa in a room off the main lounge where the others are gathered. Blonde London model girlfriend Jo Howard serves the drinks, JD on ice. They've been living together – that's Ron and Jo, not Ron and Jack – in California since Ronnie and his wife Chrissie split, and they have a ten-month-old daughter, Leah.

I feel like I'm 2000 light years from home. At least.

'In between takes, Charlie, Bill and me mucked around with some of my songs and Bill turned round and said, "Do you realize how quickly you could go through these?" And he was right. I laid down all the tracks in just ten days. And so my first solo album in four years was recorded.

'The album and tour have certainly given me a new lease of life. Getting such a bunch of guys together like that was absolutely amazing. Despite all the different managers and record companies involved the project proved to be no trouble at all. Not one single trauma. And what was so flattering was the way they all insisted on playing my songs alone. When the tour started in Toronto, I tended to let the weight fall on their shoulders because I knew they could handle it better than me. But now I understand how to approach the whole thing. It ain't as crazy as I originally thought.'

Ronnie's career with the Stones started back in 1976 after the demise of the Faces. His face popped up on the cover of the *Black and Blue* album, which confirmed he was already a member. Many argue that he hauled them out of an artistic quagmire and gave them the shot in the arm they desperately needed. 'I've always felt well at home in the Stones. After all, they always were my favourite band ... always. I've been able to do my own thing in the band. Mick and Keith will always listen to a song I've written which I think might be suitable for the band.

'So many people think the Stones' approach to everything is simple and direct. What they don't realise is in that simplicity there are so many subtleties that you've got to be on top all the time otherwise you're bound to get caught. It's not that I've helped to liven the Stones up – it's that they've helped to liven me up. There's such a tremendous democratic framework within the band. Everyone is encouraged to do what they want.'

How did they react to him doing a solo album?

'They were great,' he says, a fag in his mouth, a glass of bourbon in his hand, a one-way ticket to cloud nine in the back pocket of his jeans. 'It's really funny. Every time Mick sees me with a fag in my mouth he rushes up and grabs it, saying I'll ruin my voice if I don't stop smoking. He also says I should cut down on the ol' Jack Daniel's ... but what can a poor boy do?

'Besides, Mick would love to do a solo album himself – he's definitely got it in him – and he's also got more than enough material. And Keith is getting closer and closer to doing just that. He's written some incredible stuff recently.'

How is Ronnie coping with being a front man for a change?

'Now that took some working out. See, when you've been playing with people like Mick and Rod for years you tend to let them take the limelight. Hell, they're naturals so they're gonna take it anyway. But now I'm gradually coming to terms with it myself. I now know all the things they go through – and it's real hard.'

A-ha! An ego is born.

'Nah, I'm no egotist. I've lived with too many to be one. I guess that's why I like to show off a lot on stage – I know it don't mean anything. I could have done solo tours years ago but by now my force would've been spent and I'd just be existing. I've done it in the right way. All I've ever wanted to do is give value for money – giving just me is self-indulgent. That's why it's great to be surrounded by guys who are incredible talents in their own right. It takes you down a peg or two and you've got to come back smiling. I think the tour affected everyone like that. Keith was giving things that people could never imagine. And I broke my balls to get it right.'

Why does he think he's been dubbed rock's Mr Nice Guy?

'Dunno. Maybe it's 'cos I don't bullshit unless it's absolutely necessary. A lot of people I play with happen to be really famous and it can sound very flash when you talk about them. But it's just the same as anyone talking about their mates. It's perfectly natural. Like the other night Bob Dylan popped around my house for tea. It was on the eve of the US tour and he was checking up on me. He wasn't sure whether I'd go through with it.

'I love living on the West Coast. I like to stick my roots down wherever I am. My family lived in the same house for over twenty years, and when we moved it was just 150 yards down the road.'

He attended Ealing Art College and is an accomplished artist –

he did all the artwork on his album, which includes a brilliant self-portrait. Why didn't he bring the album out much earlier, when it had been knocking around for such a long time?

'I didn't want it to surface until it felt right. I could never have done all this eighteen months ago. It takes a certain approach – it helps if you're a little crazy – and right now I can enjoy it. I believe that's the key to lasting in this business. The Stones' longevity is down to that – approaching the right thing in the right way at the right time. That, plus the way they live. It's always been five guys and five women who are very close at all times.'

Moot point.

'They've learned to search out what's gonna be the next fashion and ride with it – very often they set the fashion themselves. And they've also got the ability to suss out anyone who's gonna try and put the spoke in.

'Would you like to meet Keith?' he suddenly asks.

Does a bear shit in the Ronnie, sorry, woods? 'Er, yes, that would be good.'

'Keith's a bit nervous about hanging with journalists after that bust in Toronto. But I don't think we'll have any problem with you.'

Try saying that to Lemmy and Chris Difford. I follow Ron through to the lounge where Keith Richards, Ian McLagan, Kenney Jones, Stanley Clarke, Bobby Keys and Ziggy Modeliste are seated on chairs or the shag-pile carpet drinking Jack Daniel's, laughing, being rock stars, smoking cigars.

The smell of dope is intoxicating and that night I snort the best coke this side of Colombia. The Jack Daniel's is premium and the grass is something else. I kinda pity people like Keith Richards. Nights such as these are customary for rock gods. For them, it's like watching *Coronation Street*. For me, it's like watching *Close Encounters of the Third Kind*. When the sun rises it's time to go.

Ron Wood still performs with the Stones and was for a while known to have a predilection for twenty-year-old Russian gals.

There's a certain person not unconnected with IPC Magazines that Alf Martin of *Record Mirror* has some sort of history with, so when Alf finds out that one of the publisher's mags, *Melody Maker*, is planning a big relaunch with an exclusive Malcolm McLaren interview as the star attraction, he has a discreet word with me. 'Can you track down McLaren and get an interview?' He was looking for a spoiler, a newspaper term for upstaging a rival by getting an exclusive on their exclusive. I have two weeks. Philip Marlowe for a fortnight.

It's a tough ask. I don't know Malcolm like I know the Pistols. Managers don't figure much in my life, probably because of my short-lived PR stint. Malcolm kinda passed me by. I talked to him backstage a few times and at the odd reception but that was about it.

I make a million phone calls. I hang around near his Glitterbest offices off Oxford Street. I go to his favourite bars and clubs. I ask Steve Jones when I bump into him at the Speakeasy. 'Never know where the fucker is. He can be hard to get hold of if he doesn't want to be got hold of, y'know what I mean?'

I do now. It's impossible to locate him. He obviously doesn't want to be got hold by me, that's for sure.

Then one fine day, spoiler deadline looming, in desperation I ring the office number a final time and Malcolm answers.

'Well, I'll say this for you,' he says. 'You're tenacious. Let's meet up.' He must know the score. He must know the *Melody Maker* relaunch hinges almost entirely on him. He must. What a smooth operator...

We arrange to meet at a Covent Garden wine bar for lunch on *Record Mirror*. Bet he doesn't show.

He does. Three hours later I have my shorthand spoiler. I split the interview into two parts and Alf splashes the first with Malcolm on the cover the week before the *Melody Maker* relaunch hits the shelves and that week we don't need to splash the final part – it's just a spread inside. That's so last week's thing. Cool, huh?

Regrets? He's had a few – but then again, too few to mention at this stage of the game. And it is a game, never doubt that.

Now, Malcolm McLaren sits in the corner of a Covent Garden wine bar eating duck, out of luck, doesn't give a fuck. He's only too willing to discuss motives, coups, idiosyncrasies, top hats and tales. Well, what else is there to do on a rainy Monday in London when you're used to perfumey Paris?

That's where his makeshift home is at the moment. But he's not there to sip coffee in the Champs-Élysées and watch the girls go by. Too unproductive for a man like McLaren. No, he's now involved in the lucrative European porn business. 'The continent has a fabulous porno film market – but they just don't make them for younger people. I want to make them with good music, good stories. They'll love 'em.'

I'm sure the kids will love anything this five-and-dime-store hero can come up with. He met a bunch in London recently. 'I expected them to slag me off. Instead they asked, "What's next, Malcolm? What are you going to do now?" I gave them something at the end of the day. They knew Johnny Rotten was simply an idea, an idea that gave them the excuse to leave their jobs and have an adventure instead of carrying on and playing safe. That's what they're grateful for.'

Gratitude is probably the last thing McLaren thought he would get when he set out on the road to ignominy three years ago with the Sex Pistols, those pig-swill idolatry bashers. It wasn't gratitude this red-haired conjuror sought. It was, he shamelessly admits, greenbacks.

'I set out,' he smiles and wipes some orange sauce from his mouth, 'to swindle the rock-and-roll industry out of one million pounds. I failed. It was just nine hundred and fifty grand.'

But wait. That wasn't all he was after. 'And I wanted to cause chaos. Cash from chaos. I use a word which the British have always found distasteful – exploitation. I wanted to make the show-business world cry. I really took that word "exploit" and bloody well pumped it dry, using it in any shape or form without mercy. I'm ruthless like that.' He orders a pot of tea. 'Every time I came up with the germ of an idea, the industry shook. I created a lot of problems both economically and philosophically. At the end of the day, I made the audience more important than the act and for that I will never be forgiven.

'I replaced the star with the image – and that was the Sex Pistols. I always made absolutely sure that the band would never be stars. When Johnny Rotten took it upon himself to be one I threw him out. And when Glen Matlock left I brought in Sid Vicious simply to procure more money.'

Well, it wasn't for his musical abilities, that's for sure.

Apparently our hero knew his cheapskate chimeras would never sell that many records. 'Out of all the money we made, only about £150,000 was profits from records. Most of the money was obtained by fabulous advances that I secured from companies at the moment of signing. By the time we brought out "God Save The Queen", which I reckon only sold about 40,000 copies worldwide, we were the number-one band. We were the great talking point, an attitude, an image. But we were never a band. Oh, there were a few cute songs like "Anarchy" and "Queen". But they weren't important. We were the fabulous symbol of ruin, of no future. The "Destroy" T-shirts I had in my shop sold like hot cakes – 50,000 in the UK alone.

'I know it's been suggested that I'm the big conman of the world. Well, let me tell you, I feel very proud to be called that. My hero is the man who "sold" the Eiffel Tower to a fool.

'I'm not a liberal. I love extremity. Most people want you to tear down things. They want you to be shocking. They don't want you to be seen shaking hands with Sir John Reid – they want to see you throw a pie in his face. They don't care if a band can play. They want to know it can't but that it's still up there, on top of that steeple, shaking music by the neck. I never allowed the Pistols to think they were good. I prevented them from becoming stars . . .'

Recently McLaren was successfully sued by John Lydon and reckons he had to pay out around £60,000 in legal costs. 'I was warned six months before the case that it would happen, but I just carried on regardless and was so ill-prepared when it arrived that I created my own burial.'

He says he can't discuss certain subjects involved in the case for legal reasons. 'I could be held in contempt of court but I don't care. I'll never go behind bars for anyone. My companies – Glitterbest and Matrixbest – are now in the hands of the receiver and my shops have been closed down. I haven't got much money left. There's some in Brazil and some in the States.'

So what happened to the proceeds from his great 'swindle'?

'I spent it all on a few hot dinners, a few plane rides, and generally having a good time. It was a shame it couldn't continue, but I suppose I had to get found out in the end.'

He attributes part of the blame for his downfall on the movie, *The Great Rock'n'roll Swindle*, the bowel-movement account of the Pistols' history. In the film McLaren tells, in a series of easy lessons, how you can swindle the music business. Examples – 'Don't play, don't give the game away' and 'Always remain a mystery.'

He says he put a lot of time and money into the project and is disappointed with the result. 'It's like a half-baked *Hard Day's Night* and all I could do to disassociate myself from it was to get my name taken off the credits.'

He sips his tea sedately and smokes profusely. His laugh is both frequent and infectious and promotes curious stares from other tables for the duration of his recital.

The movie should be released in a month or so and will no doubt raise a few eyebrows and incite deer to commit acts of atrocity since their patron saint Bambi gets topped by either a hippie (never trust them) or the Pistols, it's hard to make out which.

'I was concerned with getting money for nothing,' says McLaren, as he orders a second pot of tea. 'I'm just a good salesman, a clothes salesman.'

True, very true. But there is a little more to our silver-tongued Svengali than that. What follows is his own account of his picaresque adventures before embarking on 'The Swindle'. Of course, it may or may not be true – but I can assure you it's fun to read . . .

'I was born into a wealthy Jewish diamond-dealing family and brought up in a rambling Victorian mansion in Clissold Park, Islington. My second cousin is Danny Kaye and I believe the spectacularly ugly Marjorie Proops is some kind of niece of mine. Anyway, she was brought up in the same house. My grandmother was extremely middle-class. She taught me a lot and told me wonderful stories about how she used to sell fake diamonds to pawnbrokers and how she and Agatha Christie were the greatest of friends. My mother was man-mad and my father, whom I hardly ever saw, was involved in the second-hand car business. I haven't seen my mother for twelve years. Last time I heard she had suffered a heart attack. I never did care much about family ties.'

The family eventually moved to Hendon and McLaren remembers cleaning Bob Monkhouse's car because he lived in the house opposite. 'At the age of thirteen I was a real West-Ender. I used to go to a club where lesbians would copulate on brass bedsteads. My mother was a snob so she insisted that my first job should be a wine-taster. I became a real expert and they asked me to go to Portugal. But I didn't fancy that so I left.

'I then went from job to job *à la* Brook Street Bureau and finally ended up working for an accountancy firm in Devonshire Street, W1, a few doors away from Stephen Ward during the Christine Keeler affair. The milkman used to tell me about the goings-on he often saw.'

There followed a short stint at Fyfe's bananas where he booked people into cabins on their cargo lines.

'Then my mother decided it was time for me to learn French so she packed me off to Cannes. Upon my return I entered an art college and got involved in graphic design. I started hanging around with beatniks in coffee bars and stayed out all night on one occasion. There was a blazing row when I got home so I left. I was seventeen.'

For the next six years he attended a succession of art colleges all over the country. 'I used to obtain grants under different names. I even married a French Turk when I was twenty for fifty pounds to enable her to stay in Britain. I found myself working in galleries with people like John Lennon and Yoko Ono.

'I got involved with the French riots of '68 and helped create a huge festival when I was at Goldsmiths College in London during the week of Brian Jones's death.'

It transpires that McLaren 'gave up' listening to rock music between 1964 and 1976. 'I knew everything there was to know about rock'n'roll between '58 and '64. People like Eddie Cochran, Gene Vincent, they were the ones. The Fifties was one of the most anarchistic decades in history. But then the industry took control and throughout the Sixties and early Seventies music meant nothing.'

The day the music died for him was when the Beatles arrived on the scene. 'They were the worst thing that ever happened to rock'n'roll. All that nice-boy-from-an-industrial-wasteland nonsense. In fact, when the Pistols started being compared to the Beatles in terms of their importance their days were numbered. The Pistols' nearest equivalent was the anarchistic Fifties, not the lukewarm Sixties.'

He had built up a collection of over five thousand rock'n'roll singles and they were his only contact with music. 'But then I thought it time to pick up on the music I'd refused to listen to. I used to go around stalls in the markets listening to things like Velvet Underground. It was awful.

'Then I went to see the movie *Woodstock* and I started to realise there was a rock'n'roll revival in the air. I thought the time was ripe to create an oasis in this hippie desert. I would walk down the Kings Road looking very Elvis Presleyish and one day I was grabbed by a guy who ran the Paradise Garage. We started selling Fifties clothes and I would bring my records to the shop to provide the right background music. I started getting acquainted with the new rockers, the Rod Stewarts, the Faces. I did all the clothes for the David Essex movie *That'll Be the Day* and then the shop really caught on. Even Lionel Blair came in one day to buy a drape suite.'

He was now aware that he was in on something big. 'My ideas were strong – but they were also revivalist. I decided it was no good being retro. I had to get the feeling of the day. So I started the Sex shop. It was so obvious. There were all these designers trying to make people look sexy. All I had to do was take the crudest points of this – like tight black plastic trousers, bondage gear and so on – and adopt sex as an attitude. I needed the music, though. I needed vulgar music. Oh, sure, there were some fairly interesting things around at that time, like Iggy Pop, but it still wasn't right. So I split to New York and managed the New York Dolls for six months.'

When he came back to London he was still searching for the 'right' sound. 'I had all these kids in my shop who looked Bowieish and Ferryish, but they really didn't want to be either. Then Steve Jones and Paul Cook walked in one day ...

'I used the expertise I had obtained from working in the shop to create this band. They didn't possess much musical ability, but I realised that didn't matter. It was simply a question of selling an attitude in as hard a way as possible. I thought it must be better to make a success out of a group who couldn't play rather than a group that could – and I did.'

Er, isn't that a little callous? I venture, as he lifts his fourth cup of tea. He casually places it back in the saucer without taking a sip.

'But I am callous,' he assures me. 'It's my job to be callous. I don't set myself up to be portrayed as a nice guy. In fact, I much prefer to be portrayed as a gangster. I don't want to be associated with the Mick Jaggers and the Rod Stewarts of the world. They're another kind of gangster – the gangsters of love. They take love away; I leave it where it is. I'm more money-orientated. Those people are the music business.'

I tap my crème brûlée. It has a hard surface with a soft, creamy interior. I wonder if the soul across the table is simply a human crème brûlée.

Malcolm?

'Yes.'

Are you ... No, it doesn't matter. We sit awhile in silence. So, now he's told me his motives, though I have a sneaking suspicion that he's devoid of such artifice. Maybe it was purely a game, y'know, the one I mentioned at the start. Some he wins, some he loses. He doesn't like losing: that's why he's now talking so freely. Losing sixty grand would leave me very bitter.

And he's also told me his life story. Now seems the appropriate time for his views on one Sidney Vicious, punk of this parish, deceased.

'I wanted to make him a star.'

But you just said that you'd prevented the Pistols from becoming such animals.

'Ah, but that was before I realised people wanted a star. And the last star they wanted was Sid – that's why I would have made him the biggest star of them all. He would have been number one now, had he lived. Let's face it, he had one of the best rock'n'roll voices in years. He had the right attitude, plus the one basic self-destruct ingredient to make him the tops – he never, ever saw a red light. Only green. He would do anything, anywhere, anytime.

'Do you know the song I was going to let him sing –"Mack The Knife"? See, all the songs have been written. It doesn't matter anymore about writing. Just take the culture by its throat, like we did with "My Way". He could have competed with Johnny Mathis, Frank Sinatra, Tom Jones, all of them. I wanted to take him to Las Vegas, to let him perform in the nightclubs. But he missed the boat and so did I. I was very upset when he died. Sid was the one to be the star and he was the ideal person for me to abuse. I suppose I was partly responsible for his death. I wish I could've been there. He wouldn't have died if I'd been around. The man had to go and that was what he was destined for.

'He wanted to be accepted. He loved the razzmatazz of show business. That's why Rotten hated him. The Pistols were the ultimate showbiz group. After Sid died I tried to promote him as being *the* Sex Pistol.'

Wasn't it a big mistake to head for the States with the band?

'Of course. I was against it. I wanted them to go to Leningrad.'

East meets West with McLaren as mediator.

'It's a question of knowing what you're doing. Sometimes you work on your gut reaction, sometimes your intellect. Most times I'm able to combine the two and that's why I'm successful. I can make money,' contradiction time, 'but it never really bothers me. Oh, it does now because I don't have very much. When you're riding on the crest of a wave like I was you get to know when to seize the moment and take the initiative. Like making a record with a fifty-year-old ex-train robber.'

Are you immoral?

'Johnny Rotten was a good Catholic boy who didn't have the immorality that I possess. He had this silly idea about honour. Kids don't want to be honourable. They want to be destructive and fabulously immoral and at the same time they want to be exploited or to exploit. If they don't have the expertise for the latter they take the first choice. That's why they get onto a stage. That's a tremendous sexual release and an alleviation of all that they've lived through for the past sixteen years.

'One of the Sex Pistols' great contributions was getting rid of the music. Kids got more interested in reading about them going up the Amazon with a train robber than sitting in their bedrooms listening to bland old music. It added adventure to their lives. It stimulated them on their way to work.

'Oh, how I hate all these abominable groups. How I hate all these silly little record labels like Rough Trade. How I hate Rock Against Racism. Who cares? It just makes people join silly little armies.

'Do you know something? More hippies listen to punk now. They're the ones who buy the records. The actual punks are still on the streets, the nearest thing to the Dickensian image of the urchin. You don't see them in the shops buying Human League records – but you do see the hippies. It gets less exciting every day. It's a good job the audience jump up on stage and try to strangle Jimmy Pursey. They should try and destroy such silly people.

'I'm convinced the kids don't want that. The record industry is dying, it's not important any more. The 1980s will be the decade of the painter. There will be a big visual explosion – that's why records are appearing in a variety of colours now. If a kid can pick up a guitar he can just as easily pick up a tin of paint.

'OK, I shot my bolt, but I'm proud of it. As far as I'm concerned there is a fantastic excitement in Europe, excluding England. All those kids on the streets in France, Spain and Italy want to share in that attitude – maybe I can find a niche. The kids are bored. They don't care about these singers. They would enjoy going to a fashion show and seeing dancers with music providing just a background. They don't care who's up on that stage. Look at Ian Dury's new album – punk *à la* Weather Report. It's wallpaper music.

'People in the record industry are useless. They're only interested in pinewood furniture and getting Jimmy Pursey on the golf course. It's all so cosily liberal. That's why they hate me. I hit them where it hurts.'

So, what projects loom on the horizon?

'I'm thinking of doing a TV film on the history of Oxford Street set around child thieves through the ages. They're all in search of their mother and they find her in the end – a fabulous Faginesque character carrying twenty-five handbags. And I'd love to open a music-hall style club where the music itself would be demoted to the toilet. Kids can tune in to what they want down there while upstairs they're busy telling each other jokes and performing in front of audiences made up of themselves.'

Malcolm McLaren, punk's most famous iconoclast, has a recurring nightmare: 'I keep seeing these huge Edwin Shirley trucks going up and down the M1. Up and down, up and down, up and down.

'Who needs it?'

JULY 1979

Wayne Fontana, Gerry Rafferty, Queen

Up in my old stomping ground, Modern Publicity's Covent Garden office, I sit with Gerry Marsden and a very bald Wayne Fontana: they're promoting the Liverpool Explosion tour featuring Gerry and the Pacemakers, the Merseybeats, the Swinging Blue Jeans, the Searchers and Dave Berry.

Wayne wanted to get something off his chest. 'I became an alcoholic and everything between 1965 and 1973 is a blur. I'd disappear after a show and go on mammoth binges, drinking three bottles of brandy a day,' says the man who once fronted the Mindbenders when the band contained Eric Stewart of 10cc fame. 'Finally my stomach caved in and I had to have eight pints of blood pumped into me. I never touched a drop after that. Then I got made bankrupt, and then divorced my wife.'

Yes, yes, Wayne. But apart from all that, are you happy?

These days, it seems that if I'm not trawling across America I'm in London pubs talking to pop stars like Gerry Rafferty who appears to suffer from the same malaise endemic amongst the pot luck parvenus of the music world – presspox.

He's liable to be afflicted by this particularly virulent disease whenever a specific strain of the bacteria happens to be in the immediate vicinity.

He refuses to employ the services of a manager for reasons which will become apparent; he's articulate and far from being mysterious. Nevertheless, he's still an acute sufferer and only dares confront the germs when absolutely necessary – such as promoting a new album for example.

And his new album is 'Light Ale' ... oops, my mistake. He's drinking that in the West End bar but talking about *Night Owl*. So naturally I take the opportunity to ask him why he avoids the press like the plague.

'Many journalists try to be creative in their own right when they describe an interview. They want to come across as being terribly hip and bright. They're thinking maybe of writing a book so they want to be taken extremely seriously.'

This is starting to hit very close to home.

'And then they start to include material from previous interviews which gets a little distorted. If that trend continues for, say, three years, then an article which contains quotes by a particular artist may only be 60 per cent true.'

Grudgingly, I admit he has a point.

'Besides, I think it's terribly boring to say in interviews what colour socks I'm wearing or where I had dinner.' He's talking metaphorically, of course, because I know for a fact his socks on this occasion are black and he had dinner in the restaurant opposite the pub. 'I make music for a living – that's what's important. I won't talk about my personal affairs simply because I feel that's my business and nobody else's.'

But are you happy, Gerry?

'Everyone strives to be, in the way that everyone strives to have good relationships. It's easy to look back and say 'I was happy then' when in fact I probably wasn't. I have no pressing problems at the moment ... maybe that's the definition of happiness.' He wipes some beer foam from the top of his mouth

'People who make music for a living, who choose to make music as opposed to working in an office or factory, are happy to perform anywhere, even if it's in the local. When you're out of the public eye everyone thinks you're living this life of misery.

'During those three years I took off after the problems with Stealers Wheel, I had a pretty good time. During my first five years in the business I was away most of the time, away from my family. When there was no pressure on me from various sources, when I was doing the things that please me, I got to know my wife and daughter.

'A woman who marries a musician is like a woman who marries a sailor. It takes a special kind of person; you have to have a lot of feeling for each other at the end of the day. I knew I was lucky in that respect.'

Gerry's past has been well documented. To recap: born in Paisley of Irish father and Scottish mother 32 years ago. Stint with Billy Connolly in the Humblebums touring Scottish folk clubs. Stint with Stealers' Wheel of 'Stuck In The Middle With You' fame. Managerial problems.

Three years exile. Rebirth with *City To City* album and 'Baker Street'. A series of those 'disenchantment with the music biz' style interviews. And now, *Night Owl*.

In the light of the incredible success of *City To City* – it's sold over four million worldwide mainly on the back of 'Baker Street' – does he play safe with the new album? His rotund face, recently clean shaven, which adds a third circle to his already circular appearance (the other two being his glasses), spins as he meticulously places his pint on the beer mat.

'I obviously felt more confident when writing the songs for *Night Owl* and consequently I think they are a lot more positive. Much of the stuff I've done in the past has been too negative. I actually sing better than I've ever done before.'

Rafferty exudes confidence, a fact which manifests itself in his attitude to The Business. He refuses to enlist the aid of a manager due to a well cultivated acerbity which he has watered heavily over the years. The demise of Stealers' Wheel was due mainly to management tactics which Rafferty despised.

'I still feel the same as I always did – and now for the first time in my life I'm actually making some money out of music, all off my own bat without help from anybody. I vowed I would never have a manager and that attitude will never change. I just don't believe in them. Oh sure, they can help you in the early stages of your career, but I'm 32 now. I've been through a few in my time and I'm too long in the tooth to get one now.

'I employ a lawyer to negotiate contracts for me and a personal assistant to deal with the day to day running of my affairs. That's all I need. I don't want anybody taking decisions for me. In the past when people have done that they've been wrong.

'I don't want some mouthpiece of a manager squawking on my behalf to protect my interests.'

But by adopting such a policy, isn't he in danger of turning into the very thing he hates?

'If that was the case I'd have taken up maths at school – I was pretty good – and become a businessman. The fact of the matter is any artist who sells records in large quantities can't avoid being involved in the non-creative side of the industry.

'I'm a product of my environment and I manage to use it in whatever way I can in terms of my success and attitude,' he says. He cuts the interview short when I start to press him for details about his newly acquired house in Kent.

"It's nothing really, just a Nissen hut," he says, clearly displaying all the symptoms of presspox.

Rafferty never again hit the dizzy heights of 'Baker Street'. His final album, Another World, was released through his website in 2000. In 2008 it was reported he was asked to leave a London hotel after guests complained of his strange behaviour; shortly afterwards he checked himself into a hospital for treatment of a chronic liver condition. He died in January 2011 aged 63.

Queen are among the elite number of bands universally despised by the rock press. And the feeling is, make no mistake, mutual. When you've been on the receiving end of a stream of vitriol at the outset of your career and watched it being carefully cultivated over the next six years, you're bound to retaliate.

Queen's hatred manifests itself in their continued habit of ignoring the music press. There's the occasional token chat, as pointless as it's innocuous, but in the main requests for interviews receive a blanket, 'No.'

One of the last interviews Freddie Mercury gave was the final nail in the Perspex coffin. Under a headline that boldly asked, 'Is This Man A Prat?', the king of the leotards was demolished by one of the old-school Queen-haters and Freddie obviously came to the conclusion that interviews in future would be superfluous because he was popular enough already. It just wasn't worth the hurt.

The curtain, velvet naturally, closed. I'm intrigued.

So I drive down to Roger Taylor's very big house in the country for a chat about Freddie Mercury's balls. In fact, Roger's home is so large that when I go to the toilet I get lost. As I searched around for the door to the lounge, from which I emerged seemingly hours ago, I walk past open French windows in an endless hallway and glimpse two people playing tennis in one of the courts outside – Freddie Mercury and Brian May. Freddie waves and I wave back, and that's the closest I ever get to the guy. They may have released more than their fair share of duffers, but Queen cream is creamier than anyone else's. It's an honour to get a royal wave from the greatest showman of them all.

But when Roger saw Freddie pirouette across the stage with the Royal Ballet in a skin-tight leotard and looking for all the world like the Fonteyn of youth, he had to admit Freddie had a lot of balls.

'I was more nervous than he was,' says Roger, who's not the biggest ballet fan in the world. 'I mean, I wouldn't do it. That's just not me. But I'd like to see anyone else have the courage to do that – and carry it off as well as he did. He had a lot of bottle' (literally!) 'to go on that stage. He loves all that stuff.'

And as Freddie delighted the dickie-bow darlings with his well-developed *pas de deux* and distributed his evident terpsichorean talents liberally around the theatre, young Roger lent a hyper-critical ear to the music – orchestral versions of 'Bohemian Rhapsody' and 'Crazy Little Thing Called Love'.

He wasn't impressed. 'It was awful. Badly played, under-rehearsed, they couldn't even keep time. These guys seem to be ruled by opinions, not by music. A lot of people are conned by these classical musicians who bandy the word "culture" about so frequently. They hide behind it. Rock'n'roll isn't culture – it's vulgar, thank goodness.'

Still, you could hardly accuse Freddie of being 'vulgar' – more Olga (as in Korbut), such is his gymnastic dexterity when he leads Queen across the quiescent wastes of pomp (as in -adour) rock.

'Freddie is only being himself. He doesn't care – and it's the only way to be. Some people think that's great – others simply hate it.'

Roger, a little wary, a little weary, sits stiffly in an armchair. He seems to be the only member of Queen left who is prepared, albeit rarely, to open his mouth in the presence of a hack. 'We all sat around a table to discuss the press situation and we agreed I should be the one to represent the band. Freddie is very uncompromising and refuses to have much to do with journalists.'

Roger, too, has a very low opinion of the music press. 'Most of it is rubbish,' he says. 'There was something I liked recently, a piece on Malcolm McLaren.' (Hope it was mine.) 'I think I'm the only member of Queen to actually read the music papers.'

Why does he think the band are slagged?

'Queen have always come across as being a rather confident band and I think the press may have mistaken confidence for arrogance. Hence they became very wary of our motives, which in turn has bred a dislike for our music.'

At the risk of being sent to Coventry by my colleagues, I'd like, if I may, to come clean. I love Queen. My love affair began with a simple, pre-packed but indispensable line – 'Dynamite with a laser beam' – and has continued mainly uninterrupted right through to *Live Killers*.

Why?

Freddie Mercury's lascivious lisp – the most attractive intonation known to man; Brian May's reel-'em-off rococo riffs that could, in his capable hands, transform the music for *Coronation Street* into a masterwork; John Deacon's stoic stance; Roger Taylor's intense power, so unexpected from one so slight; the band's ability to go over-the-top without falling into the trap of caricature; a desire to give the punters what they want; their cast-iron confidence; those nine glorious winter weeks of 'Bohemian Rhapsody', which kept the cold away from my door. The monkey on Queen's back, as corpulent and cantankerous as ever, has been put there by those who firmly believe they can never emulate past achievements.

'That all began after "Bohemian Rhapsody". When it stayed at number one all those weeks, we were told that we would never be able to make another single to rival it both artistically and from the point of view of sales.'

Yet 'We Are The Champions' sold a great many more. Why did they decide to dispense with the services of a manager?

'Because we were fed up with giving other people money. I mean, everything seems so great when you get into the charts for the first time. You're living on cloud nine and nothing else matters. But in truth that hit means absolutely nothing. Oh, you think you're really living ... for a while. Somebody gets you a flat in Chelsea and it's all free. But one day the rent stops being paid for you and you realise you're skint.'

My attention is suddenly diverted.

'Forty – love.'

Wimbledon, the Persil white opiate for the suburban strawberry munchers, wrings out its perspiring petticoats on the huge back-projection TV in the next room. Roger's girlfriend, an extremely attractive French girl called Dominique, is engrossed. The couple have lived together for two years. Crippled old marriage questions permeate the air.

'I don't believe in marriage,' says Roger. 'It's simply a contract and the fewer contracts I enter into the better.'

What's it like having a bank account overflowing with money at the age of twenty-nine?

'I've completely lost touch with how much things cost. When you find yourself living in hotels for so long you never really deal in money as such. Everything is available whenever you want it – but you never see the cash actually being handed over. I've forgotten what it's like to be penniless, which Queen were for years.'

Roger is a decent chap who knows how to schmooze. In fact, most of these guys are pretty decent chaps, whether they're Bruce Springsteen or Joe Strummer, Lemmy or Johnny Rotten, Debbie Harry or Paul Weller. There's a kind of streak of decency that links them all. They are artists, masters of their crafts, confident in their ability, devout in their belief. They know what they want and they know how to get it. They don't want to destroy, they want to create. They are your friends. They help you glide through life.

A music journalist kinda destroys more than he creates because it's a lot fucking easier to write. It's one of life's tragedies.

Roger Taylor has released four solo albums – two since Freddie Mercury's death in 1991. He also released three albums with his band the Cross between 1987 and 1993. He still plays under the Queen name with guitarist Brian May, first with ex-Free singer Paul Rodgers and, more recently, Adam Lambert. Roger has been married twice and has five children.

AUGUST 1979

Whitesnake, Ian Dury

In a West End recording studio, David Coverdale twiddles some knobs, then shows me how to twiddle them. But it's all too much. Recording studios are uncomfortable buggers. They take the music out of music and bring it dangerously close to science. I'd rather not twiddle those knobs, David. I'm no scientist.

He's putting the finishing touches to *Trouble* by Whitesnake, the band he moulded in his post-Purple days. The band now boasts erstwhile Deep Purple colleagues Jon Lord and Ian Paice, leading to speculation that Purple will emerge from the ashes.

'They said exactly the same when Ian and Jon formed PAL – Paice, Ashton & Lord,' says David. 'Actually, it's a good job I didn't join the band. It would have been called CLAP! I formed Whitesnake after deciding against joining up with some established stars and forming a "supergroup". I've seen too many of them fall on their arses.'

So why have Jon and Ian in the band? Isn't that a supergroup?

'Having a keyboard player and drummer like them, you've got the best in the world. When you've worked with the best for years, you can't take second best. Purple was such a mega band. Before I joined, the biggest audience I'd ever played to was two hundred. In my first week with them I played to 350,000 on an American tour. Consequently, I never really had a feeling of contact. But now that's all changed. Instead of fleeing from the people into waiting limos we invite them into our dressing room. We're getting so many new fans.'

And I leave him twiddling into twilight.

Ian quit the band a few years later and Jon hung around until 1984. But Coverdale has singlehandedly kept Whitesnake alive. In 2008 the band received the coveted Classic Rock Best Album award; in 2015 the group released The Purple Album.

'I see myself as a member of the building trade – a rock'n'roll brickie. It all depends on just how good a brickie you want to be. If you're gonna build a Gothic tower you'll need a lot of bricks, and a lot of skill ...'

Ian Dury, man of Hod, has invited me round to his recently acquired West End flat – 'I've only got a year lease. Haven't got a fucking clue where I'll be after that.'

When you're writing the interview for *Record Mirror*, the *Daily Record* and the *Evening News*, you get bounced up to club class – invites to the homes. I've interviewed Ian once before – we went ice skating together at Queensway, believe it or not. He'd just released *New Boots and Panties*, the outlet for a townful of emotion that swirled and bubbled in Dury's jewel box.

It created a unique market. Seldom out of the charts, the album has clocked up sales approaching half a million.

The follow-up, *Do It Yourself*, was a disappointment. A bit self-indulgent maybe? Overestimating the aural intelligence of the masses? Or just plain shit? After chatting to Ian for an hour and a half, I'm still not sure what he thinks of the album.

'I think we went a bit MOR simply because we tried to be so different from *New Boots*. But it has paved the way for a lot of new songs to be written. A lot more hard work will come as a result of it. Oh, well, you can't disappoint everybody. The songs on *Do It Yourself* were more autobiographical, which may have been a mistake. Now that sounds as if I hate the album and it's not true.'

Why was the album more autobiographical?

'In a personal way I wasn't really happy last year. Everything that happened really messed up my normal life. I felt alone a lot of the time. I didn't go out; I didn't meet many new people. I guess it was obvious, in the light of that, how my songs would turn out.'

Are you a satirical songwriter?

'What's that saying ... Sarcasm is the lowest form of wit? No. Satire is the last outpost of the bankrupt middle-class public-schoolboy wanker. There's nothing very important about the entertainment industry. People worry too much about industrials. If it's entertaining and people want to see it there doesn't have to be any more reason.'

But it's true he's regarded as something of a hero by many. 'And I'm amazed by it. To think me, just another normal crotchety old bastard, could be thought of as some kind of bod to a lot of people. I mean, for a start, I'm not all that reliable a person. I don't go waving magic wands at people in real life.

'A bishop once told Mick Jagger he had a lot of respect. Jagger replied: "There is no respect attached to what I am." When I realised he really meant that I stopped loving him. The only real respect is a personal one. If someone wants to be decadent in private it's their responsibility not to make a fuss about it. It's not that wonderful a thing. In fact it's very sad – the last outpost of someone who can't relate to normality. I have a responsibility to keep myself together. Ten years ago I could like myself quite easily. Now I have to work hard at it. But I still have that self-respect. If I lost that, I'd give up. Van Morrison used to get a lot of letters from people who said his songs prevented them from jumping off bridges. After he read them he'd say, "Christ, that's another one I've stopped." I hope my songs don't stop people jumping off bridges.'

He's got a smile as blue as his baggy shirt. I've had my doubts about Dury in the past. It was that art-school/fart-school antecedence, that down-among-the-plebs pageantry. After our last interview I had a cast-iron respect, which has since rusted. But the longer he talks, the more I begin to realise he's still out there on that ledge with the rest of us, scheming and dreaming. Scheming and dreaming and screaming … But self-respect isn't the only kind, is it, Ian?

'I do respect the guys I work with, enough to want to work with them. I don't think they think I'm the best singer in the world. But I do object to being called, as I once was, the "Roy Hudd of rock". I mean, fuck me.'

Ian, do you think you're ugly?

'Nah, I'm just around the corner and three doors down from handsome, that's all. I still get my fair share of fan mail. A lot of the young ladies don't seem to mind that much. In fact, some people seem to find me attractive. I have fourteen-year-old girls writing to me asking for a photograph. And I remember the last time I played at Hammersmith, ten girls leaped on the stage to get hold of me. 'Oh yeah,' he adds, tongue in cheekily, 'I get the screamers alright. Gary Glitter watch out.'

But he also takes great pains to point out that he doesn't want to simply attract the 'TTDC – that's Teen and Twenty Disco Club. It's like

I'd rather do an interview with the *Daily Mirror* than the *Observer*. I want to reach as many kinds of people as possible. I'd be very happy if the audience was full of old-age pensioners and little kids.

'You can't attach much importance to what I do – although at the same time I hope I believe in what I do. I'm thirty-seven now. On my thirty-fifth birthday the telephone was cut off because I hadn't paid my bill. I was skint. I was very worried about that telephone bill. Very worried. I don't have to worry about the telephone bill any more. They used to say something about Keith Moon which I thought was a magnificent concept. They reckoned that if he'd left the Who at any time he would have been broke in six months. That's a great thing to remember.

'I've been in a closeted atmosphere for quite some time. Mind you, I never was one for showing my face. Don't like the scuffling it involves. I'm just not interested in that nonsense. I don't find it very interesting in the way that, say, Bob Geldof or Billy Idol seem to. Oh, I didn't have time to experience an identity crisis or anything like that. I was too bloody busy. Still am. I die when I'm alone …

'Still, I've been lucky. None of us are in debt. We've managed to stay alive by selling records. It's all quite healthy. But I think the rest of the guys still worry about their telephone bills.'

He looks a little tired. Does he get depressed?

'I usually get moody when I'm exhausted but generally I don't think there's any point in taking things seriously. If we make mistakes on stage we just laugh. We know we've done our best and there's absolutely no need to get uptight about it. The only people who know when you've played a bum note are musicians and they didn't pay to get in anyway. So it doesn't matter.

'It's important to have normal feelings. I try hard to keep myself together in that way. I'd hate to end up like, say, Bob Dylan, living in that huge West Coast mansion. One day Dylan was walking down a narrow corridor with a huge bodyguard. This little guy came rushing towards them and bumped into Dylan. The bodyguard got hold of him and said, "Hey, do you know who you've just knocked into? That's Bob Dylan." And the little guy replied, "I don't care if it's fucking Bob Donovan! Get outta my way!"

'Once I was walking down to a tube train when a mass of people suddenly swept me off my feet, and they didn't touch the ground till I reached the platform. The train was already there and in the rush I fell over. Someone saw me and helped me onto my feet, which saved me from a right good stamping. It's nice to have someone around to pick you up when you fall down. I get up quicker that way.'

Like all good circles the subject reverts back to respect. 'I just don't know why it should be that people respect me. After all, I'm only a bit of a spiv, a bit of a clown, a bit of a brat. It's always easy for an oddball to be accepted.'

The Blockheads broke up, re-formed, broke up, re-formed and gave their final performance at the London Palladium on 6 February 2000, supported by Kirsty MacColl. Ian died of cancer a few weeks later, aged fifty-seven. In my humble opinion, New Boots and Panties featured the finest lyrics ever written by a British artist.

SEPTEMBER 1979

Earth Wind & Fire, The Beach Boys, Sting

It's late – it always is in LA. No one's ever on time. Here they wait around for the leaves to fall. I've been waiting patiently for an audience with Mr Earth Wind & Fire, Maurice White, for eight days. He's as elusive as a Pimpernel but I finally nail him at a West Hollywood recording studio where he's putting the finishing touches to the Emotions' new album.

It's very late. He's expecting me. 'Maurice will be down in a while,' says the studio caretaker. 'Take a chair, sir.' I sit. Sit. Sit.

'Why don't you go upstairs and shoot some pool, sir?'

I go upstairs and shoot some pool. And some more pool. Three hours later Maurice appears. It's three am and he tells me he's been 'Dancing since noon.' Seems he's also been rehearsing with the band for their forthcoming US tour before coming to the studio around seven. 'I'm probably one of the busiest people in the world. I can go on non-stop for weeks at a time. If I'm not in the studio I'm writing or preparing for another tour.

'Having a lot of energy is like having a lot of ideas – you have to take it and channel it and make it into something. Even when I'm not doing anything I sit around looking at myself. That's a habit I got into when I was a kid. I'd sit in the corner watching myself outside of me. When you do something like I do, having that ability is a bonus.'

Maurice's pyramid of harmony rises out of a disco desert. He's built it stone by stone through eight albums stretching back to 1972.

'Each new album, each new song contributes to the whole. I've always been a loner, ever since I was a kid. I came from a big family – five boys and four girls – and only occasionally did I have the luxury of being by myself. I can speak of my experiences through my music. I try and reach the inner soul through song, through that secluded part where you talk to yourself about your decisions and how you should make your way through life. Do you understand?'

Sure 'nuff.

'We are speaking of a certain type of lifestyle and it's important the kids know what we mean – that's why we always print the lyrics on our albums. We are now in the pop market and the record buyers don't know where we're coming from. They haven't yet lived the things we speak of. I guess I mean mostly the kids from the suburbs. We are talking of things relative to the street, relative to survival, where people wait for a new day. Those kids haven't ever got up in the morning and wondered if they're going to get through the day OK. My personal past has enabled me to speak of those things.'

The title of the new album was a deliberate attempt to eradicate the diffidence in most (nah, all) of us.

'We wanted to awaken the self in everybody. You go into the record store and ask for *I Am* and that's a reaffirmation of you just by saying those two words. In the US people have certain conceptions about black groups. They think black music must be of a particular type and when boundaries are broken it's as though you did something terrible. Every time we release an album *Rolling Stone* magazine slams it. Yet every album is successful. I live in fear of them giving one of our records a good review. Then I'll know we've failed.'

Are you a pain-in-the-arse perfectionist?

'Yes. That's one of my problems. I often wish I was a lot sloppier. There are annoying little things. For instance, if my closet isn't completely tidy I go to pieces. To have an orderly closet saves time for me. I'll take out the wrong pair of pants and have to go back and change them.'

But doesn't such an attitude spill over into relationships? Perfectionists are notoriously intolerant of others.

'I've learned toleration because I had to be tolerated. Growing up in my parents' home, first in Memphis and then in Chicago, taught me that.'

Maurice is divorced. 'I never had any kids. I really don't know why I got married. I had a good home. None of my brothers and sisters are married. But we've all got time. I'm thirty-five now. I figure I've got another thirty-five years left. I still got time for all that family stuff.'

We leave the studio together, and in the car park opposite he climbs into the coolest Porsche imaginable.

Apart from a four-year hiatus between 1983 and 1987, EW&F continued to record top-notch albums and became an American institution. Maurice and the band were inducted into the Rock'n'roll Hall of Fame in 2000. EW&F performed at the 2002 Winter Olympics, Superbowl in 2005 and the US Open golf in 2008. In February 2009, they played at the White House during President Obama's first formal dinner. Maurice did indeed find the time for 'all that family stuff'.

He eventually died in February 2016 from the effects of Parkinson's
disease, at the age of 74.

I wander round the Los Angeles record companies in the hot
sunshine wearing a Journey T-shirt – cool design but I know nothing
of the band and never will. I set up a few things. I'm hot to trot. I
stay for two and a half weeks downgrading the paid-for hotels as
the interviews start to dwindle, finally ending up on the sofa in the
front room of a beachside apartment belonging to ex-Fleet Street
photographer Laurence Cottrell. Unfortunately, I leave the window
open to his apartment one morning and all his photographic
equipment is stolen. Hi, Megan, haven't seen you for a while.

Capitol records fly me out to Las Vegas to spend the night, take
in a Glen Campbell show and interview him backstage. Isn't that a
great sentence?

Now let me tell you about Colette.

Collete was a blonde singer from Orange County whom I met while
working for the *South East London Mercury* when she was fronting
a band based in Lewisham. She was stunning, foxy, real arm-candy.
Every man should have one at least once in his life. I was in a pre-
Dina no man's land and we had some fun. I took her to receptions
and concerts, and pop stars would talk to us backstage because she
really looked the part and that helped me look the part. She lived in
a bedsit in Gloucester Road and said, 'You're such a man,' when we
made love. What a nice thing to say to someone, especially to a man
when he's making love.

She was twenty and had 'l-o-v-e' tattooed across the backs of her
fingers. Colette was a mystery, a black-magic woman with a soulful
voice and a fear of audiences. After a few months she suddenly
ended the affair and went off touring with the band in Scandinavia.

I didn't hear anything from her until Christmas Day 1977 when she
rang me from Orange County. The tour hadn't worked out and she was
back home. After that call we wrote to each other fairly regularly; it

was nice to have a sexy pen-pal in California. But it gradually emerged that she harboured feelings for me. I was flattered.

Flattered enough to call her when I get to LA. I'm holed up in a tasty hotel apartment block favoured by rock-stars and hookers who'll bang you two at a time if you ask nicely.

The next evening Colette is walking towards me through the foyer. She looks healthier. The rock chick has hatched. She's a woman now without a trace of black magic. My God, she's lovely – but I can't, I daren't, go back.

She stays for a few days, we hold hands on the beach. She's got her troubles, I've got mine. The thrill is gone and when Colette finally leaves I know I'll never hear the words 'You're such a man' ever again. Mortality touches me on the shoulder. I hadn't noticed that the lights had changed.

The night Colette leaves, I get a call at the hotel and I'm Alice in Boogie Wonderland again. On a scale of one to ten, how cool is this question?

'Can you have lunch with the Beach Boys at a restaurant on Santa Monica beach tomorrow?'

'No, sorry, I'm busy.'

'Oh.' No fucking sense of humour, these guys.

'Only joking. I'd love to have lunch with the Beach Boys tomorrow or the next day or any day over the next fifty years.'

'Oh.'

And that's how I find myself sitting around a table with the Beach Boys in a beach restaurant. Brian Wilson is opposite me. He doesn't speak much. And when I try to strike up a conversation I don't quite understand what he's saying: the restaurant's too noisy and, besides, the blue litmus paper obviously turned red a long time ago and he's living the dream.

I'm not interviewing the band. This is an off-the-record get-together. Mike Love is sitting next to me (can you believe all this?) and it's easier to talk to him. After three years of speaker-grinding noise, my drums are snared and, if I'm more than a foot away from a person in a place with a lot of background noise, I sometimes can't hear a thing.

So I talk to Mike for a while and he's a really nice guy and invites me to see the band perform their new single, 'Sumahama', on *American Bandstand* in Hollywood the next day, hosted by the legendary Dick Clarke.

As the sun toasts the empty pavements, we meander through the LA heat haze in Laurence's Ford Mustang to the TV studios for an appointment with the Beach Boys on America's favourite show. And when we get there, Carl, Dennis, Al and Brian say, 'Hi, Barry,' and I wish they all could be California girls at that moment because I feel like fucking the lot of them. The Beach Boys know my name. Look up the number. It's like winning an award.

After the show I shake Dick's hand (doesn't sound right) and Mike takes me to one side. 'I understand you'd like to do an interview, Barry.'

There! He says it again.

Yes.

'Well, why don't you come out and see my home in Santa Barbara? You and I can do the interview and you can spend a little time there.'

Yes.

'Great. Make it the day after tomorrow, around midday. You can meet the family. Is that good for you?'

Yes.

'OK. I've got a little map here. It's easy to find when you know how. Look forward to it.'

Yes.

'We've got to go now. Nice seeing you again, Barry.'

Yes.

'That's a result,' says Laurence.

Yes.

OK, I might seem like a gormless dick to you, but christ, hanging out with a Beach Boy at his house in California? And with his family.

Yes.

For a few souped-up, Bermuda-short years, the Beach Boys were America. The birth of surf with all its biologically clean, large-breasted Pepsodent blondes in blue bikinis; its guys sliding out of black Elvis leather and breezing into big shirts and wide smiles; its tanful of exercise and sublime backseat drive-in sex, made everyone want to sing sweet'n'high in their flaming hot rods.

In 1965 California was the place to be. The real deal. They even told you so on *The Beverly Hillbillies* every Sunday night. The American dream. And the Beach Boys conveyed it all in three-minute pristine pop perfection. They were an enclave in the British charts surrounded by the dockyard rock of a million moptops. After all, the only thing that really bugged them was driving up and down the same old strip while here the kids were ferrying across the Mersey trying desperately to get out of this place.

They made you want to be a beach boy, to be blond and slim and get sand in your shoes and ride up and down that strip instead of getting a tube to Whitechapel every Saturday night looking for adventure and whatever came our way, though it never did.

Mike Love stretches out on a lounger three hundred feet above the Pacific Ocean at his Santa Barbara home and not a cotton field in sight. The thirty-eight-year-old Beach Boy (one of these days they're gonna have to change that name – Beach Men or better still Beach Big Boys) looks good as he sips a chocolate malt.

The demise of the Beach Boys coincided with the demise of America. Both went to pot, pieces and polyurethane. Brian Wilson – in the top three pop-genius category – appeared to crack and spent years in a wilderness inhabited by strange dreams and love letters in the sand.

But now, says Mike, 'We intend to be better than we've ever been before. Those people that have slagged us in the past are the ultra trendies who have lost sight of the fact that some things are timeless and universal – like your basic Beach Boy. Our music will be played throughout history like Beethoven, Bach and Brahms. We are into the future, we are into the now. Those who call us over the hill don't realise we are immortal. What they say doesn't mean shit to a tree.'

The chocolate malt gasps in the bottom of the carton as Mike Love sucks hard. He's telling the truth by the way. At least, that's what I think as a band of naked revellers frolics in the autumn mist near Mike's private beach directly below.

Interviewing a Beach Boy by the ocean is like interviewing a Beatle in the Cavern or Rod Stewart in bed or a Sex Pistol in the toilet. It's relevant. His home is at a spot he calls Asoleado – Spanish for a place in the sun. Like Page Three. It's little short of paradise.

After a series of indifferent albums, the band released *L.A. (Light Album)* earlier this year. It proved beyond question that the Beach Boys were still getting around, still capable of a little subtle soul seduction, still holding on to those honeydew harmonies with the less fattening centres that melt in your mouth, not in your hand.

The single 'Lady Lynda' promptly scored and 'Sumahama', although not exactly a surfin' safari of a hit, is still there among the Jags and Tourists of this world.

So why the long gap before making music again?

'Just things, y'know.' He stretches again. 'Like Carl put on a lot of weight and Dennis started drinking too much and Al had his ranch and horses and Brian went through a highly emotional state in both his mind and body and was smoking way too much. He's a sensitive, brilliant musician and pressures can sometimes manifest themselves in bad ways in people like that. We were not as cohesive as we might have been for quite some time. But now we're gonna run the group like a team again. We've been living apart for far too long.'

To get the band back on their feet, Mike has masterminded the 'Total Fitness Programme'.

'We just want to be healthier and fitter than we've ever been before. I think it's the only way we can maintain a close relationship. There's too much acid in the systems and not enough vitamins. Now we regularly go to a training camp in the mountains by the sea to work out.' Jogging like bluebirds, no doubt.

Another project in the bag is a movie, *California Beach*, which I must admit sounds great. 'It's about four girls from various parts of the States who meet out here on the beach. There's a Midwest farmer's daughter, an East Coast girl, a southern girl and a northern girl.'

Sounds familiar. 'It's just a series of sociological vignettes played out here day after day against a backdrop of Beach Boys music. Kind of like an *Endless Summer*.'

To launch the movie, the band intends to hold the world's biggest beach party next spring and they'll also undertake a 'California Beach' tour. After each show there will be a party, organised by the Playboy Club and oozing with pretty girls. 'Should keep the press interested,' smiles Mike.

So, two shots in the arm. But what of the man himself? The cousin of the Wilson brothers from clean-cut LA., Mike has lived in Asoleado for the last eight years.

'Oh, sure, I used to have a place in Beverly Hills and one in Malibu. But I got tired of all that. When I moved here I became involved in transcendental meditation and eventually became a teacher.'

Unlike so many other rock stars who prodded meditation with a superficial finger, Mike has remained loyal to his beliefs. To the extent, he assures me, of being able to levitate and disappear!

'Too many people in this business dwell on the insubstantial aspects of life – having the right car, going to the right parties, wearing the right clothes. I've just been concerned with my life, with its depth and dimension, more than my career in show business.'

Mike has his own meditation room in the building complex at Santa Barbara, which also houses his publishing company, Love Songs, and the people in his employ. 'It's very difficult to go on tour when you live here. When you look down at the sea through stained-glass windows, when the sunlight breaks through, it's so tranquil yet so energising. Who needs a hotel room?'

But Mike won't be living in his paradise home for much longer.

Asoleado will shortly be transformed into the Love Foundation Holistic Health Centre. 'It's costing a million dollars to turn this place into a centre where people can come to get healthy. To diet, exercise, even be examined by a resident MD. A lot of people get interested in health and longevity when they reach a certain age.'

Wonder what age that might be. Not 38, perchance?

Mike has just bought a two-million-dollar mansion set in twenty acres at Lake Tahoe. He'll be moving in with his four daughters and one son from three previous marriages, and his Japanese girlfriend, ex-air hostess Sumako. One of his ex-wives lives in a chalet at Asoleado. 'I'm not gonna get married again for at least two years simply because I've got so much to do in terms of my career – the movie, the records, my philanthropic endeavours.'

I wonder what his favourite periods in Beach Boys history were.

'Mmnn. The nostalgic ones, like all of a sudden being able to take a plane to Hawaii for a few days and not having to worry about the money. But the current period is the most pleasant of all because we're more aware of what we're doing. After all these years my plans and dreams are finally coming true.

'There was that bad patch when we decided to rest up awhile but we got back together again through a certain amount of pride and ego and strength and stubbornness, which are part of the characters of all of us and which have enabled us to steer a course through the shaky times and come out on top.'

God only knows what I feel about that.

Dennis Wilson died in 1983 and his brother Carl in 1998. Al Jardine then left the band and Mike retained the legal rights to the name 'The Beach Boys'. The surviving members of the Beach Boys continued to tour as three separate bands – The Beach Boys Band with Love and Bruce Johnston, Al Jardine's Endless Summer Band with Jardine and his sons, and Brian Wilson with a ten-piece band. The dream was over. But then they all met up again...

In RCA's LA office I flirt with Rita Coolidge during an interview because I seem to be able to make her laugh. I'm even on the verge of asking her out when I remember hubby Kris Kristofferson looked like a big bloke in *A Star Is Born*.

'Me and Kris speak to each other all the time when I'm on the road,' she says, in between laughs. I love this girl. 'We used to tour together a lot more but we were just getting stale. At first, people were fascinated by the two of us sharing our romance on stage but I think they got a little bored last time out. We've got to change our style if we're to continue doing concerts together.'

Alas, they never did. Things will get a little stale and the couple will split within months of the interview. I wish I'd asked her out when I had the chance. She might have even said yes. Maybe not.

Back in dreary London it's back to dreary work interviewing dreary people like dreary teacher Gordon Sumner.

But wait! Why is he running into that phone box? Why is he taking his clothes off? Why is he wearing an orange and black hooped jumper? Wait. It couldn't be. Surely not.

Not ... Sting? Not, ahem, Britain's answer to Debbie Harry? Not the Police singer – at number one this week with 'Message in A Bottle' – who now rivals Rod Stewart and Bob Geldof in the sex-symbol stakes?

'I get a lot of teenage girls chasing after me,' he tells me. 'But that doesn't make me any vainer because, as far as vanity goes, I've already reached saturation point. I am completely arrogant.'

I like the cut of this man's jib.

Sting says he doesn't want to end up like David Essex when 'Nobody takes you seriously because you're too good-looking.'

But the twenty-six-year-old ex-model – who recently starred as The Face in the movie *Quadrophenia* – has a serious side. It appears pop music isn't his only love. 'I'm thinking of taking part in a new classical opera by the German composer Eberhard Schoener in London early next year,' he says. Ooh-er.

The band's new album, *Regatta De Blanc*, ain't exactly a classical gas, but it's already emulating the success of its predecessor *Outlandos D'Amour*.

'I can hardly believe that the first album has sold nearly a million copies worldwide. We were worried about losing money on it and worked out that we had to sell five thousand copies just to break even!'

The Police have been given a transatlantic tonic with the success of their records in the States. 'We brought reggae to America in the way that the Stones took over rhythm and blues. We don't think we've ripped off black music, we've just helped to make it more palatable.'

He was originally a PE teacher in Newcastle by the name of Gordon Sumner but gigged in a local band in the evenings. 'That's where I got the nickname Sting,' he recalls. 'I used to play in a trad jazz band with a lot of old guys. I would turn up for shows in a yellow pullover with black hoops. They all thought I looked like o bumble-bee so they started calling me Sting. It's now official because even my mum calls me it.'

'C'mon, Sting, get the fockop. Yall be late fer school now, mun. Breakfast is on the teyble.'

Never was any good at accents.

OCTOBER 1979

The Jam, Andy Williams

Paul Weller appears to grow more cynical by the hour. He hits me with his rhythm stick every time I meet him. After a show in Brighton we talk half the night away in his hotel room. The interview appears in the *Evening News*, which is a real coup because Paul refuses to talk to the big papers, believing them to be the unacceptable face of capitalism. I've also interviewed him for the *Daily Star* and *Daily Record*. None of the national journos get to know these bands the way music-paper writers do. We've been on the road with these guys, got pissed with these guys, snorted drugs with (some) of these guys. The early bird catches the worms, which, incidentally, my hair has been free of since that fateful haircut late December back in '67 (oh, what a night!). So ...

Welcome to the two-tone zone.

The Jam. Two-tone mohair suits, two-tone shoes, two-tone harmonies, two-tone attitude.

A growing legion of fans has pushed their latest album, *Setting Sons*, straight into the charts at number seven. The sound is fun, young and even charming, but the lyrics are dark, set in that adolescent void hogged by Jam fans.

But that two-tone approach has finally brought the band the kind of stardom that has eluded them since the beginning, when they trod the same London pub boards as the Sex Pistols and the Clash back in 1976. Their single, 'Eton Rifles', is currently number three in the charts, and this Sunday the band start a sell-out three-night stint at the Rainbow.

Other bands from that era have since fallen by the wayside, deluded by malignant self-importance and dogged by misfortune. But the Jam, especially guitarist Paul Weller, refuse to inflict their egos on the pop public and quietly continue making a stream of classic singles.

'I suppose I've been cynical since I was fourteen years old,' says Paul, 'since my teachers kept telling me what I should know when they knew absolutely nothing themselves. All they were good at was tripping out on acid. I could tell them more than they could tell me.'

It's been four hours since the end of the show and he's been drinking solidly ever since. Paul has always maintained that his shoulder is a chip-free zone. But chips are necessary to any rock artist who's worth his salt and my guess is there's a whole plateful up there with the odd piece of skate thrown in.

'I love the English language but when I wanted to read contemporary books at school they insisted on stuffing Dickens down my throat,' he says. 'Same with music. All they played was Beethoven and

Tchaikovsky when they should have started from Elvis. Christ, I couldn't even fill in a tax form when I left school. I had to educate myself. I haven't got any special perception. Many of the letters I receive articulate my sentiments better than I do. It's just that when I was thirteen I first saw the Pistols and they blocked my brain. At last, I thought. The whole youth culture has arrived. Before that the only bands I'd seen were Status Quo and Wings. You could never be them – but you could be a Sex Pistol.'

Older stars, like Bob Geldof of the Boomtown Rats, infuriate Paul when they start spouting about the young generation. 'People like that, setting themselves up as spokesmen for the kids, make me spew. The young are the strength, the future of this country. I'm still young, I've got time on my side – what have they got?'

So how will he avoid falling into the same trap when he's twenty-seven?

'I'll know when I've got nothing left to say. Then I won't write things down any more – I'll lose my bottle.'

Surprisingly, Paul remains optimistic about the immediate future of music in Britain. Whereas contemporary observers are confidently predicting the end of the rock epoch, Paul firmly believes that the scene now is better that it was in 1976. 'There are so many great bands around that I can only foresee it getting better. Groups like the Skids, the Ruts and the Undertones point the way – barring outside interference.'

Outside interference? From whom?

'The Government. I know this will sound really stupid in print, but I wanted to send a copy of our new album to all the heads of state, just to try and make them aware of how the young feel about certain things. But I never did. I didn't think any of them would bother to listen.'

Paul and his ilk are in touch with their followers because they have largely unaffected lifestyles. He lives with his girlfriend Jill in a London flat.

'What else can you do but watch TV or go out for a drink? I do exactly the same as any other guy my age. Oh, sure, some people think you're different, but that's because they want to. Our fans know we're just three ordinary geezers.'

The following morning the band poses for some photos on the beach and I dash back to London for an appointment with Andy Williams. From Genesis to Revelation.

'Andy,' says the PR girl to Andy Williams, in his London Hilton Hotel suite, 'this is Barry who writes mainly about punk.'

'Oh, really?' he says, as we shake hands. 'What – like the Ramones and the Clash?'

Andy Williams. Shit! Who would've thought I'd be getting it on with the moon-river man himself (verbally speaking)? This guy is so laid-back he makes a sloth look like a cheetah. He caught the wind a long time ago, boxed it up and sent it second class to Saturn.

He lives in a breeze-free world that only money can buy.

Still, he's definitely top of the pops as far as his three children are concerned. Noelle, sixteen, Christian, fourteen, and ten-year-old Robert all call their dad Poppa. And he loves it. 'Their mother, Claudine, always called her father Poppa, like most French kids, and the three picked it up,' says Andy, between puffs of a giant cigar. 'I hope they never stop calling me it.'

You're it.

Andy is preparing for his first British tour in three years. It coincides with the release of his new album, *The Classic Collection*. Dressed casually in pale blue polo-neck sweater and jeans, he paces the room as he talks of his divorce from Claudine. 'The kids reacted to it very well, but then it wasn't such a bad divorce. Claudine and I were separated for several years before the final split so they were used to it. But we have remained close friends and see each other a great deal.'

After the couple divorced, Andy found himself emulating the character in one of his most famous records, 'Solitaire'. 'I was very lonely, not for a woman but for a family because, more than anything, I'm a family man,' and pretty home-loving too, I hear. 'I missed the children and Claudine. But there was never any doubt that they would live with their mother.'

Then Andy met a beautiful young actress called Laurie Wright. 'When I met her she was feeling very down because coincidentally, her parents had just divorced. 'I invited her as my guest to Las Vegas where I was appearing in cabaret. It was all above board. She slept in a spare bedroom in my suite. In fact, Laurie was a house guest for six months before we started getting involved.'

Would he consider marriage again?

'Not at the moment. She has her own career and her home in Beverly Hills. But I do like her to come on the road with me.'

During the tour Andy will be consuming large quantities of champagne and beer. 'It helps me unwind after a show. But I never take drugs. Just give me a few good friends, a decent meal, some fine champagne and I'm happy.'

When Andy returns to America he'll go straight to Aspen where he's just bought a ski lodge, and where Claudine and the children live. He'll holiday there before heading for his new home in South Carolina. Then he'll start work on his first Broadway show – in which he plays a Catholic priest. 'I'll have to grow a beard and dye my hair blond for the role. I'm excited about the whole thing.'

Andy, who's sold more than thirty-five million records during his career, hopes his new single 'Jason' will be successful – for personal reasons. 'I wanted something that tied in with the Year of the Child, and then a woman sent this song about a mentally retarded boy. When I sing it I think of my son Robert. He's not retarded but he does suffer from dyslexia. It would be great if 'Jason' turned out to be a hit for me. It's funny, the whole world is changing these days.' He stares out of the window, still talking.

'Things you read in the papers about some rock star's sexual secrets wouldn't have got in a few years back. Although I'm against censorship of any kind, the only thing that bothers me is that just because some star like David Bowie says something, young kids might be influenced by it. I wouldn't like to think that my kids were unduly influenced and that they could stand by their own ideals.

'Look, I'm not against homosexuality. I think my children can take care of themselves in life and if one of them came to me and said he was homosexual I'm not going to beat him up. Life is over for me now. By that I mean I'm very content in doing what I'm doing. I have no more worries.'

No worries. He did marry again (not to Laurie but to Debbie Meyer) in 1991. He died in 2012 aged 84; his birthplace in Iowa is a tourist attraction.

NOVEMBER 1979

The Specials, The Selecter, Madness

Souped-up ska has arrived – punk lyrics skanking on a Jamaican beat played by black and white bands in sharp mohair suits. It's a cliché, but in an original kinda way. The Specials are the trailblazing Seventies ska band and the first to appear in the charts with 'Gangsters'. They set up the Two Tone record label and originally signed both the Selecter and Madness – though Madness have now gone to Stiff. The Specials are from Coventry and have received the most attention of all, even tempting Elvis Costello to produce their first album. They herald the return of live dance music to the scene after the recorded doldrums of disco.

'There are so few bands now you could really go out and dance to,' says singer Terry Hall. 'And that's what people who love music like to do. It's a Moonstomp party.'

The only blot on the good clean fun of rock steady is the reputation the gigs have for attracting violence.

'Oh, sure, there's rivalry between certain groups in the audiences, but that's mainly just the skinheads-versus-everybody-else syndrome.

I've been a skinhead since I was ten. Pork-pie hats, polished brogues, button-down shirts, razor-parted hair. Kids have been trying their best to look scruffy for the last few years. It's time for change.'

The band are currently headlining the Two-Tone tour supported by the Selecter and Madness

The Selecter, at seven in the charts this week with 'On My Radio', are the odd man out – they have a girl singer, Pauline Black.

So what's it like travelling the country with twenty men?

'No different from travelling with twenty women,' says twenty-six-year-old Pauline. Mmnn, I sense the force with this one.

Pauline hates it when their music is described as revivalist. 'People who say that have obviously never seen us play. They've missed the skinhead ska of the Sixties because they were too busy being old hippies. Our songs are very different from those of that era. We've had the benefit of that whole punk experience. And all the bands are different. Madness are like Ian Dury, the Specials are more punk, and we're more reggae.'

Why do the bands have so many members? 'Because it's more fun visually and better musically.'

Camden Town-based Madness call their music the nutty sound and describe themselves as the only band in the world with six and a half members. The half is non-musician Chas Smash, who announces the band and demonstrates his bananas brand of skanking throughout the set.

'We're having a great time,' says sax player Lee Thompson, the star of their hit single 'One Step Beyond'. 'The other bands seem to row with each other quite a bit, but we get on very well. Madness ain't as serious as the others. We're just a lot of fun. But there's no rivalry.'

Lee knows that the revival could end as quickly as it began. 'I've had a laugh and that's all that matters. I could go back to playing tiny places tomorrow and it wouldn't bother me. It's all happened too fast for me to take it seriously anyway.'

The Selecter broke up in 1982, and Black went on to forge an acting

career in TV and the theatre culminating in the Time Out 1991 award for Best Actress as Billie Holiday in the play All Or Nothing At All. The Selecter re-formed that same year, made several albums and toured extensively until finally calling it a day in 2006. The Specials shocked the pop world by splitting in 1981 at the height of their popularity with the No. 1 classic 'Ghost Town'. Terry Hall formed Fun Boy Three with fellow Specials Lynval Golding and Neville Staple while Jerry Dammers, who started the Two-Tone record label, continued with Special AKA, scoring with 'Free Nelson Mandela'. The band, minus Dammers, reformed in 2008. Madness have continued, on-and-off, ever since and have become a British institution.

DECEMBER 1979

Alex Harvey, The Damned

Old soldiers never die. Take Alex Harvey who's once again on the glory trail after a year in the wilderness. His new album released this week, *The Mafia Stole My Guitar*, shows that, despite all the health rumours, Alex is fighting fit.

'I can run half a mile and swim half a mile right afterwards,' Alex tells me at his north London home where he lives with his wife and two children. 'I know some people think I'm a bit of a nutcase but, let's face it, the oldest cliché in the book is you have to be a nutcase to play rock'n'roll. And that's the only life I know.'

Alex was plagued with problems after his manager, Bill Fehilly, was killed in a plane crash three years ago. First the Sensational Alex Harvey Band split, then Alex became involved in a series of legal battles that still continue and which have made him a very angry man.

'I'm 45 and I've been through an awful lot. Can you imagine how bad it was for me when Bill was killed? But you know something

– I'm winning. I loved the band, loved 'em – but I mustn't get over-emotional. It's finished. When I started in this business I knew a lot of kids. Now they're all dead. I'm the only one left. I'm unique.'

Alas, Alex ain't so unique any more. He died of a heart attack not long after that interview while on the road. So much for running and swimming.

The Damned have gone off the radar, love. 'New Rose' is now as dry as a bone, 'Neat Neat Neat' has lost its lovin' feeling, Brian James is living on Dead End Street and even love couldn't keep Captain and Tennille together.

But Rat Scabies's cock is a sign that the best is yet to come.

It was when he pulled it out in front of a bunch of open-mouthed studio technicians during a session for Capital Radio that I realised just how much I'd missed the Damned. Noticing its lack of petrification, I remembered how flexible the band were – eccentric one minute, devout rockers the next. Its jaundiced appearance reminded me of how colourful they were; the presence of varicose veins was redolent of their energy; the lack of any noticeable discharge their discipline (for, despite views to the contrary, the Damned never indulged in more than a controlled chaos); the odour their strength.

Yes, the Damned were, and are, unique. Forget what critics would have you believe: Messrs Scabies, Sensible, Vanian and new boy ex-Saint Alisdair Ward, are back in business with the release of their new album *Machine Gun Etiquette*.

The Damned always did defy the rules, not because of an adopted pose but because the individuals themselves defied description. If any band deserved the appendage 'punk', it's this collection of crazy pavings. Other bands who hiccuped during the winter of '76 only got so far before drinking water from the wrong side of a glass and regaining their equilibrium. The Damned had no equilibrium. They didn't hiccup, they BURPED. A thick, rheumy, brown ale of a burp that rejoiced in its own noise. It was tragic to see them go. It's glorious to see them return.

The sight of Captain Sensible sitting alone in the Capital Radio studio playing lead guitar would have been little short of miraculous two years ago. One thing the Damned never got was praise for their musical capabilities.

'You look around at other people,' says Sensible, 'and then you think, "Who's better than the Captain? Nobody."'

Dave Vanian cups his black-gloved hands around a glass of Scotch and Coke. 'We're so much better than we ever were. We actually talk to each other now. I never knew we would get back together again. But I'm very glad we did. We haven't got the limitations we had before when we were stuck in one little hole. Even though the reviews haven't been that favourable for the new album, I know we've shocked people into realising that we can play. I wouldn't change a thing.'

It's at this point that Rat brings forth the spider from the fly. 'I've written eight songs this week,' he says, accompanied by the sound of Sensible's guitar and the crackle of a downward-moving zip.

Ex-Saint Alisdair, recovering from laughing at the sight for sore eyes, sits next to me. What did you do when the Saints split?

'Got drunk on all the money.' So that's two pints and a Scotch. 'Now I'm in a band I like. I really am.'

'Shit,' interrupts Rat. 'He won't even talk to us. He costs us a fortune in extra hotel rooms cos he refuses to sleep in the same room as the rest of us.'

More laughter. 'Nah, this is a band I can talk to,' says Alisdair. 'We all speak the same language, have the same sense of humour. The Damned is more like a religion among its fans. And there ain't much humour around these days.'

Alisdair is convinced music goes in seven-year cycles. 'We've got another four years to go before something new comes along.'

So, who'd have thought it? The Damned, the first punks to make a single 'New Rose', the first punks to make an album, *The Damned*, the first punks to tour the States, the first punks to split, the first punks to re-form. And maybe the last punks. Ever.

But the burning question remains: would you let your daughter marry one of them?

And will plonkers be next year's big thing? Er, you can put it away now, Rat.

'It's nice out today, ennit?'

A few days later, Rat sips tea in a North London caff – and I do mean caff. The sandwiches have as many cracks as the cups. He looks healthy, which is amazing, considering his lifestyle. Rat probably instigated the Demise of the Damned Mark One, which followed the release of their second album *Music For Pleasure*. Why?

'I got bored with it all. Oh, sure, it was great being a pop star at first – but it ain't what it's cracked up to be. It got to the stage where I just couldn't go out in public. In fact, it got so violent I wasn't even able to go down my local boozer. I took a bird down the Hope and Anchor one night and she got glassed in the face by someone who had a grudge against me. And I got beaten up twice through no fault of my own. But I was drunk both times so maybe it was my fault. I can't remember now.

'The songs were rotten, too. Brian James, who'd written most of them, had achieved his aim and, in my mind anyway, dried up. I reckon we'd all got as far as we could musically. After all, you can only take a nurse's uniform so far. And our reputations were getting out of hand. I was being accused of the most ridiculous things.'

So Rat vamoosed.

'I needed to get completely away from the rock world. I thought I was gonna have a nervous breakdown. My whole personal-defence mechanism decided it was time for me to call it a day.'

For Rat to pack it in is rather like Hartlepool winning the Cup – it just ain't gonna happen.

So he formed Whitecats. Flop. Meanwhile, across the teeming metropolis, Captain Sensible formed King. Flop.

The two flops joined forces. 'Captain wanted to work with me again. So we had a walk round the block and decided to do a tour. The only problem was, who could we get as a singer? We looked around, then finally came to the conclusion that the best we were ever likely to get was Dave Vanian.'

Vanian had left the Doctors of Madness and spent his days reading the grotesque in his Islington house with the black walls and blacker ceilings, and remembering yesterday. He was ripe for a reunion.

'My attitude has changed now,' says Rat. 'You get used to people staring at you. You stay in places where you're known.'

On their last US tour Rat banged nineteen girls in twenty-two days. 'That's my record. The only nights I missed out were when we arrived – I had jetlag – and when we had to drive to a gig. If I wasn't in the Damned I wouldn't pull nearly as much.'

An honest man is Rat.

The Damned have continued to tour and record with a number of different line-ups. Dave Vanian and Captain Sensible are the only two original members still playing in the band..

Dina decides to return to Cyprus. It's over two years since I'd proposed and for the last year or so we've been virtually living together, although all my belongings are still at home with Mum and Dad, along with the dirty washing and a lot of food. I can't really give her the life she wants, she knows that now. She packs in her job as a PA at Henley's, spends Christmas Day at my mum and dad's, buys me my first electric typewriter and flies home three days later.

She's gone, but it don't worry me none.

And then it does.

I love this woman and I'm sure, almost, that she loves me. I know I'll never love anyone more.

Shit, it looks like the beginning of 1980...

Record Mirror readers' top singles of the decade

'Mull Of Kintyre'
'Rivers Of Babylon/Brown Girl In The Ring'
'You're The One That I Want'

Record Mirror readers' top albums of the decade

Bridge Over Trouble Water
Greatest Hits: Abba
Tubular Bells

Record Mirror readers' 1979 Awards

Best band: Police, Blondie, Queen
Best male singer: Gary Numan, Bob Geldof, Sting
Best female singer: Kate Bush, Debbie Harry, Judie Tzuke
Best single: 'Are Friends Electric'
Best album: *Regatta de Blanc*
Best gig: Led Zeppelin

JANUARY 1980

AC/DC, The Stranglers, The Clash

Time to get back out there on the road, to a place where you can rub your guitar for hours and it won't go limp. Just get harder. And more potent. Where you can stick it in every conceivable orifice known to man and hammer away till the hole becomes raw and painful but it'll come out, strings glistening, still unsatisfied, still fretting for the ultimate release. And the amps perish in the heat and the stage turns to lava and wrists run dry and hearts burn up and still the G shaft remains erect, taut, firm and famished. A kind of highway to hell.

But down at the Angus Steak House at midnight, where you won't find any veg, just pert young rumps, scientists believe they have come up with a solution. They claim to have discovered a formula that will provide the guitar with what they term an OE – orgasm explosion. It's called Project AY. On the surface is appears to be simple enough. A young Australian Scot – a combination the scientists believe to be the perfect catalyst for the experiment, one down under, the other well done – dressed in a schoolboy outfit, fed bags and bags of sweet lollies, chocolate nuts and liquorice-flavoured chewing gum, rolled around in a vat full of regurgitated sweat, shown film after film of Billy Dainty, Chuck Berry and the Penguin and all the while receiving crippling electronic shocks. Then hand him a guitar and let him loose on the world.

Angus Young sucks another lolly on the way to Brighton, where the mods come from. There's an air of limpness on the coach. AC/DC are entitled to get limp – they've been gigging solidly since 4 May.

'The longest break we had was three days while we travelled from one country to another,' says Angus, popping yet another chocolate into his mouth. 'When you're touring so much it's hard to prevent yourself getting stale. So I like to think bad. MEAN! Think mean, play mean. We like to get the tension up really high and leave it there. Townshend is always violent on stage. He must feel that way to look it and carry it off every time. Sometimes, when I've been playing particularly mean, I have to be guided back to my dressing room because I can't see where I'm going.'

As he talks, *Monty Python* is being particularly mean on the in-coach video system. Classic sketches like 'The Larch' and 'Spam' wrap themselves around the rest of the band like university scarves. Angus ignores the daftness of the diversion. 'When I'm on stage I'll think of anything to keep going as long as it has dynamics or can make me moody. Sometimes I might think, What would Humphrey Bogart do in this situation? Sometimes I even think of jokes. The kids in the audience have come to see you do something wild, so you try to oblige. They always want to see you perform better than the last time they saw you. You have to keep proving yourself.

'We were playing Reading Festival in '76 when all of a sudden this girl with enormous tits walked past the stage at the front. Everything seemed to stop as the crowd watched this massive pair wander past. There was only one thing I could do – I dropped my trousers. It seemed to work too.

'If I paid money to see B. B. King I'd like to see him play, sure, but I'd also like to see a bit of an act even if it was only watching him hold the same note for ten minutes. But at the same time too many bands rely on special effects to see them through. Apart from a bit of dry ice we don't have anything you could term a "special effect". But we try to make a song exciting. When we play "Sin City" we want to make it sound like something really fucking sinful.'

I'd like to say at this point Bon Scott put his foot through the coach window, followed by another unmentionable part of his anatomy. But the singer was feeling a little low. It seems he pulled a muscle on the band's last French tour and it became inflamed the day before the Brighton gig when they were due to play Southampton. The show was cancelled, despite Scott receiving the same freezer jabs that enabled Bjorn Borg to play the '78 Wimbledon final.

And before you know it – Brighton. The Centre. The sea front.

'ANGUS! ANGUS!' chants the crowd, and after thirty minutes they get him, enveloped in smoke during the opening chords to 'Livewire' perched behind drummer Phil.

Watching the five-foot-three-inch nomad, satchel strapped across his back, socks around his ankles, tight, tight shorts, one cannot help but marvel at the ingenuity, the breathtaking brilliance of the idea.

Every schoolboy with a brain in his head and a bulge in his Y-fronts would love to be a guitar hero; to stand twelve feet above his contemporaries wielding a force he never could in the showers after football.

But when the average guitar hero is stripped of his leopardskintight strides and musketeer shirt, what's left? Nothing more than a schoolboy who shaves.

Angus bridges the gap. You actually think he is a schoolboy reliving his fantasy on stage and the effect is shattering. It makes him the most stunning guitarist around today.

During 'Bad Boy Boogie', when he actually circumnavigates the hall on Bon's shoulders, the whole concept is developed. For not only is the schoolboy indulging in fantasy before your eyes, now he's right there beside you in the audience playing, just like it was your mate who's been mimicking him throughout.

'Every time I ever saw a band, they seemed so far removed from me, so untouchable, that it never seemed completely real,' says Angus, on the coach back to their hotel in London. 'We've been determined to steer away from that. We're real, not a mirage. We're still as raw as the day we started and that gives people value for money. For so long now, fans have been subjected to second-rate bands. Kiss, who only filled a gap left by Bowie, and Nugent and Van Halen, who filled a gap left by Zeppelin. People want the real thing, not imitations. That's why bands like the Who can still sell out Madison Square Garden for a week whereas Kiss can't. Those bands simply used the time in between the tours of bigger groups to their own advantage. They weren't doing anything new.

'But AC/DC has a definite image, a definite style. We don't fill any gaps. Oh, sure, if Zeppelin toured every week we probably wouldn't do so well. But we've always thought we were in the first division, even when we were playing small clubs back in Australia. We never wanted to compete with the local bands – we wanted to compete with the world. Put us on a stage with anybody and we'd hang on in there. Even if we weren't going down well we wouldn't give up.'

Mind you, looking at the tired faces as they watch yet another episode of *Python*, it seems as if they gave up a long time ago.

'Oh, don't let that fool you,' says Angus, breaking open another packet of sweet lollies. 'When roused we can be hell-raisers. During the last French tour one big newspaper said that any girls who came into contact with AC/DC should visit their nearest VD clinic. And that's just 'cos one of us went to a doctor for a penicillin jab while we were there. All that association with shady ladies came about because we once all stayed in the same house and were visited by a whole lotta girls and VD ran amok. Hence the song "She's Got The Jack". Sure, most other bands experience the same things. The only difference is we write songs about it.'

Has the band's attitude changed with the rise in their popularity?

'It's not that we've changed, it's just that we meet a better class of women these days.'

They don't meet them at their gigs, that's for sure. You can count the number of girls among the tattooed, denim-clad audience on the fingers of one hand.

'Women only like to go and see pretty people play and young girls like to think they're older so they'll go to a disco with their friend. Most of the boys that turn up want to be guitar heroes. I love seeing kids, really young kids, being dazzled by it all. In fact I'd rather see them at gigs than going to youth clubs. They can learn by going to a show.'

So how come young Angus made the grade when thousands didn't?

'I had drive. I wanted to do it and I knew I'd do it. I just wanted people to sit up and take notice of me. It was a challenge. I never mellowed, I never changed. I just stuck at it. I was an unhappy schoolboy. Always played truant. I was a bad pupil and only really liked art because you could do what you liked. My school was the third worst in the state. Many of the kids ended up in reform schools. It was so military. They seemed to take great pride out of keeping you in the dark. They didn't want you to know what was going on in the rest of the world. I was really surprised at the way people lived outside Australia when I left it. People were getting away with a lot more than I ever did.'

As the coach pulls up outside the hotel, the Glasgow-born guitarist reveals that he's a little worried about his looks.

'One magazine invited readers to vote for the face of 'seventy-seven,' he recalls, picking the remnants of a strawberry lolly from his teeth. 'My arse came ninth . . .'

Because Bon Scott is feeling under the weather, I don't really get the chance to talk to him. As we alight from the coach outside the Holiday Inn in Swiss Cottage, I realise it's three am and I haven't got nearly enough money for a cab. Shit.

'What's up, mate?' It's Bon.

'Er, nothing.'

'Where do you live?' I think he's sussed.

'Kings Cross.'

'How you getting back?'

'Not sure.'

'I've met you before, haven't I? I mean, before today.'

I remind him I once went to the flat they all used to share in Earls Court – where else? – in '76 after seeing them live at the Marquee and interviewing them for the *South East London Mercury*.

He says he remembers but doesn't look as if he does. Why should he? I'm just a man, an average man, doing the best, the best I can.

'Got enough for a cab?'

'Er, no.'

'Here, take this.'

He slides me a tenner. I decline but he insists and I grab. Quick.

What a nice bloke, and how obliging of him to die a few weeks later after drowning in his own vomit in a car before I had the chance to repay him.

Ex-Geordie vocalist Brian Johnson replaced Bon and later that year they released their most successful-ever album, Back In Black, which sold nearly 50 million copies. They've been going ever since and have shipped over 200 million sales. Johnson was forced to take a break from live singing in 2016 after medical warnings that he was at risk of going totally deaf.

On the day that Hugh Cornwell gets a two-month jail sentence for drug possession, Harry Casey of KC and the Sunshine Band tells me he collects parrots. 'I have fifty in my bedroom at home. One, Sparky, can sing all my hits. The parrots are more intelligent than a lot of people I've met in the music business.'

I think it's a travesty of justice – Hugh, not the parrots – and smacks of one of those make-an-example-of sentences, given purely for the sake of publicity, I used to see a lot as a court reporter.

Hugh had tiny amounts on him when randomly stopped in a car he wasn't even driving, amounts for which anyone else would've been fined or even conditionally discharged. It's anti-punk hogwash. Hugh doesn't have a bad bone in his body. The Stranglers' tough stance and despicable reputation is derived almost entirely from Jean-Jacques Burnel; Hugh is more big softie than arch-villain but his fierce intelligence helps him adapt to any situation.

I feel so strongly that I write to him in prison and he writes back. His letter is long and intimate – unlike many of his interviews – and he mentions he'd like to talk to me about the whole experience in an extended interview when he gets out.

Until then I think it's time to renew my acquaintance with the Clash, who are growing bigger by the minute.

The James Cagney of punk, Joe Strummer – stone-faced, steel-capped, stacked high – sneers and stares, as usual. He's holed up in the Clash house, a terraced tenement twenty-four hours from Tulse Hill. He sticks his gun out of the window. 'Political power grows from the barrel of a gun,' he screams. And smiles.

Next to him Mick 'Humphrey Bogart' Jones is looking depressed. Maybe, he thinks, he wasn't really cut out for this. Casablanca is a million miles away and Claude Rains supreme.

Paul 'Muni' Simenon – or Skaface, as the Streatham Locarno lotus-eaters dubbed him – sits patiently in a corner. He never did like Mondays anyway.

'Edward G' Headon works flat out in the basement supplying the ammo. He smiles. Whatever else may happen, the humdrum will never snare him now.

Outside they put the batteries into the loudspeaker.

Next door Lester bangs on the wall. It's raining. Naturally.

The guy holding the loudspeaker is wet through.

'Come out with your hands up.'

'Come in and get us, Topper – sorry, copper,' says Joe. 'There's no way we're gonna appear on *Top of the Pops* alive. You won't get us standing there like pricks propping up a load of old shit. How can we bash our guitars with passion when they ain't even plugged in? How can we sing when the mic is phoney? The show's like an anaemic rice pudding. Give me *Tiswas* any day.'

Mick turns to Joe. 'But we do lose out by not playing on it. I can't see us ever having a Top Ten single as a result.'

'Mugs!' The word leaps from the loudspeaker and reverberates around the street.

'We'll never change our attitude,' screams Mick, changing his attitude. 'We'll never prostitute ourselves.'

'You might as well go and give someone a blow-job for ten bob than appear on *Top of the* fucking *Pops*,' yells Joe.

Lester bangs on the wall again. 'Hey, you guys, will you shut your fucking noise?'

The loudspeaker guy decides to goad the band. Snipers are positioned on rooftops,

'Your new album's crap.'

'The world is full of assholes,' screams Joe. 'No matter what you do or which way you turn, there's always twenty people ready to slag you off – and they're always the fucking loudest. Well, they can all go fuck themselves. Imagine if you saw your imitators getting hits and glory with their imitations? Wouldn't you feel like leaving them to it and moving onto a new pasture? It makes me sick, watching all these blokes in zipped pants piss-arsing around.'

Mick lights a cigarette and talks through the smoke. 'Maybe we should've brought the first album out again for these idiots, blue eyes.'

'No,' says Joe. 'Maybe we should've brought out a hammer. A nice hammer. Those people who were expecting something heavy from *London Calling* probably think we sound like Frank Sinatra. But it's a damned sight better than most of the other plastic shit like PiL or the Jam. I don't get any kicks out of listening to that.'

'Yeah, but that's you,' says Mick. 'I don't think these bands should be lumbered together just because they don't move you emotionally.'

'I'm not lumbering them together. They're just examples. It's their style of rock – bam bam bam.'

Joe aside: 'I certainly feel better these days. I'm more in touch with reality, the reality of all this monkeying about. Before, we were losing a ton of money, packets of it. On our first tour everyone would just jump into the nearest hotel and smash it up then leave. It never occurred to me that they'd send the bills to just us 'cos everyone was smashing it up – all the support acts. No, we got all the bills for it. That brings you down.'

Mick aside: 'I used to be optimistic. Not anymore. Maybe it's because they wouldn't give me a mortgage. I'm just a misery guts these days. I guess it happened ever since I started getting involved in the Clash.'

In the flashing blue moonlight, Loudspeaker Man calls: 'You can't stay in there for ever.' There's no reply from the house. 'You're just a bunch of publicity-seeking losers.'

'The press love us,' says Joe. 'They're orgasmic about the Clash. That's because we're not dummies. Like with Lester Bangs – he ended up driving round in our van for six days. He must've revelled in it. But I thought all that stuff he wrote was rubbish. You must be able to say it better than that.' Lester stops banging.

Family priest, Spencer Tracy, tells Loudspeaker Man he's going in. He dances in and out of the puddles that lead like a daisy chain to the Clash house. The band watch him enter.

'This is no place for you,' says Joe, as Father Tracy walks in.

'Bejasus, we all became too complacent too fast.'

'I've never been complacent,' says Joe. 'I'd be scared if we had a mammoth hit. Is there anyone in the whole world who can write a good song after selling a million? You can't say John Lennon. You can't say Bob Dylan. The proof is, as soon as they make it they don't seem to be able to write decent songs anymore.'

Father Tracy fondles his rosary. 'But, boys, don't you think you write better songs if you suffer?'

'If you suffer and write bad songs you're suffering even more,' replies Mick, philosophically.

'Yes, my sons,' says Father Tracy. 'But a lot of people have lost faith in you. The band are now doing everything they once vilified – like touring America.'

'Look, Father, we've got to take care of business,' says Joe. 'Instead of sitting in this shithole not selling records, we might as well go to that bigger shithole over there and not sell any. We haven't been to anywhere like Japan yet but we're certainly gonna try to get there this year. I hear it's a bit creepy over there.'

'It's only creepy,' insists Paul, 'because they're all down there and we're all up here.'

'But what about the things you said? People believed in you,' says Father Tracy.

'That was business,' says Joe. 'I don't care about business. I piss on it from a great height. I'm only interested in the music. If that's going great that's all that matters. It's depressing when you lose a lot of dough or when something goes wrong. But it doesn't really affect me as much as the music. If that's cool it dictates all the rest. You've got to realise that I love music. I'm obsessed with it. Surely you don't think I wander round worrying about the economy all the time. Look, if I had a weekend off I'd spend it twanging a guitar, not going to Karl Marx's grave to make a brass rubbing.

'People took us the wrong way. When I sang "Sten Guns In Knightsbridge", it was about them shooting us. But people started saying, "Yeah, the Clash have got the Sten guns." We haven't got any Sten guns, the army have. I tried to make that point clear in interviews afterwards but it was no good. They still kept saying, "If you ever keep that promise to go to Knightsbridge with Sten guns we'll be with you." And then everyone thought we used to wear army fatigues. They weren't. They were Clash trousers.'

'Yeah,' says Paul. 'We designed them with so many pockets so you could hide your dope easily. And they were better than the bondage trousers 'cos you could run in them and hop over walls. With bondage ones you kept tripping over the chains.'

'But the songs on *London Calling*,' says Father Tracy, 'they're not as emotive as before.'

'We're just expanding our subject matter,' replies Joe. 'We don't want to repeat ourselves – that's the most heinous crime you can commit. I mean, do we have to be like the Ramones and release seven albums of the same stuff? If people want that all the time they can get it from the Ruts or the UK Subs. There's plenty of groups playing good head-banging music. *London Calling* is a musical shark attack. The saxes on it are great. It's best not to tart the songs up too much. I mean, I wouldn't put horns on everything. But one day I'd like to have a horn section on stage, not standing at one end all night just blowing but like when they have a funeral in New Orleans and walk in a long line. I'd like them always walking, maybe out into the audience.

'I'm getting nervous now ... Here's looking at you, kid,' he says to Father Tracy.

'But I'm supposed to say that,' says Mick.

'Well, there's no way you're gonna get me to say "you dirty rat".'

'You fucking dirty rat,' says Mick.

By 1983 Mick Jones and Topper Headon had left the band and three years later the Clash were no more. Joe died in 2002 and the band was inducted into the Rock'n'roll Hall of Fame in the following year. In 2004 Rolling Stone ranked 'London Calling' the fifteenth greatest song of all time.

FEBRUARY 1980

The Stranglers

I tell Tim, who knows how much I yearn for Dina, that I'm going to Cyprus to try and persuade her to come back. I never knew I could miss someone so bad.

I book a flight for 14 February – a little different from the Ford Consul trek of seven years earlier – and check into a hotel in the centre of Nicosia. I don't know where she lives and my only lead is the surname of her close friend Haroula, an air hostess for Cyprus Airways whom I met frequently on her many trips to London. I ring head office and the receptionist knows Haroula and has heard my name mentioned, so, obviously being an incurable romantic, she gives me the address. I buy some flowers for Haroula's mum and Dina, and take a cab to the apartment.

The mum opens the door.

'Hi, I'm Barry – Dina's friend from London?'

'My God! Barry! Come in! Come in! Flowers! Thank you! Dina's out with Haroula but I'm expecting them soon! Sit down! Sit down! Dina will be so pleased to see you.'

'You think so?'

'Oh, yes.'

Wait a minute. Her last two sentences didn't end with an exclamation mark. That's kinda worrying. Or is the lack of emphasis a deliberate sun-kissed Mediterranean way of saying she really does miss me?

We have Greek coffee and she's easy to talk to, as most Greeks are, and I can tell she knows the way to Amarillo and understands my pain. I'm standing in a kitchen helping a stranger wash some dishes in the shadows of love in a strange town, but it feels right.

A key turns in the lock.

'Ah! They're here! Quick, go into the living room.'

Do I sit? Do I stand? Do I kiss her on the lips? Do I hold her hands?

Do I ... God, she's beautiful.

'Barry!'

'Hi. Er, Happy Valentine's Day.' I give her the flowers.

She looks a little embarrassed, but not displeased. I have to hug her, and she hugs me back. She loves me, she loves me not.

I check out of the hotel and move into an apartment, which is a lot cheaper and a lot roomier. The weather is cold and damp and over the next nine days I proclaim my undying love: in empty tavernas on the road to Larnaca where we eat fresh-off-the-charcoal *souvla*; in busy Nicosia cafés; in the car on the way back to my apartment from her friend Nora's place where, with Nora's husband Richard, we play Cluedo till dawn; and in my apartment, where she can only stay for a few moments. It's a Greek thing.

Yet I still don't know what she'll do as I board the plane back to London. It's a woman thing.

The first person I interview back at the ranch is Kenny Rogers over lunch in Langan's. He tells me he has an eleven-seater jet, fifteen bodyguards, a priceless collection of antiques, a $4 million colonial mansion in Bel Air with six bedrooms and thirteen baths. 'I have a great fear of reaching seventy and being flat broke,' he says. No chance of that Kenny. 'Money is a form of freedom. I have sacrificed a lot of people for my music, including my ex-wives.'

Standing in front of the imposing gates of Pentonville Prison at six am in the bitter cold, waiting for Hugh Cornwell to emerge after his short but not so sweet jail stint, is an experience I'd rather not repeat in a hurry.

I'd been invited down by the Stranglers' management – I live around the corner – and the place is swarming with reporters and paparazzi as a pale but palpably untampered-with Hugh, emerges. A car is waiting outside to collect him, and as he pushes aside the microphones and shorthand notebooks and flash guns – it's still dark – he catches sight of me and pulls me into the car. Hazel O'Connor is sitting in the back and they fall into each other's arms. I was never sure about that relationship and kinda thought it was more publicity than synchronicity.

We drive to a flat in the West End for coffee and a shitload of smack – only joking. Hugh never touches the stuff again. 'Do you know, I spent the whole time inside cleaning toilets and washing floors – twelve hours a day, seven days a week? I wasn't allowed any exercise and granted only two visits in six weeks. I don't regard prison as a rehabilitating place, just demoralising. All it does is make you more bitter towards the system. It's a complete waste of human activity.'

Hugh and I arrange for me to visit him at his place in Bath a few days later for the interview while the experience is still fresh in his mind.

After spending the day at his home in the hills, where he tells me he's stopped drinking and smoking before seven p.m., I set about transcribing and knocking into some semblance of shape around three hours of tape. It's an erudite, honest, sometimes shocking account.

An excerpt:

I missed the guitar. I wanted to write and play music, but I couldn't.

I didn't see what right they had to deprive me of that. I asked for a guitar and they said, 'We've got bus drivers in here, and they can't have buses.' These were unnecessary restrictions . It doesn't seem to have any positive effect. It just makes you feel bitter, not, 'Oh, I'm going to be a good boy now.'

It makes you even more anti the system than you were before.

I missed not drinking at first, but I got used to it. I never missed taking drugs. Once temptation is removed you're not tempted any more. It's only when you know they're available that you miss them. You forget what it's like to have a drink. After a few weeks it seemed as if I'd been there months, which is frightening. You get accustomed to it. A lot of guys asked me, 'Have you started dreaming about being in here yet?'

It's really worrying when that happens. In all my dreams, and I had a lot, I was going round visiting people on the outside. They'd say, 'What are you doing here? You're supposed to be inside.' And I'd spend the whole dream wondering how on earth I'd got out, and that I had to get back before morning. It was like time travelling.

I remember seeing my mum and saying, 'I've got to be back soon before they find out I've gone.' And I'd wake up wondering how I did it. My mum and dad were very good about it. I didn't want them to come and visit me though. Visits were great because that's when you found out what was going on. The solicitor came every week and told me what was happening and gave me any messages.

You can have any publication. I had a paper every day. But you don't get it until the afternoon. You can have a radio. But you can't have more than one to a cell. One guy I shared with also had a radio. When I said, on leaving prison, that it was the most humiliating, degrading experience of my life, I was referring to when the screws were psychologically trying to cut me down, trying to destroy my personality, depersonalise me. Nobody's got the right to do that, whatever you've done. It can really affect you.

I send it to him to check over and meanwhile juice up the *News of the World*, who are salivating at the prospect of a two-part feature. A couple of weeks go by and I hear nothing from Hugh. The *News of the World* is starting to lose interest. Then I get a parcel hand-delivered to the office containing half a dozen copies of a slim but professionally produced book entitled, *Inside Information* that turns out to be my draft transcript of Hugh's interview. I'm credited inside as transcriber.

So what am I gonna do? Sue them? The publication is given away free to members of the Stranglers' fan club and that's the death knell for any national newspaper interest and any big bucks for me. Ah, well, I guess there's no such thing as a free lunch after all. But I've seen a few things with these boys and it's a relatively painless payback.

Only goes to prove that in the land of big softies I'm the biggest.

Nothing from Dina.

I kick make-believe tin cans around my bedroom while my mum and dad watch telly next door. I'm nearly twenty-eight. This doesn't feel right any more. Nothing feels right any more. I've got this glam life yet I still live at home and never have to iron a shirt. And the woman I love has rejected me. I know I'll never see her again. It's as final as, well, me ever ironing.

I take a month off. I can do that now.

APRIL 1980

Spandau Ballet

I write yet another letter to Dina but her love for me is dying. I know it. Dying. Everything is dying – look at punk. .

Dig the new breed who are still pretty much the old breed with the occasional knob on. The Jam, the Clash and the Stranglers are no longer punk bands in any sense of the word. They've 'progressed'. A straight punk band isn't cool any more. Ska has wrestled the scene away from punkified London and carried it off to a ghost town in the bleak midwest for a bleak midwinter.

The papers search lustily amongst the pretty young things for the next musical twirl to generate a fashion quirk that can fill an empty white page with a flourish. Goths are drab, punks passé and two-tone is too grey.

The New Romantics are tailor made to be the next big thing – all masculine coquettishness and afternoon delight; bright and breezy with lashings of sauciness and doomed to the lifespan of a mayfly.

Any Technicolor light at the end of a decaying tunnel will do and I toddle along to see the darlings of New Romanticism, Spandau Ballet, play a rare live show at Scala, now home of ambiguous celluloid once but once called the King's Cross Gaumont where my nan and granddad fell asleep in the darkness either side of me as I watched The Absent-Minded Professor and Whistle Down The Wind.

Spandau Ballet? Shit name. New Romantics? Dubious movement that reeks of hype and kilts. When I discover the band went to my school, I became even more sceptical. Owen's may have had a great reputation as a top class grammar taking only the best students locally, but many a rogue came out the other end, intelligent but still a rogue. The school was slap-bang in the middle of some of the toughest council estates in London, what did they fucking expect? Islington is a shithole.

I'd missed the Spandau guys at school by the wrong side of five years and didn't know them from Adam, but they sounded like a bunch of middle-class chancers; the school also had its fair share of those. They'd been wearing disguises for four years – first as pseudo-rock band The Cut, then early punk outfit The Makers, who actually played The Roxy, only to change again to power-pop band Gentry. All this New Romantic shit is just another disguise.

They're the spokesmen for the variegated peacocks that inhabit the translucent world of London's clique-clubs like Blitz and St Moritz and Gottheshitz and the band crack their bone china hearts.

When I arrive at Scala in my jeans and T-shirt, I feel remarkably underdressed in the face of the jamboree bags out in force to see their heroes play and who pump some Hollywood juice into that seedy Kings Cross night. The clothes are unacceptable in bleak mid-London but unspeakably cool nevertheless and the make-up is Louis XVI meets Marilyn Monroe on acid.

If the band look anything remotely like this lot, what the fuck are they going to sound like? I haven't heard a note of their music – a record deal is yet to be signed – but I figure it will be pretentious tosh with frilly bits and perish the moment it drips out of their limp instruments.

But there's no denying the whiff of old-fashioned excitement in the air before the band are due on stage, fashionably late of course. This is outstanding hyperbole engineered by manager Steve Dagger and his crew and even I get a few butterflies.

And everyone smells so nice.

It begins in darkness, taut waves of sound stripped of melody yet still retaining depth in the black. The riff is repeated over and over but it isn't repetitive, it's infectious. And then a voice as unexpected as bishop in a brothel surges forth.

'Soldier is turning / See him through white light'

Instead of the uptight nasally bollocks usually associated with electronic music, it's full-on croon with soul. I've never heard a voice like it in rock before, so incongruous yet so harmonious. It's Kraftwerk with a northern soul and you can really dance to this shit.

Their stage presence, hewed by four years of pushin' broom, is compelling. Tony Hadley is a giant of a man with a giant of a voice and boy, they sure know how to play.

They only perform a short set, but I've seen enough. Spandau Ballet are a cool band and head honchos of a new, romantic sound that is the twirl required to generate the fashion quirk. This is the real deal.

I have to interview Gary Kemp after the show in an office at Scala and I'm not enamoured with the idea. I still believe he's a middle-class wanker. I think they all are. Any cunt could be a punk but it took a swish cunt to be a New Romantic. I was quite happy seeing them live and taking that memory home and I don't want to be disappointed like I often am when I meet the perpetrators of wonderful music. My problem, not theirs, I guess.

But orders is orders, captain, and I sit in the office, waiting to be disappointed. Gary swishes in. I stand up and we shake hands.

He wears a plain white shirt, black watch tie and grey trousers with large window pane check and an obligatory sporran. 'The shirt cost a fiver from M&S, the trousers are from Modern Classics in East London and the tie is from the Scotch House. I got the brogues from a market stall for seven quid.' The whole ensemble for under thirty pounds. So he watches the pennies.

'It's not hard to look smart anymore. Oh sure, you can go on about how kids have got nothing and come from deprived backgrounds. But surely if you've got nothing you've got to look smart – cos that's ALL you've got .

'If you can't make money to buy your way out of your present life, if you can't play a guitar or write a book or paint a picture, then the only alternative is to take pride in your appearance. It's your strength.'

The moment he opens his mouth, all my pre-conceptions go out the window. Gary is an Angel face from exactly the same background as me. Spandau Ballet may look like dilettante dandies carved out of cold middle-class stone. But they're not. They may easily be mistaken for the offspring of 'professional people' who, after cultivating a chic intolerance to their milieu since mid-teens, fly their Habitats and slide into metrosquats where they become, er, predictably hip. But they're not. In the downrush, in the waterfall world of decibels, pork-pie hats, black leather jackets, two-tone tremors and surrogate quiffs, Spandau Ballet are a big splash that hasn't finished climbing yet.

The band are from Islington and classed as working. They're the end product of a highly stylised, high-rise tradition. Like great eagles circling the grey skies of pre-rock'n'roll London, the borough councils plucked us from bathroom-less slums and flew us way up into the clouds before dropping us onto tower blocks, where we feathered our nests in flats with bathrooms and mirrors and hatched cults and trends in the shadows of Elvis and the Beatles. Working class kids plus bathrooms equalled style and innovation. Seeing our reflections regularly helped to change the world and the demise of once-a-week bathing made us confident and clean and enabled us to create the sixties, the most crucial decade in history simply because for the first time the working classes could determine their destinies.

For the last twenty-five years the working classes have been the most fashion-conscious by being the most extreme. Spandau Ballet ride the fashion stagecoach on top and up front, cocksure but always romantic.

'Working-class people have always been into style,' says Gary with the familiar accent, mine. 'They've always wanted to look good. Always the only people who could dance to black American music.

'We were always down the clubs, having our hair cut into wedge shapes, dancing. It was always soul music, never rock. Even though they don't look it, our audience is essentially made up of soul and style boys. There's no comparison between us and anybody else. We're not the product of the middle-class rock press who, for the first time, have been able to dictate to the working-class kids how they should be dressing. That's disgusting.

'The middle-classes have never been able to cope with working-class elitism. That's why they can't get into mod or soul boys. That's why they won't get into this.'

So how come a bunch of hyperactive WC kids ended up in fancy-pants soluble clubs like Blitz? 'We just didn't want to hang out at the Lyceum every weekend,' said Gary. 'We've always been ahead of fashion. Things I wore in the summer and had the piss taken for wearing are now available in the chain stores in watered-down versions.

'It's not the music so much as the fashion. Clothes have been progressing but recently took a bad turn when they reached the science-fiction stage. They looked cheap. The reaction against that was very simple – a return to the decadent forties. But that only lasted a couple of weeks. You have to be prepared to change very quickly. Now we dress very, very romantically. We want to be dandies not clones.'

'Everyone is sick to death of rock. I detest the word. It's been going on for twenty years. We play dance music, regimental structures on the rhythm, laid-back guitar, and a voice you can actually understand. For the last two years I've been trying hard not to listen to too much music. We never go to see bands play. We simply don't see ourselves as a "band" in that sense.'

He firmly believes that people had been misinterpreting the scene. 'Punk was simply a piece of fashion designed to last a few months. But everyone turned it into a tradition. Rock music has got nothing to do with politics. You can't change the world in a song. But you can change people's attitude to music. Punks are the hippies of the Eighties.'

Gary is adamant that in the hierarchy of things, fashion

predominates. 'If I had a choice between fashion and music I'd go for fashion. The people that go to clubs like Blitz are not gay just because they dress strangely. It's not a question of sex at all. The guys like to look at themselves more than at girls. They can fall in love with their friend's clothes. It really is a working-class thing, no matter what you think. The designers, the musicians – they're all working class.'

Whether or not Spandau will prove to be harbingers of an erudite era remains to be seen. But they can pirouette past my place anytime.

Spandau went from strength to strength throughout the 1980s but broke up in 1990. They sued the pants off each other during the next ten years, but eventually re-formed in 2009. Pop's a funny ol' game. Gold has been played four billion times on American radio.

MAY 1980

Barry White, Devo, Mrs Constantia Cain

A few choice words told to yours truly down the telephone line . . .

Dexy's Kevin Rowland: 'Rock is totally dead. It's been going for twenty-five years, and if it's not dead it's high time it was. I haven't heard a decent rock song for five years. Music went wrong after Sixties soul broke down.'

The Blues Band's Paul Jones, who hangs up on me when I press him about his private life: 'Music was full of angry young men singing about depressing things. We wanted to bring some fun back to the scene. Blues zooms in on the emotions.'

Hot Chocolate's Errol Brown: 'I watched *TOTP* and thought I'd never appear on it again. Then a friend saw a huge light over Hampstead and was convinced it was a UFO. When he told me I started to write "No Doubt About It" and it was our first number one.'

I also get to have a chat with Johnny Mandell who wrote the

M.A.S.H. theme, 'Suicide Is Painless' and a particular favourite of mine, 'The Shadow Of Your Smile'. Old, romantic and tender. And the song's not bad either.

The thing about Barry White's house is the water. It's everywhere, cascading from fountains in hallways, meandering through rooms in tasteful streams before flowing into the vast swimming- pool outside.

Barry White's water ain't wet. It's cool. Real cool.

'I like water. It's soothing, sensual, a constant reminder of God. It flows.'

The last word seems to last forever as it drifts out onto the dance floor looking for romance.

The thirty-seven-year-old undisputed king of aural sex is sitting opposite me at a table by the side of his Olympic-size pool in the backyard of his house in the Hollywood Hills. He's slimmed down after doctors warned him his excess weight would kill him if he didn't act now.

More people must've made love to Barry White than any other singer. His voice – a cocktail of obscenity, serenity and inevitability – has been known to make some girls go weak at the knees and strong at the thighs. 'You're The First, The Last, My Everything' and 'Just The Way You Are' are two of the finest moments ever committed to vinyl and wonderful to dance to with the girl you love.

He singlehandedly got a generation of British guys to say, 'Oh, baby,' when they screwed. My old man would never have dreamed of saying it to his wife and my grandfathers in their flat caps had never said 'baby' in that context in their lives.

I don't know which is more exciting – being Barry White's guest or finally meeting a superstar called Barry. His wife, Glodean, brings out a jug of iced tea . She was originally a singer in Barry's backing band – only Barry White could be married to someone from something called Love Unlimited.

'Making love to someone you love is the most beautiful thing you can ever do,' Barry tells me. 'Why shouldn't I sing about that? Every act has a thing and my thing is love. Physical, sensual love.' When he talks I feel like I'm being seduced. He really should have a licence for that voice. It's like a soulful sax in a smoky club.

Glodean smiles knowingly.

'I really don't think enough people quite understand the power of love,' says Barry. 'I hope my music has gone some way to enlightening them. I know my songs have echoed around a million bedrooms during that mystical, magical moment. Guys have told me they thought I was in the room with them. Do you know, in 1974 loads of babies were christened "Barry"? There was a Barry boom!'

I must admit, I haven't come across any five-year-old boys called Barry. Then again, I don't really get to hang out much with five-year-olds. I understand they don't drink alcohol.

Before becoming the ultimate aphrodisiac, Barry looked as if he might enter a life of crime. He was brought up on the tough streets of downtown LA with his younger brother Darryl. 'I was in a bad gang and at the age of fifteen I went to jail for stealing tyres.'

He turned to music for salvation. 'Music was an integral part of my home life. My mother Sadie was a piano teacher and she'd play classical records all day long. I became fascinated by the melodies and the structure. When I was barely out of nappies my mother would sing to me and I'd sing the counterline. It just came naturally.'

Barry, who cannot read or write music, recalls that his brother was into fighting while he was into music. Sadie, an ex-movie actress, was the single biggest influence on Barry's life. 'She taught me all the important things – decency, morality, how to treat a lady. I'll treasure her memory for ever.'

Barry's brother Darryl was slain in a gangland related incident three years after that interview. In 1993 Barry's beautiful home was destroyed in an earthquake. He never again touched those magical highs of the mid-Seventies but was still a well-respected artist who picked up thirty-

seven platinum and over a hundred gold records. He died in 2003 at the age of sixty after suffering a stroke.

Devo are wearing Bill and Ben flowerpots on their heads when I meet up with them the next day on a movie set at Universal Studios. I don't like to say anything – the daft todgers might take offence and boot me in the flubberglub. It's perfectly obvious to them what those pillar-box red plastic hats signify.

Winkies!

Or, to be more precise, Aztec Winkies!

Hats, it seems, are merely penile projectiles in the Devo dictionary of daffy definitions.

'They are the sign of a man's sexuality. They represent the energy of the organ,' says Gerry Casale, without the slightest hint of a smirk.

Brings a whole new meaning to giving head.

And, like all Devo concepts, the hat-wearing has a dualistic connotation, or the Tweedledum and Tweedledee syndrome.

'They are festive hats,' continues Gerry. 'We wear them to create a party atmosphere. We want to be the life and soul of the party, like the guy who gets drunk and sticks a lampshade on his head to get a laugh.'

Mark Mothersbraugh gives one of his customary tag lines that always seem to crystallise a particular facet of Devo psychology in one searing, succinct sentence. 'David Bowie used to wear a plastic hat too . . .'

I'm being treated to a preview of their new show – the final one before they embark on a world tour to promote their new album, *Freedom of Choice*. It's remarkable. The speakers double up as the light show to produce some stunning monochrome effects and the encore, a medley of songs from Stevie Wonder's *The Secret Life of Plants* using the flowerpots to maximum advantage, has to be seen to be believed.

After they finish, the band wander up and down Sunset Strip wearing grey vinyl suits. It's so hot you can actually hear their feet squelching in their pillar-box red shoes. And naturally they wear those hats. They're posing for a photo session and attract the attention of T-shirted LA types noticeable by their dumb expressions and limited stoned-clad vocabulary.

'Hi. Hey. Wha' . . .? Hey. Hi. Devo, huh? Shit. Hi. Hey. Mind if I, er ... Yeah? No kiddin'. Hey. Hi . . .'

The articulate Devo, gleaming metallic sex pistons of techno-brash, provide a sharp contrast to this ring of mediocrity.

What lurks behind the clinical, boiler-suited exterior? Do their hearts pump blood or BP? Are they just a bunch of Dunlops rushing in where angels fear to tread, or are they the harbingers of a duty free *Tomorrow's World*?

Devo are an exquisite enigma. Or is it enema? Whatever, they have confused and confounded the British press who seem incapable of accepting them on any serious level.

And nobody could believe it when these strange, fragile-looking beings appeared not to see the joke. Oh, sure they would, as they do now, sit with you and mock a quasi-intellectual article rejoicing at their 'reductive synthesis', but if you went away and wrote a piece with tongue firmly in cheek, they seemed to get hurt.

'We answered questions in earnest,' says Gerry, sipping a glass of Californian champagne. It's now midnight. We're in a downtown bar and they're still wearing fucking flowerpots on their heads.

'The British seem to lack a sense of humour about it all. We were just stirring things up for fun. Devo are just playing with reality.

'In the end, everyone resorts to religion, right-wing politics and disco. Devo are observers of the human condition. But the joke is, we're part of that condition too.'

What does Devo-lution mean, Gerry?

'Stripping away the shit. When Bob Seger writes, "I like to watch her strut", you tell him that's a fucking joke. You tell him that's a fucking stupid line. That's my freedom of choice. Don't expect me to wear gypsy leather trousers and go out and sing, "I like to watch her fucking strut". I'm confident that there's a whole segment of society that doesn't want to hear about girls strutting or pulling triggers on devils' guns.'

'Devo's programme is the alternative to sock-in-the-crotch rock. Our sexuality is more like Henry Ford and the assembly line. We are sexual in a powerfully clean, technological way. Devo is the cleansing agent for all the awful records out there. Devo presents you with a pure and healthy sex. I've never been able to understand why a woman wants a man with a great big hairy belly. They must have a perverted and demented view of sex.'

So that's why Dina stayed with me.

'A lot of people represent the medieval kind of sex, like Rod Stewart, while we represent the new sex. Girls in Spandex pants are turned off by Devo because they are into medieval sexuality. After the A-bomb and A-rseholes, Devo will emerge as heads of the post sexual revolution.'

And now we must go because the man from the house is walking down the garden path and will be here any moment.

Hurry, he's about to open the door of the greenhouse.

W-e-e-e-e-e-d!

Devo released three albums in the 1980s, then stopped performing and recording in 1984. Three years later they emerged from a self-imposed hibernation, released two more poor-selling albums, embarked on a world tour and broke up in 1991. Mark Mothersbaugh wrote the music for Rugrats. They re-formed in 1996, and in 2006, under the name Jihad Jerry & the Evildoers, the band released the EP, 'Army Girls Gone Wild' followed by the album Mine Is Not A Holy War. Alas, drummer Alan Myers died in 2013 aged 58 and Bob Casale passed away the following year aged 61

From weeding to wedding.

I get married. Straight up.

Dina has come down the garden path. It's me! Again! Me over the sunshine, the laughter, the comfort of family and friends with a clear blue sea and pine-clad mountains never too far away. Me.

I'm at Heathrow, again, waiting for her plane. Waiting to hear her say, 'Barry,' before we kiss at the arrivals gate, the most romantic place in the world. Waiting to hold her close and whisper in her ear, 'I love you so very much. Never leave me again.' Waiting to hear her say, 'Never, my love'. Waiting to hear the Association sing it over the loudspeaker ...

'Would a Mr Barry Cain kindly make himself known to airport security?' My reverie is broken. Jesus. The whole airport just heard my name. Do I have any drugs on me? Nope. Guns? Nope. Am I illegally parked? Nope. Then what the hell?

'Oh, please follow me, Mr Cain,' says the airport security guy. I follow him into airport security territory and then a swift left, slap-bang into the Immigration Office. Dina is seated at a desk, behind which sits an older, wiser airport security guy without the uniform. I haven't seen her in three months and she's just too good to be true.

I think the guy saw the look of love but procedure is procedure.

'You are Mr Barry Cain, is that correct?'

'Yes.'

'Have you some form of ID?'

I had a cheque guarantee card, a library card and a membership card for the Zanzibar in Covent Garden.

'And you know this woman?'

'Yes.'

'Her name?'

'Miss Dina Constantinou.'

'No, it's not Dina,' says Dina. 'That's not on my passport.'

'Sorry, yes – it's, er ...' Cantstandyou, Constanya '... Constantia.' Not a good start.

'Well, it appears that Miss Constantinou's entry visa expired some time ago and she was staying in this country illegally. I've explained to Constantia that we can't really let her into the country.'

I've never heard anyone call her by her real name before. It sounds strange.

'Under any circumstance?' I tentatively ask.

'Well, if Miss Constantinou can find a guarantor, she can stay for seven days and apply for a visa.'

'But visa applications can take weeks.'

'I know. It's really rather a *Catch-22* situation. Besides, the fact that she broke the visa rules means they may well decide not to issue her with one.' He pauses and looks at me carefully – or, as my nan used to say, in an old-fashioned way.

'There is an alternative. But it's a long shot.'

'What's that?'

'Well, if you were to get married, the authorities might – I say *might* – be inclined to look more leniently on the situation.'

'What? Get married in seven days?'

'I'm afraid so. And even then it's only a slim chance that she'll be allowed to stay.'

I turn to Dina. 'Dina, Constantia, I know I asked you three years ago to marry me. Will you? This week?'

'Oh, I don't know. Let's just see what happens in the next few days.'

She still hasn't said, 'Barry.' We still haven't kissed.

I sign a few forms, and the immigration officer tells us we have to report back to him one week from today.

'Good luck,' he says, as we get up to leave.

'I think we'll need it,' says Dina.

I don't. Six days later we get married at Finsbury Register Office. In the meantime I contact our respective local MPs, who send us letters of encouragement and bring the matter before the immigration minister who informs them he will look into our situation.

On our wedding night, after I've written up the Barry White interview for the *Daily Record*, Dina and I dine at Langan's. It almost feels like the Last Supper: we have to report to the immigration officer tomorrow and his 'slim chance' pessimism pervades each course, each

288 Varieties of Talk Soup

glass of wine, each loving word. This time tomorrow Dina could be boarding a plane for Larnaca at a foggy Heathrow and I'll be walking back out of the terminal building with the immigration officer telling me, 'This could be the start of a beautiful relationship.'

'Well, you've certainly got some friends in high places,' says the immigration officer, the next morning. He's wearing a different suit and a different smile. 'It seems, Miss – or should I say Mrs? – Constantia Cain can stay. But if you ever leave the country there might be a problem when you come back through Immigration, though hopefully you'll find a sympathetic person that day. Congratulations to you both. I'll hope you'll be very happy together. At least now you've got a story to tell your grandchildren.'

If he only knew the half, I think, and look at him in an old-fashioned way.

A week later we have the wedding reception upstairs at a friend's pub just off New North Road in Islington, and later end up at another friend's impressive house around the corner that one wag describes as decorated in 'gangster chic'.

So, now I'm married and I can sense my travelling days are numbered.

But who wants the world when you've got Malcolm McLaren?

JUNE 1980

Malcolm McLaren, Don McLean

I'm sitting in the office when the phone rings. It has a habit of doing that. Must get it fixed.

'Hello, is that Barry?'

'Yes.'

'Great. My name's Jamie Reid – I did a bit of artwork for the Pistols.'

A bit? He was responsible for all of the Pistols' graphics. What on earth is the man who invented punk art doing ringing me?

'I'm just standing here in Covent Garden with Malcolm and he suggested I give you a call. Malcolm's thinking of writing a book about the whole Pistols shebang and he wondered if you might be interested in getting involved.'

Of all the gin joints in all the world he decides to walk into mine. This is a great honour. McLaren is one of the hottest tickets in town – everyone wants to interview him. But a book. And maybe written by me. Yabbadabbadoo!

The three of us meet up the next day in a pub near the office. I suggest that instead of a book about the Pistols, why not his autobiography, which I could ghost-write? Malcolm, who spends about 80 per cent of the time smiling, likes the idea and Jamie, reserved but genuinely interested, is a sweetheart from head to toe.

It's all agreed, and Malcolm contacts his lawyers. Love is in the air. A week later I haggle with him over the contract in a pub off Fleet Street and a favourite haunt of *Evening News* reporters. As I walk in with Malcolm I spot John Blake sitting with a few guys at a table in the corner. The moment he catches sight of us he starts denouncing Malcolm, who gives as good as he gets. And it makes me look pretty cool having the cutest girl on the hot story beach on my arm.

John is one of the smoothest operators I've met and it was a privilege to work alongside him at the *News* for his Ad Lib column. I became wise to the do-re-me of cutting-edge journalism under his tutelage but that's part of my past now. It's difficult to justify a week's shift on the *News* these days while trying to build the Farringdon Agency into the top pop news agency.

A top pop agency that gets an exclusive interview – by a hotel pool in Tel Aviv – with Mr Don McLean.

Now, I remember, a long, long time ago, when his music used to make me smile. Now he makes me weep with a glorious version of Roy Orbison's peach, 'Crying', currently at number one .

The thirty-four-year-old singer who tasted superstardom at the turn of the Seventies with classic records like 'Vincent', 'And I Love You So' and, of course, 'American Pie', looked to be all washed up eight years ago. He couldn't buy a hit.

Anyone who knows anything about pop would put 'Vincent' and 'Pie' in their all-time best-records list. I'd never before heard lyrics quite like, 'portraits hung in empty halls, frameless heads on nameless walls with eyes that watch the world and can't forget'. I believe 'Vincent' contains the finest words ever committed to a number-one record. That kind of talent can never die while the artist still draws breath. It was only a matter of time.

His decision to record a version of Roy Orbison's classic tear-jerker 'Crying' – a song Don had included in his stage show for many years – has made Don McLean hot property once more. It's like the Bible tells you so.

Well, isn't romance kinda wonderful . . .?

'It's like 1971 all over again,' says Don, as he lazes poolside on a sunbed beneath a burning sky at the Tel Aviv Hilton where he's basking in his new success before flying back to his native New York. He's trim in trunks and the oily rays loosen him up. 'I hear all these twelve-year-old kids walking around singing "American Pie" in the streets and I think, My God, that's amazing. It's great to think that just one generation liked your music – but now it's starting all over again. I've done a lot in this business and this is the most incredible thing that's ever happened to me.'

Don may have been out of the spotlight for the last eight years but he was seldom out of the limelight. 'My career is playing my music to people,' he says. 'I've been packing out concert halls all over the world for years. Just because I've been out of the charts it doesn't mean I've not kept on playing. I'm a born survivor. I enjoy the struggle of continually trying to get my music across. You read of people in this business who've committed suicide because they couldn't cope with that struggle.

'I guess I'm lucky to have escaped in one piece. Right now I feel very happy about my life and my career. In fact, I don't seem to have any problems at all. But I can't deny that you do get a lot of scars over the years.'

One of those scars was a broken marriage. Don was divorced at the tail end of his first flush of success. It's left him with a bitter taste. 'After that there was no way I could think the marriage system was right. Marriage just doesn't fit in with my way of life – which is pretty peculiar anyway, what with travelling all the time and having hundreds of people trying to contact you every day.'

But Don does have a new girl in his life. She's a beautiful young Israeli called Orly, which accounts for his Tel Aviv holiday. 'We met six months ago but then she was conscripted into the Israeli Army. I'm just visiting her for a few days. My life has enabled me to have friends, very close friends, all over the world. It's funny, I don't make friends very easily, just that kinda guy, I guess. But when I do they're usually for life.'

His songs are often accused of being too maudlin and sentimental, which he accepts.

'I seem to be more effective when I sing about gloomy things. I guess that's only because I read the newspapers. It's very difficult for me to provide escapist entertainment these days. People are more aware of what's happening in the world and it's making them feel pretty sad. I just reflect that. I leave "entertainment" to others. I've always wanted to be different. I think my singing is very similar to method acting. You reach inside yourself and get lost in a particular emotion. And I seem to find myself reaching a gloomy emotion easier than any other. But don't get me wrong. I'm a pretty happy guy. That's why I never stopped playing my banjo at shows!'

And what about that sentimentality?

'Well, isn't romance kinda wonderful . . .?'

Don has continued to perform and his last album, Addicted To Black was released in 2009. In 2004 he was inducted into the Songwriters Hall of Fame. He has two children and lives with his wife Patrisha in Maine. The handwritten lyrics for 'American Pie' sold at auction for £1.3 million.

JULY 1980

The Stranglers

The phone rings at six a.m. It's Saturday morning. Who's ringing me at this unearthly hour? I slide out of bed, careful not to disturb my wife of two months who is probably dreaming of me (?).

'Barry, hi, it's Ian Grant.'

The Stranglers' manager? What does he want with me?

'Look, the band has just been arrested in Nice for inciting the fans to riot at their concert. Can you get any publicity for us? It'll help their cause.'

I manage to get through to the news desk at the *News of the World* and end up speaking to Sue Carroll, who used to knock around with Ros and Sheila from *Record Mirror*. I tell her what's happened and go back to bed.

The next morning the story is splashed across the front page. Sue makes sure I get a cheque for seventy pounds, which ain't bad for a phone call. Good job I've got some Inside Information.

A week later – would you believe? – I'm in Rome with the men in black themselves. Mmmnn, smells like teen spirit . . .

'Friends, Romans, countrymen – lend us your ears.'

A creditable Cornwellian preface to the Stranglers' first gig since their not-so-Nice within these walls residency.

An unlikely setting – a far from verdant park in the middle of a babbling metropolis overlooked by a towering Castel where popes of old sought refuge from irate parishioners by nipping along an underground passage connected to the Vatican nearby.

By ten p.m., the park is overflowing with eight thousand roaring Radis raring to root, toot and generally get down to the band, whose pasta exploits have made them a household word in every prison in Europe and Top of the Popes in Italy.

The Stranglers have reached a Spaghetti Junction in their career. Unaided by airplay, their last few singles have plopped in and rippled out again. Their credentials as first-division rock maestros have taken a battering.

But under the stars in Cornetto Land they prove once more – after a shaky start – that live they not only still cut it, they disembody it, skewer it and burn it over red-hot coals.

Previous alfresco Stranglers' gigs have been dismal affairs. They found it difficult to breeze with the sleaze among the birds, bees and smell of burning grass. But in in Rome they slaughter the Italians who, in the end, refuse to leave after the stipulated one encore. They bombard the stage with cans of Peroni and empty Chianti bottles until the band return with a bare-chested Jean-Jacques causing a few macaroni madonnas to actually scream.

If a spell in the nick does this, I hope they get solitary next time.

But let's not dwell on past misdemeanours.

There is an inveterate terror of the Stranglers within the media and the business.

'People are frightened of all sorts of things – the dark, crossing the road, spiders.' Jet Black, his customary drawl slowly filling the room like an inflating dinghy, sits on the edge of a Roman bed. It's three am and Hugh Cornwell lounges on a pillow at the other end.

'Our black clothes are not meant to evoke fear. Have you ever been frightened by a priest walking down the street?' asks Hugh. Joyce and Jung were – but that's another story.

Dave Greenfield sits cross-legged on the floor of the hotel room. The Mephistophelean motor madmen of the Mediterranean are all asleep in the ancient city, dreaming of hooters and scooters.

Next door Jean sleeps.

Earlier in the day the following 'interview' took place, Jean recumbent in his bedroom, me sitting on the edge of his bed, tape machine whirring conspicuously, preventing the pre-gig snooze he so obviously wanted.

Why are the Stranglers always finding themselves in trouble?

'I don't think about it. Past caring.'

Do you go looking for it like a lot of people assume?

'That's their problem. I can see this one's gonna be a good 'un. I'm only gonna keep you for half an hour.'

Er, aren't the band after the maximum amount of publicity?

'It really doesn't bother me if people think that or not.'

So, come on, Jean, have you changed in any way over the last year? I haven't seen you for ages.

'We've provided you with some good fucking gigs in the last few years.' True. I hate the Stranglers, really. I only made out I liked you so you'd take me to Japan, Iceland, France and now Italy. But, em ... Shit, it's hard asking questions when I've asked so many in the past.

'So why are you bothering?'

The entire music press hates you.

'Great. Maybe we're the plague. Maybe they're shit scared of us. I really don't know and I really don't care, to tell you the truth.' .

I bet you do, really.

'No, I don't.'

I don't believe that. You still must be concerned about your image.

'No, not at all. How can we be concerned about an image when everyone knows about us anyway?'

Do you think you're as popular as you were?

'Of course not.'

Why?

'Every band has fluctuations.'

Do you worry about getting old?

'Getting old? I worry about my faculties diminishing.'

Are you a different person than you were a year ago?

'Yeah.'

Why?

'I'm a year older.'

That's not an answer.

'It is. It'll do for now. Look, the Stranglers' music has mellowed out. The Stranglers have gone the opposite way.'

Opposite way of what?

'Mellow. What's the opposite to mellow? Rougher. Yeah.'

And you?

'I'm not really important.'

I feel as though I'm disturbing you.

'You've got nothing to talk to me about.'

It's true.

Back in that bare, boiling bedroom, I ask Hugh how he felt about his rapid rise to the position of prison veteran. What was it like when the door slammed behind you for the second time in a matter of months?

'I thought it was ironic. You appreciate everything that happens to you when you come out of the nick simply because you're denied so much. I was just getting back to enjoying freedom when suddenly it all happens again.

'At first when you're inside you have to adjust. It's hard but when you've got a hand on that you're OK. But if you have to keep adjusting that's gonna lead to long-term mental damage. I derived many benefits from that first spell inside. I got nothing out of it in Nice.'

You've perpetrated some pretty nefarious deeds– dirty ones done dirt cheap, in fact.

'Such as?'

Intimidation, violence, kidnapping, and then there are the really bad things...

'Who can honestly stand up and say that at one point in their life they haven't intimidated someone?' asks Hugh.

'What is misunderstood,' says Jet, 'is the fact that we happen to have a sense of humour. But very few people see that and predictably the wrong conclusions are drawn. It's an occupational hazard.'

The band are also in Rome mixing their new album, *Meninblack*.

'One of its themes,' says Jet, Disney starlight piercing the window, 'is the Men In Black, mysterious people connected with interstellar travel. We've been planning this album for a long time. Look at the window on the cover of the *Rattus* album . . .'

'The unknown,' says Hugh, 'is one of the fundamental points of interest of the band. In our conceit, we consider ourselves to be artists, and when we do something we do it for a reason that we understand. That really is all we want to do – explore our art form as we see it.

'I hope we're not an average band. If we are then we're not artists. We're probably the most different band there is. Most groups are of a similar age. They're brought up together and have the same musical and lyrical ideas. We're just so different it's ridiculous – Hugh and Jean are academics, Dave is a statistical whiz-kid, I'm just thick. It simply shouldn't work, but luckily we happen to be four people who understand each other.'

'We came,' says Hugh, 'from four different directions but we ended up in the same state of mind.'

Jet: 'I think the only common denominator about the Stranglers is we were all brought up in England.'

Hugh quit the band in 1990 to pursue a solo career and the other three members have continued to perform and record to the present day. Jet Black is 109.

AUGUST 1980

Bow Wow Wow

Bow Wow Wow's Annabella is the last person I'd ever interview for *Record Mirror*, and the iniquitous influence of McLaren looms large.

If only I had a sweaty packet of old boiled sweets in my crusty pocket. Instead, I'll just have to make do with rabid puppy love and half a pound of lumpy, cold voyeurism.

Annabella, I think I'm in love. I don't care about Bow Wow Wow, home taping or piracy. I don't care that you've allowed that malevolent Eighties Fagin, Malcolm McLaren, who makes a living out of misanthropy, to inveigle his way into your life.

I don't care.

That's all behind us now. Before us? Sun, sea and piracy.

She sits, this Captain Kid, in the Vivienne Westwood/McLaren designed pirate clothes – baggy orange shirt with blue polka dots and fluffy sleeves, sash, hair ribbon.

'I'm going to have ringlets in my hair too, like the pirate women had, and a Napoleon hat. It's not punk, it's pirates.'

And I'm all at sea. Annabella is half Burmese. I'm half pissed. The girl that brought you 'C30 C60 C90 Go', the girl who follows in the footsteps of Sid, is cute with a kapital K.

Her face is sexy with hint of roly-poly voluptuousness. Annabella, I think you're attractive, they think you're attractive, but do *you* think you're attractive?

'Me? Attractive? Nah. When I look in the mirror I think eeerrrgh! You know, I always wanted to look like someone in *Charlie's Angels*.'

Who, Farrah Fawcett?

'Ergh, nah. Not her. I dreamed of looking like Sabrina – Kate Jackson. She always looked so nice. When I was younger my favourite pop star was Cliff Richard. I used to think the people on the television could also see you, so before Cliff came on I'd brush my hair and get all dressed up to prepare myself for him. Now when I look in the mirror I just ask myself if I look decent enough to go out into the street. That's my gauge of attractiveness. I can't ever imagine somebody looking at me and thinking I'm sexy.'

I used to think that about me too. But you soon realise how wrong you can be.

Annabella Bess Mann, or, if you prefer Burmese, Myint-Myiante Aye, has an intense desire to be alone, like a teen Garbo from West Hampstead.

'At one time I was really very popular at school. I don't know why but I found myself walking around all day saying, "Hi," to so many people. A friend of mine told me she heard people discussing me and saying I was like a craze, y'know. I didn't know what she was talking about.

'Maybe it was to do with my haircut. Every time I put it in place it stayed the same. I used to have really short haircuts, I'd get DAs done at Vidal Sassoon's modelling school and have it flicked a lot so everyone called me "Soul Girl". Everyone said my hair was really lovely and all that stuff. But now it's a mess 'cos I had it permed.

'Anyway, I knew all these people, but then I started getting less popular. It coincided with the time I joined Bow Wow Wow. My teachers told me that withdrawing from my friends was just a sign that I was going through adolescence. 'Cos, y'know being a girl is so difficult. I really hate it sometimes. Girls are so bitchy. They're always trying to compete with each other. If there's one popular girl they'll always try and bitch about her, but what I say is, if a person's popular it's them, it's their personality. They can't make you be unpopular, not unless they spread rumours or bully you, which is really unfair.'

Ever felt like a dirty old man? These trial-and-tribulation puppy-fat tales are in no way prevarications or deliberate digressions. They are uppermost in the Bow Wow Wow singer's mind.

Listen to this tragic tale of unrequited love among the text-books and ink stains.

'I've never had a boyfriend. I don't really know why – I guess I never really liked anyone that much. Well, there was someone. He was two years older than me. His sister was at my school and she was the same age as me. He was the big heart-throb of his year. Anyway, my friend liked his friend and that's how I got to meet him. Everyone began to know about my friend and the other guy so it was kind of quiet about what was going on between me and him.'

And what exactly was going on between you and him?

'Nothing. Oh, well, one day I'd ignore him, then the next day he'd ignore me, and the day after that we'd both feel guilty and smile at each other. Like I said, he was this big heart-throb and everyone liked him. But it wasn't just 'cos he was good-looking that I liked him. There was something about him. I'd wanted to talk to him for ages but I'm old-fashioned and think it's the boy who should make a move first. He was like John Travolta in *Grease*, very popular. He was cute, sweet, shy. He was the only boy I ever really liked. But he was just as nervous as me. We'd just talk a little bit and say, "Hi," to each other. Our relationship went on like that for two years.'

Then what happened?

'He left school and became an apprentice professional with Tottenham Hotspur.'

I wonder if, when he's cleaning Glen Hoddle's boots, he'll remember this beauty from West Hampstead and weep.

When he went out of her life, Annabella took a good look at herself and decided she was boring. 'The highlight of my social life outside school was going shopping. I just used to walk to all the shops in the West End and Swiss Cottage. I didn't have the money to buy anything. I had a friend who used to get fifty pounds every month from her dad and it got so depressing watching her buy so many new clothes. So I decided to get a job. My mum heard about one going down at the local dry-cleaner's on Saturdays. At first I couldn't do it, although it was very simple to do. I got really nervous in case they'd decide to sack me and I'd lose out on the eight pounds a week I was paid. But I eventually got the hang of it and stayed there for seven months. I spent all my money on shoes, shirts and jewellery, especially earrings.'

And then it happened. One day this strange man with a shock of red hair and a Mephistophelean look in his eye walked into the shop.

'Hello, little girl, what's that you're singing?'

'Oh, I'm just singing along with the radio. It's nothing special.'

'Do you sing a lot?'

'Well, yes, I suppose I do.'

'Would you like to audition for me?'

'And that was how it happened, really. I honestly thought the guy was some nutter, to be honest. He said he needed to hear me sing before I did the audition and that he'd send somebody round to pick me up and take me to the place where the band were rehearsing. When he left, one of the guys who worked in the shop said to me, "Christ, what a weird bloke."'

Annabella's hobby is singing. 'I've been singing for as long as I can remember. My friend and I would sing Abba songs in her bedroom with the windows open. The neighbours used to hear us and come out into their gardens and clap at the end of the song, It was great: we had this tremendous feeling of being able to sing, although we couldn't really. It was like letting the music flow into our souls.'

You tell it, girl.

She decided not to take up Malcolm's offer of an audition because she thought he was a 'bit of a weirdo'.

'But it was the holidays and I was really bored. So I took a friend along with me to the rehearsal room for a giggle. I had a really bad cold and kept telling them that but they insisted on going through with it. Also, I heard they were auditioning other girls at the time and that they already had another singer, and she was aged fifteen. I felt really bad about doing this behind her back. Anyway, I sang "YMCA" and "Wedding Day". When I left they said they'd get in touch. And they did.'

The innocent abroad was concerned not about her role in the band, but whether or not they were punks.

'I sat in the car on my way to the audition while a friend of Malcolm's drove. That was when I first found out exactly who Malcolm was. When I realised I thought, Punk rock? No way. See, I never liked punk and I hated the Sex Pistols. I could never understand what they were singing about. Their music was too rough. My friends didn't like them either. I much preferred Abba. But my real favourite was Stevie Wonder. I think the only punk rock group I didn't mind was the Stranglers – but only their first album. I used to like Blondie too, till somebody told me they were punk. I just kept hoping Malcolm wasn't trying to get me into a punk group.'

Malcolm, fresh in from France and feeling particularly shiny and black, had other ideas. Adam and the Ants were behind him. He still had Matthew Ashman on lead guitar, Dave Barbarossa on drums and bassist Leigh Gorman in his knapsack. And in Annabella he got the affirmative. Fourteen, Burmese, a girl who had never seen a band live in her life, whose only previous experience was singing to Stevie Wonder on the radio in her bedroom, with its Abba and John Travolta posters on the pink walls to hide the stains, and a friendly rag doll on the bed. A girl who desperately wanted to be an air hostess until she found out she needed too many O-levels.

'It was the only way I knew how to travel round the world. But you need O-level maths and I'm hopeless at that. In fact, I'm hopeless at most subjects, really. And do I hate homework.'

A girl so ordinary she makes Mavis in *Coronation Street* look like Catherine Deneuve.

And the most obvious girl in the world to have in your band.

Only McLaren, the Red Rob of rococo rock and the man who sold London Bridge to an entire record industry, could come up with a song about the most controversial issue in the flagging music business and get them to release it.

A song about home taping – sung by a fourteen-year-old home taper who actually taught herself how to sing while she was home taping.

In five hundred years' time there seems little doubt that Malcolm McLaren will be regarded as the da Vinci of the twentieth century. Apart from the painting.

But what does this ordinary girl think of her mentor?

'He's nuts. I don't know how I got mixed up with this. He has the strangest ideas. Like yesterday I did a video for the record in a bedroom dressed in a nightie and he wanted to surround me with forty poodles. Can you imagine having all those dogs trampling over you when you're trying to sing? And the other day he got us all dressed up in these pirate clothes and took us out into the street but refused to walk with us 'cos he was too embarrassed.'

But, Annabella, say he asked you to appear in a porno movie?

'I wouldn't do it. I think he knows that too. I have my limits and that's one. I'm sure he does too. I don't care what's gone down about him in the past, I'm not going to hold that against him. As long as he's OK with me, that's fine. It's his life, nobody can hold that against him.'

Wasn't your mum a teensy bit worried when she discovered you were about to involve yourself with the man who founded punk?

'You know what mums are like – and mine's really old-fashioned. Her main worry was that I'd be dressed up in leather. That was the first thing she asked Malcolm – would I be wearing leather?'

Annabella has been sacked from the band twice. 'When it happened again I was really upset. By then my life had changed and nothing seemed important but the group. After that sacking I went home, burst into tears and started singing "I Will Survive". My mum asked me what was wrong. I told her and she said, "Right, I'm going to see that McLaren and have a go at him for upsetting my daughter." And I got back in.'

Annabella remains pessimistic about the future. 'I don't think I'm going to be a success 'cos there are too many things against me. Like a lot of girls my age would see me and get a bit jealous. I think everyone's going to hate me. But I'm not going to be a Debbie Harry or a Wendy Wu clone. I don't know if I can cope. God, I don't know.'

Annabella doesn't take drugs, shuns alcohol, thinks smoking is silly, eats calorie-counter food, like cod in butter sauce and chilli – 'I burnt the pan today and Mum, who's a nurse, will kill me when she gets home' – and likes *Dallas* and *Soap*.

She never goes to discos – 'Went once with my older brother but I got bored' – and turns down offers of dates because it brings memories flooding back of the Spurs apprentice.

She still wouldn't mind being an air hostess – but at the same time she desperately wants to be successful as a singer.

'See, I'm really just ordinary. In fact, I'm the most ordinary fourteen-year-old girl you'll ever meet. God, what a weird place to start – a dry-cleaner's in Kilburn.'

At an after-gig Spandau Ballet party backstage in Wembley Arena ten years after that interview, Annabella appeared out of the crowd and breezed over. 'Hi, Barry. I just wanted to say that the interview you did was my very favourite.' What a sweet twenty-four-year-old she'd turned into. And she still made me feel like an old perv. After splitting from Bow Wow Wow in 1983, Annabella pursued a solo career. In 1994 her single, 'Do What You Do', was a big dance hit. She reunited with Leigh Gorman for the Bow Wow Wow tour in 1997. Her music has been featured in several movies. She still continues to perform, under the title 'Annabella Lwin of the original Bow Wow Wow'.

SEPTEMBER 1980

Malcolm McLaren, Ozzy Osbourne

For the next few months I entertain Malcolm McLaren.

Most nights he grabs a taxi to my flat in Hampstead Road, lies on the sofa, smokes a twenty pack of Marlboro, drinks Screwdrivers until the vodka runs dry and tells me the complete, unexpurgated story of his life. I feel like Boswell recording a great man's thoughts. This is something quite extraordinary. I tape each and every word, my recorder a thief in the night, stealing the diamonds that fall from his mouth.

I like this guy, this weird, wonderful guy. But then again, I'm as corny as Kansas in August. He begins the beguine and as his story unfolds, this gullible soul is hooked, line *and* sinker.

God knows what Dina, my wife of three-and-a-half months, thinks about it all. I assure her it will be my fortune, but she's not convinced. In fact, I'm not even sure if she knows who Malcolm is, and that's why I love her.

But big wheels keep on turnin'.

The last of the great I rock 'n' roll hell-raisers is back in window-wrecking, bar-brawling form! Ozzy Osbourne, whose paranoid voice took heavy metal heroes Black Sabbath to the top of the charts all over the world, is now hell bent on emulating that success with his new band, Blizzard of Ozz.

A two-year break hasn't dulled Ozzy's wild-man edge. 'I'm looking forward to raising hell,' says the 31-year-old singer.

'I don't plan these things, they just seem to happen. I might be sitting quietly at a table one minute, and smash it up the next. It's just my way of relieving frustration–but I don't want to end up like Keith Moon.'

Ozzy's over-the-top antics once resulted in a crazed crowd completely demolishing a concert hall in America.

'On the eve of a show, I returned to what I thought was my hotel room. It turned out to be someone else's room, and I slept undisturbed for 24 hours, missing the show as a result.

'The 18,000 audience went mad and caused 44,000 dollars' worth of damage while I slept quietly on!' But even then his days with Sabbath were drawing to an end. 'It was like a marriage going on the rocks.

'After nearly twelve years with the band, I'd fulfilled all my ambitions. It was time to do something else.'

So Ozzy took a long, well-deserved holiday and got to know his wife, Thelma, and their three children all over again.

'I started getting restless. I have a hate-hate relationship with music. I hate it when I'm doing it and I hate it when I'm not doing it.'

Ozzy formed Blizzard with guitarist Randy Rhoads, ex-Rainbow bassist Bob Daisley and ex-Uriah Keep drummer Lee Kerslake. Their first single 'Crazy Train' is poised to enter the charts – where, funnily enough, Black Sabbath's first single, 'Paranoid', is enjoying a new success.

Ozzy is married to a judge on a talent show, one that Britain's got, apparently, and America.

OCTOBER 1980

Randy Crawford, Malcolm McLaren

Randy Crawford reveals three secrets during our little chat. The Crusaders gave her a BMW as a thank-you present for singing 'Street Life'. Her idol is Shirley Bassey. She's addicted to Yorkshire puddings. 'I have this thing about them and it's bad because you just can't get them back home in Georgia.' Heading for the Frisco bay? Meanwhile, Buster Bloodvessel of Bad Manners reveals five secrets during our little chat. A huge fry-up for breakfast. Three Big Macs and fries for lunch. Another three for tea. Home to a slap-up meal. Ten pints of Special Brew down the pub. 'That's when I usually fall asleep.'

Malcolm continues to enthral. He introduces me to his girlfriend, a gorgeously exotic 19 year-old French girl who dresses like a million dollars. Jamie Reid occasionally accompanies Malcolm to the flat and every time I see him I like him more. TV reporter Robin Denselow is producing a documentary on Malcolm and comes around to film me interviewing him for the book. So much for being a ghost writer.

Forty-seven cassette tapes later the first stage of the book is complete. Now I have to transcribe every word, put them into readable shapes and send it swiftly over to Malcolm so he can give me the go ahead, which I do.

The Sun is desperate to serialise it and a lucrative publishing deal is in the pipeline. But Malcolm's busy with Bow Wow Wow and I'm not convinced he's even looked at it. He really does float like a butterfly and sting like a bee. I kinda get the feeling I caught Malcolm 'in between jobs' when we did the book and now it's way down his list of priorities.

We still keep in touch but when he decides to set up home in Hollywood the book effectively grinds to a halt. It's a big loss.

Maybe I can save it for a rainy day...

NOVEMBER 1980

Adam Ant

Onwards and upwards. What about Ant music for sex people?

The slightly-built, intense twenty-five-year-old Cockney who is Adam Ant made it into the top five with his last record, 'Dog Eat Dog'. Now the much-maligned swashbuckling Zorro of the stage can tell all his critics to go fuck themselves.

Not that he would. Adam's onstage bark is far worse than his bite. He's a softly spoken, nervy, bespectacled bank clerk of a bloke. He neither drinks nor smokes, and sips water at CBS headquarters in Soho Square. His one driving passion is his music, which somebody once described as 'a celebration of life as a virtual art form in itself rather than just a mad, grim parody towards death'.

Adam merely describes his songs as being 'Antmusic'. 'It's exciting, fresh and alive. No way could anyone call it rock'n'roll.'

I see. But why ants?

'They're so strong and intelligent. People are scared of insects – especially the ant.' Speak for yourself.

'Because of that they try not to recognise their existence. That's what happened with us in the early days. But now you either love or hate Antmusic – but you certainly can't ignore it. There's even an Ant underground movement with its own Antzines. And there are the Ant fans.' And if a couple of Ant fans decided to run away together and get married I suppose you'd call that an Antelope.

'The people that come to our gigs are very provocative. They get a kick out of looking good and are dressed to kill. None of them are plain Janes, that's for sure. Our shows are more like happenings. The atmosphere is electric. People leave our gigs exhausted. That's how it should be. My audience is a truly colourful, honourable and proud group of peacock people.'

And Adam likes to do this proud group proud. 'I think it's extremely important to look romantic on stage. After all, it's only fair to the kids who could've been waiting months to see you. That's why I wear things like my hussar's jacket. It's essential that you look as good as your music.'

Yet only a few months ago the future looked bleak for our hero. The rest of the band quit and defected to Malcolm McLaren and his Bow Wow Wow Pistols project.

But Adam, like the true blue ant he is, bears no grudges.

'I have a great respect for Malcolm. The man was born out of his time. He's like a modern-day Colonel Tom Parker. I'll never forget the time I was at art school studying graphic design. I formed a band and we once played at another college in London. Our support band that night was the Sex Pistols. It was their first ever gig and when I saw them I was shell-shocked. I decided to throw the towel in for a long time because I realised I just wasn't in the same class.

'When I got the opportunity to be managed by the man who gave the world the Sex Pistols, I leaped at the chance. It was incredible.'

In fact McLaren only managed the band for a month before taking the other three away with him. Since then controversy has raged as to who discovered the driving drum sound favoured by both Adam and the Ants and Bow Wow Wow.

'We put the emphasis on drums and voices in our music. It's much more provocative,' says Adam. 'I was inspired by the chants of the Burundi tribe from Africa. It's very exciting music.'

After the split, Adam teamed up with guitarist Marco Pirroni of Banshees and Models fame. They re-recorded an earlier Ants track called 'Cartrouble Part 2'.

Together, they're determined to put ants into everybody's pants ...

Adam, real name Stuart Goddard, was once voted Sexiest Man Alive in a US poll. The Ants were squashed in 1982 and Adam pursued a solo career. After some initial success his pop-star status went into the doldrums after performing 'Vive Le Rock' at the Band Aid concert in 1985. He acted for a while and had one last hit with the album Wonderful in 1995. Adam had a few run-ins with the law and was charged with affray on two occasions. He also spent time in a psychiatric unit. He made a complete recovery and his autobiography, Stand and Deliver was published in 2006. He is once again touring solidly and an album, Adam Ant is the Blueblack Hussar in Marrying the Gunner's Daughter, was released in 2013.

Magazine Publishing

There's a chill in the air. Something's afoot...

If you've made it this far then you three guys deserve a medal. We're now about to enter the twilight zone of my fifth, and final, career in music, again as a result of the Debbie Harry interview – now rapidly becoming my ultimate Megan Moment.

As I grow older I've come to realise that I'm the guy who makes appearances in other people's dreams because I've got none of my own. They're all used up. I got paid to go around the world and see a lot of things and meet a thousand pop stars. What the hell are you supposed to do when dreams you never dreamed of come true and you've still got the rest of your life to live?

You go for the money. Then the show.

I can't live without dreams so I hitch rides on other people's. It's called going with the flow and it floats you to nowhere but, hey, I'm busy making nowhere plans for nobody anyway, so what the fuck?

And occasionally, just occasionally, you get to have a ball . . .

1980-1981

Flexidiscs, pop mags, Sex Pistols

David, the madcap magazine publisher who's still paying the Farringdon Agency a small fortune to write the copy for his one-shot magazines, comes into the office with a glint in his eye.

'How would you boys like to start up a monthly pop mag? I'll get it printed and distributed and pay you a fee.'

Tim has always wanted to publish his own magazine and immediately sees a way of achieving just that. 'How about we publish it and pay you for print and distribution?' he asks.

By the end of the conversation, Tim and I own half of a monthly pop magazine and by issue five we own it all, after starting a company called Colourgold. It takes some doing but we have the funds and the nous to oust David, who turns out to be the front man for an East End printer who publishes the one-shots along with a lot of soft porn.

Me? I never dreamed of publishing a magazine.

Tim and I discover just how lucrative one-shot publishing can be when John Lennon is murdered two weeks after the first issue of our new pop baby hits the streets. While we're all sitting in the office that morning stunned by the death, Gerry, who appears to have taken over from David, storms through the door.

'Gerry, have you heard the news? Unbelievable.'

'Yeah, yeah. Now let's get a fucking magazine out. Quick!' Boys to men. This is lateral thinking above and beyond the call of duty. Idol + death = dosh. They never taught me that in algebra lessons.

That night I write an entire thirty-two-page John Lennon magazine, relying solely on my memory and the Beatles publications I still possess and which I vowed – thank goodness – I'd never let go. Tim sources the photos from Rex Features, whose studios are just across the road. Comag, our distributor, makes sure we're the first on the newsstands, beating the *Melody Maker* special – which has an exclusive Lennon interview given just before Lennon's death – by five days. That's Barry 2--*Melody Maker* 0, by my reckoning.

John Lennon: A Legend sells nearly 80,000 copies with an 85p cover price of which we, that's us and the East End printer, get around 35p a copy. Not too shabby in dark and doomy 1980.

Flexipop is born in November 1980 at the end of punk, in the middle of a ska revival and at the start of New Romance, all set against a backdrop of tarty charts teeming with tarty acts.

Consequently, *Flexipop* is a tarty magazine. It's the first publication to have a flexi-disc featuring an exclusive track from a major chart act taped to the cover of each issue. Tarty or what?

To steady the gaily coloured disc on the turntable, we advise people to place a 10p piece on the bit in the middle of the record that states, 'Place coin here'. This really is pure pulp for pinheads. And they play like a dream. Some are double-sided. Some are EPs!

Tim and I have both had enough of interviewing pop stars, in the traditional sense at least. It was becoming like any other job, a chore. Pop music had started to get up itself. It needed taking down a peg or two and, occasionally, ridiculed. Pop went poncey and that was never the plan. Sure, it was poncey back in the Fifties and Sixties, but it was poncey with soul and, besides, it was brand spanking new then. Eighties pop is developing a paunch and a receding hairline.

Bands are discovering the new electronic gadgetry. Playing music is easier than ever before, a whole lot easier than the bass they expected Sid to master in '77. Ultravox's 'Vienna' epitomises the techno boom. It would've cost a lot more to make that record three years before. It was good while it lasted but now it means nothing to me. Like a nice meal you had once in a restaurant the name of which you can't remember.

Punk has stuck some bollocks into a discofied, moribund music scene and paved the industry's streets with gold. Record sales are up, the coffers are full. Let's pump up the volume and paint the town red to match the gold. Let's get as much shit out as possible and dress it up in as much MTV finery as we can afford. Video may have killed the radio star, but it's created pop as visual art and taken away its mystery. Now the song is imagined for you, someone else's interpretation of it is in your head.

When you listened to the lyrics on a Beatles track as it danced on the turntable, you could see the disillusioned girl writing the early-morning letter to her parents in the kitchen before meeting a man in the motor trade; you could see Rocky Racoon falling back in his hotel room and Eleanor Rigby on her hands and knees, and the bells on a hill and Kansas City and the USSR, see them all across the universe to Strawberry Fields forever. You could even smell Mr Kite's benefit at Bishopsgate and feel the cold in that bleak Norwegian Wood bathroom.

MTV will donate its organs to the music business and singlehandedly keep it alive and kicking for simple minds. Pop as visual art has given rise to a shitload of pretentiousness. Bands have become either peacocks, running like girls down misty streets, or audacious cocks who chew gum, smoke fags and embrace style over content. The shit really is hitting the fans.

It's time for a slap down. It's time for *Flexipop*.

Tim and I have absolutely no idea how to produce a magazine but that doesn't stop us producing a magazine that looks like it's been produced by someone who has no idea how to produce a magazine. Thank Christ it has an exclusive version of 'On My Radio' by the Selecter on the cover or it would've sold a great deal fewer than the 48,000 copies it finally ships. We printed more than 140,000 on a sale or return basis, so, to our amateur eyes, it looks like a meagre return and we both arrive at the conclusion that, for the first time in our professional lives, we've failed. Big-time. Fail or return.

Tim takes it particularly badly when we get the numbers from Comag and he wanders out of the office like Captain Oates, into the frozen wastes of a docile December afternoon in Mount Pleasant, not to be seen again until the next day.

The magazine is essentially a dodgily printed 60p ad-free picture fest – black-and-white photo stories starring the Selecter, the Specials and Bad Manners plus colour specials on UFO, the Jam's current favourite songs (Paul's top two are 'Christine' and 'Happy House' both by Siouxsie and the Banshees) and Madness lifelines.

We even organise a fashion spread, via McLaren, with Annabella from Bow Wow Wow, and I do the shoot in a studio with Vivienne Westwood, who is odd and witty and knows exactly what she wants. She's designed the whole Annabella pirate look and it's a strong image.

It's strange seeing her in the shadow of Malcolm's words. He's told me some very intimate things about their relationship and it's like meeting, in person, the main love interest from a picaresque novel.

The only real articles in *Flexipop* with 'proper' words are 'Testament of Youth' and 'Welcome To The Working Week'. They are to be regular features, in which a star, Ian Gillan and Kate Bush in this case, talk about their private lives..

When we discover the level of returns, Tim and I decide to change some of the content although, to be honest, we don't need to worry too much. The exclusive flexi on *Flexipop* issue two features two tracks from the Jam – a new version of 'Boy About Town' and 'Pop Art Poem'. And the Jam are the biggest band in the land.

We cut the number of photo stories to a main one over three pages – the Damned star in Rat Van Winkle – and a day-in-the-lifestyle two-pager on Hazel O'Connor. Reluctantly, Tim and I both admit we need to do interviews, so between us we 'do' Adam Ant, Buster Bloodvessel and Andy McClusky from Orchestral Manoeuvres in the Dark.

We're still running the Farringdon Agency so it's pretty easy to get access to almost anybody – private holiday snaps from the Police, Siouxsie in 'Testament of Youth' and Francis Rossi in 'Welcome to the Working Week', another new, self-explanatory, addition. To complement the flexi-disc with a feature, I spend a Sunday with the Jam and their girlfriends at Paul Weller's house in Woking and end up getting pissed down his local pub. Rob Hope, the photographer, a friend of mine from the *South East London Mercury*, takes the pix.

That's the thing with *Flexipop*: virtually every photo used in the magazine is exclusive. And many of them make the artists look pretty ridiculous.

The result? We print 125,000 and sell 65,000. Now we're getting there.

The magazine's designed by ex-*Sounds* man Dave Fudger, and he's really starting to understand it. Alas, other commitments mean he can only stick around for the first two issues.

Enter former *Record Mirror* cartoonist, the Dickensian Mark Manning, complete with a deep Bradford accent, a bulldog called Baxter, a ring at the end of his knob, a God-given talent for drawing caricatures and a desperate desire to become a rock star, which he eventually becomes for a twisty wee while.

Mark, who's never designed a magazine before, joins an outfit that's never published a magazine before. It's the way of the world and sometimes it works.

The third flexi-disc is by flavour-of-the-month the Boomtown Rats with an odd ditty called 'Dun Laoghaire' (pronounced Leery) after the Irish port. In that issue we run a special Sex Pistols feature after I track them all down and ask them the same questions:

1. *Why do you think the Sex Pistols broke up?*
2. *What did the band achieve?*
3. *What do you think would have happened had the band continued?*
4. *What's your favourite Sex Pistols' record?*
5. *What was the biggest mistake the Sex Pistols ever made?*
6. *What do you think of the other members?*
7. *What did you feel when Sid died?*
8. *Who was responsible for the success of the Sex Pistols?*

Johnny Rotten

1. They just decided to leave me stranded and that was that. It needed to end. It was turning into the Rolling Stones.
2. Not very much. It was a start, I guess.
3. It just could not have continued.
4. 'Problems', which was about how I felt being in that band, and 'God Save The Queen'.
5. Signing me.
6. They were all right for a bit. Funny how none of them are doing much at the moment. I hear Matlock's got religion and now he's claiming he wrote some of the songs. Huh, do you know he walked off stage once when we were playing 'God Save The Queen' out of sheer disgust?
7. How would I get to the funeral? But there wasn't one.
8. Quote me: 'He says nothing but the smile gives him away.' They'll get it.

Steve Jones

1. We'd all had enough of it. We were getting on each other's nerves. We hated each other so much.

2. A lot. There just wouldn't be any new bands around if it wasn't for us. Things would be exactly the same as they were five years ago.

3. We would be the biggest band in the world.

4. 'Bodies'.

5. Having Glen Matlock in the band.

6. Rotten – he was all right but you couldn't tell him anything. He knew it all. Sid – he was all right too. But stupid. Matlock – a mummy's boy. Paul – he's my mate. McLaren – he's just a conman.

7. I was pretty pissed off because he could've been a real star. He was dense but I liked him.

8. Me.

Glen Matlock

1. Pure hatred of each other.

2. We paved the way for a lot of new talent. OK, we didn't achieve that much – except a breathing space.

3. I can't imagine that ever happening.

4. 'Submission'.

5. Two big mistakes – getting rid of me and going to America.

6. Rotten – very talented but lazy. Always used to go on about things in the most obtuse way. I suppose that's strange coming from me. Sid – he embodied the Pistols image. Steve – slovenly. Paul – good drummer and a regular geezer. McLaren – the perfect opportunist but always lets himself down. He treads on too many people's toes and so ends up with no friends. You can only do that a few times. Most people who work with him end up getting fed up with him.

7. I was very sad. He believed his own publicity and got caught up between the fact and the fiction.

8. The greyness of the era.

Paul Cook

1. Just a classic case of too much too soon. We found ourselves in a position we weren't ready for and personality clashes abounded.

2. We changed people's attitudes to music and life.

3. It would have got really boring and we would have split up anyway. We couldn't take it any further.

4. 'Bodies'.

5. Going to America.

6. Rotten – he's a really nice, self-centred bloke. Sid – he was a really nice, self-centred lunatic. Matlock – nothing. Steve – I love him. McLaren – I like his ideas and his politics. I think everyone does.

7. Remorseful, relieved and relaxed. And upset, of course.

8. Me.

Malcolm McLaren

1. Because Rotten became a policeman and took us to court. And we went to Brazil and Sid died.

2. Anarchy in the UK, for a moment.

3. We would have had our own TV station by now.

4. Sid singing 'Mack The Knife'.

5. When they started to think of themselves as musicians and not stars.

6. Rotten – too Catholic but a great poet. Sid – pure art. Steve – England's problem. Paul – a typical good worker. Matlock – too good for the Sex Pistols.

7. How great he was and what a funeral.

8. Need I answer?

The fourth flexi blows us all away. Adam and the Ants sing Village People! They record 'A.N.T.S.' to the tune of 'Y.M.C.A.' and it's brilliant. We even start to get airplay on Radio 1 – they review it on the Friday-evening new-release show – and the magazine sells more than 90,000 after printing 105,000.

The fifth disc is a double-header, 'No Respect/Just Pretendin' by

Bad Manners, whose lead singer, burger king Buster Bloodvessel, has become the *Flexipop* mascot. The cover pic is a disgusting close-up of Buster's grinning face smothered in baked beans. You can almost touch the sauce-coated hairs inside his far from inconsiderable nostrils. The photo story features the cool XTC dressed up in ludicrous *It Ain't Half Hot Mum* uniforms for a ditty entitled 'Virgin Soldiers' and is shot on location in Swindon with photographer George Bodnar, me and a hastily written script.

The Pretenders version of the Small Faces classic, 'What You Gonna Do About It?, backed with a new version of 'Stop Your Sobbin'', graces the cover of issue six. These records are hot stuff. The bands are taking it all very seriously and the 'singing' magazine is flying off the shelves.

During this freneticism, the *Flexipop* team is swollen by the addition of Huw Collingbourne – Cambridge English graduate, sophisticate, gay blade, renaissance man of mystery, cynic. The perfect credentials, in fact, for the chief interviewer of a down and dirty magazine like this. Huw asks the questions that no one else dares to. He has no compunction about making some lip-pursing, baggy-trousered popette with delusions of grandeur look like a complete tosser. It's his forte and he's a genius. And there's an element of sleaze about him that Tim, Mark and I readily identify with, sleaze that sorts the boys from the boys, sleaze that pleases, cerebral sleaze with knobs on. *Flexipop* to a tee.

Huw first spots the magazine on the newsstands and it's love at first sight. He rings, makes an appointment, comes to the office, and it's love at first sight. He writes like a dream.

Our gang continues for another twenty-six issues of pure delight that give offence but hurt not. A succession of the coolest continue to supply exclusive tracks, acts like Depeche Mode, Thin Lizzy, Genesis, The Cure, Motorhead, Toyah, Blondie, Soft Cell, Madness, the Associates and Altered Images.

The features are scatty and surreal – I take Kim Wilde and Simon

Le Bon on a blind date, fly up to Glasgow with resident *Flexipop* photographer Neil Matthews to do a ghost photo story featuring Altered Images; stick Dave Gahan in a coffin between two real live dead bodies; dress Annie Lennox up as a corpse; get caught standing on a stool in a public photo booth with my hand on my crotch as if someone just kicked it, and a telephone wrapped around my neck while trying to give readers ideas for a Photo Booth Act Out the Song competition ('When I Need You' and 'Hanging On The Telephone' in case you're wondering); re-enact *The Sound Of Music* movie on Primrose Hill with Angelic Upstarts; creep around Highgate Cemetery with Dave Vanian and the Polecats, have the run of Stamford Bridge for a sexy photo story with all-girl band the Bodysnatchers.

The comic strips – Martyn Lambert's 'Trunkie The Toilet' and Mark's 'GruntWazzock Pork, The Existentialist Sleaze Surfer' – are fucking bizarre.

We even manage to open a *Flexipop* office in Los Angeles after teaming up with an LA-based attorney and his younger brother who open an office on Beverly Boulevard that Tim and I fly over to check out.

We're picked up at the airport in a limo and taken to a five-star hotel overlooking the ocean in Santa Monica. Neither of us can quite believe it. We're greeted with open arms by the attorney, and his younger brother, at his huge Beverly Hills pad, and taken out for sushi and slipped crafty joints and fine white lines by well-meaning dudes in designer jeans, and generally shown a pretty good time.

At one stage I take my place, along with twelve other guys, at the kind of boardroom table you only see in *Dallas*, to discuss the future of *Flexipop* and its imminent Stateside success. Would be nice to have a well-meaning dude in designer jeans on hand to slip me a crafty joint because this is mind-blowingly surreal.

The younger brother runs the office but he appears to be as clueless about the US magazine market as Tim and I are. The whole exercise is a flop and we end up footing the bill for the flights, the five-star Santa Monica hotel and even the fucking limo. Now I know what it's like to be a rock star.

A publication has to be promoted to survive, and spending money to boost circulation was never part of our publishing philosophy. We manage to sell a few ads but it's very much hit and miss. By the very nature of magazine distribution, without promotional support, orders are reduced on each successive issue. We're oblivious to this but we're holding our own. The orders drop gradually, which means it's still selling, still poking jabs, still growing like a weed on the shelves of the big-shot pop mags. Still crazy after two years.

Then Tim and I make a grave error. We decide to go on holiday at the same time and leave Huw and Mark in control. The lunatics take over the asylum. The photo story – 'Bad Bax' – featuring a band called the Meteors, and directed by Mark, Huw and resident *Flexipop* photographer Neil Matthews – is a graphic, bloody, cannibalistic gore-fest, using entrails donated by a local butcher (we plug him at the end in return for the organs) and shot in full colour.

In the same issue Martyn Ware of Heaven 17 is asked what he thinks Hell is like and he says that for breakfast you'd have basted babies served on toast. All this going on inside a magazine with a free transparent Buck's Fizz single on the cover slapped across a cutie-pie pic of Haircut 100.

By the time I get back from holiday, it's too late to make any major changes without shelling out some serious, film-changing money. So we go with what we've got and, Bob's yer fucking uncle, some granny in Blackpool complains to WH Smith after buying it for her granddaughter and it's immediately taken from the stands and banned for two issues.

We never recover.

We're forced to drop the flexi when it just gets too expensive to produce, and let *Flexipop* stand on its own two feet. The first issue of the 'new look' flexi-free *Flexipop*, issue twenty-eight, has Paul

Weller, a big fan of *Flexipop*, on the cover dressed up as a mad scientist and besmirching my good name in an exclusive interview. But it's not enough to stem the flow of falling orders. Ex-*ZigZag* magazine supremo Kris Needs is appointed editor as Tim and I take a back seat to develop a new one-shot magazine company.

Kris does a great job, but as a result of the ban the magazine is in freefall. Kris's tastes are a little too esoteric for a mainstream pop mag, and the final issue contains a major article on Britain's most famous warlock, Aleister Crowley, and is numbered 666.

A magazine like *Flexipop* was meant to love and kiss like a toothless vampire for eternity, but it's finally become unprofitable and we close it down after limping on to issue thirty-three.

Flexipop could never have been a *Smash Hits*, or the lesser spotted *Number 1*. These were the big guys and they weren't singing from the same hymn sheet, although a music writer who attended the very first editorial meeting of *Number 1* later told us the message was, 'Be more hard hitting than *Smash Hits*. Read *Flexipop*.'

1982

The Jam, John Denver

In the autumn of 1982, the Jam announce they would split later that year. I meet up with Paul and Rick in a pub to find out why. Bruce isn't in the mood to discuss the reasons and is a no-show.

OK, so how do you feel about it, Rick?

Rick: I personally think we could have had more to contribute but at the back of my mind I knew we shouldn't go on forever. We all knew it would happen eventually.

But you would rather it happened later rather than sooner?

Rick: Depends how you think.

But if Paul hadn't decided to end it, the Jam would've continued?

Rick: Yeah.

Paul: I told Rick and Bruce in the middle of August. In my own mind, I've been thinking about it for some time. There are a lot of contributory factors as to why, but it's mainly on a personal level, the way I feel as a person. That's what really made my mind up. One day I just woke up and thought about the whole secure situation the Jam was in and it terrified me. The fact that we could go on for another ten years and have hits and be successful, which we know we could do, really frightened the life out of me. I'm 24 and here I am SECURE. That's when I decided I wanted it to end.

What do you mean, 'secure'?

Rick: To know what's going to happen to you in the future.

And you don't like the idea of that?

Rick: No. It's similar to the feeling people get when they suddenly realise they've done everything that's required of them in normal circumstances – marriage, house, children, job. And then you get to thinking it's gonna be that way for the rest of your life. That's all there is left.

But the Jam has given you both security which in turn has enabled you to do what you're doing now.

Paul: Right and I'm not knocking any of it. I can understand if Rick and Bruce are pissed off about the split. That's fair enough. But at the same time, I don't want to get too sad about it. We've really achieved a lot in six years. We've done everything a group could do.

Rick: I haven't got anything to be sad about at all.

Paul: It's best to quit while you're on top. You can't go much further than the Jam. Splitting now means you can hold your head up high. I hear the Who are going to split up soon but who really cares? I'd hate us to go on like that because people don't look at all the good things you've done. They just focus on the crap. All the good you've done gets cancelled out. To me, the Jam will always mean something and it will never lose that meaning.

How did you break the news to Bruce and Rick?

Paul: I just told them.

What was their reaction?

Paul: Hard to say. You'll have to ask them. I think they took it pretty well.

Were you worried about telling them?

Paul: Yeah. It's a difficult thing to do.

What did you say? Was it something like, 'Look, I think we've come to the end and it's time we did something different.'?

Paul: Something like that

Were they surprised or were they expecting it?

Paul: They were surprised.

I heard they were expecting it.

Paul: That's crap. All these papers talk crap. It's like all these 'close friends' we've suddenly acquired. Y'know – 'A close friend of the group tells me.' Utter crap.

But you're upsetting a hell of a lot of people. Doesn't that concern you at all?

Paul: Sure – but you've got to put yourself first. Look, if I carried on doing what I've been doing over the last few years – touring, releasing albums, choosing the singles – I'd go mad. I need time to get out of this whole insular set up. We're not public property. Never have been and never will be.

But isn't that a selfish attitude?

Paul: Yeah, maybe it is. But at the same time they are important reasons to help me keep sane. Oh sure, aside from that I still firmly believe that we've achieved everything. Sure, if we didn't give a fuck about it and decided we were only in it for the money we could plough on forever. But the Jam has always been much more than that. Right from the start it has always transcended just being a group and just being music. It's much, much stronger.

In what way?

Paul: The whole feel about it. The contact with our fans or always trying to stand by what we've said or always remaining the same people. I'm proud of what we've done.

But hasn't the fact that you haven't sold records outside of the UK in any significant amounts played a part in the decision to split up?

Paul: No! I read something in the *Sun* that said I want to expand and have a brass section and girl singers and that Rick and Bruce want more success in America. That's bullshit. Never believe the rumours. The fact that we haven't been successful elsewhere is just hard luck on those people. We've always played whatever we wanted and if people pick up on that, great. We've never tried to change to capture another market.

Have the personal relationships between the three of you – which have remained something of a mystery – had any effect on your decision? Have your attitudes towards each other changed much?

Rick: Obviously they do. At the start you're mates and then as it grows you become business colleagues. You're there for a different reason then when you started the band.

Can you honestly describe yourself as friends?

Rick: I think we could. OK, so we don't socialise. But we're still friends.

Paul: If anything, our relationship has gone onto a more polite level which in a way is a bad thing. When we first started out we used to hang out with each other all the time and get on each other's tits and argue and say exactly what we felt. A lot of it was to do with our age. We were so young. But now our relationship has mellowed and as a result, maybe it's lost some of its edge.

Can you talk to each other or are there embarrassing silences?

Paul: Don't you think that happens with everybody? We all live in different areas, we've all got girlfriends, we've all got our own circle of friends. You haven't got so much to talk about. It's not that the band falls apart, it's little things like when one of you meets a girl so you wanna be with that girl as much as possible. In fact. I'm the worst offender for that. When I first met Jill I totally cut myself off from Rick and Bruce which I now kinda regret.

Why?

Paul: Because I think we could have been, well…we are still mates, still close, ain't we?

Rick: Yeah and we always will be.

Paul: When it boils down to it, I guess you're talking about going out and getting drunk together which ain't so very important.

But can you honestly say now you've split up you'll remain friends?

Paul: When you've worked with people for ten years you're bound to.

But people work in jobs for that length of time, build up close relationships with their workmates yet when they leave they never set eyes on them again. Doesn't it worry you that that might happen?

Paul: I haven't thought about it.

What are your plans?

Paul: No concrete ones. The last thing I want to do is go out and get a really tight, insular thing again. I certainly don't want to recreate what we three have done.

Will you ever work together again?

Rick: It's possible but I can't see it happening, to be honest. The break will give us breathing space. I suppose we can do anything we like. But most problems you don't see until they happen.

Won't you be lost without Paul? After all, you're used to being part of a band where one member is so obviously the front man.

Rick: Well, if I just sit back and wait for something to happen it's going to be a lot worse. There are lots of things I want to do.

Like what?

Rick: Photography for one thing. And seeing friends. I guess they'll be the first things I'll take off the shelf.

Paul: Music will be first with all three of us because it's in our blood. The big mistake people make is adopting the 'I'll be all right' attitude. The Jam was a group. OK, I was projected as the front man but it was still a close knit group. The letters from the fans reflect that.

But you alone have been promoted as the Jam.

Paul: The fans don't see it that way. A lot of people, record company included, think I'm gonna blast in where the Jam left off and go straight to number one. That's bullshit. It just won't happen that easily and why should it?

But you do get pissed off when a Jam record doesn't get to number one.

Paul: You've got the wrong man.

But I know you think it deserves to be there.

Paul: Oh, I think all our records deserve to get to number one and I always have done since 'In The City'. But it doesn't choke me if they don't.

But how are you going to feel if you don't achieve the success in the future you achieved with the Jam?

Paul: But that's just what I've been talking about. That'll do me good and that's not because I'm arrogant. I'm less arrogant than all the other pop stars around. I simply need the challenge as an individual. It's not the success; perhaps I can't articulate it properly. Let me give you an example – when a Jam record gets to number one I can't find it in myself to be as elated and I should be.

Highs and lows of the last six years. What was the best time?

Rick: When we started off doing places like the 100 Club. When it was so fast it was unbelievable.

Paul: That era was the best. All the club dates. Everything was really moving. Not just us, everything. 1976 was so exciting.

Favourite Jam records?

Paul: The first two singles. *All Mod Cons* which was a whole new step. *Sound Affects*, the chain of singles from 'Tube Station' to 'Going Underground' which all had a similar sound.

So, you think Jam music was becoming a bit samey, a mite predictable and that might be another reason to quit? A lack of ideas?

Paul: I'm not sure about the lack of ideas. As a group we could go no further. But as individuals…

Rick: Though I do think about all the things we could have done, in the future. Maybe a change of direction.

Paul: Yeah, but then we could have ended up our own arses doing that.

You said earlier you hadn't changed over the last six years. Is that really true?

Paul: In some ways, maybe it isn't, but there's been no major change. I've always tried to stick to my word.

I don't think there's another band that would split up at this point in their career.

Paul: Right! No-one. You'll see the Clash celebrating their twentieth anniversary like the Stones are now. To me, that's disgusting.

So, what now? A low profile? It's been impossible to pick up a paper in the last two years without something about the Jam inside. I thought you decided a while ago to stop doing interviews.

Paul: I only ever do the ones I feel like doing. I haven't done *NME* or *Sounds* for a very long time.

Why?

Paul: Because I don't agree with their policies. Most of them stink. It's the same with the national press. I'll do *Flexipop* and *Smash Hits* because I like them.

Will your dad, John, still manage you?

Paul: He understood the the reasons behind the break-up. Him and me will always carry on – it's a partnership. We'll never split up.

Do you think the band will ever get back together again?

Rick: That would be a mistake. The only reasons would be either trying to recapture a memory which is impossible or for the money. Both would be wrong.

Paul: I know people will say it's easy to talk like that now and that we will get back together in the future. But those same people were saying I'd gone back on my word and that the Jam will never end. Well, they can now eat their fucking words.

In 2010 Bruce played bass and sang on Weller's Wake Up The Nation album. Later that year he joined Paul on stage at the Royal Albert Hall for a short Jam medley. It was the first time they'd been on stage together in nearly thirty years. In 2011, Rick Buckler formed the band If with Tim V from Sham 69. Paul goes from strength to strength and, like Mike Oldfield, has no less than seven children. John Weller sadly passed away in 2009. He was a one-off and is sadly missed)

I'm still writing the pop column for the *Daily Record* and meet a feisty John Denver in his London hotel room who tells me he has just suffered the worst year of his life.

The thirty-nine-year-old singer, who still only looks nineteen, has watched his marriage – to the girl he made a household name with the haunting 'Annie's Song' – crumble. And today the couple finally divorced. I'm the first journalist to talk to him since the news came through. In fact, he's holding the notice in his hand as I walk into the room.

Result.

John, in town for a concert at the Royal Albert Hall and a spot on a TV chat show, reveals how his sixteen-year marriage fell apart.

'I love Annie. She's a wonderful woman,' he says. 'It breaks my heart to think that we can't live together any more. We just seemed to drift apart. I guess I kinda blamed her and, my God, actually thought she was a real fucking bastard for screwing everything up. But I realise now it was all my fault. Everything's been crazy for a while now – tours, movies. I was never home. It's a wonder Annie stayed with me for as long as she did. The break-up of my marriage has been the supreme sacrifice in my career.'

When John moved out of the family home in Aspen, Colorado, he found life alone desperately difficult. As well as Annie, he had to leave their adopted children, Zachary, nine, who is half-Native American, and Anna Kate, six, who is Japanese.

'I got a little house on the other side of town but it was just terrible,' he says. 'And when I did visit the kids, taking them presents, putting them to bed, kissing them goodnight and then having to go, it was the worst thing that's ever happened to me. In fact, I was hitting the bottle a lot and even started eating meat, which I never do. My whole life was turned upside down.'

But John's relationship with his children hasn't been affected by the break-up. 'I love them so very much and the time that I spend with them is terribly precious to me. My inability to have children had absolutely no effect on our marriage. Annie and I had the most wonderful experience throughout the adoption process and the kids are so much ours and so much a brother and sister. It's really been a pretty miraculous thing. But since the divorce has become final, I feel that a great weight has been lifted from my shoulders.'

There's nobody special in John's life at the moment. 'I haven't met anyone I thought I could take home,' he says. 'I've really been totally alone. There have been a few one-night stands, I must admit, but that is definitely not the most satisfying experience. It's no way to live.

'My fans had a real good feeling about my relationship with Annie through the songs I wrote. I want them to know that, as hard as it's been, Annie and I are now in really great shape and the future is going to be good for both of us.'

John married Australian actress Cassandra Delaney in 1988.They had a daughter named Jesse Belle, after he had treatment for infertility. They divorced in 1993. Denver and Annie Martell were rumoured to be getting back together until John's death at the age of fifty-three in 1997 while flying his jet off the coast of California.

In September 1982 I marry my wife for the second time in a Greek Orthodox Church in Nicosia. We've been married for two years and still haven't been to Cyprus to see Dina's folks. For all I know, she hasn't even told them.

Then, out of the blue, Dina tells me we're going to Cyprus for a big church wedding. I ask my mum and dad to come but they're terrified of flying. They've never been abroad in their lives and Nicosia at that time of year is about treble the heat they can cope with and far too big a culture shock. It's a no-no. In fact, none of my family or friends come to the wedding. I guess I cheated my mum and dad out of a lot of things by marrying Dina, but I live with it. What else can you do?

Because I was never christened – my dad was Catholic and my mum C of E – in order to get married I have to become Greek Orthodox and spend every night for a month being indoctrinated into the religion by one of the few priests on the island who can speak English with sufficient fluency. Father Andreas is an angel of a man, and beneath a star-filled Cypriot sky we talk long and hard about Adam and Eve and Darwin and Old Testament prophets and the history of Orthodoxy, and his beard is shot with moonbeams and his smile is one of love. I've never met a saintlier man.

At the culmination of these 'lessons', he christens me Joannis (my middle name is John, there is no Greek equivalent for Barry) in front of a church full of well-dressed, well-meaning Cypriots – all total strangers – while I stand in a bowl of water with just a pair of white cotton M&S Y-fronts and a hot flush separating me from God.

Two days later he marries me to my wife in front of a church full of well-dressed, well-meaning Cypriots – all total strangers – while I wear a cream suit bought in Chapel Market, a million miles from me now. The reception, by a hotel swimming-pool, is magical, not least because as we greet each member of the considerable queue of guests from our podium (I feel like we're the couple on top of the wedding cake), somebody thrusts an envelope full of cash into my hand. Apparently, the traditional pinning of money to the wedding outfits of the couple as they dance only takes place in villages these days – oh, and the 'Charlies' (Cypriots who live in London) still do it in Haringey halls and Enfield hotels.

I'm relieved to discover I don't have to dangle the bloodstained sheet from our wedding-night bed out of my hotel-room window the next morning to prove to the world that my wife was, indeed, a virgin.

After the reception we go to a house where tables are laid in the back garden for about fifty people to sit down and feast on *souvla* and *sheftalia* and *kolokassi* and *macaronia tou fournou* – and it's just struck midnight. This is the best wedding I've ever been to, and it's all mine. We drink beer till the cocks crow and I feel like a king.

I wish Mum and Dad could've been there.

For some reason, the next day Dina informs me that if she dies in London she wants her body to be flown home to Cyprus because the idea of eternity in the English cold terrifies her. I tell her the Greek bugs are bigger and would devour her shrivelled carcass quicker than you can say Nana Mouskouri, but she insists she'd rather Greek bugs than English winters.

Despite the fact that I can't speak a word of Greek, I guess I'll end up buried among a *meze* of Cypriot strangers in some Orthodox cemetery in north London. I'll be stuffed into a huge pita bread, garnished with tomatoes, lettuce, cucumber, parsley and maybe a little coriander, liberally sprinkled with lemon juice instead of holy water and dug deep into the damp earth.

And not a soul to bring me flowers.

Not even a fucking lemon.

1983

Last ever interview: Hall & Oates

In May 1983, not long before the last issue of *Flexipop*, I go on my first foreign music-press trip in three years, arranged, fittingly, by Alan Edwards. It's also the final music interview I ever do and some of the quotes make it a fitting finale.

The most amazing thing about the whole trip is that no one takes any drugs. And we're in Miami! Jeez, things are changing...

What, I hear pinhead pundits up and down the country exclaim, are such a wholesome Ariel-clean pair like Hall and Oates doing in a septic tank of a mag like *Flexipop*?

Well, let me state categorically here and now that it has got nothing, absolutely nothing, to do with the trip to Florida the duo's record company have very kindly laid on me to see them in action. I'm very much against the kind of duplicity I know other journalists indulge in, and would never dream of entertaining the idea of pushing sycophantic hogwash simply because I get the opportunity to laze around a luxurious hotel pool sipping piña colada, and spend long, balmy evenings in al fresco restaurants overlooking the warm bit of the Atlantic, eating juicy steaks washed down with expensive, robust burgundies. I'm just not built that way. It's by sheer coincidence that I happen to think Hall and Oates are a shit hot act.

Again I hear some of the more intransigent among the three of you rebuke my sincerity. Oh ye of little faith. OK, I admit the swordfish steaks are superb and Jack Daniel's is a most welcoming host, but it takes a lot more than a plate of Key West oysters and a succulent lobster to sway me.

Hall and Oates are good. Really. In fact, they're about the best thing to come out of America since Blondie.

The States has a long heritage of singing duos – Sonny and Cher, Sam and Dave, Simon and Garfunkel, the Everlys to name but two.

Compare that to our great British pedigree – Flanagan and Allen, Peters and Lee, Pearl Carr and Teddy Johnson – and it doesn't take a genius to realise that in the dyad market the Stars and Stripes have got it sussed. Daryl Hall and John Oates are now the most successful vocal partnership bar none. A chain of mellifluous singles has seen to that. Numbers like 'Private Eyes', 'I Can't Go For That', 'Kiss On My List' and 'Family Man', have endeared them to both hack and hick alike. Not only are their records infectious, they're plausible, unlike

99 per cent of the dross that slithers out of the US Hot (?) Hundred.

Yep, as I sit back in my seat at the Miami Civic Center, engulfed by the suntanned hysteria of the cute fifteen-year-old Florida chicks around me, the clam chowder and fresh crab I had for dinner still teasing my palate, I think, These boys are great.

With a fire that would bum bands half their age (both men are thirty-three), the pair ride tandem across an inexorable barrage of hits that leave you with the thought, Fuck, is it really that many? Each song has a black soul with a white heart, and therein lies the secret of their astonishing success.

The next day at the Fontainebleau Hilton I sit around a table with the boys after a particularly tasty lunch involving a large number of scallops and a rack of lamb.

Hall and Oates are very much the odd couple, Daryl the tall blond Adonis, and John a portable Burt Reynolds – hispid and acute. Both, it transpires, are particularly articulate, a little unusual in the world of FM ephemeral rock. And both are looking a little shell-shocked after a gruelling eight months non-stop on the road.

A few lifelines first...

Daryl: single, born in Philadelphia, lives in Greenwich Village, likes motorcycles and reading and is a pretty rich dude.

John: single, born in Philadelphia, loves racing cars – 'Cars are my therapy. They cleanse my mind. Some people talk to psychiatrists, I race cars.' He's also a pretty rich dude.

So, how come you're not like the rest of the American acts that permeate the airwaves? You know, the overall feeling of hip that envelops you? I think that's a pretty reasonable opening gambit. I'm a little out of practice.

Daryl: 'We're more in touch with the rest of the world than most American bands. We don't insulate ourselves. Our roots are American but our experience has altered our sensibilities. There seems to be a lot of indolent people here.'

Why do American records have so little meaning? It's a candyfloss culture, right?

Daryl: 'Americans are very complacent. They just don't wanna be stirred much. It's unfortunate for us because we both believe our responsibility is to stir people. I guess Americans don't really care much about being enlightened by music 'cos it's not that bad a way of life here. Basically, everyone has an opportunity.

'There's a very small number of people that don't have what they want and even those people are brainwashed into thinking they do. The bottom line isn't that far down over here.'

John: 'When the gas price went up to a dollar fifty that was still half the price than in any other country – yet people still complained.'

Daryl: 'You can't move people emotionally when they're not desperate. In England, because it's smaller, people are in touch with each other. The English are capable of being more aware but they're stymied by cultural barriers.'

John: 'Music isn't taken seriously enough here. It's been relegated to the shopping-centre syndrome. When you're inundated with it, it ceases to have any meaning. Like, you can turn a TV on at any time of the day and hear a rock song.'

Daryl: 'TV here sucks. It's numbing. Complacency can be directly attributed to TV. People here are gorged with media, with the arts, with music, and consequently none have any significance any more.'

The death knell of the teenager?

Daryl: 'Rock 'n'roll isn't a teenage phenomenon any more. It's strictly for adults in America. Teenagers are a lost group. Video zombies.'

John: 'Music isn't the rallying point of kids any more. It's sports and video games.'

Daryl: 'In the Fifties, when the term 'teenager' was coined, it was a strange time and place. Between 1950 and 1975 teenagers were the most significant members of society. They weren't before that era and they're not now. They're a dying breed.'

John: 'Maybe there will be a rebirth, who knows?'

They didn't look like they were dying at the Civic Center last night where all the girls dreamed that they'd be your partner. So how come two, ahem, slightly older gentlemen are getting it on in front of pubescent girls? I thought rock'n'roll was teenagers playing to teenagers.

Daryl: 'It must be our energy they relate to.'

John: 'We try and transcend it. We write of teenage adolescent emotions with adult sensibilities simply 'cos we're not teenagers any more.'

But what were they like when they were? All those Philly fillies and gang fights, huh?

Daryl: 'We were both in neighbourhood gangs. But I was a devout coward so I never printed the name of my gang on the back of my leather jacket. That way I was assured of complete anonymity.'

Hall & Oates have had thirty-four hits on the US Billboard Hot 100 singles chart, six hitting the top spot. They also have seven platinum and six gold albums. The duo have continued to record and tour. Pretty rich dudes.

1983–1988

Let's make lots of money

Tim and I have bought the freehold of a shop front and basement, with a maisonette above, just off Marylebone Road. We use the lower floors as offices – Mark in the basement with Baxter the dog, spray mount and the odd mind-bending substance – and rent the flat to a friend of innovative publisher Felix Dennis, the man who invented the poster magazine. He visits the office and I give him a guided tour, which takes about thirty seconds. We're no threat, despite our brand new red-and-white Suzuki jeeps parked prominently outside, and I never see him again.

We're living the Thatcher dream. It's not *Flexipop* that makes money for us, it's the legion of one-shot pop mags, mainly posters, we start to churn out on a monthly basis. The first one is on Adam & the Ants.

The Burundi beat boy dominates the charts and the Prince Charming image sets the tone for the infectious gimmickry of the Eighties.

We sell a staggering 60,000 out of a 65,000 print run, swiftly followed by another with the same result. This is serious money. Adam's lawyers tell us politely, because, I guess, of our journalistic credentials, to refrain from doing any more and we comply, although in all truth they don't have much of a case legally. It's all about copyright, and if a band hasn't trademarked their name, and most don't, you can legally bring out a magazine on them. Their lawyers cite 'passing off', that someone buying the magazine would reasonably expect it to have been produced by the act themselves seeing as it bore their name. So we just put 'unofficial' on the cover. Fuck you.

The bigger the act, the more muscular the lawyer. They bully and harass but they know they can't do a thing about it.

So out they come, two, three, sometimes four mags a month, and it's like that for the rest of the Eighties – Culture Club, Wham!, Duran Duran, Spandau, A-ha, Frankie Goes To Hollywood, Madonna, Bros, Kylie and Jason. It's like a fucking sweetshop. The kids can't get enough. And the bigger the order, the lower the percentage of sales needed to break even – sometimes as low as 12 per cent on an order of 60,000. The rest is pure profit.

And then there's the Sting.

It goes like this...

Instead of publishing a one-shot mag on Wham! and calling it *Wham!, An Independent Publication*, you publish a mag of exactly the same spec called, say, *Hit Machine* and slap 'No. 1' on the cover. It's been sold into the distribution trade as a regular monthly title on a sale or return basis. The first order is, say, 80,000. The next two are 75,000 and 69,000. By the time it reaches issue four, I change the publication from sale or return to firm sale, which means everything ordered is paid for.

Thing is, it takes several months to process the sales levels, so by the time issue four comes along the trade is still not finally aware of the sales of the first – it's like they're using carrier pigeons. So the order could be as much as 45,000 all on a strictly no-return, firm-sale basis. It takes another three or four issues before the sales figures are known so the orders remain unfeasibly high. And even when the title eventually finds its level you can coast on the back of that firm sale for months on end. Then, when *Hit Machine* finally bombs out, you replace it with *Pop Double-Up* or *Metal Fury* and the whole cycle starts again.

No wonder some of the richest men in the world are publishers. At least, they certainly were back then...

After the demise of *Flexipop*, the office is never the same again. Tim announces he's had enough of publishing for a while and becomes a full-time student at the London School of Economics. We agree that I have his salary but he still gets 50 per cent of the profits and in return he works during his summer break.

When he completes his degree I can, if I want, take some time off. I'm thirty, married but childless, still footloose and fancy free. I'll be thirty-three when he finishes. I could maybe do a degree, or apply to RADA. I never lost that luvvie feeling. The RADA option is just a year, and I reckon if I can build up the business, Tim could take it over for just a year, then I'd come back and we'd do something big.

OK, so Paul and Andrew, my twin sons, come along in 1984 – near the end of Tim's first year. I can still do this. I'm still footloose, although the fancy free is in handcuffs. I farm everything out – the writing is done by Huw, the design by an outside company. I visit the photo agencies and select all the pics. Choosing a poster is a very tricky business but I know what I want and I know how to get it. The basement office is now occupied by old mates Jan Moir and Jon Futrell, who run a PR set up. Mark is taking the first steps to pop stardom and eventually metamorphoses into Zodiac Mindwarp with his Love Reaction. He asks me if I'll be his manager but I politely decline. I'm not manager material.

I'm also not publisher material. I feel like Bobby Charlton without the comb-over – he couldn't make the transition between footballer and manager and I can't between journalist and publisher. Sure, I earn a few bob, but it just doesn't feel right. It's uncomfortable.

Can't stop it, of course. Wife, kids, mortgage, responsibility – I've moved to a three-bed semi in Muswell Hill that cost £41,500 and we borrowed £37,000. One building-society manager refused to give me a mortgage, despite my good credit, after I showed him copies of *Flexipop*, which he deemed 'unsuitable' for children. Children! I told him to stick his money up his arse. Funny how cash brings confidence to the table.

Still, some day my prince will come and take me away from all this. I'm thinking like a girl as far as Tim is concerned. It's like he's away at war or in prison and I'm waiting for his return. I don't want to do this anymore. I spend my life looking at photos and reading, and sometimes writing copy that I think will appeal to teenage girls.

Remarkably, it appears to work. So much so that Pineapple, the dance studio and clothing company, is on the verge of making an offer for the business. Every magazine we publish makes a profit. I conceive and design a magazine that opens out into a board game and Pepsi Cola use it in a promotion.

The Eighties are a goldmine for pop periphery.

While pop burns up, a load of fiddling Neros suck and shit, suck and shit. Sweet 16 Pop Music has been snatched off the street and gang banged in an alley 'til she can't scream no more, and I'm in the queue.

To the victor, the spoils. Tim, holidaying in New York at the end of his first year at the LSE, rings and says Costa Rica is the place to be, so I load up the truck and fly to San Jose where he's waiting. I'd only just returned from my three-month-old sons' christening by Father Andreas in Cyprus and also the honeymoon we never had – five days in Cairo while Dina's mum looked after the boys – to see the Pyramids across the Nile.

It's the rainy season in Costa Rica. We spend our time taking strange train rides through rainforests, travelling on strange, packed ferries and buses and drinking in strange bars while watching sloths taking it easy in the trees of Puerto Limon. We're the only Europeans for miles.

The rain drives us out and we fly to Mexico to see the Pyramids before heading off to Cancún for some R&R. And the most amazing thing of all – we're paying for it! The whole shebang! Not a record company in sight! Jesus, one phone call I make to the office from a hotel in the middle of nowhere costs eighty-four pounds. Lobster and champagne in a beachside restaurant is a cool hundred. Money is losing its value.

To the victor, the spoils. I buy a Porsche, get all my clothes at Brown's in South Molton Street, take a six-week holiday in Cyprus, spend a month in Bangkok, Hong Kong and Bali, and buy a larger house in Muswell Hill. Tim moves into a flat in Notting Hill and drives a brand new Peugeot.

He's the only other person in the world who can run the company. It's very much hands-on. Hence we only need the services of a secretary, Judy. The rent from the flat upstairs pays the loan on the building so our overheads are next to nothing. If there's an easier way to make money I've yet to see it.

I receive an application form from RADA and get accepted into Middlesex University to read English and Philosophy. I haven't told Dina yet because I know she'll hate the idea and insist I continue to run Colourgold even with Tim around. It's of no consequence. After Tim gets his degree he falls into a trough of depression that is tragic to witness.

Just as he's starting to recover, his mother commits suicide. It's safe to assume he won't be checking into our office for a while. Tim has since written of those days with a lyrical solemnity seldom bettered in his wonderful autobiography, *The Scent of Dried Roses*.

All I hear is RADA ga ga, RADA goo goo. Someone still loves me.

And all the time Babylon's burning. Madonna is proving to be a big seller, but Kylie Minogue sells more, especially when she's on a cover with Jason Donovan. The next big thing is always just around the corner and in the late Eighties the streets are short and the corners are massive. Bros really bring it home. A combination of a couple of Bros mags, a Kylie special and one of the regulars nets a cool profit of nearly fifty grand in one month alone in 1988.

It's time for a new kind of pop magazine, especially now Wet Wet Wet, Stock Aiken Waterman and the Goss boys are shooting high. And especially as singalonga-*Smash Hits* is now selling nearly one million copies every fortnight.

It's time for *Pop Shop*.

Link-up, Pop Shop, Michael Hutchence, Jason Donovan

One of my regular monthly titles is called *Link-Up*, a poster magazine of the latest flame with a few interviews but mainly featuring free classified ads for penpals, swaps, buying-and-selling and personal messages. It's the most successful of all the "sting" titles I've published but still ends up all at sea under that ol' firm-sale devil called love again.

It gives me an idea. At the end of 1988 I launch *Pop Shop* with the help of ex-IPC publisher David Curtis. It's a thirty-two-page, slightly -bigger-than-A4 magazine, on cheap-quality gloss paper with an eight-page pink newsprint section of free ads I cull from the leftovers of *Link-Up* and 'mail mate' applications from a school where David's brother-in-law is a teacher.

Four days after *Pop Shop* appears on the street we sit in the office and await the post. Seven letters drop onto the mat and a tsunami wave of depression sweeps across us all. An hour later the doorbell rings. I open the door and there's a Royal Mail van parked outside.

'Are these the offices of *Pop Shop*?' asks Mr Postman.

'Yes.'

'Then these are for you,' and he and his mate unload three full sacks of mail from the back of the van. It's a magic moment.

I print 140,000 copies and sell nearly 50,000 – a "failure" in those bygone *Flexipop* days but not too shabby now after the experience of eight years of magazine publishing. We're deluged with mail and I enlist the aid of my mum and dad who sort it all, index each letter, then send out the replies. The free ads are just another flexi-disc, the copy is watered-down *Flexipop*. It's all still pure pulp for pinheads.

But I sold it in as a "sting" title and that means it goes firm sale at issue four – 70,000 copies. It's an amazing order, but unless I pump up the volume and start advertising and promoting and thinking big, *Link-Up* will go the way of all Colourgold publications, down the shitter. But why change the habit of a lifetime? I'll simply surf 'n' turf till I can't bump no more and move up the queue in that alley.

In issue three, I stick the pink pages into a poster magazine that opens out into a full-colour calendar featuring everyone who's hot to trot and put the price up to 75p for one month only, even though a poster mag is much cheaper to produce than a thirty-two-pager. We sell 55,000 copies.

By issue six we're doing 30,000 and the number of pink pages has increased to thirty-two. We feature an interview with INXS legend Michael Hutchence...

Let's talk about your body. You have some rather unusual...

'Distinguishing features? Yeah, I have three parallel scars above my heart which I like to call my "urban scars". I carved them about ten years ago with a knife. It was a pact with my friends and I thought it was much better than a tattoo.'

Do you find it necessary cover up your naughty bits?

'Well, sometimes I wear boxer shorts, sometimes underpants, but mostly I wear nothing. I have a rule that I never wear any underwear when I'm wearing boots. I know it's strange but it's served me well in the past. Sometimes when I'm performing I feel like machine-gunning everybody ... taking all my clothes off and not telling my parents.'

Do you languish in front of the mirror, flexing your pecs?

'I hate looking at myself in the mirror. Honest, it's my neurosis. As for keeping fit, well, I try to, otherwise I'll never last out when we're on tour. I swim, run and do as much yoga as I can to make me relax. Mind you, those difficult positions can be a bit of a problem. I'm a pretty straight person generally. I'm not trying to be Rambo but I try to stay in good condition. There's nothing worse than seeing a tubby, unfit blob trying to wheeze his way across the stage.'

Do you go out of your way to be sexy on stage?

'I can honestly say that nothing about what I do is contrived. It's just "me". I don't wiggle my hips to look sensual, it's just the way I happen to move. I suppose there aren't many singers who are like me these days. Most of them look like accountants. I happen to prefer wearing leather trousers because I don't have to wash them!'

Have you got a big bed?

'Yes, an enormous one and it's very comfortable. It has to be because I spend a lot of time in it.'

Why do plenty of people seem to find you sexy?

'I take anything like that with a large pinch of salt. Being this supposed "sex symbol" is a real strain because there is so much poncing about involved. I don't know why girls scream and stare at me all the time. Maybe it's because I'm stupid. Actually, I think I look OK but nothing great. I hate it when fans give me things like cuddly toys but what can I do? Say to them, "I don't want your teddy?" I usually chew their crotches out and throw them back!'

What are your favourite romantic indulgences?

'Erm, well, I love to go skinny skiing, which is skiing without any clothes. Yes, I'm quite partial to that. I've just found the best place in the world to do rude things. It's this beach in Sydney where the land juts out right into the ocean and there's just the sound of waves crashing on the shore . . .'

Didn't you once have a weird experience with a condom?

'I've had many weird experiences. Actually, I'm not wild about condoms because they tend to break when I use them. Once we were playing in Queensland and I heard that this fascist bastard MP had banned condoms being sold to teenagers. I got really angry, slagged the guy off and threw a lot of condoms into the audience. Needless to say, I was arrested.'

You've had many female admirers – Paula Yates, Koo Stark, Belinda Carlisle. What sort of girls are you attracted to?

'I love all sorts of women – preferably thin, beautiful and with long blonde hair. I think Princess Diana is very, very sexy. Pity she's spoken for. I look for intelligence in a woman, a sense of humour and the ability to hold an interesting conversation. There are many layers to a woman. Unfortunately some women get stuck on the wrong layer. English girls are the most fun. American girls never understand my jokes. I don't think any woman with sense would want to go out with me. I'm too much hassle. I wouldn't want to go out with me. Besides I've had too many relationships disintegrate because of the pressures of my career.'

Do you ever get broody?

'Sometimes, yeah. I'd like a baby, but not just one woman. Maybe five women. I guess I'd have to come to some kind of arrangement.'

Do you lead a rock'n'roll life style?

'I used to but I've cleaned up my act a lot. I used to be Mr Fun Time, drinking and indulging, but I realised I was destroying myself. Now I'm Mr Clean – no sex, drugs or drink. Honest.'

Do you ever get fed up with being in the spotlight?

'All the time. Sometimes I wake up on tour and I think, I want to be lazy today. Why should I have to work? But I can't get out of it.

You have a duty to your fans and you can't disappoint them. It's not like a normal job where you can ring in and say you're sick. There's nothing good about being a pop star except for the free drinks, free food and adoring women!'

Are you self-obsessed?

'It's so easy to let fame go to your head and start acting all selfish and spoilt. Everyone imagines they'll be able to cope with stardom – but nothing can prepare you for what happens to you. It's a weird feeling.'

Do you ever get bored with talking about yourself all the time?

'Most definitely. It gets to me after a while and drives me nuts. I want to stop the interviewer and start asking him questions about his life. Why should I keep talking about me? It gets so boring. The funny thing is, I don't think anyone really knows me – the true me. Even I find it hard to differentiate between the man and the myth sometimes . . .'

Especially when he was found hanging with a belt around his neck seven years later in the wardrobe of a Sydney hotel room, looking for adventure.

I figure we can hang on until maybe issue twelve and then close it. But with this one I feel a little sad. The letters are pouring in and my mum and dad are snowed under and that makes them feel important. Plus, they do it for nothing.

The staff, all freelance, are cute and cuddly and I'm the only man and it's mighty weird but nice. The lovely Judy, my secretary, the gorgeous Luxmi, whom I make editor – I'm too busy writing replies on our problem page and far too old – the fast-talking honeypot about town and shit-kickin' journalist Anna, and the fascinating, sexy Jill who sells the space

They talk about things most boys don't talk about and I love it. This is a whole new world for me and I'd like to keep it hanging on, but that firm-sale black hole beckons.

Maybe if we could raise a little money. Who knows?

David does. He sends over a copy of the mag to a friend of his at Maxwell Consumer Magazines and says we're looking for investment. The contact rings back within an hour of receiving the copy.

'No, David, we don't want to invest in it, we want to buy it.'

A week later David and I are sitting in the office of Terry Humphries, MCM's MD, and selling him the magazine for a heavily negotiated six-figure sum. The only problem is, I have to stay on as editor. OK, they offer me a £30K salary, company car and expenses, but what about Colourgold? I can't give that up.

Terry magnanimously agrees to let me continue publishing my own magazines from their offices and the deed is done. In May 1989 I join Maxwell as the editor of *Pop Shop*. Anna gets a job as a staff writer and Jill joins the sales team. My Colourgold overheads are expunged overnight and the Bell Street offices are closed indefinitely for the holidays. The company gas, electricity, water, telephone and messenger charges are now a thing of the past.

And Dina loves the car, a brand spanking new Rover.

My office, just large enough to accommodate Anna and myself, is squeezed between Fleetway Publications – responsible for a host of state-of-the-art graphic novels, *2000 AD* starring Judge Dredd, and *Wedding & Home*. I guess this is how a *Smash Hits* editor must feel, although I've only got a staff of one. We settle in and continue to bring out the magazine every month. The free ads are handled by a distribution company Maxwell has just purchased.

Because of the immense reader response *Pop Shop* generates, we're able to build up a pretty accurate reader profile. The average age is sixteen with a twist more girls than boys so I tone down the more infantile *Pop Shop* name on the cover and go heavy on the *P.S.* They're also articulate, potty about Then Jerico and don't think the Queen should abdicate in favour of Prince Charles and Princess Diana.

I know all this because on the free ad application coupon we always include a topical question. After a year, we get Jason

Donovan to answer the same questions and to guess the results, just
so we can bung him on the cover with the line 'Jason Donovan on
sex, AIDS and drugs!'

If there was a general election and you were able to vote, who
would you vote for?

'I studied politics at school – just domestic politics – and I don't
believe in voting for the sake of it. It's compulsory in Australia to
vote, so you have to make a stand about the way you feel.'

Jason's guess: 'I think 30 per cent would vote for the Green
Party and 20 per cent for your Labour and Liberals. But I think the
Conservatives would get the majority.'

Poll results: Labour 42 per cent, Greens 34 per cent, Tories 16 per
cent, Various 8 per cent.

Do you think the Queen should abdicate in favour of Prince Charles?

'Royalty should be kept fresh. I certainly think it wouldn't cause
an upheaval if he was to come in now. And Diana's fantastic! She's
amazing! They're a young, trendy couple, and I think the country
needs that. No disrespect to the Queen, but we need to get new ideas.'

Jason's guess: 'Yes, 50 per cent; No, 50 per cent.'

Poll result: No, 60 per cent.

Where did you first find out about the facts of life and how old
were you?

'I don't think I ever actually found out formally. My dad never sat
me down and told me them, that's for sure, and I tend to disagree
with parents who do. I think it's something you pick up in the
school playground.'

Jason's guess: 'You start to become aware of it around eleven and
from the schoolyard.'

Poll results: Under 10, 35 per cent; 10—13, 59 per cent; 14+, 6
per cent. Found out from: teacher, 36 per cent; friends 21 per cent;
mother, 23 per cent; father, 5 per cent; other, 15 per cent.

In the light of the recent AIDS problem, would you like to see the age of consent raised?

'No, I don't think that's going to solve anything. I don't want any pressure groups jumping on my back, but I think Aids is a message to people to slow down. Don't get me wrong, I don't believe that people should be going out there telling everyone what to do. At sixteen, kids just do what they want to do.'

Jason's guess: 'No, 70 per cent, but maybe even higher.'

Poll result: No, 69 per cent.

Do you think conscription should be reintroduced?

'I can't stand the idea of conscription. Why should I be made to go and kill myself because some idiot is involved in a dispute with someone else? I'm as patriotic as the next man but I'm not going to fight other people's battles.'

Jason's guess: 'No, 80 per cent.'

Poll result: No, 80 per cent.

Do you think capital punishment should be reintroduced?

'Yeah. If someone goes out and kills someone and it's proven 100 per cent that they killed someone, then they should be killed themselves. I don't think that sitting in jail for thirteen years does anyone any good.'

Jason's guess: 'No, 60 per cent.'

Poll result: No, 57 per cent.

Do you believe in God?

'I believe that at some stage there was a person around who touched history like no other person before or since and his life was documented in the Bible. I don't practise religion.'

Jason's guess: 'Yes, 80 per cent.'

Poll result : Yes, 68 per cent.

Do you think that Britain should get rid of all its nuclear weapons?

'I think the whole world should give up its nuclear weapons, not just Britain. It's all down to trust. I prefer to see the £20 billion spent on weapons being used to help the homeless or protect the environment. But I would never, ever want to live in a socialist society...'

Jason's guess: 'Yes, 71 per cent.'
Poll result: Yes, 82 per cent.

Terry Humphries walks into the lift at Greater London House in Mornington Crescent where the company is based. It's lunchtime and he sees me standing in the corner clutching a leather-bound copy of *Little Dorrit*. I purchased the complete set of Dickens when I got my cut of Maxwell's money and grab a few pages at every opportunity. I read my first Dickens book, *A Tale of Two Cities*, just six months ago and I'm utterly hooked. Where was this guy all my life?

'The figures on *Pop Shop* – or should I say *P.S.*? – are looking good,' he says. 'The free poster magazine stitched inside has worked really well. Every promotion we do seems to pay off with an increase in sales. Good stuff. Keep it up.'

Dina hates my idea of inserting a poster mag on one particular act over several issues because she thinks it will impact on the sales of Colourgold titles. She's probably right. But it's a mighty fine feeling to have a hit on your hands and to have the resources to keep it going. So in go huge, juicy poster mags of Then Jerico, Stone Roses, Wendy James, Kylie, Bros and Bon Jovi. Sales are creeping up to 65,000 a month. Ad agencies start to get interested because of the age range of the magazine – it's older than *Smash Hits* with a different vibe altogether.

Alas, *P.S.* is a victim of its own success. A lot more people at Maxwell's are noticing it and want a piece of the action. A new title that's to be the focus of a major launch has been postponed and *P.S.* takes its place. After a round of meetings, in which I sit in relative silence and bow to superior knowledge of promotions and big business, it's decided to push the *Pop Shop* name again, reduce the size of the magazine to *Smash Hits* proportions and turn it into a fortnightly.

I hate every decision but understand that the company is looking at the wider, big-money picture and I'm Joe Schmuck, cowboy one-shot publisher from Palookaville with one foot in the grave as my fortieth birthday approaches like a runaway train.

But I do sense this is my golden opportunity to set in motion an idea I've harboured for a while. I've always believed it's possible to create a pop group in a magazine of the same name. Like, for example, P.S. the band. You feature a soap-like photo story of the problems they face, and at the end of each episode you invite the readers, who are essentially the band's managers, to decide their fate by offering several alternative scenarios and asking them to vote. P.S. is the perfect vehicle because we can include the votes on the pink-page form.

I get the go-ahead to run with the idea and place an ad in the *Melody Maker* classifieds. After a round of auditions, I find four likely lads and proceed to groom them for pop stardom on the back of Maxwell's millions.

I also stand down as editor and promote Anna to number one. My new role is editorial director, but I keep involved mainly to promote the band.

The new look *Pop Shop* is launched in spectacular fashion with a clumsy, ill-conceived TV ad that must have cost a fortune to put together and is aired during the break on *Coronation Street*. The ad is a cliché from start to finish but it's serious shit. Mark Neeter, the in-house publisher of the magazine, has negotiated a deal with Virgin Records to slap on the lipstick and eye-shadow for the first issue with a cassette on the cover featuring some cool acts including Neneh Cherry. The print run is a staggering – to me – 250,000. What a way to promote P.S. the band!

I get the four guys firmly ensconced in a rehearsal studio in Croydon where main-man Dave lives and Maxwell's quite happily pick up the bill. They even pay my petrol money for the weekly drive down to check on their progress. The band are turning into a talented bunch of young, good-looking desperadoes and the response to the photo story is impressive. It's spread across two pages and at the end of each issue there's a dilemma to overcome and choices for the reader to make. My plan is to get a cassette of three tracks recorded by P.S. (the name chosen by the readers out of five other names) and give it away free with *Pop Shop*, asking the readers to vote for the one they'd like released as a single.

Mark knows record producer Gwyn Mathias, and I get the band into a recording studio to lay down three tracks for the cassette. A few days later I'm playing the tape in the office of the head of A&R at EMI and explaining the concept to him. He's interested. Who wouldn't be? It's all about the idea.

'Can I come down and see them rehearse?'

How's that particularly relevant? He's heard the tape. They sound OK and one of the songs is a belter. Anyway, it's all about the idea. But I say nothing and we agree a time later in the week.

The band are ill-prepared and nervous and don't need this. They perform all three songs indifferently but surely he can see the spark. It doesn't really matter, though, because it's all about the idea.

Not, it seems, to the man from EMI. 'They need to play some gigs,' he tells me, in the bitter cold in Croydon. 'Let me know how they're progressing.'

I can't believe it. As he walks away I feel like screaming, 'BUT IT'S ALL ABOUT THE FUCKING IDEA!' I don't.

Where was the creativity, the vision, that Monkees' spirit? Oh, well, it's still all about the idea and there's plenty more fish in the sea.

I leave the magazine just before the Italia '90 World Cup, but I still retain the rights to the band. When it's discovered that the first issue of the new look *Pop Shop* sold "only" 120,000, Mark Neeter is asked to leave. Anna follows a few weeks later and, as a result, the magazine suffers badly. I'm invited to return as a consultant, which is just about the nicest word in the English language, along with 'free'.

They end up paying me more money than before, but the damage has been done. There are new faces prowling the Maxwell corridors and plans afoot to replace *Pop Shop*. In a night of the long knives it's finally closed down and *Rage* magazine is released. Despite employing the talents of DJ Gary Crowley as a consultant, it lasts just two issues. Publishing a successful pop magazine is not as easy as it seems.

The rot is beginning to set in. This is no way to treat a lady. Too much diversity is robbing pop of the cohesion essential to its pertinence. The Sixties and Seventies and, to some extent, the Eighties, fuelled an eternity of dross – but the hymn sheet was the same. The core, the focus of everything, was always just a handful of people – bands, singers, producers, heads of record companies – who knew what they were doing and steered the new big bright green pleasure machine through uncharted waters.

Just look at this list of the top ten selling singles of 1990:

1. Righteous Brothers – Unchained Melody
2. Sinead O'Connor – Nothing Compares 2U
3. Elton John – Sacrifice /Healing Hands
4. Adamski – Killer
5. Vanilla Ice – Ice Ice Baby
6. Maria McKee – Show Me Heaven
7. Beats International – Dub Be Good To Me
8. Madonna – Vogue
9. England World Cup song – World In Motion
10. Snap – The Power

It's kinda dancey, kinda ravey, kinda ballady, kinda showy, kinda jokey. In other words, it's kinda nothing. Real nothing. The nothing bit in 'All or Nothing' ain't as nothing as this nothing. In fact, it's nothing compared 2 this. Elton John gets his first number one in the nothing year of 1990. And whatever happened to Adamski, Vanilla Ice, Sinead O'Connor, Maria McKee, Beats International and Snap, crackle and pop? 'World In Motion' is the real standout and that's a fucking football song. One of the Righteous Brothers has been dead for years; he should've been the *Ghost*, not Patrick Swayze.

1991–1992

18 Rated, Zodiac Mindwarp, Elvis Aris

Heigh-ho, heigh-ho, it's back to work I go. My office hasn't been touched since I moved out eighteen months ago. I feel like Pip visiting Miss Havisham as I open the door, half expecting to see a twenty-five-year-old wedding cake surrounded by cobwebs and more than a few dirty rats.

I have great expectations. I'm about to publish a new magazine and I'm joined in the venture by Huw Collingbourne, whom I roped into *Pop Shop* as the resident astrologist writing under the apt pseudonym Quentin de la Folle. Over a few bottles of red in a Greek restaurant during my last days at Maxwell's, we think up zany ideas for magazine covers and the stand-out is a man's hairy arse made up to look like Elvis Presley. From that image we develop the idea for an entire magazine of the bizarre and extraordinary called *18 Rated*.

I can honestly say that this ill-fated mag gives me some of the strangest experiences of my life.

The first forty-eight-page issue, a £1.50 bi-monthly, features Richard 'Rocky Horror' O'Brien getting his crystals in a maze at a transvestite shop off the Euston Road and looking very sexy; an interview with horror writer James Herbert and the *18 Rated* 'Knob Survey', which involves Anna Martin, recently resurrected from the dead, wandering around the West End in broad daylight asking complete strangers the size, shape and wow factor of their cocks.

She then contacts a number of celebrities through PRs, record companies, personal secretaries, mums, dads and pet poodles to answer one question: what is the size of their knob? We call the double-page spread Personality Plonkers...

Boy George: 'It looks much bigger when it isn't wearing a hat.'
Matt Goss: 'They don't call me the human tripod for nothing.'
Luke Goss: 'I don't like to boast, but I used to keep it in a greenhouse.'
Julian Clary: 'I'm hung like a draught-excluder for a cat flap.'
Jason Donovan: 'Just like my part in *Joseph* at the moment, it's of Biblical proportions. But then I was always big down under.'
Arnold Schwarzenegger: 'It's in proportion with the rest of me.'
Screaming Lord Sutch: 'It's a monster. Whatever John Major says, I'll double it.'
Tony Blackburn: 'I'm very fond of mine and find it very useful in winter as I can wrap it around my neck and use it as a scarf.'
Richard O'Brien: 'Ask anybody.'

But the two features that create the most unbridled joy are a regular photo story set in the future called 'The Vicky Venus Killings'; and a profile of bum impersonator Elvis Aris.

The photo story stars all-girl trio Cherry Bomb & the Bombshells and is another attempt at manufacturing a group on the back of a magazine. Instead of using *Melody Maker* to recruit members I place an ad in *The Stage* magazine asking for girls aged sixteen to nineteen.

An endless stream of wannabes comes to the office, where I sit alone most days, and audition just for me. Some sing, some dance, some unhook their bras and show me their breasts when I mention the job might involve nudity, and some will never see thirty again. The three girls I select become Cherry Bomb, a seventeen-year-old with, it has to be said, breasts that would make Russ Meyer salivate; Val Policella, a stunning blonde eighteen-year-old Italian, and Grace Elegy, barely seventeen but already a veteran of fashion shoots for teenage mags.

I bet if the head of A&R at EMI sees them he'll finally realise that it really is all about the idea.

Elvis Aris, on the other hand, is a figment of a boozy session in Camden Town. The problem is, how do we persuade someone to let us turn his arse into a star-studded event? And how do we persuade someone else to do the turning? Actually, the second one is a no-brainer. Zodiac Mindwarp, a.k.a. Mark Manning, was just about the finest caricaturist around when he designed *Flexipop*, so I contact him out of the blue and ask if he'll take a moment out of his Love Reaction and draw famous people on someone's backside.

He's actually a bit shocked. This bearded, booted, fearsome-looking death punk whose single, 'Prime Mover', crashed into the Top Twenty a few years earlier, is a little shocked. But he agrees, for old times' sake.

And does Zodiac know anyone who might let us abuse his bum for a couple of hours?

'No way. This is weird enough without fucking painting a mate's arse. Nope, you'll have to sort that out yourself.'

In desperation, we reply to a few classifieds in *Gay News*, and that's how we come across Robbie – along with a thousand other guys – the middle-aged rent-boy from Baker Street. We talk on the phone and he's happy for Mark to paint his bum and for us to take photos. His voice is gentle and refined and he charges sixty quid an hour. Call it our promotional budget.

We arrange to meet at his smart mews house on a bitterly cold morning three days before Christmas. Huw and I, armed with all kinds of everything, are the first to arrive. Robbie opens the door gingerly. He's naked apart from a tiny, tight red leather thong and a welcoming smile.

'Come in, come in.' He's well into his forties but slim and still fairly attractive. 'Well turned out', I guess, would be the best way to describe him. He leads us into the living room. The heavy curtains are drawn and the room is lit only by fading flames in a fireplace, their shadows flickering across a sheet nearby that's spread out on the carpet. Strange electronic music drifts in the air and freezes the moment.

'Sorry I haven't had time to change – I've just this minute been entertaining a client.'

This is surreal.

The bell rings. Enter Zodiac Mindwarp.

'Robbie, this is Zodiac. He's the man who'll be painting your bum.'

'Hello, Zodiac. I hope your brush isn't cold.'

This is seriously surreal.

Robbie pulls open the curtains and pours Mark a large whisky. He still hasn't slipped out of his thong.

'OK, I'll just go and change. But I must insist that my face is never seen.'

'Robbie, it's not your face we're after. And I can assure you that your face will not be shown.'

'I've always looked after my bum,' he says, out of the blue. 'It's as taut now as it's ever been because I exercise it all the time. Even when I'm standing on a station platform I keep flexing the muscles there. I think you'll be pleasantly surprised.' He smiles and goes upstairs.

Meanwhile, photographer Robin appears on the scene, having just finished shooting a school nativity play. He starts setting up his equipment, if I can say that, and thinks that we've laid the sheet on the floor. 'As it's white, he can lie on that and it'll work as a backdrop. Good idea. What's his name?'

'Robbie,' says Huw.

Mark is sorting out the paints while Huw and I rifle through the extras – microphone, false noses, wigs, Elvis Presley's white Las Vegas suit, can of spinach, bow tie, sailor's hat, bowler hat, pipe and a massive Havana cigar.

Robbie comes down the stairs in his outfit for the session, a black leather bondage mask and absolutely nothing else. 'Like I said, it's imperative that my identity is never revealed.'

'Right, er, Robbie. This is Robin, the photographer.' What with this whole secret-identity thing I feel like saying, 'Robin, this is Batman.'

'Hello, Robin, I hope your aim is true.'

'Er,' says Robin, clearly shellshocked, 'pleased to meet you.' As they shake hands Robbie's bollocks swing vigorously.

'Now, where do you want me?'

Stand-out moments over the next couple of hours are the expression on Zodiac's face when he accidentally touches a patch of dried spunk on the sheet, and me inserting the cigar up Robbie's backside for his Churchill impersonation.

'Is that all right, Robbie?' I ask, as I slowly push it in.

'Stick it up as far as you like, Barry. It's no problem at all.'

The pictures are sensational – Elvis Presley, Churchill, Popeye and Gazza.

Comag order 70,000 copies, but we can't find a printer in the UK who's prepared to take on a magazine with a picture of a man's arse dressed up like Elvis Presley on the cover, so we're forced to use a company in Boulogne. The French, it seems, don't have a problem with hairy arses.

When *18 Rated* finally hits the streets, WHSmith and Menzies are distinctly jittery about displaying it. In some branches it's kept under the counter and is only available to anyone who specifically asks for it, which kinda defeats the object. In order for people to ask for it, we need publicity. From out of nowhere we get three big hits.

Paula Yates, who took over from Juicy Luicy as the *Record Mirror* gossip columnist back in 1978, presents an early-evening magazine show on ITV and flashes a copy of *18 Rated* on screen telling everyone to go out and buy it. I only met Paula a few times when she worked on *Record Mirror* and she was as sweet as candy kisses. She remembered.

The *Sunday Sport* editorial team go ape-shit over the mag when we send them a copy. They inundate the office with calls asking about Elvis Aris and beg for the photos. I actually have a drink with the features editor at a pub near the *Sport*'s office and he tells me the staff on the paper think *18 Rated* is the funniest magazine they've ever seen. They splash Elvis across two pages and even give a teaser on the cover.

One morning, about a week after the magazine has been hidden under counters in high street newsagents, we get a phone call from the producer of TV's *The James Whale Radio Show*. 'Our new series starts next week and we want the first show to go with a bang. We want Elvis Aris. Can you get hold of him?'

Have we pulled the wool over some people's eyes!

'I don't know. I'll make a few enquiries and get back to you.'

'I need to know within the hour as we're planning schedules now.'

'Oh, I don't know,' says Robbie, on the phone a few minutes later. 'I'm absolutely paranoid about anyone recognising me.'

'You can wear your bondage mask all the time. In fact, I think it's a good idea. It'll make you look more mysterious.'

'But they'll want me to perform.'

'It'll only be a small spot. We've got over a week to rehearse something.'

'Sixty quid an hour.'

'But, Robbie, we've got to drive to Yorkshire Television in Leeds and back. Can't you think of it more as an adventure than a job? When will you ever again get the opportunity to show your bare bum in front of millions of people?'

He finally agrees to do it for a knockdown price and even throws in three nights of rehearsal at the office.

The spot on the show is bigger than we thought. We decide that Robbie's bum will mime to three songs – 'Crocodile Rock', 'Get Into The Groove' and Elvis's 'Hawaiian Wedding Song'. When he pops into the office in the evening, we paint a couple of eyes and a mouth on his bum and he stands stark bollock naked in the middle of the room attempting to move his 'taut' arse, which is a little frayed around the edges, in time with the words.

But Robbie is tone deaf and keeps trying to move his arse in time with the music. We bark out orders and he gets a little flustered and I always end up convulsed with laughter. One night my dad drops by and creases up saying it's the funniest thing he's ever seen. It's obvious Robbie won't master this in three days and it takes a week, at no extra charge, before we've got a halfway decent act to present to the nation.

The day before we're due to drive up to Leeds disaster strikes. Yorkshire TV says they cannot get permission from any of the music publishers to perform their songs from a bum. 'You'll have to do something else.'

We're screwed. We hastily arrange three sketches – Winston miming to his 'We shall fight them on the beaches' speech, complete with cigar, one involving the Queen Mother having afternoon tea, and Elvis dying after consuming a dozen Big Macs. Robbie doesn't need to do anything but move his arse when I speak off camera. It's shit compared to the TV gold we'd created in a week but it's still a plug.

Four of us drive up to Leeds – Robbie, our ad man Bill, who volunteers to drive and is a dab hand with a brush in the absence of Zodiac, and Fiona, a twenty-four-year-old *Sun* Page Three girl, who came to the office to audition for the photo story and insisted I touch her breasts because she'd just had them enlarged and wanted my opinion. Straight up. I liked her style. Plus, she's prepared to work for nothing. It's the least I can do.

She's Elvis Aris's sexy stage assistant and will appear as a hula-hula girl in the Elvis sketch.

As we near the TV studios Robbie slips on his bondage mask. He's starting to panic. It's finally beginning to dawn on him what he's let himself in for. 'I can't go through with this. I'll be recognised, ridiculed, shot.'

'Pull yourself together, man, or I'll get angry,' I say, though I'm probably panicking more. 'And you won't like me when I'm angry. Nobody will recognise you. You're not going to say one word.'

That seems to pacify him for now. After picking up a dozen Big Macs, we park at the studios and make our way to Reception. As Robbie walks through the doors, one of the guys behind the desk looks up and calls to his mate in the office, 'Hey, Dave, quick, it's Elvis Aris.'

Dave comes running out. 'Hello, Mr Aris. We've been expecting you. Are these people with you?'

'Yes,' I interrupt. 'We're his assistants.'

Elvis nods and we're shown to our dressing room. 'Here we are, Mr Aris.' And there on the door in gold lettering are the words, 'Elvis Aris'. I swear I see a tear fall onto the bondage mask's brass mouth zipper. I would've said he had a lump in his throat but I guess Robbie usually did on a Friday night back in Baker Street where the sheets come from.

The room is huge and there's a jaunt in Robbie's step as he walks up and down excitedly, checking everything out. He's beginning to feel like a star. 'Tonight, Matthew, I'm going to be ... Elvis Aris!'

The producer comes in. 'Hi, guys, pleased to meet you. Look, sorry about the mix-up over the songs, but I'm sure you'll still go down a storm. Oh, and we've got to drop the Queen Mother sketch. So we'll start with Winston and do Elvis at the end of the show and James will be interviewing you or, rather, your bum.'

'Interview?' says Robbie.

'Yes. Must rush.' (Is that the bum's rush?) 'Good luck, Elvis.' He leaves.

Robbie is shellshocked. 'Nobody told me about doing an interview.'

'Don't worry, Robbie,' I say courageously. 'I'll be your bum's voiceover.'

Bill starts to frantically paint a picture of Winston Churchill on Robbie's backside, and when he finishes, Fiona, now dressed in a grass skirt with a pair of very large coconut shells for a bra, follows Robbie to the studio, carrying a Homburg, huge cigar, shirt and bow tie. Robbie is wearing a silk robe, which he removes when he walks into the studio, forgetting that he's naked underneath.

'Quick, do something about his fucking bollocks,' I hear someone shout, and I quickly head off to the Green Room fearing the worst, determined to drown my sorrows and acute embarrassment in free wine. It's busy but I can't bring myself to speak to anyone. What on earth am I doing? This is a total mistake. Robbie's going to fuck everything up and it's all my fault. Instead of selling more copies of *18 Rated*, people who have already bought the mag will take it back and demand a refund. What was I thinking? Is this the Megan to end all Megans? I'll look like a laughing stock.

The lights go down in the Green Room and the TV flashes on. Is that my entrails I'm sitting on?

'Guess who's back?' asks the ITV announcer. 'Live from Leeds, it's The James Whale Radio Show.'

Suddenly the whole screen is an arse dressed as Winston Churchill, complete with hat and cigar, miming to a recording of Winston Churchill's 'Fight them on the beaches' speech. Robbie is cheek perfect.

'Fuck!' says the awestruck American guy sitting next to me. 'I've never seen anything like that in my life.' He's a little drunk but, still, I feel proud. We manage to bring to life a non-existent arse impersonator in the shape of bum bandit Robbie and fool all of the people some of the time on a cult ITV Friday-night show. Robbie appears again at the end dressed as Elvis Presley and Fiona proceeds to ram home the Big Macs and it's all a bit of a shambles. The interview doesn't really come off as I attempt to answer James's questions via Robbie's arse before the credits roll.

But none of that matters. For one brief, Churchillian moment, we manipulated the media. Malcolm McLaren would have been proud. And if Robbie had been allowed to perform 'Crocodile Rock', 'Hawaiian Wedding Song' (great routine with Fiona) and 'Get Into The Groove', just as we'd rehearsed it, *18 Rated* would've taken off with a Christmas number one in the offing. No kiddin'.

It's all about the idea.

Two months later we publish issue two but WH Smiths and Menzies both refuse to handle it because of the cover – a hunky, nude male model adept in the art of 'priamorphism', the ability to transform his penis into a multitude of shapes. He's standing side-on, his privates covered with a small white screen, which reflects a silhouette of his penis. We put a finger puppet of a dinosaur on the end of his knob so the silhouette looks like a creature reminiscent of the shadow shapes performed by hands on bedroom walls.

'Knobby Burns – He's Got A Monster!' screams the cover line. Alas, no customer of WHS or Menzies gets a chance to see Knobby's nuts turning into helicopters, St Bernards, Barry Manilow, Dennis Norden or, best of all, Jimmy Hill.

Neither do they get the chance to see the Treacle Tart story about a new sex craze sweeping the suburbs. While Dina's at work, Huw comes round to my house with a camera and Fiona. She strips off completely and I cover her naked body with two tins of treacle while Huw snaps away. When we finish I usher her into the garden because the treacle is dripping everywhere and she rinses her body with a hosepipe of cold water in the warm sunshine. God knows what the neighbours will think if they see her.

The *Sport* picks up on the story and Fiona gets paid to have treacle thrown over her in a photo shoot. That's the way of the world. The order for issue two is just 21,000, distributed entirely through independent outlets. *18 Rated* needs a little tenderness, a shoulder to cry on, encouragement, money.

So we pull it.

That's the way of the world, or my world anyway. I never invested money in any of the titles I produced. But I did invest my time and my talent. And it's evidently never been enough. Not by a long chalk.

1992-1998

Property ads, Princess Di and the death of pop

In between churning out pop magazines at an alarming rate – some winning, more starting to lose – and thanking God for Comag, my distributor and all-round good guy, and Take That, the natural successors to New Kids On The Block for whom I also once thanked

God, I watch my twin boys grow and publish a free local magazine, *Northbound*, covering Muswell Hill, Crouch End, East Finchley and Highgate. My partner in crime this time is David Orme, originally a director at Comag who lives just around the corner.

We're in the middle of one of the worst recessions in history, which is hardly the best time to bring out a magazine relying almost entirely on property ads, but we do OK. Not liveable wage OK, but OK. Our days are spent visiting local retailers and selling them space. It's a first for me and I find it surprisingly exhilarating walking out of an estate agency after they agree to pay a grand for a full-page colour ad.

Much of the editorial content is geared towards the advertisers. But it's bright and lively and people seem to like it. However, after two years, what *Northbound* really needs is a little tenderness, a shoulder to cry on, encouragement, money.

So we pull it.

My only true love is Colourgold. I continue to publish magazines out of the office as a total one-man band. I don't see a soul for weeks on end. To cut costs I'm writing all the copy myself and start doing hard deals on production and photo costs. When the Internet enters my life, I sit at home and do the same. The 'Sting' scam is no more as the wholesalers wise up with computers, so I have to take chances and publish magazines on anyone who I think might push a few copies.

Some do pretty well – Boyzone, Madonna, Peter Andre (though the third one flopped), Spice Girls (but nothing like Take That), East 17, Elvis, Robson & Jerome, Bon Jovi, official Chippendales' poster, 5ive, Backstreet Boys and a Freddie Mercury memorial. Some do so-so – All Saints, Keanu Reeves, Oasis, Blur, Verve, Blue, Beatles. Some do pretty shit – Robbie Williams, Hanson, Cliff Richard, official Michael Jackson, Gary Barlow, Michael Owen, official Right Said Fred. Some are ridiculous – the Spice Girls management sue me for publishing a poster of the gals because I really, really, really want to and I end up writing a cheque for £1000 made payable to 'The Spice Girls', which they cash.

And some are catastrophic . . .

I get an order from Comag of 170,000 copies, the biggest I've ever had, for *Funeral of Princess Diana*, a thirty-six-page 'luxury' magazine. Comag can get it into the shops within two days of printing – and that's just three days after the funeral. Everything is time-sensitive but, for the first time ever, the paper won't take the ink and the whole operation is aborted at the print stage. I end up in the High Court for disputing the paper supplier's bill and it's a nightmare.

On my way home, having settled on a figure and having realised that the writing is on the wall, I walk through Lincoln's Inn. The sun is blazing through the trees. Its lunchtime leaf-caressed fingers of burning gold are enticing all the sexy and intelligent from out of their masters' chambers and onto the grass, gleefully clutching small bottles of Evian and M&S sandwiches before clutching their knees and talking shop.

I remember how much I enjoyed that feeling of sitting outside with workmates and chewing the fat and loving the job and getting paid monthly and not worrying about tax or numbers or bills or distant drums. I try to sprint away from some memories, but they're always tucked in just behind me, like tricky Kenyan 10,000-metres runners, ready to pounce at the sound of the bell.

I suddenly see that for far too many years I've actually been a pimp Miss Havisham, earning money from my first love but deserted by my intentions and left to rot. Even though I work from home, I'm always in that office, alone, watching pop music slowly die, no matter where I am or who I'm with.

It's the numbers that tell me it's dying – what else? The numbers that I've always loathed telling me it's the beginning of the end for a music business spawned in the Fifties and shagged to within an inch of its life by the time it hit forty.

Maybe Blue Oyster Cult's Allen Lanier was right back in 1978:

'Rock and roll was all about a frustrated generation of kids hating their mothers and fathers and getting wrecked,' he told me. 'But those revolutions have been won and it now reflects in the music – soft and radio playable.'

Maybe Jim Steinman was right when he said, the very next day, 'Everyone got older and left rock behind them. They've dispensed with the heroics and are now dealing with interior forces. We all live too comfortably. That's why we like FM radio.'

Maybe Kevin Rowland was right when he stated, back in 1980, 'Rock is totally dead. It's been going for twenty-five years and if it's not dead now, it's high time it was.'

Maybe Darryl Hall was right when he told me, back in 1983, 'Music has been relegated to the shopping-centre syndrome. When you're inundated with it, it ceases to have any meaning. '

Debbie Harry told me, in that fateful interview all those years ago, 'Rock'n'roll is a part of everyone's life now, no matter how you react to it and what your age might be.' Rock'n'roll was a part of everyone's life in 1978. It's not any more.

The kids just ain't that interested in this fat, middle-aged bastard that can't get it up any more. It's not about the music now: it's about pose and exposure. You really can fool some of the people all of the time and that's all you need to get by. Forget the sweet morning dew.

The female answer to Boyzone is the subject of my final pop magazine. It's 1998, the Year of the Tiger. B*Witched: they'rrre grrrreat! But the magazine isn't. It seems only about two hundred people out of 75,000 in the UK, France, Germany and Italy would be happy to pay the equivalent of £1.95 for a poster magazine of B*Witched, despite the fact that I've arranged to have the copies translated for each country.

The teenage punters are latching on to the fact that this year's pop star is usually next year's turd in the hole and will stink the place out if you hang them on your wall. They've got the Internet now and cute little mobile phones and Sky TV, and they hear the music but don't really want to listen. It's gone from being a tourniquet keeping your guts in, to underarm deodorant.

As Roy 'Bladerunner' Batty said, 'Time to die.'

Oh, maybe Colourgold could continue with a little tenderness, a shoulder to cry on, encouragement, money. So it's obviously time to pull it. I've been pulling it all my life and it really does make you go blind.

That's it. Game over. Pop music is out of my life.

And the main lesson I've learned?

Only ever snort other people's coke.

Goodnight, Megan. Turn out the light.

77
SULPHATE
STRIP

AN EYEWITNESS ACCOUNT OF THE
YEAR THAT CHANGED
EVERYTHING

FEATURING:
SEX PISTOLS
THE STRANGLERS
THE CLASH
THE DAMNED
THE RAMONES
THE VIBRATORS
THE TUBES
THE JAM
BLONDIE
X-RAY SPEX
SHAM 69

THE BOYS
THE DRONES TELEVISION
GENERATION X
THE HEARTBREAKERS
ALTERNATIVE TV
IAN DURY
RADIATORS FROM SPACE
AND MANY MORE

BARRY CAIN

The acknowledged seminal work on punk: a fast-paced trip through an extraordinary year. This book includes major new interviews with Paul Weller, Johnny Rotten, Strangler Hugh Cornwell and Rat Scabies of The Damned.

www.redplanetzone.com

ROCK ATLAS
UK AND IRELAND SECOND EDITION

*800 great music locations and the
fascinating stories behind them*

Rock Atlas is more than just a guide to over 800 music locations. You can visit many of the places or simply enjoy reading this extraordinary fact-packed book's fascinating stories. Some are iconic, others are just plain weird or unusual, such as Bob Dylan turning up unannounced on a public tour of John Lennon's childhood home or the musical park bench commemorating Ian Dury's life that plays recordings of his hits and his appearance on Desert Island Discs.

Providing insights into many performers' lives, Rock Atlas includes artists as diverse as The Beatles, Sex Pistols, Lady Gaga and Lonnie Donegan. Presented in an easy-to-read, region-by-region format, every entry provides detailed instructions on how to find each location together with extensive lists of the pop and rock stars born in each county.

Illustrated with hundreds of rare, unseen and iconic colour and black and white photographs, Rock Atlas is a must for anyone with an emotional tie to contemporary music and the important places associated with it.

On sale now

For information on Red Planet books visit www.redplanetzone.com

Heddon
Street,
London
David
Bowie
poses for
the iconic
Ziggy
Stardust
album
cover

ROCK ATLAS

800 great music locations
and the fascinating stories
behind them

Written and res... by David Roberts

PLACES TO VISIT

Album cover
& music
video
locations
Statues,
graves
memorials &
plaques
Venues,
festivals and
places that
influenced songs

Hundreds
of new
photos
and facts

www.redplanetzone.com

www.redplanetzone.com